TRANSITION AND INSTITUTIONS

UNU WORLD INSTITUTE FOR DEVELOPMENT
ECONOMICS RESEARCH (UNU/WIDER)

was established by the United Nations University as its first research and training centre and started work in Helsinki, Finland in 1985. The purpose of the Institute is to undertake applied research and policy analysis on structural changes affecting the developing and transitional economies, to provide a forum for the advocacy of policies leading to robust, equitable, and environmentally sustainable growth, and to promote capacity strengthening and training in the field of economic and social policy-making. Its work is carried out by staff researchers and visiting scholars in Helsinki and through networks of collaborating scholars and institutions around the world.

Transition and Institutions

*The Experience of
Gradual and Late Reformers*

Edited by
GIOVANNI ANDREA CORNIA
VLADIMIR POPOV

*A study prepared for the World Institute for Development Economics Research
of the United Nations University (UNU/WIDER)*

OXFORD
UNIVERSITY PRESS

OXFORD
UNIVERSITY PRESS

Great Clarendon Street, Oxford OX2 6DP

Oxford University Press is a department of the University of Oxford.
It furthers the University's objective of excellence in research, scholarship,
and education by publishing worldwide in

Oxford New York

Athens Auckland Bangkok Bogotá Buenos Aires Cape Town
Chennai Dar es Salaam Delhi Florence Hong Kong Istanbul Karachi
Kolkata Kuala Lumpur Madrid Melbourne Mexico City Mumbai Nairobi
Paris São Paulo Shanghai Singapore Taipei Tokyo Toronto Warsaw

with associated companies in Berlin Ibadan

Oxford is a registered trade mark of Oxford University Press
in the UK and in certain other countries

Published in the United States
by Oxford University Press Inc., New York

© The United Nations University, 2001

World Institute for Development Economics Research of the United Nations University
(UNU/WIDER) Katajanokanlaituri 6B, 00160 Helsinki, Finland

The moral rights of the authors have been asserted

Database right Oxford University Press (maker)

First published 2001

All rights reserved. No part of this publication may be reproduced,
stored in a retrieval system, or transmitted, in any form or by any means,
without the prior permission in writing of Oxford University Press,
or as expressly permitted by law, or under terms agreed with the appropriate
reprographics rights organization. Enquiries concerning reproduction
outside the scope of the above should be sent to the Rights Department,
Oxford University Press, at the address above

You must not circulate this book in any other binding or cover
and you must impose this same condition on any acquirer

British Library Cataloguing in Publication Data

Data available

Library of Congress Cataloging in Publication Data

Transition and institutions: the experience of gradual and late reformers/
edited by Giovanni Andrea Cornia and Vladimir Popov.
p. cm.—(Studies in development economics)
Includes bibliographical references and index.
1. Asia—Economic conditions—1945– 2. Europe, Eastern—Economic conditions—1989–
3. Former Soviet republics—Economic conditions. I. Cornia, Giovanni Andrea.
II. Popov, Vladimir Mikhailovich. III. Series.
HC412 .T728 2001   338.947—dc21   2001021639

ISBN 0-19-924218-6

1 3 5 7 9 10 8 6 4 2

Typeset by Newgen Imaging Systems Pvt. Ltd, Chennai, India
Printed in Great Britain
on acid-free paper by
Biddles Ltd., Guildford & King's Lynn

Foreword

The transition to the market economy of the former socialist countries has generated an intense debate on the factors and policies that facilitate their successful transformation into vibrant market democracies. To a large extent, this debate has been inspired by the macroeconomics of stabilization, neo-classical trade theory and the theory of private property rights, while the dominant prescriptions which have emanated from such analysis have emphasized rapid stabilization, liberalization and privatization. This study argues that a broader explanation of the phenomenon at hand drawing also on other theoretical insights might better explain the complex process of transformation underway in these countries.

A broader analytical approach is essential, in particular, to understand the transition experience of countries with structural characteristics and institutional setups very different from those of the better analysed and understood economies of Central Europe. Indeed, while considerable literature has appeared on the transition experience of the latter countries, much less is known about the case of the gradual, partial or late reformers such as China, Vietnam and Laos, the Central Asian economies, the European successor states of the former Soviet Union and south-eastern Europe. With few exceptions, these countries have followed transition strategies different from that of the countries of Central Europe. Even less is known about the structural and institutional conditions of the two countries—Cuba and North Korea—that are still operating under central planning, about the timid market reforms they have introduced so far, and about the reform paths they might follow in the future given the existing institutional, economic and political conditions.

Our study argues that insights from the new institutional economics are particularly relevant in explaining the pattern and pace of reform in late, gradual or partial reformers. It also helps understanding the impact of differences in income inequality, social norms, institutional development and initial structural conditions on their performance. An area of particular attention in our study concerns the nature and efficiency of unconventional property right regimes. The traditional view about the alleged superiority of private property rights is not clearly borne out by the experience of these economies. Likewise, the study focuses also on the role of the state in transitional economies. While there has been unanimous agreement on the need to reduce the role of the communist state, little has been said about what the new state should be or do. With hindsight, it appears that an excessive reduction in the size of the government might have affected institutional continuity and policy credibility.

This study aims at contributing to the ongoing debate on the transition by highlighting the importance of factors and experience of geographical areas which have been broadly neglected so far. As such, I recommend it to the economists, policy makers and practitioners in the field of transition.

Giovanni Andrea Cornia
Director, UNU/WIDER

Acknowledgements

The editors would like to thank a host of persons who helped both directly and indirectly in bringing this research project to final fruition. Firstly, sincere professional gratitude is extended to the whole project team, especially to the chapter authors and the participants to two project meetings held in Helsinki during November 1996 and May 1997. We sincerely believe this volume has benefited much from the scholarly debate which took place on those two occasions and from the suggestions and advice received from them at a later stage. As this volume was being written while events were actually unfolding, frequent updating and revisions were called for. We are, in no small measure, appreciative of the patience shown by contributors in producing two revisions of the initial drafts.

Throughout the life of this research project we were also furnished with the constructive comments of several current and former colleagues at UNU/WIDER (Tony Addison, Juha Honkkila, Gregorz Kolodko and Renato Paniccià, to name a few) and from several other institutions including the World Bank, the United Nations Economic Commission for Europe and the European Bank for Reconstruction and Development. These colleagues provided insightful comments and wise advice on the scope and structure of the volume and on several specific issues. We are also deeply indebted to three anonymous referees for their critical and helpful comments on an early version of this manuscript. Thanks to their constructive criticism, a substantially more focused and polished version of our study has now seen the light.

We also wish to acknowledge with gratitude Liisa Roponen of UNU/WIDER for her expert formatting of the manuscript, for keeping continuously up to date on chapter versions and revisions, and for providing us with a cheerful face in spite of numerous amendments in the book typescript. Thanks go also to Robert Zimmermann who helped with the final English editing of a few final chapters. And finally, special thanks go to Lorraine Telfer-Taivainen, the project secretary, who administered the project, arranged the related meetings, kept calm during turbulence, and even had some left-over energy to regularly supply us with cups of tea and sympathetic smiles.

Giovanni Andrea Cornia
Vladimir Popov

Contents

List of Figures	ix
List of Tables	x
List of Contributors	xiii

Part I. Introduction and Overview

1. Structural and Institutional Factors in the Transition to the Market Economy: An Overview 3
   Giovanni Andrea Cornia and Vladimir Popov

Part II. Lessons from Selected Country Case Studies

2. Russia: Inconsistent Shock Therapy with Weakening Institutions 29
   Vladimir Popov

3. Reform Paths in Central Asian Transitional Economies 55
   Richard Pomfret

4. The Chinese Road to the Market: Achievements and Long-term Sustainability 78
   Fan Gang

5. Vietnam: Transition as a Socialist Project in East Asia 94
   Manuel F. Montes

6. The Tortuous Road to the Market in North Korea: Problems and Prospects 114
   Keun Lee

7. Cuba: The Stalled Transition 132
   Manuel Pastor Jr

Part III. Changes in Key Institutions

8. Economic Performance in Transitional Economies: The Role of Ownership, Incentives, and Restructuring 153
   Derek C. Jones

9. Unorthodox Ownership and Governance Structures in Transitional East Asia   171
   Laixiang Sun

10. Transition Approaches, Institutions, and Income Inequality   192
    Giovanni Andrea Cornia

11. Informal Institutions, Social Capital, and Economic Transition: Reflections on a Neglected Dimension   218
    Martin Raiser

References   240
Index   263

List of Figures

1.1.	Relation between the extent of liberalization and economic performance in a cross section of economies in transition	7
1.2.	Relation between the extent of export orientation and economic performance in a cross section of economies in transition	22
2.1.	Aggregate distortions in industrial structure and external trade before transition and GDP change during transition	31
2.2.	Government revenue and shadow economy, 1989–1996	38
5.1.	Graphical representation of Vietnam's transition and development paths	96
5.2.	Gross output of selected sectors	104
5.3.	Growth rates and 1985 industrial weight	106
5.4.	The changing structure of exports	107
7.1.	Exports and imports in Cuba, 1989–1998	134
7.2.	Budget deficit, 1989–1998	136
7.3.	Real GDP index, 1989–1998	137
7.4.	Tourist flows and revenue, 1989–1998	138
11.1.	Representation of the interrelationships between formal and informal institutions	222

List of Tables

1.1. GDP change in transition economies, 1990–1999	4
1.2. Results of the regression of the log of GDP 1996/GDP 1989 on non-policy and policy-related factors	9
1.3. Results of the regression of the log of GDP 1998/GDP 1989 on non-policy and policy-related factors	14
1.4. Results of the regression of the log of GDP 1998/GDP 1994 on non-policy and policy-related factors	15
2.1. General economic and social indicators, Russia, 1989–1999	37
2.2. Employment, capital stock, and output in major industrial sectors, 1995	39
3.1. GDP growth and inflation in the Central Asian republics	59
3.2. Allocation of general government spending in USSR, Kazakhstan, and Uzbekistan	60
3.3. Demographic change in the CARs and Russia during the first half of the 1990s	66
3.4. Lending operations of the World Bank in Central Asia	69
4.1. Change in the economic structure of China, 1978–1998	79
4.2. The development of non-state sectors, 1980–1997	80
4.3. Reduction of planned production and sales, 1978–1994	83
4.4. Trade openness and external balance, 1978–1997	84
4.5. Growth in the coastal regions, 1981–1994	85
4.6. Financial performance of major state enterprises, 1978–1997	86
4.7. Evolution of the official formulation of the reform objectives since 1978	89
5.1. Gross domestic product by ownership in Vietnam, 1986–1995	99
5.2. Recent macroeconomic data, 1991–1995	100
5.3. Transfers between state enterprises and the state budget, 1987–1994	101
5.4. Distribution of gross industrial output by management level, 1985–1995	102
5.5. Distribution and growth rate of gross industrial output by economic sectors, 1985–1995	102
5.6. Number of non-state industrial establishments by types of ownership, 1985–1995	103
5.7. Average annual growth rates of gross real industrial output by sector over selected periods	105
5.8. Employment statistics by type of enterprise, 1988–1994	109
5.9. Growth rates of labour force, employment, and unemployment, 1985–1995	110
6.1. Overall economic performance by sector in North Korea, 1990–1996	120
6.2. Long-term trend of economic growth	121
6.3. Food grain situation, 1996 and 1997	121

List of Tables

6.4.	Industrial structure in 1989–1990	124
6.5.	Foreign investment in the Rajin-Sunbong free trade zone as of June 1996	129
7.1.	Structural indicators: Cuba versus a sample of comparable reference countries	141
9.1.	The output, employment, and number of rural enterprises in China, 1995	184
9.2.	Private and household industrial establishments in Vietnam and China, 1985–1995	186
9.3.	The features of heterodox ownership and governance structures versus the J-firm and the A-firm	189
10.1.	Income inequality indexes in Eastern and Western Europe, 1986–1987	193
10.2.	Changes in Gini coefficients due to redistribution in Eastern and Western Europe, 1986–1987	194
10.3.	*Ex ante* expectations about the impact of the transition on income inequality	199
10.4.	Gini coefficients of the distribution of net per capita disposable household income in 16 countries in transition of Eastern and Central Europe and the former Soviet Union, 1989–1997	202
10.5.	Income shares of population quintiles, Russia, 1970–1995	203
10.6.	Structure of personal income by income types, Russia, 1990–1995	204
10.7.	Share of income transfers in total household income in selected countries of Eastern and Central Europe and the former Soviet Union, 1989–1993/1994	204
10.8.	Evolution of the Gini coefficients and income gap in China, 1978–1995	205
10.9.	Gini coefficients of the distribution of gross monthly earnings in 16 countries in transition of Eastern and Central Europe and the former Soviet Union, 1989–1997	208
10.10.	Average wage by sector in relation to the national average wage, Russia, 1990–1995	210
10.11.	Minimum wage as a proportion of the average wage in selected countries in transition, 1989–1994	211
10.12.	Changes in the concentration coefficients of social transfers in selected countries in transition, 1989–1993	212
10.13.	Changes in the concentration coefficients of property and self-employment incomes in selected countries in transition, 1989–1993	213
10.14.	Decomposition of the increase in the Gini coefficients of the distribution of household incomes between the pre-transition period and the years 1993–1996 for selected countries in transition	213

List of Tables

11.1.	Selected performance indicators in state-owned enterprises, community-owned enterprises, and town and village enterprises, China, 1983–1993	225
11.2.	Perceptions about external environment and attitudes towards means of financing: East versus West German entrepreneurs	228
11.3.	'Unofficial' payments by enterprises for official permits, Ukraine and Russia survey results, 1996	230
11.4.	Mean trust in political and civil institutions in selected countries	234

List of Contributors

Giovanni Andrea Cornia is currently Professor of Economics at the University of Florence. Between 1995 and 1999 he was the Director of UNU/WIDER. Prior to this he held research positions in a few United Nations agencies and taught at the Universities of Pavia and Florence. His work has focused on macroeconomic, distributive and human capital issues in both developing and transitional economies.

Fan Gang is the Director of the National Economic Research Institute of China and Professor of Economics at the Graduate School of the Chinese Academy of Social Sciences. His main research interests are in the field of macroeconomics and the economics of transition.

Derek C. Jones is Professor of Economics at Hamilton College. He undertook some of the first empirical analyses of worker cooperatives and employee ownership. His current research examines diverse issues for transition economies. Another area of interest is economic development in depressed communities including an investigation of employment practices in firms in central New York. Finally, he has a growing interest in internet economics.

Keun Lee is Professor of Economics at the Seoul National University and holds a Ph.D. from the University of California at Berkeley. He has been a lecturer at the University of Aberdeen in Scotland and a Research Fellow at the East-West Center in Hawaii. His current research focuses on corporate governance and growth, industrial policy, and innovation and technology policy in Korea and China.

Manuel F. Montes is Program Officer for International Economic Policy at the Ford Foundation. Prior to this, he held research positions at the East-West Center in Hawaii and at UNU/WIDER in Helsinki. From 1984 to 1991 he held a chair in money and banking at the University of the Philippines. He has written on balance-of-payments crises, development policy and transitional issues with special reference to South East Asia and Indochina.

Manuel Pastor Jr is Professor of Latin American and Latino Studies and Director of the Center for Justice, Tolerance, and Community at the University of California in Santa Cruz. His research focuses on issues of macroeconomic stabilization and distribution in Latin America and urban development in the United States.

Richard Pomfret is Professor of Economics at the University of Adelaide in Australia. He was previously at Kiel University (1974–6), Concordia University (1976–9) and the Johns Hopkins University (1979–91), and has also worked for the United Nations and the World Bank. His research is in economic development, with a focus on Central Asia.

List of Contributors

Vladimir Popov is presently Head of the Research Sector at the Russian Academy of the National Economy in Moscow and Professor of Economics at Carleton University in Ottawa. He was Senior Research Fellow at UNU/WIDER in Helsinki and has held Visiting Professorships in universities in Canada, Germany and Japan. His research centres on the economics of transition, the Russian economy and comparative economic systems.

Martin Raiser is Principal Economist at EBRD. Among other things, he is currently working on Central Asia and acting as an Editor to the Transition Report published by EBRD. His research interests are in institutional change, social capital and economic performance in transition economies.

Laixiang Sun is Senior Researcher at the International Institute for Applied Systems Analysis (IIASA) in Laxenburg, Austria. He is also affiliated with the UNU/WIDER in Helsinki and the Guanghua School of Management of Peking University in Beijing, China. His research has—*inter alia*—focused on microeconomic incentives, property rights regimes and economic development.

PART I

INTRODUCTION AND OVERVIEW

1

Structural and Institutional Factors in the Transition to the Market Economy: An Overview

GIOVANNI ANDREA CORNIA AND VLADIMIR POPOV

1.1. INTRODUCTION

Despite widespread hopes for a rapid move to political democracy and economic prosperity, the transition to the market economy has brought about a large and abrupt recession and significant increases in unemployment in most countries of Eastern Europe and of the former Soviet Union. In contrast, the reforms introduced since 1978 in China and 1987 in Vietnam were accompanied by a sharp acceleration in the growth of output and rapid improvements in living standards. The move to the market is thus characterized by considerable cross-country variation in policy approaches and outcomes.

With the exception of China and Vietnam, all former socialist economies experienced a severe recession during the initial phase of the transition to a market-type economy. In Eastern and Central Europe the contraction of output lasted for three to four years and ranged from 20 to 30 per cent, while in most CIS countries output continued to fall for seven years in a row and is now less than 50 per cent of the pre-downturn level (Table 1.1). Among the European countries, Poland is that which has registered the most satisfactory performance. The slide of output was stopped already in 1992, and since 1993 GDP grew at a rapid pace while inflation and, to some extent, unemployment were simultaneously reduced, state enterprises started to be restructured, and market institutions built.

Most studies on the impact of the transition have attributed these variations in economic performance to three sets of causes: (i) the policy approaches followed in the field of stabilization, liberalization, and privatization; (ii) differences in initial macroeconomic conditions; and (iii) the availability of external finance. This approach, however, does not explain why apparently different strategies have produced similar results under similar initial conditions (compare, for instance, the cases of gradualism in China and shock therapy in Vietnam), or why better results were achieved under supposedly inferior approaches (compare Uzbekistan and Kyrgyzstan), or why several countries (Moldova is symptomatic of such a situation) which realized important

Table 1.1. *GDP change in transition economies, 1990–1999 (1989 = 100)*

Countries/Years	1990	1991	1992	1993	1994	1995	1996	1997	1998	1999
Eastern Europe and Baltic countries[a]	*93*	*83*	*80*	*81*	*84*	*88*	*92*	*95*	*97*	*99*
Albania	90	65	58	65	72	78	85	79	86	93
Bulgaria	91	80	74	73	74	75	67	63	66	66
Croatia	93	74	66	65	66	67	71	76	78	78
Czech Republic	99	87	84	85	87	93	96	97	94	94
Estonia	92	82	70	65	64	66	69	76	79	79
Hungary	96	86	83	82	85	86	87	91	96	99
Latvia	103	92	60	51	52	51	53	57	59	60
Lithuania	95	89	70	59	53	55	58	62	65	65
FYR Macedonia	90	83	77	70	69	68	69	70	72	72
Poland	88	82	84	88	93	99	106	113	118	123
Romania	94	82	74	75	78	84	87	82	76	73
Slovak Republic	97	83	78	75	79	84	90	95	100	101
Slovenia	95	87	83	85	89	93	96	101	105	108
CIS states[a]	*96*	*90*	*78*	*70*	*61*	*57*	*55*	*56*	*54*	*54*
Armenia	93	77	36	31	32	35	36	38	41	42
Azerbaijan	88	87	67	52	42	38	39	41	44	46
Belarus	97	96	86	78	70	63	64	71	78	79
Georgia	88	69	38	29	25	26	29	32	33	34
Kazakhstan	100	87	84	76	67	61	62	63	61	60
Kyrgyzstan	103	98	79	67	53	50	54	59	60	60
Moldova	98	80	57	56	39	38	35	35	32	30
Russia	96	91	78	72	62	60	58	58	55	55
Tajikistan	98	91	65	58	47	41	39	40	42	44
Turkmenistan	102	97	92	83	66	63	58	42	44	52
Ukraine	97	85	74	63	49	43	38	37	37	36
Uzbekistan	102	101	90	88	85	84	85	87	90	93
China	104	112	127	145	162	178	195	213	229	246
Mongolia	98	88	82	81	83	88	90	94	97	—
Vietnam	105	111	120	130	141	155	169	183	193	—

Note: [a] Weighted average.
Sources: EBRD (1999); for the Asian non-CIS economies, World Bank (1996*a*) and Asian Development Bank (1999) (Key Indicators).

progress in all three above areas, now have domestic markets dominated by highly protected privatized monopolies little regulated by formal institutional arrangements, limited 'new entries', no growth and extremely high inequality.

While these analyses have served their purpose during the stabilization phase of the transition, their present usefulness is limited. The explanation of the success in containing the transformational recession, restarting growth, and developing appropriate economic structures must, therefore, be sought elsewhere, i.e. in factors which often cut across traditional taxonomies.

Factors in the Transition to the Market Economy 5

This volume attempts to fill—however partially and imperfectly—this gap. It discusses the causes of the observed differences in economic performance and optimal policy responses for the future. Its main conclusions are that differences in output performance are explained by variations in initial 'structural' and 'institutional' conditions and in institutional developments during the transition, i.e. factors that are usually thought to be of secondary importance, such as the preservation of adequate capability of the state, the establishment of competitive markets, the expansion of the new private sector, the introduction of adequate incentives and maintenance of an incentive-compatible distribution of income, and so on. In contrast, factors such as the speed of liberalization do not matter as much, or the evidence on their role is not conclusive.

The volume also tries to fill a second gap in the transition debate. While a considerable literature has appeared on the experience of the transitional economies of Eastern and Central Europe, much less is known about the case of the gradual, late and partial reformers of Asia (including Central Asia) and of the former Soviet Union. With rare exceptions (Kazakhstan and Kyrgyzstan), these countries have followed a transition strategy very different from that of countries of Central Europe. Countries such as China, Vietnam and, to some extent, Uzbekistan—for instance—have been cautious liberalizers and slow privatizers. With the introduction of new forms of ownership, their economies now simultaneously comprise a variety of property rights regimes. In spite of problems met in the initial phases of the reforms, they have been able to sustain the public provision of social services and contain the rise of income concentration within reasonable limits (regional inequality surged in China after 1990).

By managing to preserve the institutional capacity of the state, these countries avoided the institutional collapse which, in most CIS countries, outweighed the positive impact of liberalization. For instance, as Pomfret points out in this volume, Uzbekistan's gradual reform strategy proved superior to that of Kazakhstan which followed a more liberal approach but was unable to create a well-functioning market economy, and is in danger of ending up with a market model in which cronyism and organized crime play a more significant role than the price mechanism.

With the view of filling, if only in part, the 'geographical gap' of the transition literature, our study includes six national case studies which deal mainly with less well analysed nations. Besides the 'classical' models of gradual institutional development (China) and inconsistent shock therapy with weakening institutions (Russia), the volume includes the less studied and understood cases of the Central Asian economies and Vietnam, which, as it turns out, allow the shedding of new light on old transition questions. All case studies focus on the extent to which differences in performance during the transition may be explained by uneven initial structural and institutional conditions and the development of institutions during the transition or should be attributed to other factors.

The two countries that are still operating under central planning—Cuba and North Korea—are also included in this analysis. This provides the opportunity to speculate on what lessons these economies can draw from the transition experience elsewhere, and on how long they can stall a deepening of reforms. As noted by Pastor (this volume), Cuba has already begun a 'transition to somewhere', adjusted to the massive loss of Soviet subsidies, and engineered some output recovery. Yet, there are clear limits to its present minimalist approach to reforms, and it is possible that the country will sooner or later be forced to accelerate policy changes in this area by another economic slowdown. North Korea has also introduced some modest changes in the light industrial sector and agriculture (Lee, this volume). However, the situation is rapidly worsening, and the rationality of this 'extreme gradualism' is getting increasingly difficult to accept.

1.2. NEGLECTED FACTORS IN THE EXPLANATION OF THE TRANSFORMATIONAL RECESSION

The conventional wisdom has probably been best summarized in the 1996 World Development Report *From Plan to Market*, which basically stated that differences in economic performance were associated mostly with 'good and bad' policies, in particular with the progress in liberalization and macroeconomic stabilization: countries that are more successful than others in introducing market reforms and bringing down inflation were believed to have better chances to limit the reduction of output and to quickly recover from the transformational recession. 'Consistent policies, combining liberalization of markets, trade, and new business entry with reasonable price stability, can achieve a great deal even in countries lacking clear property rights and strong market institutions'—was one of the major conclusions of the WDR 1996 (p. 142). Thus, countries that are more successful than others in introducing market reforms and bringing down inflation are believed to have better chances to limit the fall of output and quickly recover from the transformational recession.

While this may well be true as a general theoretical statement, the devil is in the details which often do not fit into the generalizations and make straightforward explanations look trivial. Take the example of Vietnam and China, two countries that shared a lot of similarities in initial conditions and achieved basically the same results (immediate growth without transformational recession) despite different reform strategies. While the Chinese reforms are normally treated as a classical example of gradualism, the Vietnamese reformers introduced a shock therapy in 1989 and still managed to avoid a slump in output (Montes, this volume).

Or, take the example of the differing performance of the states of the former Soviet Union. The champions of liberalization and stabilization in the region are definitely the Baltic states (with a 1995 EBRD cumulative liberalization index ranging between 2.4 and 2.9), whereas Uzbekistan (with an index of 1.1) is commonly perceived to be one of the worst procrastinators. However, in Uzbekistan output fell by only 18 per cent over 1990–5, the economy started to grow again in 1996 and in 1999 was only 7 per cent below its 1989 level, while in the Baltics output fell in the early 1990s by 36–60 per cent and in 1999, five years after bottoming out, was still 21–40 per cent below its 1989 level (Table 1.1).

At a first glance, there seems to be a positive relationship between liberalization and performance (Fig. 1.1). However, a more careful consideration reveals that the link is

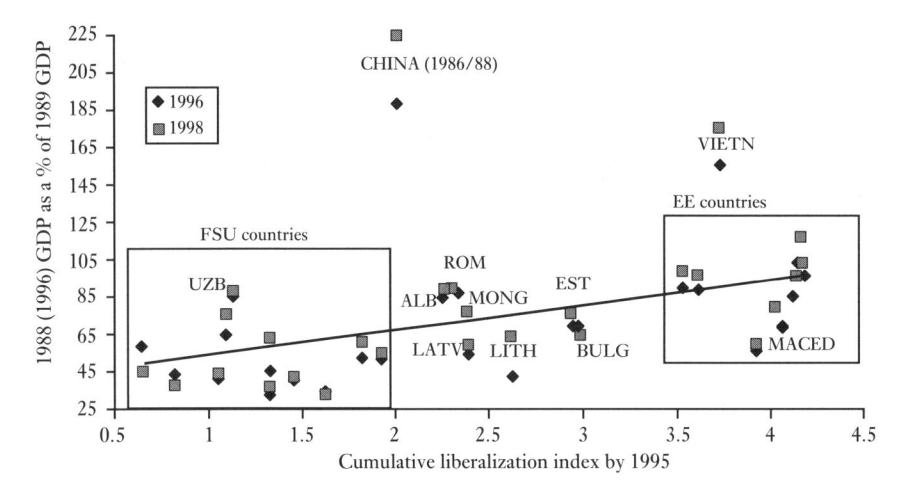

Figure 1.1. *Relation between the extent of liberalization and economic performance in a cross section of economies in transition*

just the result of a sharp difference in the magnitude of the recession in EE countries, as a group, and FSU states, also as a group. Within these groups the correlation, if any, is much weaker, not to speak about China and Vietnam, which are outliers. Similarly, there is no correlation between liberalization index and performance, as measured by changes in industrial output and GDP, for over 80 regions of Russia (Popov 1999*c*).

Overall, attempts to link differences in output changes during transition to the cumulative liberalization index and to macro-stabilization (rates of inflation) have not yielded satisfactory results: dummies, such as membership in the rouble zone (i.e. FSU) and war destruction, have been shown to be much more important explanatory variables than either the liberalization index or inflation (Åslund *et al.* 1996). Other studies that tried to take into account a number of initial conditions (repressed inflation—monetary overhang before deregulation of prices, trade dependence, black market exchange rate premium, number of years under central planning, urbanization, and per capita income) found that in some cases liberalization becomes insignificant as well (De Melo *et al.* 1997, p. 25).

1.2.1. *Initial Structural Conditions*

A substantial portion of the variation in output performance during the transition may be explained by the distortions in the industrial structure and trade patterns inherited from the centrally planned system. The socialist economies differed considerably among each other in terms of the importance of the military sector, extent of over-industrialization, underdevelopment of the service sector, 'under-openness' of the economy, and share of exports to the Soviet republics and among socialist countries. The greater these structural distortions (measured by an aggregate indicator expressed as a percentage of GDP), the more difficult it was to sustain output during restructuring. After accounting for initial structural conditions, the conventional picture of relative significance of various policy-related factors changes considerably.

This explanation—which emphasizes the difficulties faced in restructuring the supply side of the economy—implies that market imperfections hamper the reallocation of resources across sectors, causing in this way a temporary loss of output as the decline in the production of non-competitive industries is not offset immediately by an increase in the production of competitive ones. This asymmetric effect is due to the existence of barriers to capital and labour mobility, poorly developed banking systems and securities markets, uncertain property rights, lack of easily enforceable and commonly accepted bankruptcy and liquidation procedures, the underdevelopment of housing and labour markets, and so on.

In view of this, a low level of economic development (in particular, lower capital/output ratios) may represent a certain advantage, as the resources to be reallocated from the declining to the expanding sector of the economy are substantially smaller. According to this explanation, the Vietnamese and Chinese reformers were therefore less penalized by the legacy of socialism, thanks to the relatively modest weight of the distorted industrial and agricultural structure they inherited from the socialist era. The Chinese communes had little fixed capital stock and proved to be much more amenable to reform than the Soviet and East European state farms which comprised a huge centralized infrastructure poorly suited to family farming.

In contrast to China and Vietnam (and, to some extent, Albania and Mongolia), the East European, Baltic and the CIS states entered the transition with huge accumulated investments in fixed capital stock and were thus doomed to experience a more pronounced transformational recession. Among the countries with modest structural distortions (less than 30 per cent of GDP), one finds Slovenia, Croatia, Macedonia, the Czech and Slovak republics, and Hungary. All these countries, with the exception of war-affected Macedonia, performed better than most other transitional economies (Table 1.1). On the other hand, among countries with aggregate distortions of over 50 per cent of GDP one finds all the former Soviet republics except Russia (where aggregate distortions amounted to 39 per cent of GDP). Taking into account the other two non-policy factors characterizing the initial structural conditions, one finds that about half of the variations in performance may be explained by the level of development, aggregate distortions, and the war dummy variable (Cornia and Popov 1998; Table 1.2, regression 1). Even in China, large state enterprises in heavy industry proved to be a bottleneck to the reform process, as indicated by the negative correlation found between the share of state enterprises in total output and the rates of economic growth by province.

After factoring in the regression equations that explain output performance the initial structural conditions, the addition of the liberalization index and of the rate of inflation increases R^2 only modestly (Table 1.2, regressions 2, 3, and 4). In addition, the coefficient of the liberalization index is not significant and has the wrong sign.

In other words, the differences in performance may be explained in good part by differences in initial structural conditions, and the role of traditional 'good policy'

Table 1.2. *Results of the regression of the log of GDP 1996/GDP 1989*[a] *on non-policy and policy-related factors (all coefficients are significant at the 5 per cent level except those in parentheses)*

Equations	1	2	3	4	5	6
Number of observations	28	28	28	28	17	17
Constant	5.23	4.96	5.55	5.71	5.91	6.07
Distortions, % of GDP[b]	−0.01	−0.01	−0.01	−0.01	−0.001	−0.001
1987 PPP GDP per capita, % of the US level	−0.01	−0.02	−0.01	−0.01	−0.02	−0.01
War dummy[c]	−0.63	−0.58	−0.40	−0.40	0.26[d]	0.27[d]
Decline in government revenues as a % of GDP from 1989–91 to 1993–6	−0.01	−0.01	−0.01	−0.01	—	—
Liberalization index	—	(0.07)	—	(−0.4)	—	(−0.05)
Log inflation (% a year, 1990–5, geometric average)	—	—	−0.12	−0.14	−0.12	−0.14
Shadow economy as a % of GDP in 1994	—	—	—	—	−0.02	−0.02
Adjusted R^2	0.75	0.75	0.85	0.84	0.92	0.91

Notes: [a] For China, all indicators refer to the period 1979–86 or similar. [b] Cumulative measure of distortions as a percentage of GDP equal to the sum of defence expenditure (−3 per cent regarded as the 'normal' level), deviations in industrial structure and trade openness from the 'normal' level, the share of heavily distorted trade (among the FSU republics) and lightly distorted trade (with socialist countries) taken with a 33 per cent weight. [c] Equals 1 for Armenia, Azerbaijan, Croatia, Georgia, Macedonia and Tajikistan, and 0 for all other countries. [d] Significant at the 8 per cent level.

Source: Authors' calculations.

factors is limited. Yet, it would be wrong to conclude that liberalization does not matter at all, since all major explanatory variables (structural distortions, liberalization, and inflation) are correlated with each other. However, controlling for uneven initial structural conditions is a natural step when evaluating the impact of policy measures introduced at a subsequent stage.

There is therefore some, though not very conclusive, evidence that performance depends also on the progress in liberalization. However, even if this impact is real, it is not strong and is overshadowed by other factors. If a lesson is to be derived from this analysis, it is that liberalization by itself does not matter much and works only once the initial structural distortions have been corrected, at least partially, and in a competitive environment with strong state institutions (see later).

1.2.2. *Initial Institutions and the Decline of Institutional Capabilities during the Transition*

In the best of all possible worlds, an efficient state should provide public goods (rules and norms, law and order, contract enforcement, defence, R&D, and so on), goods with large externalities (education and health care), and basic social transfers. The impact of public institutions on development is not necessarily measured by its public expenditure/GDP ratio, since the money could be used to subsidize inefficient industries, or for excessive defence buildup, and so on. The concept of 'ordinary government expenditure' (Naughton 1997) is more suited for the purposes of the current analysis as it excludes defence outlays, investment financing, subsidies, the servicing of the public debt, and social transfers financed from off-budget funds.

The former socialist economies presented considerable variation with respect to initial institutional conditions and their subsequent evolution during the transition. Indeed, accounting for economic performance on the basis of factors discussed above (structural distortions, the level of development, war, inflation, and liberalization) leaves a considerable amount of variance unexplained. This residual appears to be strongly correlated with the efficiency of state institutions. In relation to the predictions of the basic model, China and Vietnam did much better than expected, Central Europe and Baltic states somewhat better than expected, and most CIS states much worse than expected. Exceptions within the CIS prove the rule: Uzbekistan, a country that has adopted a slow approach to the reforms but preserved strong state institutions, performed considerably better than all other CIS countries (Pomfret, this volume).

The decline of the state capacity to implement consistent economic policies has possibly contributed a great deal to the worse than expected economic performance of Russia and most CIS states. In this volume, Popov argues that the collapse of output in the former Soviet Union cannot be attributed to the speed of reform *per se* but to the institutional collapse of the late 1980s/early 1990s. In contrast, it is precisely a strong institutional framework that explains the success of the gradual reforms implemented in China and of the shock therapy adopted in Vietnam (in both cases central planning was not dismantled before new market institutions were created), and for the relative success of the radical reforms in Central Europe, where new market institutions emerged quickly.

The importance of the institutional factor was pointed out more than once for various countries and regions, including transitional economies (Polterovich 1998). Rodrik (1996*b*) found that nearly all variations in the rates of growth in labour productivity in Southeast Asian countries in 1960–94 can be explained by per capita income in 1960, average length of education, and the index of the quality of institutions derived from surveys conducted in the 1980s. Similarly, it was found that 70 per cent of the variations in investment in 69 countries can be explained by only two factors—GDP per capita and institutional capacity index (World Bank 1997). Stiglitz (1998) talks about emerging post-Washington consensus with the greater emphasis on the role of institutions, whereas Holmes (1997) believes that the major lesson to be learned by Western democracies from recent Russian developments is exactly the one about the crucial importance of the state institutions: whereas the Soviet Union proved that the non-market economic system with the strongest state cannot be efficient, Russia today is proving that the market without strong state degrades to the 'exchange of unaccountable power for the untaxable wealth' leading to economic decline.

The efficiency of state and non-state institutions is not easily measurable. In most CIS and Balkan countries, the collapse of the state and the limited development of market institutions is well illustrated by the dramatic spread of the shadow economy and the parallel decline of revenue/GDP ratios; by the inability of the state to deliver basic public goods (e.g. health, education, law and order) and set up an appropriate regulatory framework for the enforcement of property rights, bankruptcies and contracts; by the accumulation of tax, trade, wage, and bank arrears; by the demonetization, dollarization, and barterization of the economy; by the decline of bank financing as a proportion of GDP; by an increase in crime rates; and so on. Most of these phenomena can be defined quantitatively. However, the construction of the aggregate index of institutional capacity is problematic as there is no clear rationale for the selection and weighing of its various components (Campos 1999*b*).

A partial measure of institutional efficiency is offered by the trust placed by businesses and individuals in state institutions. If this approach is followed, the CIS states rank much lower than the Central and Eastern European countries in all polls. In a recent survey of the credibility of state institutions in 69 countries, the CIS states had the lowest score, lower than that of Sub-Saharan Africa (World Bank 1997, pp. 5, 35). Especially striking was the gap between Central and Eastern Europe and the CIS countries.

A synthetic measure of the institutional capacity of the state is the revenue/GDP ratio. Though past analyses rightly emphasized the excessive role of the state (and of the communist party) in the former socialist economies, the downsizing of the state that took place in many CIS states during the recent years has likely gone too far. During the transition, tax/GDP ratio decreased in all former socialist economies. However, the Central European countries and Estonia managed to arrest this decline after only a few years, while Russia (together with Lithuania, Latvia, and several Southeast European and Central Asian states) experienced far greater reductions. In Vietnam the tax/GDP ratio grew by 1.5 times over 1989–93. As planned, the revenue of the Chinese central government as a percentage of GDP fell markedly after the introduction of the fiscal decentralization reform at the end of the 1970s, but this was compensated by an increase in the revenue and quasi-revenue of regional government institutions.

In most CIS states, the reduction of government expenditure proceeded without any coherent plan and did not involve the reassessment of government commitments. Instead of concentrating the limited revenue collected on a few priority programmes, the governments decided for generalized cuts across the board which kept all public activities half-alive, half-financed and barely working. This process has led to a gradual but substantial decay of public education, health care, infrastructure, law and order, R&D, and so on.

Low tax/GDP ratios, and the ensuing weak capacity of the state to regulate and deliver essential programmes, are related to the spread of the shadow economy. To be sure, the expansion of the shadow economy renders revenue collection more complicated. At the same time, weak administration and regulation act by themselves as a potent stimulus to the development of unregulated businesses. Whatever way the causation runs (most probably it runs both ways), there is some evidence that a one percentage point reduction in the share of tax/GDP ratio is accompanied by a similar increase in the share of the shadow economy (Cornia and Popov 1998). In other words, the recent changes in the share of government revenues in GDP are a rather accurate predictor of the ability of the state to enforce rules and regulations.

Institutional capacity is influenced also by the nature of the political system underlying the economy. Using the terminology of political science, it is appropriate to distinguish between strong authoritarian regimes (China, Vietnam, Uzbekistan), strong democratic regimes (Central European countries), and weak democratic regimes (most FSU and Balkan states). The former two are *politically* liberal or liberalizing, i.e. protect individual rights, including those of property and contracts, and create a framework of law and administration, while the latter regimes, though democratic, are not so liberal since they lack strong institutions and the ability to enforce law and order (Zakaria 1997). This gives rise to the phenomenon of 'illiberal democracies'—countries, where competitive elections are introduced before the rule of law is established. While European countries in the nineteenth century and East Asian countries recently moved from first establishing the rule of law to gradually introducing democratic elections (Hong Kong is the most obvious example of the rule of law without democracy), in Latin America, Africa, and now in CIS countries democratic political systems were introduced in societies without the firm rule of law.

Authoritarian regimes (including the communist one), while gradually building property rights and institutions, were filling the vacuum in the rule of law via authoritarian means. After democratization occurred and illiberal democracies emerged, they found themselves deprived of old authoritarian instruments to ensure law and order, but without the newly developed democratic mechanisms needed to guarantee property rights, contracts, and law and order in general. No surprise, this had a devastating impact on investment climate and output. There is a clear relationship between the ratio of the rule of law index on the eve of transition to democratization index, on the one hand, and economic performance during transition, on the other. To put it differently, democratization without strong rule of law, whether one likes it or not, usually leads to the collapse of output. There is a price to pay for early democratization, i.e. introduction of competitive elections of government under the conditions when the major liberal rights (personal freedom and safety, property, contracts, fair trial in court, etc.) are not well established.

As noted, after adding the decline in government revenues variable to the ones that characterize initial conditions (level of development and distortions) and external environment (war dummy variable), the explanatory power of the regression covering the period 1989–96 (1979–86 for China) reaches 75 per cent with satisfactory t-statistics (regression 1, Table 1.2). And it is quite remarkable that the inclusion of liberalization variables at this point does not improve regression statistics (regression 2, Table 1.2). Factoring in inflation allows one to improve the explanatory power to 85 per cent (regressions 3 and 4, Table 1.2). The correlation coefficient rises further up to 92 per cent, if other indicators of the institutional capacities, such as the share of shadow economy, are added, though the number of observations in this case is only 17 because of the lack of data (regressions 5 and 6, Table 1.2). Similarly, Campos (1999*a*) found evidence that government expenditures are positively, not negatively, associated with economic growth in transition economies, i.e. lower expenditures contribute to economic decline in transition economies.

Running the same regressions over the period 1989–98 produces similar though somewhat weaker results (Table 1.3). Again, after factoring in distortions and the decline in government revenues, the liberalization coefficient becomes insignificant, although the explanatory power of the regressions does not rise higher than 80 per cent. These results do not support therefore the arguments about the 'threshold' levels of liberalization, i.e. the fact that liberalization starts affecting performance only after a certain time, or about the lagged impact of the liberalization.

To sum up, there is evidence that, after factoring in initial structural conditions and environmental factors, differences in economic performance during the transition depend mostly on the strength of institutions and not so much on the progress in liberalization *per se*. This said, we still have to explain why the results for the period 1989–98 are less satisfactory than the results for the period 1989–96. To solve this puzzle, we rerun several of the regressions in Table 1.2 over the 1994–8 period. The results (Table 1.4) are substantially different from those reported in Tables 1.2 and 1.3: the coefficient of the variable 'initial structural distortions' has the wrong sign, the t-statistics of many other variables deteriorate sharply, and about two-thirds of the variations in economic performance over 1994–8 remains unexplained by the variables considered so far.

This suggests that the causal factors at work during the initial five to six years of the transition had become less relevant during the subsequent quinquennium. Indeed, by the mid-late 1990s many countries had started recovering from the transformational recession, and the impact of initial distortions in the industrial structure and trade patterns was being felt less intensely. Although only four years of observations are obviously not enough to draw final conclusions, the regression results of Table 1.4 are consistent with this explanation.

1.2.3. *Changes in Property Rights Regime and Microeconomic Incentives*

One of the comparatively few institutional changes promoted by the dominant approach to the transition is the establishment of a private property rights regime. The theoretical justifications offered for this recommendation generally revolve around the alleged superior incentive structure and access to credit markets that private property exhibits in relation to other forms of property.

The differences in approaches to privatization followed in the economies in transition allow one to verify the validity of these arguments. In fact, despite a comparatively short transition, the former centrally planned economies (CPEs) already exhibit considerable variation in terms of prevailing property rights regimes. On the one side, in Azerbaijan, Belarus, Tajikistan, Turkmenistan, Ukraine, Uzbekistan and—until recently—Romania, the state still controls well over 50 per cent of the industrial companies and practically all the land. This group includes Vietnam which introduced, however, a major commercialization of SOEs in cooperation with several

Table 1.3. *Results of the regression of the log of GDP 1998/GDP 1989 on non-policy and policy-related factors*[a] *(all coefficients are significant at the 5 per cent level except those in parentheses)*

Equations	1	2	3	4	5	6	7	8
Number of observations	28	28	28	28	17	17	17	17
Constant	5.30	4.88	5.68	5.73	5.74	5.43	5.86	6.08
Distortions, % of GDP[b]	−0.01	−0.01	−0.01	−0.01	−0.01	−0.01[d]	(−0.00)	(−0.00)
1987 PPP GDP per capita, % of the US level	−0.01	−0.02	−0.01	−0.01	−0.01	−0.02	−0.01[d]	−0.01
War dummy[c]	−0.67	−0.58	−0.38	−0.37				
Decline in government revenues as a % of GDP from 1989–91 to 1993–6	−0.02	−0.01	−0.01	−0.01				
Liberalization index		(0.11)		(−0.01)		(0.11)		(−0.06)
Log inflation (% a year, 1990–5, geometric average)			−0.15	−0.15			−0.13	−0.16
Shadow economy as a % of GDP in 1994					−0.02	−0.02	−0.01	−0.02
Adjusted R^2	0.67	0.69	0.80	0.80	0.72	0.73	0.82	0.81

Notes: See Table 1.2.
Source: Authors' calculations.

Table 1.4. *Results of the regression of the log of GDP 1998/GDP 1994 on non-policy and policy-related factors (all coefficients are significant at the 15 per cent level)*[a]

Equations	1	2	3	4	5
Number of observations	28	28	28	28	28
Constant	4.51	4.25	4.56	4.32	4.60
Distortions, % of GDP[b]		0.004	0.005	0.003	0.003
War dummy[c]			0.15		
Decline in government revenues as a % of GDP from 1989–91 to 1993–6				−0.003[d]	−0.004
Liberalization index	0.07	0.12	0.09	0.10	0.07
Log inflation (% a year, 1990–5, geometric average)			−0.06		0.04
Adjusted R^2	0.21	0.27	0.37	0.29	0.33

Notes: [a]For China, all indicators are for the period 1984–8 or similar. For notes [b] and [c] see Table 1.2.
[d]Significant at the 21 per cent level.
Source: Authors' calculations.

multinational corporations. A second group, including China and a few CIS states, has developed a large 'quasi cooperative sector' comprising workers' collectives and town and village enterprises (TVEs) (Sun, this volume). In contrast, in Central Europe and Russia a large chunk of SOEs has been transferred to the private sector, though also in this case there are differences between the insider privatization followed in Russia, the rapid sales of SOEs to foreign companies adopted in Hungary and the slower approach followed in Poland where the marketization of SOEs was given greater priority (EBRD 1999).

The current evidence shows that the attribution of private property rights is, by itself, far from sufficient for engendering adequate incentives and growth. At the macroeconomic level the relation between privatization and economic performance is blurred at best, and is starkly put into question by the comparison between the highly developed but inefficient Russian private sector and the highly successful Chinese TVEs, joint ventures and other firms operating under different types of property rights regimes.

At the microeconomic level, it might be too soon to draw conclusions based on empirical analyses of privatized firms, not least because of the massive scale of the privatization experiment carried out in the former socialist economies. As noted by Suutela (1997), while some 6,800 enterprises were privatized in the non-transition economies of the world between 1980 and 1991, more than 45,300 large and medium-size firms were divested in the transition countries of Central and Eastern Europe and the former Soviet Union by the end of 1994 alone. In addition, actual outcomes of different privatization approaches are still unclear, as secondary and tertiary redistributions of property titles continue, and the time needed for the privatization–restructuring impact to work through is not yet past. Empirical evidence on the relation between privatization and microeconomic efficiency is therefore highly preliminary. Be as it may, these initial analyses cast some doubts on the alleged positive relation between private property and efficiency. To start with, Jones (this volume) shows that the privatization processes in Russia, the Baltic Republics, and other transitional economies have unexpectedly resulted in a substantial amount of employee ownership, but not in worker control. These findings suggest that privatization did not produce fundamental changes in inherited patterns of corporate governance, but that it rather served to strengthen managerial control. While it is often argued (Raiser, this volume) that the range of feasible privatization alternatives was sharply restricted by the initial informal institutions such as the implicit distribution of property rights before the transition, the incentive and efficiency problems caused by insider privatization remain.

Before–after efficiency studies of privatized SOEs are inconclusive, as privatization has not always given rise to restructuring. Most studies confirm what was discussed above, i.e. that TVEs and cooperatives are more efficient than SOEs, whether privatized or not. Finally, a few studies show that auction-privatized firms are generally more efficient than insider-privatized firms, though no one knows whether this is due to causation or self-selection, and that privatization by direct restitution creates disincentives because of the unclear property rights and high litigation costs this approach often entails (World Bank 1996*a*). Indeed, the main message of all these analyses is that the institution of proper incentives for all economic actors involved should take precedence over the establishment—*per se*—of any given property right regime.

1.2.4. *Changes in Asset and Income Inequality*

Another neglected factor in the analysis of the differential performance of the economies in transition is the level of income and asset inequality—and its change during the transition itself. While it can be argued that in the initial years of the transition, growth collapse and large rises in inequality were co-determined by third factors (including differences in the initial structural and institutional distortions), it is equally plausible to argue that, once it did stabilize, inequality affected subsequent growth in a significant manner.

The transition was expected to bring about a closer relation between human capital, effort, and monetary rewards than during the socialist era. But in many countries it brought about much larger increases in inequality than expected (i.e. Gini coefficients of the distribution of disposable income equal to or greater than 35–40). These surges in inequality proved to be detrimental to long-term growth. There are three sets of theoretical arguments supporting this contention. To start with, high inequality (particularly when it arises from undeserved accumulation of assets and opportunities, the erosion of labour institutions, rent seeking and predatory activities) erodes microeconomic incentives, reduces work effort, and increases labour shirking and the cost of monitoring and supervising labour performance. Second, high levels of income inequality create socio-political instability and social tensions which reduce the savings ratio (Venieris and Gupta 1986) by driving away domestic and foreign investment, erode the security of property rights, augment the threat of expropriation, and increase the cost of business security and contract enforcement (Benabou 1996). Finally, the political economy of high inequality may also lead to slow growth: for instance, under democratic rule, countries characterized by a high degree of asset and income inequality are expected to grow less rapidly than more egalitarian countries as high inequality leads to the election of governments which favour redistribution through high marginal tax rates which, in turn, depress private investment and growth (Alesina and Rodrik 1994; Alesina and Perotti 1996). In a sense, redistributive policies of this kind were implemented in the democracies of Central Europe, but not in 'illiberal democracies' such as Russia. In this class of models, high income inequality reduces also progress in education and human capital accumulation, as financial markets are incomplete and governments are unwilling or unable to tax the wealthy to expand public education.

Even a cursory look at the data shows that the recent trends in income and asset inequality tend to correlate with economic performance (Milanovic 1998; Cornia, this volume). On the one side, the better performing economies of Central Europe have caught up with the level of inequality observed in the Western European market economies. These countries contained the cuts in the tax/GDP ratio, and were thus able to maintain a fairly comprehensive welfare state. Even more important, in these countries earnings inequality rose only moderately despite a full liberalization of the labour market.

On the other hand, in the collapsed economies of the former USSR and South Eastern Europe Gini coefficients rose by 10–20 points (despite large under-registration of high incomes), i.e. two to three times faster than in Central Europe. In these countries, the transitional recession, fall in the wage share, and rise in earnings inequality were very pronounced, the volume of social transfers collapsed and their composition and targeting deteriorated (Milanovic 1995), and privatization was much less egalitarian than in Central Europe (Honkkila 1997).

Though inequality rose also in Vietnam and China, such a rise followed a different pattern less likely to affect incentives and social cohesion. In China, inequality rose imperceptibly (from very low levels) during the years of rapid agricultural growth of 1978–84. Overall income concentration rose somewhat faster between 1985 and 1990, and much faster after 1990. The rise in income disparity which began in 1985–90 can be traced to the rapid expansion of industrial and commercial activities in the urban centres and coastal regions, which exacerbated regional inequality and the urban–rural income gap (Ping 1997; Cornia, this volume). Fiscal decentralization and an industrial policy favouring explicitly urban areas and coastal provinces accentuated markedly this disequalizing trend. While the public policy of the last two years is trying to address this imbalance, it is noteworthy that the surge of inter-regional inequality of the 1990s did not affect growth. In fact, the rise in inter-regional inequality was accompanied by much less pronounced increases in intra-regional inequality. A lower local-level inequality, and continued control of domestic migration, have thus affected little local-level work incentives and social cohesion.

1.3. KEY POLICY CHOICES: POSSIBLE ELEMENTS OF AN INSTITUTIONS-FOCUSED TRANSITION STRATEGY

Mainstream economics argues that the optimal policy approach to the transition should include immediate price and trade liberalization, subsidies removal, unified and competitive exchange rate, rapid privatization of SOEs, elimination of barriers to FDI and portfolio investments, a 'small state', development of the financial sector, and reform of the social sector and taxation. The evidence included in this volume indicates that these measures are not sufficient to ensure a good performance, and that other factors necessary for a successful transition have been neglected. In addition, the mainstream approach does not spell out an explicit 'transition strategy' (in terms of engine of growth, incentives, leading sectors, key actors, role of the state, and so on). It focuses on some necessary conditions (as in the case stabilization) but does not say much about other necessary and sufficient conditions. In addition, it overemphasizes the macroeconomy, while ignoring microeconomic and structural reforms, equity and sectoral policies, and the institutional aspects of the transition. Some of the key ingredients of an alternative 'post-Washington strategy' to the transition are reviewed hereafter.

1.3.1. *Macroeconomic Approach*

1.3.1.1. *Macroeconomic Stabilization and Inflation Control*

Even a cursory review of the literature indicates that high inflation affects adversely economic performance. However, there is no evidence that inflation rates below 40 per cent a year damage growth, while it has been suggested that inflation rates below 20 per cent may even be beneficial to economic activity (Bruno and Easterly 1995; Bruno 1995; Stiglitz 1998). Though this chapter does not explicitly try to identify the 'threshold' below which inflation is not detrimental to growth, it may be argued that in transitional economies such a threshold is actually higher than in other emerging markets because of the numerous structural rigidities inherited from the socialist era. In Uzbekistan, one of the most successful reformers, inflation never fell below 20 per cent a year during the first five years of transition, while in China, the rate of inflation exceeded 20 per cent a year in 1988–9 and in 1993–5 without only modest effects on growth (see Chapters 2, 4, and 5 in this volume).

1.3.1.2. *Exchange Rate Policy*

There is a long-standing debate among economists about what kind of exchange rate policy is most suitable to the economies in transition. The conventional shock therapy approach to stabilization recommends fixing the nominal exchange rate, which operates as a nominal anchor. Others claim that it is the real exchange rate that should be kept stable so as to ensure that the actual rate remains below the PPP rate needed to stimulate export and growth. The Czech Republic, Estonia, Latvia, Mongolia during 1991–4 and, more recently, Russia tried to maintain a stable nominal exchange rate despite persistent high inflation, thus allowing the real exchange rate to appreciate. In contrast, in Poland, Romania, Slovakia, Slovenia, Ukraine, and Belarus the real exchange rate was more or less stable during the same period while the nominal exchange rate depreciated considerably.

Each of these two approaches has its own advantages. The first may be useful in reducing rapidly high inflation (wherever it is possible) during the initial stages of macroeconomic stabilization, while the second may be better suited for overcoming transformational recession and promoting economic recovery by facilitating the transfer of resources from domestic demand to exports. With an appropriate monetary policy (such as the partial sterilization of increases in the money supply caused by foreign exchange reserves buildup) the inflationary pressures arising from this policy can be controlled, as proven by the example of many emerging market economies. Though several economists favour exchange-rate-based stabilization (Bofinger *et al.* 1997), others find that money-based stabilization was successful in quite a number of countries (Albania, Slovenia, Croatia, FYR Macedonia) and there is no evidence that this is an inferior strategy to pegging the nominal exchange rate (Zettermeyer and Citrin 1995).

However, the exchange rate is far too important a tool to be used only for fighting inflation. Indeed, a policy of managed real exchange rate, aiming at the stability of the real rate at a parity substantially below the PPP rate, is better suited for promoting economic recovery and exports. And the desirability of continuing a strong currency policy after macroeconomic stabilization is achieved is highly questionable because of the adverse effects it produces in terms of exports, interest rates, and foreign debt. In particular, such a policy tends to push up domestic interest rates at a time when exactly the opposite is needed.

1.3.1.3. *Government Revenues and Expenditure*

Maintaining the share of government revenues in GDP at an adequate level is essential for output growth. As argued in Section 2 of this chapter, an excessive reduction of public expenditure on 'ordinary government' activities undermines the provision of public goods, social cohesion, capital productivity and growth, and in some instances may lead to the paralysis of the state machinery. The example of Russia—where inadequate tax collection led to the near collapse of the state, the erosion of an already weak social protection system, the massive buildup of government arrears and a large domestic and international debt, and the instability of the rouble—offers a vivid illustration of the perils implicit in such policy. The Russian pattern of institutional decay proved to be extremely detrimental for investment, and, most important, to capital productivity and growth. It must be underscored that the fulfilment of the obligations of 'ordinary government' still leaves considerable room to reduce the inefficient public expenditures (in the field of defence, production and consumption subsidies, and some public investment) inherited from the socialist era.

The objective of sustaining basic public expenditure at adequate levels has been achieved both under authoritarian and democratic regimes, and under a variety of administrative arrangements. For instance, in China while the expenditure on 'ordinary government' of the central administration as a percentage of GDP was much lower than in Russia and Poland, it was sufficient to preserve the functioning of public institutions since the financing of social safety nets by the central government was traditionally low, and since local authorities were transferred some of the functions of the centre after 1978. Besides, due to the fast rise of GDP, during the first seven years of the reforms the absolute level of expenditure for 'ordinary government' doubled. In Russia, in contrast, though such expenditure did not look much lower than in Poland, its pace of decline during the transition exceeded that of GDP. To put it differently, while in Poland 'ordinary government' financing in real terms grew by about one-third over 1989–95/6, in Russia it fell by about three times.

1.3.2. *Microeconomic, Institutional and Industrial Policies*

1.3.2.1. *Establishing Competitive Markets*

The first and foremost task of market reforms is the creation of effective competition in each market, regardless of the property rights regime prevailing in such markets. Establishing a competitive environment and avoiding monopolistic, oligopolistic, or free-riding behaviour should thus take precedence over any other policy objective, including privatization. In the absence of competition, de-monopolization and anti-trust legislation, privatization can lead to worse economic outcomes than during socialism, mainly because of lack of control and coordination failures. In a sense, the emphasis on competition and on market environment is consistent with the emerging 'post-Washington consensus'. China managed to sustain double-digit growth by extending the scope of competition, without privatizing state-owned enterprises (Stiglitz 1998). In Vietnam, privatization was not necessary to create competitive markets and install incentives for reorienting the supply side of the economy and increasing output (Montes, this volume).

One way to achieve competition is allowing free trade. But, as noted by Stiglitz (1994, p. 256) 'there might be cases where there is sufficient internal competition and where, apart from political economic concern, ... a convincing "infant industry" case for protection can be made. Thus ... this needs to be taken into account in the process of privatization or reorganising of state enterprises, as well as in the laws allowing the formation of firms, co-operatives and partnership. The government must take action to minimise barriers to *entry* (emphasis added).' Another way to create a competitive market environment is to allow for *exit* through bankruptcy, liquidation, and consolidation of non-performing enterprises. This approach can be staggered over a fixed schedule, so as to give the 'ageing industry' the time to adjust. Finally, competition requires the creation of efficient asset, credit, and insurance markets, to avoid that only those with cash can bid in the markets for privatization or retrading, to allocate assets to the most efficient producers and to reduce risk aversion. Under these conditions (which are difficult to achieve), the creation of markets where to re-trade land, assets, securities and housing would improve efficiency substantially.

1.3.2.2. Export Orientation

Since the inception of the transition, considerable divergence has developed in this area. Countries such as Turkmenistan, Belarus, and Ukraine have adopted autarkic trade regimes characterized by the exclusion of competing imports and overvalued exchange rates. A watered-down version of this approach is observable in Russia where average tariffs are low (15 per cent), but where, at 70 per cent of its PPP level in 1995–8 (before the August 1998 crisis), the exchange rate is comparatively overvalued in relation to the 50 per cent level prevailing in Central Europe, and where declining sectors such as machinery and agriculture receive public subsidies. This import-substituting-industrialization (ISI)-like approach is sustained by the export of gas, oil, and other primary commodities which account for 75 per cent of Russia's export basket. However, the long-term impact of this approach is unlikely to be positive. Indeed, the literature indicates that while focusing on primary commodity exports hampers long-term growth and diversification of exports, in the presence of skilled labour, an open trade regime and a neutral industrial policy favour the diversification of exports and promote growth (Mayer 1997).

The export promotion strategy followed by the Asian transition economies (for instance, by maintaining a strongly undervalued exchange rate) exhibits features more akin to that of the 'Asian tigers' (Rodrik 1996*a*) than of the countries of Eastern and Central Europe. Export promotion was not accompanied by simultaneous import and capital account liberalization. Montes (this volume) argues that Vietnam (and the other economies in this group) is likely to follow an Asian model of development, in which the trade policy is at the service of industrialization, and focuses on the protection and subsidization of sectors with growth potential, export promotion, and invitation of foreign investment to raise resources and obtain technology for industrialization.

In transitional economies, the argument in favour of export-oriented growth is particularly compelling. The long isolation of these economies from the world market led to the emergence of a perverted industrial structure doomed to collapse once exposed to international competition. The convertibility of national currencies and lowering of trade barriers made it impossible to rely on the previous model of collective import substitution. In addition, the promotion of exports has been rendered necessary by the depressed state of domestic demand. Thus, the only hope to outweigh the decline of the traditional domestic sector is by rapid export expansion. Policies to support non-competitive industries at the expense of competitive ones do not pay off.

The empirical evidence supports this viewpoint. Indeed, in all fast-growing transitional economies the export sector was a main contributor to growth (Fig. 1.2). Countries with an industrial policy designed to favour export-oriented industries (China and Vietnam) were more successful than those which did not adopt an explicit industrial policy (the Central European and Baltic countries), and far more successful than those (the CIS countries) that continued subsidizing non-competitive industries.

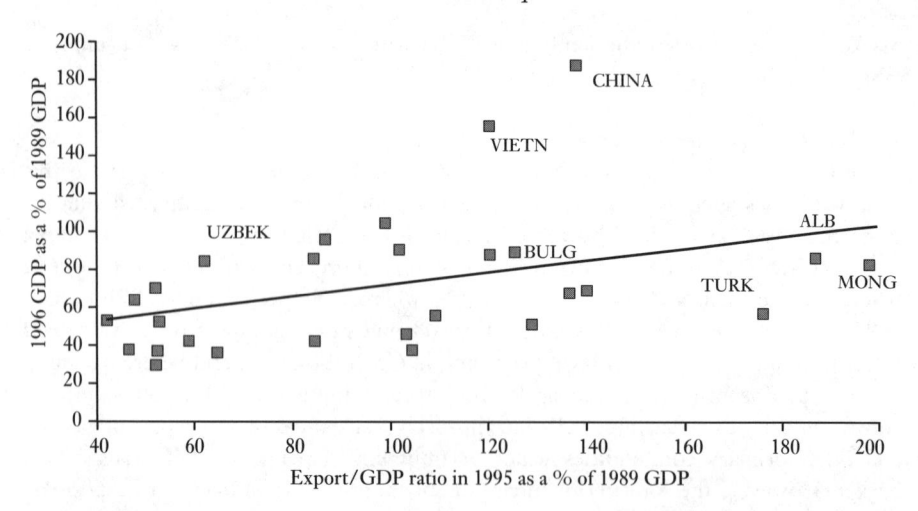

Figure 1.2. *Relation between the extent of export orientation and economic performance in a cross section of economies in transition*

1.3.2.3. The Development of the New Private Sector

Much of the discussion about the privatization of the economy has focused on privatizing the old SOEs. Yet, it now appears that effective privatization, an equitable distribution of assets, and growth may require an expansion of a new private sector (NPS). A preliminary comparison between the successful transitional economies (China in Asia, and Poland in Central Europe) and Russia provides empirical support to this view, but needs to be tested more rigorously.

Theoretically, the new private sector presents a series of advantages in relation to the SOEs and privatized SOEs. First of all, NPS firms generally exhibit better incentive structures for both managers and workers. In addition, supervision costs are lower than in other types of firms, there is no 'path dependence' vis-à-vis old work habits (which are more difficult to eradicate in state-owned enterprises, even after they have been privatized), and the risk of adverse selection of management and governance problems are lower. In many cases, managers and owners are the same people. In others, the small size of NPS firms better allows the owner to persuade the managers to act in the best interest of the firm, to monitor their performance, and to remove them if necessary. Third, some of these advantages (lower cost of supervision and greater incentives) are further strengthened by the smaller size of the NPS in relation to that of the privatized SOEs. The risk of monopolistic behaviour is therefore smaller and the inclination to compete (rather than seek rents) higher. Fourth, NPS firms have generally higher total factor productivity and lower capital/worker ratios than the SOEs and privatized SOEs. Their expansion might thus improve the allocative efficiency of the scarce investible funds available. As the development literature shows, however, these small new enterprises may face greater costs or tighter rationing in some input markets (credit), and greater difficulties in the penetration of export markets (Stewart 1987). However, experience from several developing economies, and mounting evidence about a few transitional economies (such as the Czech Republic; see Nesporova 1997) show that successful policy responses to these problems are possible.

While the development of the new enterprises across countries is not yet well understood, it is clear that without an increase in their number it might be difficult to privatize–restructure the SOEs. An increase in the number of NPS firms can indeed facilitate the absorption of labour and assets shed by the restructuring of privatized SOEs. Failure to absorb workers made redundant by the restructuring SOEs will either slow down the restructuring process, or increase the volume of transfer payments on account of unemployment benefits of early retirement schemes (possibly crowding out public investment and employment creation over the long term), or generate large political costs which may be politically destabilizing.

1.3.2.4. *Microeconomic Incentives and Governance Issues*

Governance and incentives issues are themes which theorists in comparative economics have long pointed to as being of crucial importance in influencing economic performance. Lack of incentives was certainly one of the major problems faced in the socialist enterprises. A current belief is that privatization will automatically take care of this problem. This volume argues, however, that microeconomic efficiency crucially depends on the explicit introduction of adequate incentives/sanctions for all stakeholders (managers, local authorities, national government, owners, and workers). As several studies now show (see, among others, the chapters by Jones and Sun in this volume), the imposition of a hard budget constraint, the genuine threat of bankruptcy and adequate microeconomic incentives prove to be more important for restructuring and performance than changes in the form of ownership. The excellent performance of the Chinese TVEs, for instance, may be attributed to the compatibility of incentives among community members, township and village governments and the TVE management, and to the fact that community governments are effectively monitored by assemblies of community members. The evidence also indicates that efficiency improves with the introduction of schemes which provide for earnings related to firm performance. Jones (this volume) shows that in both China and Bulgaria there is a link between the pay of the senior management and firm productivity.

At the enterprises level, careful attention must thus be paid to the design of compensation packages, whether wage based, piece rate based, or enterprise performance based, to the participation to profits and bonuses by managers and workers, to the rules on the dismissal of management and labour. As noted, these measures maximize reward to effort, minimize labour shirking and free riding, maintain the cost of supervision within acceptable limits, and reduce the agency problems between management and ownership. Improvements in incentives and governance require also the establishment of clear and certain property rights (of whatever nature they are) so as to keep transaction and enforcement costs low, and, in the case of SOEs, to establish transparent corporate governance structures. SOEs and TVEs necessitate the introduction of the hard budget constraint and the removal of subsidies (including 'hidden subsidies' such as tax and inter-enterprise arrears). This imposes restructuring and acceptance of enterprise risk.

1.3.2.5. *Privatization Approaches, Property Rights Regimes, and Efficiency*

Do efficiency and growth depend on privatization? From a theoretical perspective, this is not the case whenever the markets for credit, insurance and assets, as well as regulatory institutions, are weak or absent. It can also be argued that efficiency depends on the pattern of privatization: for instance, insider privatization (by which assets are obtained by ascription and asymmetric access to information) leads to adverse selection, and to a dilution of the incentives to make assets fructify which were acquired at no cost. Indeed this approach may even encourage firm cannibalism and asset stripping. In turn, the sale of SOEs to foreign investors (who allegedly have the ability to restructure/supervise/modernize) may face political difficulties (as this approach would create a brand of dependent capitalism), and would entail large social transfers needed to support the labour shed by the new foreign-owned companies. Third, the efficiency of privatization varies considerably depending on the scale and structure of the enterprises considered: for instance, strong incentives and lower monitoring costs are more typical of the small-scale sector than of large enterprises which tend to suffer from governance, agency, and incentive problems. Fourth, cooperatives can be more efficient than private companies.

Rapid, mass privatization has become widely applauded. Yet, the analyses in this volume suggest that quick privatization is generally inferior to a more cautious approach, both in terms of raising economic efficiency and containing the surge in inequality and poverty. Fast give-away privatization is now perceived as less efficient as it provides little revenue, and can create negative incentives and governance problems, which can be very costly over the long term. Direct sales through auctions may provide revenue to the state budget but limited domestic savings reduce local buying ability, while a glut on the asset market may reduce privatization proceeds. So the form and pace of privatization matters, while privatization *per se* (or at any cost) does not. The idea that any privatization is better than no privatization should thus be rejected. In many cases marketization and the institution of appropriate incentives are more essential.

1.3.3. *Political-economic and Institutional Factors*

1.3.3.1. *Stable Leadership and Institutional Continuity*

In democratic and authoritarian regimes alike, good performance appears to be related to stable leadership, institutional continuity, and the capacity of the state to guide the transition process over the medium term. Such capacity ensures policy stability and predictability, the prioritization of reform measures, the optimization of choices over a longer time horizon and, as a result of all this, greater policy credibility. The latter is key to attract FDI and access international financial markets at rates incorporating low country risk premia.

Thus, the most essential feature of a policy approach is not the speed of implementation of the reforms but the fact that these will not be reversed and will be sustained in the foreseeable future. The state administrative, regulatory, and policy-making capacity must therefore be strengthened, for instance through the reform of the civil service, to achieve the goals of policy stability and efficient policy implementation. And so must its ability to initiate new investment in infrastructure and to preserve and retrain the human capital inherited from the socialist regimes.

Interestingly, the sustainability of reforms has often proven to be greater when these avoided radical shocks. Fan Gang (this volume) notes that China started its economic reforms because of widespread dissatisfaction about the shortage of consumer goods and the inefficiency of state enterprises. However, a radical change was never contemplated, and never seemed necessary as the economy kept growing fast, particularly after the introduction of the initial reform package.

Commitment to reform and policy continuity (for instance in the area of social protection, preservation of human capital, and equity) can be observed in countries with different political regimes and reform approaches—the Czech Republic and Hungary on the one side, and Uzbekistan on the other. The same can be said for lack of commitment, which is observed in both democratic and autocratic regimes. An area in which policy commitment is key is that of equity and social cohesion. Excessive inequality is likely to reduce incentives, increase the demand for public transfers, erode support for the reforms and, possibly, lead to an increase in crimes motivated by material reasons.

1.3.3.2. *Formal and Informal Institutions*

Over the last few years the transition debate has increasingly emphasized the role of the legal, administrative and regulatory framework in the development of the former socialist countries (EBRD 1995). Ever more frequently, attention is also being paid to the problems connected to the enforcement of such rules. Less attention has been placed, however, on the relation between enforcement of formal rules and informal institutions, and on the long-term impact on economic efficiency of the evolution of informal institutions (North 1990). Theoretical, historical, and cross-country evidence suggests that relations of trust and cooperation are essential to keep transaction costs low, facilitate economic exchange, support self-enforcing rules of the game, and foster trust in third-party enforcement through the state. Analytically, it is therefore essential to look at the state of and recent changes in informal institutions, and to their relation to microeconomic efficiency and implementation of formal rules.

In this regard, Raiser (this volume) shows that the transition process has largely been influenced by the inherited informal institutions. In most centrally planned economies, and particularly in the former Soviet Union, the communist regime had weakened the relations of solidarity within the family and society, instilled a strong sense of dependence on the state, suppressed entrepreneurship, and eroded the relations of trust and cooperation among microeconomic agents. Recent work (Poznanski 1996) underscores, however, that there were considerable differences in this regard among the former socialist countries. If his analysis is correct, the comparatively superior performance of Poland can be explained by the better 'initial institutional conditions', in particular by the ability of her citizens to play the market, take risks, maintain a cooperative behaviour, and so on. Similarly, the case of the Chinese TVEs has shown that relations of trust and cooperation among economic agents are key to the successful development of a sophisticated system of incentives linking managers, workers, and government officials. And the stability-cohesiveness of the extended family (as in the Caucasus or rural China) and the strength of the organizations of civil society such as trade unions, neighbourhood associations, churches, etc., have been shown to affect favourably economic performance and welfare.

The implications of the institutional analysis for the future of the transition economies are that the Central European nations, firmly rooted in informal institutions supportive of market behaviour and social solidarity, may rapidly return among the group of advanced industrial nations. Further East, the prospects look much bleaker as state capacity has been eroded and institutional power at times has been taken over by criminal organizations. These countries are in danger to revert to an archaic situation of institutional competition among 'roving bandits' (Borner *et al.* 1995, cited in Raiser, this volume) which is likely to drive the economy underground for a considerable period of time.

All this implies that there cannot be one optimal strategy for institutional reform, and that the strength and legitimacy of the state, and the state of informal institutions have to be taken into account in designing policies for institutional reform. Raiser (this volume) argues that trust and cooperative behaviour will grow out of an articulated civil society and depends positively on the existence of a universal morality at the level of the nation state. While governments cannot directly influence trust in public institutions, they can do so indirectly through reforms that limit the scope for predatory behaviour by public officials, improve political and economic performance, and favour the development of the organizations of civil society.

PART II

LESSONS FROM SELECTED COUNTRY CASE STUDIES

2

Russia: Inconsistent Shock Therapy with Weakening Institutions

VLADIMIR POPOV

2.1. INTRODUCTION

Was there an alternative to the economic reforms of Gorbachev and Yeltsin in the late 1980s and 1990s in the Soviet Union and Russia? There is hardly any scholar that would give a negative answer to the question. The ubiquitous and virtually universal feeling is that 'things went terribly wrong' and that with different policies it could have been possible to avoid most of the misfortunes that struck the former Soviet republics in the 1990s: the disastrous collapse of output, the decline in living standards, the rise in mortality, and so on. After all, most other transition economies did better than the former Soviet Union (FSU) states, and it is difficult to accept the idea that the exceptional length and depth of recession in post-Soviet states were predestined and inevitable.

However, when it comes to the discussion of particular policies, there is much less agreement among scholars. The question why FSU had to pay a greater price for economic transition is answered differently by those who advocate shock therapy and those who support gradual piecemeal reforms. Shock therapists argue that much of the costs of the FSU reforms should be attributed to inconsistencies in the policies followed, namely, to the inability of the governments and the central banks to fight inflation in 1992–5. In contrast, the supporters of gradual transition say exactly the opposite, blaming the attempt to introduce a conventional shock therapy package for all the disasters and misfortunes.

The alternative explanation of the collapse of output in the FSU proposed in this chapter is that the speed of reform *per se* (shock versus gradual transition) did not matter a great deal. The unique magnitude of the recession was caused primarily by two groups of factors: (i) by greater distortions in the industrial structure and external trade patterns on the eve of the transition; and (ii) by the collapse of state and non-state institutions that occurred in the late 1980s to early 1990s and that resulted in chaotic transformation through crisis management instead of organized and manageable transition. It is precisely this strong institutional framework that should be held responsible for both: for the success of gradual reforms in China and shock therapy in Vietnam, where strong authoritarian regimes were preserved and institutions of the centrally planned economy were not dismantled before new market institutions were created, as well as for the relative success of radical reforms in East European, especially in the Central European countries, where strong democratic regimes and new market institutions emerged quickly. And it is precisely the collapse of strong state and institutions that started in the USSR in the late 1980s and continued in the successor states in the 1990s that explains the extreme length, if not the extreme depth, of the FSU transformational recession.

To put it differently, the Gorbachev reforms of 1985–91 failed not because they were gradual, but due to the weakening of the state institutional capacity leading to the inability of the government to control the subsequent flow of events. Similarly, the Yeltsin reforms in Russia, as well as the economic reforms in most other FSU states, were so costly not because of the shock therapy, but due to the collapse of the institutions needed to enforce law and order and carry out a manageable transition.

The other crucial issue of the Russian transition, also addressed here, is the relatively less discussed question of why Russia failed to introduce one of the two sets of clear-cut policies (either shock therapy or the gradual approach), but instead followed a middle-ground inconsistent shock therapy. Why in quite a number of areas (macroeconomic stabilization, industrial strategy, etc.) were Russian policy choices clearly suboptimal? Obviously, it was not a conscious choice of the policy makers, but an undesired final outcome, which makes it no less puzzling since this 'neither–nor' approach is not advocated by anyone, but on the contrary is criticized by proponents of both schools of thought. This brings about the distinction between the first best set of transition policies and feasible policies. It is argued that the combination of large pre-transition distortions and weak institutions precluded optimal policy choices in many areas, which in turn further undermined growth and investment.

2.2. REASONS FOR POOR PERFORMANCE: POLICY-RELATED VERSUS NON-POLICY-RELATED FACTORS

The initial conditions for market-type reforms in Russia were not so favourable as in the countries of Central and Eastern Europe on the one hand, or in China and Vietnam on the other. Indeed, if the transformational recession is viewed as a supply-side phenomenon, as a structural adjustment process resulting from the need to overcome distortions inherited from the centrally planned economy, then the high militarization, over-industrialization and underdevelopment of the service sector, the 'under-openness' of the economy, and the perverse structure of trade among former Soviet republics and among socialist countries obviously put the pre-transition Russian (and Soviet) economy at a disadvantage (Fig. 2.1 and Chapter 1).

In all the centrally planned economies, the share of investment in GDP was higher than in market economies. Owing to low capacity utilization and high inventories, capital productivity was low, so to maintain reasonable growth rates a large proportion of GDP had to be devoted to investment. The Soviet economy was thus extremely capital intensive: the share of investment in GDP in the 1980s was in the range of

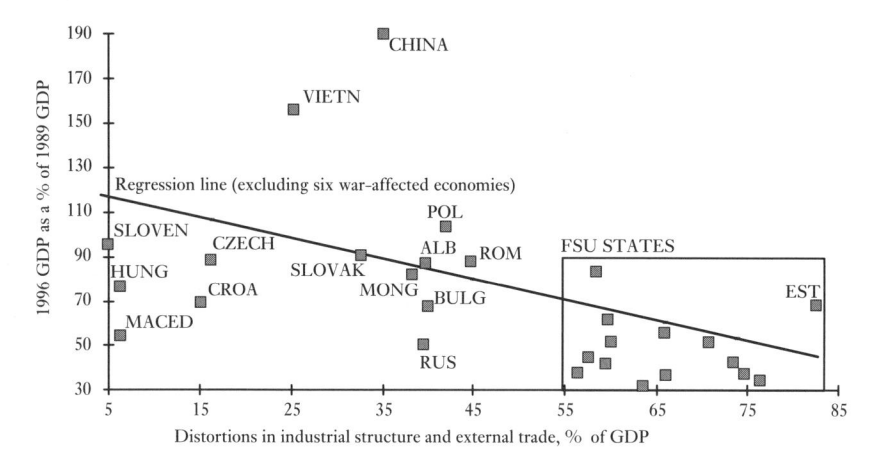

Figure 2.1. *Aggregate distortions in industrial structure and external trade before transition and GDP change during transition*

30–35 per cent, as compared to about 20 per cent in the USA and 25 per cent in Western Europe. In addition, a much higher share of GDP was absorbed by defence expenditure: about 15 per cent in the USSR in the 1980s as compared to 1–5 per cent in the major Western countries (Shmelev and Popov 1989).

All centrally planned economies were over-industrialized at the expense of the service sector, especially at the expense of trade and financial services, which were relatively underdeveloped. The Soviet economy, however, was more defence and investment oriented than other socialist economies, and the Russian industrial structure was 'heavier' than that of other Soviet republics. While the share of industry in GDP in Russia before the transition was not that different from that of other countries, the share of the least efficient industries (machine production) in total industrial output was markedly higher. In 1990 engineering accounted for 46 per cent of the employment and 31 per cent of the output of the industrial sector—more than even in the most industrialized country of the Eastern bloc (in Poland, for instance, these values were 32 and 28 per cent, respectively).[1] In the other Soviet republics, the share of the machinery and equipment industries in total industrial employment in 1990 was also lower (less than 30 per cent, if Ukraine and Belarus are excluded).

Another distortion inherent to Soviet central planning—the productivity gap between resource-based industries and secondary manufacturing—was virtually absent in other centrally planned economies. Due to its greater endowment of natural resources, the Soviet and, especially, the Russian economies were more resource oriented than those of other socialist economies, and the resource industries developed into the most efficient part of the Soviet industrial potential. Compared with world standards, their productivity was several times higher than that in secondary manufacturing. Changes in relative prices during the transition—to bring domestic prices in line with world prices—caused much greater adjustment problems in the FSU than in the East European countries, in which domestic resource prices were kept roughly at the world level.

Also, the collapse of the inter-republican trade that contributed considerably to the depth of the recession in the former Soviet republics should be attributed not to the breakdown of the Union itself, but to changes in relative prices, which made it impossible for the fuel-importing republics to finance their trade deficits with Russia.

As the data show,[2] when trade flows among former Soviet republics are recalculated at world prices, Russia had a surplus of about 6 per cent of GNP, whereas 10 of the remaining 14 former Soviet republics ran trade deficits in the range of 9–30 per cent of GDP. It is no surprise, therefore, that changes in relative prices resulted in a tremendous reduction of Russian exports, from 13 per cent of GNP in 1988 to about 4 per cent in 1995. While exports of resources to republics were mostly diverted to other countries, the sharp reduction in the exports of finished goods (mostly machinery and equipment) triggered a steep decline in output.

To summarize, the legacy of central planning in the former Soviet republics proved to be much worse than in the East European countries: restructuring and adjustment proceeded on a much greater scale and hence were associated with a larger reduction in output. Given a Keynesian multiplier of 2, the reduction of defence expenditure (by 10 per cent of GDP) and inter-republican trade (another 10 per cent of GDP) alone should have caused a 40 per cent decrease in GDP. In other words, supply shocks may explain the bulk of the Russian recession.

Distortions at the macro-level (militarization, over-industrialization, etc.) and at the micro-level (the size and specialization of enterprises) are more difficult to overcome if they are embodied in fixed assets and if these fixed assets are sizeable compared to GDP. It may be argued that in poor agricultural economies distortions were not 'set in stone', since the limited capital stock was less susceptible to distortions and was not so large in comparison to GDP and investment as it was in more advanced industrialized transition economies.

Ceteris paribus, a low level of economic development (in particular, a low capital/output ratio) is an asset rather than a liability, i.e. there are some 'advantages of backwardness'. The conventional understanding of this term introduced by Gerschenkron implies that countries with lower levels of economic development (lower GDP per capita) can benefit from the technological achievements and the experience of richer countries through international trade and hence may enjoy higher rates of growth that allow them to 'catch up' with the richer countries. With respect to the transition economies, this general argument has an additional dimension. Because of distortions in infrastructure and other fixed capital stock created by decades of central planning, the magnitude of the needed restructuring was greater in the socialist economies with higher capital/output ratios, i.e. a higher level of economic development.

China largely managed to escape the restructuring problem due to 'advantages of backwardness' resulting from the low level of economic development. Its economy was mostly based on agriculture (Sachs and Woo 1994), and the capital/labour ratio was low, so central planning did not create too many distortions in the stock of fixed capital (simply because there was not a lot of it around). Chinese agricultural communes with little fixed capital stock (except land) proved to be much more reformable than Soviet and East European collective and state farms with a huge centralized infrastructure poorly suited for family farms, whereas the township and village enterprises that became the major growth sector of the Chinese economy emerged mostly from scratch[3] (see Sun, this study).

The Chinese economy would have probably done no worse than it actually did if shock therapy (the immediate deregulation of prices and the withdrawal of subsidies) instead of gradual reforms had been introduced in the late 1970s. This argument is supported by the example of Vietnam, which followed a different reform path (overnight deregulation of most prices and unification of multiple and black market exchange rates in March 1989), but also managed to avoid a transformational recession (see Montes, this study).

To what extent did the pre-transition structural distortions contribute to the extreme magnitude of the Russian recession and to what extent was this exacerbated by poor economic policies? Attempts to separate non-policy from policy factors by running multiple regressions produce some statistically satisfactory and economically meaningful results (see Chapter 1).[4] These results suggest that the usual argument (Åslund et al. 1996; De Melo et al. 1996; Breton et al. 1997) linking the better performance of the Central European countries as compared to the FSU to better economic policies (greater liberalization and lower inflation) does not necessarily hold. Indeed, it may be shown that the identification and decomposition of the 'FSU effect' may be carried out more effectively by including in the equation not only policy variables, but non-policy factors, such as the initial conditions (the pre-transition level of development and relative magnitude of the distortions in trade and industrial structure) and the impact of war (see Chapter 1).

Thus, in a sense, the FSU countries were doomed to undergo a deeper recession than other states. This is not to say that government policy in general does not affect performance, but to admit that the conventional understanding of the policy factors (progress in liberalization and macroeconomic stabilization) is not enough to account for the variation in performance. It may well be that the most important policy factors that affect performance are not associated, despite popular beliefs, with the speed of liberalization, but with policy measures that preserve or create strong and efficient institutions which facilitate the functioning of a market economy.

The efficiency of state and non-state institutions is not easily measurable. In most FSU and Balkan countries the collapse of institutions is observable in the dramatic increase in the share of the shadow economy; in the decline of government revenues as a proportion of GDP; in the inability of the state to deliver basic public goods and an appropriate regulatory framework; in the accumulation of tax, trade, wage, and bank arrears; in the demonetization, 'dollarization', and 'barterization' of the economy, as measured by high and growing money velocity, and in the decline of bank financing as a proportion of GDP; in the poor enforcement of property rights, bankruptcies, contracts, and law and order in general; in increased crime rates; etc. Most of these phenomena may be defined quantitatively, with the remarkable result that China and

Vietnam are more similar in this respect to countries in Central and Eastern Europe than to those in the CIS (Naughton 1997). However, the construction of an aggregate index of the efficiency of institutions is problematic because the rationale for choosing weights is not clear.

One possible general measure is the trust of businesses and individuals in various institutions (see Chapter 1). Another good proxy for measuring the institutional capacity of the state is the financial strength of the government—the share of state revenues in GDP. Though much has been said about 'big government', by now it is obvious that the downsizing of the government that occurred in most CIS states during the transition went too far. Indeed, the dynamics of the share of government revenues in GDP in transition economies are a rather accurate measure of the ability of the state to enforce rules and regulations. The larger the decline in government revenues, the greater the chances of poor performance.

To sum up, there is enough evidence that differing performance during the transition, after factoring in the initial conditions and the external environment, depends mostly on the strength of institutions and not so much on the progress in liberalization *per se* (Chapter 1 presents an empirical test of this proposition on a cross section of countries).

The results of this regression analysis predict, for instance, that the 48 per cent decline in GDP in 1989–96 in Russia could have been limited to 35 per cent if the share of government revenues in GDP had remained unchanged (in reality, it fell by 19 percentage points). And if, in addition, inflation in 1990–5 had been kept at a level of, say, Hungary (about 20 per cent per year) instead of the actual rate of over 500 per cent, the 1996 GDP would have been no more than 10 per cent lower than that in 1989. These numbers are, of course, no more than hypothetical projections, but they help to perceive the relative importance of the factors that contributed to the decline of output in Russia.

2.3. THE RUSSIAN TRANSITION PATH: FIRST-BEST VERSUS FEASIBLE POLICY OPTIONS

2.3.1. *Liberalization*

Though recent research seems to indicate that the speed of liberalization is by no means a key factor explaining performance (De Melo *et al*. 1997; Kruger and Ciolko 1998; Popov 1998*a,b*; Heybey and Murrell 1999), it is still of interest to ask why Russia did not proceed with liberalization as quickly as the Central European countries. It has been suggested that the speed and extent of liberalization may themselves be endogenous to the model, i.e. liberalization policy may depend on the initial conditions, and the magnitude of the decline in output is a result of liberalization (Ickes 1996; De Melo *et al*. 1997; Kruger and Ciolko 1998; Heybey and Murrell 1999). It has been shown that liberalization itself depends on the initial conditions and on political change (as measured by the Freedom House political freedom index, see De Melo *et al*. 1997). Kruger and Ciolko (1998) have demonstrated that the hypothesis of the endogeneity of the liberalization variable cannot be rejected. The worse the initial conditions for transformation, the greater the probability of the deep transformational recession and hence the more likely are delays in liberalization.

Hernandez-Cata (1999) shows that 85 per cent of the variations in liberalization indices may be explained by geographical proximity to market economies, an index of political reform, the size of the shadow economy, and different regional dummies. The political scientists seem to follow a different approach, trying to explain cross-country differences in reform efforts by political–social–cultural factors, such as the degree of democratization (political freedom), the outcome of the first elections, the dominant religion, the ethnic composition of the population, and the type of government (presidential versus parliamentary democracy). So far, the available evidence suggests that the key variable that overshadows all the other social–political factors is the outcome of the first post-communist elections: if reform parties do well at these elections, a steep trajectory of economic liberalization is predetermined (Fish 1998*a*). What is more, the outcome of these first elections appears to be a good predictor of future political liberalization, with the result that both the economic reform path (economic liberalization) and the path of democratization are shaped by and large by this single crucial event on the eve of transition (Fish 1998*b*).

Whether economic liberalization slows down or not because voters facing a large reduction of output change their attitudes to reforms remains an open issue, even though the anecdotal evidence seems to be pretty strong: in many East European countries and FSU states, radical reform parties that introduced shock therapy packages were voted out of power. This was once among the major concerns of the 'big bang' theorists, so they were putting a heavy emphasis on working out the blueprint for reforms in secrecy and introducing the whole reform package at once to ensure that it became too late and too costly to reverse the reforms. In Russia, the poor results of reforms certainly caused the strengthening of the left opposition and the slowdown in the liberalization process after the 1993 and 1995 parliamentary elections.

The experience of other countries, however, does not confirm the anecdotal evidence. In the first half of the 1990s, when radical reform parties in power contested elections, they won in three of five cases, whereas slow-reform parties lost in four of four cases, and ex-communist parties lost in two of four cases (Åslund *et al.* 1996). Also, in Russia there appears to be some correlation between the preferences of the electorate (as measured by the results of the mid-1990s regional and federal elections of both legislatures and of governors and president) and the reform-oriented economic policies of the regional governments. A study of Russian regional voting patterns found that the reform policies of the regional governments are not rejected, but supported by the voters at the polls, even when 'objective' factors such as urbanization, education levels, the reduction of income during reforms, wage arrears, and alcohol consumption are controlled for and an instrumental variable for reform efforts is used (Warner 1997).

This way or the other, even if the reasoning that the high costs of reforms (an output fall leading to real income reductions and unemployment) forces the public to reconsider previous reformist perceptions and to vote out governments which are too radical is accepted, this reasoning would not carry us too far. First, even assuming that the pace of reforms slows down, this should not be the issue of major concern, since there is far too much evidence today that the speed of liberalization influences performance little as compared to other factors such as institutional collapse. Second, in retrospect, the perceptions of the public and policy makers on the eve of transition were so different from today's knowledge based on the decade-long transition experience that it is difficult to see how rational choices could have been made at that time.

2.3.2. Institutional Decline

Institutional capacity started to weaken back in the late 1980s under the Gorbachev reforms, and the process gained momentum after the USSR fell apart in December 1991: the credibility of the state was undermined by numerous cases of government failure, and the provision of public goods and the enforcement of law and order became notoriously inefficient. Government revenues and expenditure as a per cent of GDP decreased in most republics 1.5–2.5 times; regionalization and tensions between central and regional authorities were growing in most CIS states, while the central government's share in total revenues was decreasing; payment discipline weakened, and trade, tax, wage and bank arrears persisted despite all efforts to deal with them (see Table 2.1). Because of high inflation, the demonetization of the economy progressed at astonishing rates: monetary aggregates and bank credits as a per cent of GDP fell massively; the shadow economy, which accounted for about 5 per cent of GDP in the early 1980s and 10 per cent in the late 1980s in the USSR, expanded to at least 25 per cent, causing in this way a major loss of state revenue (Fig. 2.2); and crime rates, including murder rates, grew two times. It is quite remarkable that in all of the above areas the FSU states on average were doing worse than either China with its gradual transition strategy, or the countries of Central Europe with their shock therapy.

The actual policy followed since Russia became an independent state in 1991 has been a peculiar mixture of shock and gradual approaches. In most cases this policy has reflected compromises and crisis management more than any clear-cut approach to the transition. The approach in fact was adjusted to Russian conditions in such a way as to make it practical and implementable. The unfortunate combination of large distortions in industrial structure, the trade patterns inherited from the era of central planning and the weak institutions (which precluded explicit subsidization of weak sectors) proved to be the key determinant of the suboptimal choices in industrial strategy, macroeconomic and social policy, and perhaps in the privatization area as well.

A decade ago, the research on the macroeconomics of populism in Latin America concluded that redistributive policies arise for at least two reasons: sharp asset and income inequalities and the sharp division between, on the one hand, the export sector for primary products that is controlled by the traditional oligarchy and, on the other, the employers and workers in industry and services (Kaufman and Stallings 1991). In small, open European economies the expansion of the welfare state, which permitted a painless adjustment to the costs of internationalization, represented an

Table 2.1. *General economic and social indicators, Russia, 1989–1999*

Indicator/Year	1990	1991	1992	1993	1994	1995	1996	1997	1998	1999*
GDP, 1989 = 100	96	91	78	72	62	60	57	58	54	55
Gross fixed investment, 1989 = 100	100	85	51	45	34	30	25	23	22	22
—as a % of GDP	29	24	25	21	22	21	21	—	—	—
Employment, 1989 = 100	100	98	95	94	91	88	87	86	85	—
Unemployment rate, %	—	—	4.7	5.5	7.4	8.5	9.6	10.8	11.9	12.5
Government revenues, % of GDP	41.0**	—	44.2	36.1	34.6	32.2	30.4	—	—	—
Inflation (CPI, annual average, %)	6	93	1,526	875	307	198	48	17	60	40
Share of resource industries*** in total industrial output (current prices), %	24.2	23.7	43.9	43.8	46.5	48.1	51.1	—	—	44.6
Exports (billion US$)	140.1	108.5	80.7	63.6	64.9	81.1	88.6	88.2	74.2	—
to non-CIS countries	63.2	50.9	42.4	44.3	49.2	63.7	69.3	—	59.9	—
Real personal disposable incomes, 1990 = 100	100	116	63	74	83	72	72	77	64	—
Gini coefficient (income)	—	26.0	28.9	39.8	40.9	38.1	37.5	37.5	—	—
Average pension as a % of average wage	33	33	26	34	34	38	38	34	36	—
Average pension as a % of average income	47	40	38	44	37	34	39	36	40	—
Share of wages and salaries in GDP, %	48.8	43.7	35.5	38.5	38.2	30.0	26.5	27.5	27.0	—

Notes: *Estimate. **1989. ***Fuel and energy, steel and non-ferrous metals.
Sources: EBRD (1995, 1996, 1997); ECE (1997); Goskomstat; PlanEcon.

important political support for liberal trade policies. In the East Asian countries the political weight of urban popular groups (pressing for the redistribution of export revenues in their favour) was counterbalanced by the presence of the large class of independent farmers or small export-oriented manufacturing firms. In contrast, in Latin America the state had a much more limited capacity to tax income and assets directly, and the export-oriented oligarchy was not willing to share its revenues, but at the same time not able to resist the pressure for redistribution because of political isolation.

The heritage of central planning places the FSU economies into a situation somewhat similar to that of Latin American countries. Whatever the reasons for the wide-scale redistribution of income under the communist regime, after the deregulation of prices, these FSU countries experienced a dramatic and rapid increase in the inequality of the distribution of personal income and of the sectoral profitability of firms. Previously, under authoritarian regimes, the government had been strong enough to impose substantial transfers on the producers (the government revenues in

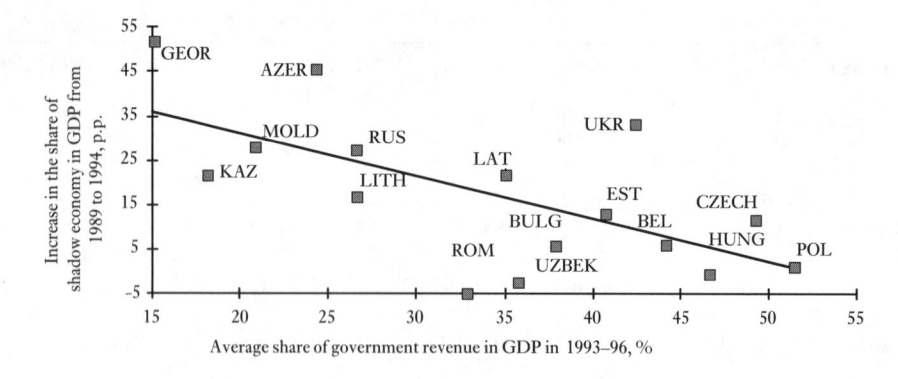

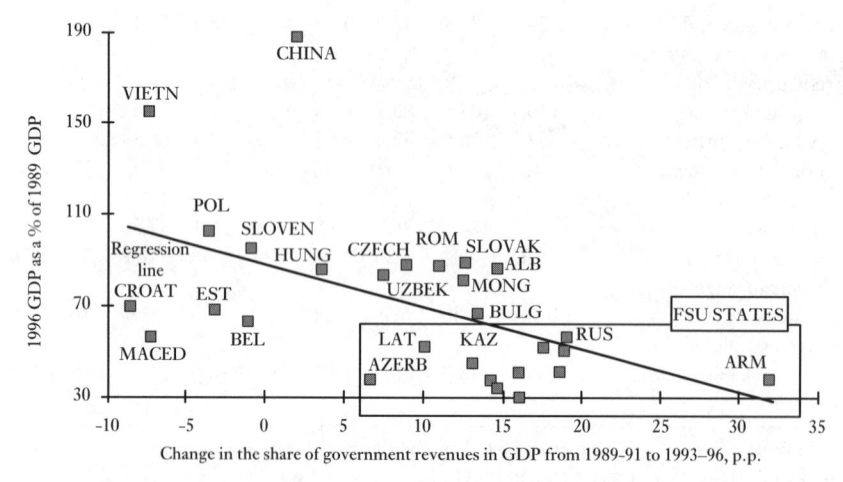

Figure 2.2. *Government revenue and shadow economy, 1989–1996*

the Soviet Union were above 50 per cent of GDP). Weak democratic governments, however, faced with falling budget revenues, were not in a position to maintain large-scale subsidization and had to choose between gradually eliminating the bulk of all subsidies and finding alternative ways of financing them (price controls, inflationary financing, building up domestic and foreign debt, maintaining an overvalued exchange rate, or depleting foreign exchange reserves).

The crucial choice between cutting subsidies to reasonable levels, carrying out open redistribution, and resorting to 'surrogate' financing was probably determined by at least four circumstances: (i) the magnitude of subsidization on the eve of the transition (which was larger in the FSU countries, mostly due to greater price distortions); (ii) the increase in income inequality during the transition (which created a greater need for income transfers); (iii) the magnitude of sectoral differences in productivity and competitiveness; and (iv) the strength of the government, reflecting the degree of consensus in society and the ability of conflicting lobbying groups to come to an explicit agreement. In Russia, a huge sector comprising inefficient enterprises became loss making after the deregulation of prices and the declining institutional capacity of the state. Yet, the government was not capable either of eliminating wide-scale subsidization to this sector once and for all, or of collecting the necessary taxes for exercising such redistributive policies. Hence, implicit—rather than explicit—redistribution became the logical outcome.

2.3.3. *Industrial Strategy*

In addition to some common patterns of structural change observed in all economies in transition (rapid growth of the service sector, especially of trade, banking and financial services, reduction of the share of investment in GDP and greater emphasis on consumer goods, conversion of defence production, etc.), the Russian restructuring was associated with a massive and unique reallocation of resources from secondary manufacturing to raw materials industries.

In Russia the resource sector (fuel and electric energy, steel and non-ferrous metals) employed in 1995 only three million workers, but produced nearly as much output as machine building, light industry and agriculture combined, which, together, employed 17 million workers. Labour productivity was over five times higher in the resource sector than in machinery and equipment and in agriculture. Surprisingly, even capital productivity was slightly higher (Table 2.2). The actual productivity gap is even greater than suggested by the data in current prices presented in Table 2.2, because domestic fuel and energy prices in 1995 were still only about 70 per cent of world prices.

Table 2.2. *Employment, capital stock, and output in major industrial sectors, 1995*

Industries	Employment, annual average, million	Fixed capital stock, trillion roubles*	Gross output, trillion roubles	% of national average	
				Labour productivity	Capital productivity
Resource sector (fuel, energy, metals)	3.0	2,319	418	326	72
Machinery, equipment, and light industry	6.7	1,265	175	61	56
Agriculture	9.9	1,805	276	65	60
Total economy	67.1	11,504	2,870**	100	100

Notes: *After revaluation of 1 January 1996. Breakdown by branches of industry (energy, fuel, etc.) is estimated from 1994 data. **Estimate derived from the ratio of gross output to GDP in 1994 (1.73) and GDP for 1995 (1,659 trillion roubles).

Source: Goskomstat.

After the deregulation of prices in January 1992, fuel and energy prices were controlled directly and, later, indirectly (through export quotas and export taxes), but nevertheless were allowed to increase from 3–5 per cent of the world price level in January 1992 to 30–40 per cent of the world level in 1994 and to about 70 per cent in late 1995. Export taxes on resource goods were gradually lowered and finally abolished on 1 April 1996 (export tariffs for oil were eliminated from 1 July 1996), whereas the prices for fuel exports to the near abroad increased to 75 per cent of the world price for gas (40 per cent for oil and coal) in 1994 and to about 70–80 per cent in 1995. After the devaluation of the rouble in August 1998 domestic fuel prices decreased dramatically in dollar terms; in 1999 export taxes were reintroduced.

Due to the changes in relative prices favouring the resource sector, its output has been falling more slowly in recent years, and exports have increased in a number of cases. As a result of price and output shifts, the share of the resource industries in total industrial output increased from 24 per cent in 1991 to 51 per cent in 1996 at the expense of the reduction of the share of secondary manufacturing, mostly machinery and equipment and light industries.

The resource sector, in fact, has already become the backbone and most important staple of the Russian economy. It accounts for 75 per cent of total exports to the far abroad (50 per cent for fuel and energy, 25 per cent for metals and diamonds) and for an even greater share of the exports to the near abroad. The share of the fuel and energy sector alone in total capital investment in goods-producing industries increased from 20 per cent in 1991 to about 40 per cent in 1995. Gas and oil industry workers enjoy the highest wages in the country: about $500 per month compared to about $250 in banking and insurance, $150 on average, $100 in machine building, $50 in light industry, and below $50 in agriculture in 1996.

Taxes paid by Gazprom, the largest Russian company producing about 600 billion cubic metres of gas (worth around $50 billion at world prices), provided 26 per cent of all federal budget revenues in 1996, while the taxes paid by the energy sector as a whole accounted for 69 per cent of the total (compared to less than 20 per cent in 1990).[5] Taxes on oil and gas production and oil refining amounted to over 50 per cent of gross output in 1996, whereas in the US the comparable figure was 25–30 per cent.[6]

On the other hand, machinery and equipment and light industries were rapidly losing their share of the domestic market to foreign competitors. The share of machinery and equipment in total Russian exports decreased from 17.6 per cent in 1990 to 3.7 per cent in 1995. In 1994 alone the output in machine building and light industry fell nearly by a half, and now these two branches produce less than 40 per cent and less than 15 per cent, respectively, of what they used to produce before the recession. Whereas employment in resource industries rose by nearly a half-million, employment in machine building and light industry dropped by over five million in 1990–5.

The most heavily subsidized sector was agriculture. In 1995 it received about $2 billion from the federal budget and another $3 billion from regional budgets, i.e. an amount equivalent to the monthly wage bill of agricultural employees. If tax concessions and government and Central Bank credits (which are periodically written off) are taken into account, the total amount of transfers to agriculture increases to over $14 billion, or nearly one-quarter of the gross revenues of the whole sector.[7] Because the bulk of all transfers goes to former collective and state farms that in 1995 produced just slightly over half of the total agricultural output (peasant households accounted for another 43 per cent of output, and independent farms for 2 per cent), it turns out that the value-added in large agricultural enterprises is close to zero, if not negative.

Before the introduction of the reforms, the inefficient sectors of the Russian economy were subsidized directly and indirectly, the indirect subsidies occurring through perverse price structures. Because of the magnitude of the problem, it was unrealistic to eliminate subsidies all at once: agriculture, machine building, and light industry employed over 20 million workers, nearly 30 per cent of the total. The actual policy of the gradual removal of subsidies to inefficient industries was thus, if not optimal, the best feasible option. However, the form in which these subsidies were being provided (price subsidies, not direct subsidies to producers for restructuring) was anything but optimal.

When subsidization is carried out through price controls, price distortions worsen the allocation of resources. In all countries, where energy is cheap, the energy intensity of GDP is high: state electricity consumption per $1 PPP GDP is nearly two times higher in FSU than it is in the countries of Central and Eastern Europe, whereas in the countries of Central and Eastern Europe it is two times higher than in Western Europe (EBRD 1998, p. 47). Consumer subsidies have a similar effect. They favour consumption over savings and lead to the inefficient use of subsidized goods (housing, energy, etc.). In addition, consumer subsidies are generally socially regressive, since most of them go to high-income households.

Overall, the Russian policy in this area turned out to be a failure because it took the highly inefficient form of price subsidies (instead of income subsidies) and because it did not succeed either in supporting investment and output in competitive industries, or in allocating funds to those few high-technology industries (e.g. aerospace) that had good prospects for becoming competitive. Instead of becoming an open economy, in the 1990s Russia opted for an import substitution policy that hindered restructuring in inefficient industries and suppressed the growth potential in relatively efficient sectors.

2.3.4. Macroeconomic Policy

The inability either to cut the subsidies inherited from the era of central planning, or to provide them in an explicit fashion, observed mostly in the CIS region, was the major reason for the macroeconomic instability experienced by these countries in the form of budget deficits, inflation, growing domestic and foreign indebtedness, and overvalued exchange rates leading to currency crises.

Empirical evidence from other countries suggests that bringing inflation down to a level of about 40 per cent is unambiguously good for growth, while the effects of reducing it further are less clear.[8] The debate on whether the monetary restrictions which had been introduced were excessive or not is thus understandable in the Central and Eastern European countries, where inflation ranged between 10 and 30 per cent per year and was close to the lower limit of cost-push inflation fuelled by imperfect competition. However, this was not the case in Russia, where, until 1996, inflation was running at rates of hundreds and even thousands per cent per year.

No doubt, the high inflation of 1992–5 contributed to the sharp decline of output. The highly inflationary environment dampened savings and investment, including foreign investment, held back the development of capital markets, and, more generally, created an atmosphere of economic uncertainty which contributed greatly to the magnitude of the Russian recession. Having been caused by the inability of the government to control the deficit and by the expansionary monetary policy of the Central Bank, the Russian inflation was indeed monetary in nature and hence should be viewed as the major policy failure (Fyodorov 1994; Gaidar 1995; Illarionov 1995).

At the same time, the conventional monetarist explanation of the high Russian inflation—pure mismanagement and the irresponsibility of the government and the Central Bank (and the mistaken perceptions of the electorate who failed to elect a better government)—is not completely persuasive, since high inflation continued for years in quite a number of countries in transition.

Though the Russian inflation was predominantly of monetary origin (Koen and Marrese 1995), there were, nevertheless, other powerful factors at work that made macroeconomic stabilization less successful in Russia than it was in Central and Eastern Europe and the Baltic States (Popov 1996). The Russian political economy proved to be more complex in several respects: it was more difficult to work out a consensus on how to cut the budget deficit (partly because of the stronger position of the communists and nationalists, partly due to disagreement between powerful industrial lobbies); it was also more difficult to ensure a solid inflow of revenues to the government budget (because of the larger size of the shadow economy and poor tax administration), and, finally, it was more difficult to overcome the 'non-conventional' reaction of enterprises to demand restrictions (the accumulation of arrears instead of holding down prices and wages: see Lahiri and Citrin 1995; Rostowski 1993).

Though shock therapy worked in other countries, in Russia it resulted in a sort of 'stop and go' policy approach: the tightening of fiscal and monetary restraints resulted in greater tensions among conflicting parties, in a fall in budget revenues, and in non-payments, which led to another round of monetary crises. Given the structural macro- and micro-rigidities of the Russian economy, it was counterproductive to try to fight inflation over several months: two such attempts created unnecessary political and social tensions and resulted in two payment default crises (summer 1992 and summer 1994), which forced the authorities each time to relax restrictions, thus undermining trust in the idea of macroeconomic stabilization itself. It was therefore suggested that the best policy for fighting inflation in Russia was not the conventional stabilization package (relying on the pegged exchange rate as the nominal anchor), but consistent, though gradual, efforts to bring down the budget deficit and slow down the rates of growth of the money supply (Desai 1994).

Because quick exchange-rate-based stabilization was not a feasible option for Russia anyway, it probably made sense to maintain a considerably undervalued exchange rate so as to encourage exports, restructuring and growth, while fighting inflation through tight fiscal and monetary policy (the sterilization of increases in the money supply caused by the growth of foreign exchange reserves) and not through a highly priced national currency (Zettermeyer and Citrin 1995). The sort of crawling peg established for the rouble from mid-1995 proved to be an important device in fighting inflation in the second half of 1995, but Russian domestic prices were rapidly approaching world levels, and since 1996 a strong rouble has undermined exports and economic recovery.

An overvalued rouble and growing government indebtedness became an alternative to inflationary financing in 1995–8, when inflation was brought under control, but finally resulted in the August 1998 currency collapse. At the end of the day, the appreciation of the real exchange rate cannot go on infinitely, and, when this goes too far, it leads to crisis. From early 1992 to late 1995 the real exchange rate of the rouble grew more than sevenfold (more than 600 per cent), more than the growth in the exchange rate in other transition economies and more than enough to kill the increase of exports, to cause an unaffordable rise in imports and to cause a fall in the trade and current account surplus, leading to a rapid decline in reserves (Montes and Popov 1999).

Overall, inflation (as well as debt accumulation and overvalued exchange rates) turned out to be a symptom of tensions and contradictions among interest groups and perhaps even played the role of the 'safety valve' that allowed the government to function despite the disagreements among major parties. As Russians put it, 'inflation is a substitute for civil war' and 'nobody has died yet from inflation'.

The problem, of course, is how can one measure the degree of consensus among 'the major interested parties' and distinguish between 'truly weak' and 'seemingly weak' governments, that is between governments which would inevitably fall once they reduce redistribution and those governments which can accomplish this, but prefer to rely on populist policies to boost their ratings at the polls. Once the government perceives a need to redistribute income in favour of the poorest social groups and weakest enterprises, and at the same time is unable to raise enough taxes for this purpose, the story unfolds pretty much in line with Latin-American-style macroeconomic populism (Dornbush and Edwards 1989; Sachs 1989). Constrained by the inability to raise tax receipts and the simultaneous need to maintain redistribution in favour of particular social groups, the governments are left with few options for the indirect financing of subsidies.

The first one is to retain control over particular prices. Controls over the prices of non-resource goods do not solve the problem completely, since they require explicit subsidies from the budget to cover the losses of the companies producing the goods. In contrast, price controls for fuel, energy, and other resource commodities effectively take rents away from the resource sector and redistribute them to consumers. The redistribution of rent in this case does not require the counter-subsidization of the resource sector, especially if the sector is more efficient than the rest of the economy. This option is available to resource-rich countries, which may be an additional explanation why the resource endowment is found to have a positive effect on the shadow economy and corruption and a negative effect on growth (Sachs and Warner 1996). The second alternative way to maintain subsidies under budget constraints is to resort to the inflationary financing of the government budget. The government in this case compensates for the shortfall in tax revenues by imposing a ruinous inflation tax on everyone.

The third way is debt financing: either domestic, or external borrowing. Debt financing makes sense when it buys time for maintaining subsidies while conflicting parties are negotiating the way to get rid of them. If it continues too long, however, it only makes things worse, since debt-service payments impose an additional burden on the government budget. Finally, the fourth way to continue redistribution with no funds in the budget is to maintain an overvalued exchange rate that favours consumers over producers and exporters over importers and leads to a rise in consumption at the expense of savings. Consumption rises in this case due to an increase in imports financed through external borrowing or foreign exchange reserves and obviously provides only a temporary solution, leading to a balance-of-payments crisis in the longer term.

This is another reason why exchange-rate-based stabilization is quite risky for transition economies with a poor consensus on how to cut inflation (Montes and Popov 1999). Opening up the possibility for the appreciation of the real exchange rate (and ensuring equilibrium only through a balance-of-payments crisis), these arrangements also allow for the continuation of populist policies—redistribution of income from producers to consumers. At the end of the day, inflation has to be dealt with at its source, i.e. the high budget deficits, the unregulated banking systems and the fragile revenue collections, so exchange rate management as a weapon to fight inflation can play only a limited role (Desai 1998).

Different countries in different periods have resorted to one or more of the above mechanisms of implicit redistribution. In Russia the government initially (1992–4) relied on controlling the prices of basic resources (oil, gas, and so on) and on inflationary financing. Since 1995, when exchange-rate-based stabilization was carried out and the rouble reached 70 per cent of its purchasing power parity value, the government relied mostly on domestic and foreign debt financing and redistribution via an overvalued exchange rate. However, since the 1998 financial crisis, which led to the collapse of the exchange rate and to the cessation of international and domestic debt financing, the government has had to rely largely on price controls (via export taxes and export restrictions) on major tradable goods (oil and gas).

There seems to be two logical ways to deal with the populist redistribution and to ensure a stable macroeconomic environment: (i) to eliminate the need for redistribution, i.e. to alleviate social and sectoral income inequalities, which is of course the task for the long run; and (ii) to strengthen the government, so that it can redistribute income explicitly (direct subsidies) rather than indirectly, or cut the magnitude of redistribution altogether. The research on Latin American and other countries has proven that the 'transitional democracies' are less efficient than either authoritarian regimes, or well-established democratic regimes in resisting macroeconomic populism (Kaufman and Stallings 1991).

2.3.5. Employment and Social Policies

The dismantling of the previous social safety net has been another manifestation of the decline in the institutional capacity of the Russian state: incapable of maintaining an extensive welfare system and a balanced budget, the government had to resort to price controls (on energy, housing, and transportation services), to inflationary and debt financing, and to supporting consumption through an overvalued exchange rate. Such non-selective income redistribution, however, failed in containing growing income differentials. While the greater magnitude of the Russian recession and the greater increases in income inequality led to a considerable reduction in living standards for the majority of Russians, the Russian government did less to mitigate these unfavourable developments than did the governments in Central and Eastern Europe (see Cornia, this volume). Spending on pensions has stayed at a level of about 6 per cent of GDP during the transition (Table 2.1), whereas in the Central and Eastern European countries it rose substantially, not to speak of the spending on family allowances that declined greatly in Russia, but remained constant (2.5 per cent of GDP) in the Central and Eastern European countries (see Cornia, this volume). By allowing the socialist system of social guarantees to disintegrate, the Russian authorities missed a chance to build up support for reforms and weaken social tensions.

2.3.6. Privatization and Capital Markets

The first crucial choice for transition economies was whether to privatize at all. It is now widely acknowledged that the Chinese strategy of 'growing out of socialism', i.e. the creation of the non-state (including private) sector from scratch at an accelerated pace (see Sun, this volume), is superior to large-scale privatization. Numerous studies aimed at exploring differences in the performance of firms owned or controlled by the state, managers, workers, outside investors, and *de novo* companies (Earle *et al.* 1995; Jones, this study) have not found clear-cut proof that efficiency and restructuring depend on ownership and control, but have demonstrated that new companies that have emerged from scratch are appreciably more efficient than 'old' companies. Also, it is generally recognized that one of the important factors contributing to the more successful performance of the countries of Central and Eastern Europe relative to the CIS states is the rapid development of the small enterprise sector. In 1997, in Hungary and Poland the total number of legally registered enterprises per 100 inhabitants was about 10, i.e. close to Western averages, whereas in Russia it was less than 2 (Åslund 1999*a*).

It seems, however, that the choice of not privatizing was available only to more or less authoritarian regimes like China, Vietnam, Tajikistan, Turkmenistan, Uzbekistan, and Belarus. Indeed, in all other transition economies (except war-torn Azerbaijan, Bosnia-Herzegovina, and Moldova) more than 50 per cent of GDP by mid-1998 was being produced by private enterprises. Given the fact that the share of the private sector on the eve of the transition was very low in all communist countries, this means that all democratic regimes carried out large-scale privatization programmes.

Nevertheless, countries with strong democratic governments (such as the Central European ones) managed to create a much better business environment for the growth of the new private sector than did the weak democracies, like Russia, where property rights were poorly protected and contract enforcement was little ensured.

With regard to privatization itself, the choices were mostly among marketing the assets to the highest bidder, distributing property vouchers, and giving property away to the workers. The first method of privatization (auctioning property for money) was believed to be preferable on economic grounds: it gave control over enterprises to efficient owners—strategic investors, domestic or foreign, willing to proceed with restructuring; besides, it allowed the state to obtain some proceeds for the budget. The second method of privatization (auctioning property for vouchers) was virtually as good as the first in economic terms (except that the government was not getting any additional revenues) and was even better on social grounds, since it allowed a fair distribution of property among citizens free of charge. The third method of privatization (giving away property to work collectives) was considered as inferior to the first in economic terms (because work collectives normally were not efficient owners) and inferior to the second in social terms (because the assets per worker and the profitability of particular enterprises varied enormously, whereas teachers, doctors, and research fellows did not receive any property at all).

However, it is exactly this third method of privatization that was largely supported by Russian managers ('the red directors'), by the workers in profitable industries, and even by the workers in unprofitable enterprises (partly due to misunderstandings, partly because work collectives, who obtained a large stake of their enterprises, were able to control or at least to influence managers). The rationale for this method of privatization could, perhaps, be found in the belief that, under greater distortions and hence greater potential reduction of output and unemployment in Russia, the major gain from privatization to the workers comes not in a monetary form, but in the form of stronger guarantees of employment in difficult times.

The Russian privatization scheme was different from that in the Central and Eastern European countries in that the workers were entitled to get a huge share of the total assets nearly for free. The Russian privatization model was certainly a compromise between economic and social goals. About half of all small enterprises (mostly in trade, public catering, and personal services) were leased to work collectives with provisions to buy them out later at discount prices (the other half were mostly sold at auctions at market prices), whereas in most large enterprises work collectives received considerable blocks of shares (up to 51 per cent) at prices well below the market level (the rest of the shares were sold at market prices for vouchers and money). The World Bank estimates that 55 per cent of the large and medium-size enterprises in Russia were privatized through management-employment buyouts, whereas the comparable ratios for other economies in transition were typically below 14 per cent.[9]

By accepting the idea of giving away up to one-half of total assets to workers nearly free of charge, the government managed to increase prices for another half and, more important, to avoid accusations of 'selling off the motherland to the new millionaires and to foreigners'. The major issue of privatization, who gains control over the enterprises—outsiders (the new rich or foreigners) or insiders (management and work collectives)—was resolved in favour of the insiders: they established their control over nearly all large enterprises and over about half of the small enterprises. A random survey of 439 enterprises conducted by the World Bank in 1994 revealed that workers and managers were dominant owners in 70 per cent of all non-state enterprise or in 84 per cent of all non-state privatized enterprises (excluding new firms that had emerged from scratch).[10]

Post factum, it looks like this was the most feasible way to privatize state property, though asset prices were extremely low in Russia partly because of the lack of domestic savings, partly because of the poor investment climate which suppressed foreign investment. As a result, the book-to-market ratio for companies subject to privatization was somewhere in the range of 50 : 1 to 100 : 1, i.e. the actual value of assets in current prices was about 50–100 times higher than the market price of company shares.

The drama of privatization in post-communist economies was driven by the huge gap between the demand for and the supply of assets. The approximate supply of assets—the book value of the property to be privatized, however uncertain the estimates of the book value are—is comparable to the size of annual GDP; the approximate domestic demand for assets is equal at best to several per cent of GDP because it is financed from the limited pool of national savings, which altogether usually amounts to 20–30 per cent of GDP. These savings are mostly absorbed by investment, the government budget deficit, and the current account surplus.

In carrying out privatization—the most important institutional reform—the Russian government gave work collectives larger concessions than did governments in the Eastern European countries. By doing this, it emphasized political feasibility over equity and economic efficiency. It seems, however, that the game was worth the candle: massive and quick privatization became socially acceptable and politically feasible at the cost of establishing the control of insiders over most privatized enterprises. As shares were traded, strategic investors from the outside gained control over enterprises. While in large, but not the largest, privatized Russian companies, outsiders owned only 31 per cent of the shares in 1996, with 59 per cent of the shares belonging to insiders and 9 per cent to the state, outsiders owned on average 57 per cent of all shares in the 100 largest Russian companies (insiders: 22 per cent; the state: 21 per cent) (Blasi *et al.* 1996).

2.4. WEAK INSTITUTIONS AND EMERGING RUSSIAN-STYLE CAPITALISM

At least at the intuitive level, it seems that the Central and Eastern European countries and the Baltic States are heading in the direction of market models that currently exist in Western Europe. Even more, it seems that they are aiming at becoming members of the European Union (EU), which requires them to harmonize their policies and institutions with those of the EU. It is also natural to assume that China and Vietnam are developing a type of market economy that is broadly consistent with that existing in the region.

With regard to Russia, the future patterns of development are much less clear. Overall, Russian public opinion appears to be more polarized than that in Central and Eastern European countries and the Baltic States, where a broader agreement on major economic reform issues exists. Communist ideals are deeply rooted in Russian history; geographical, ethnic, and economic diversity contributes to contradictions among major regional and industrial elite groups. Besides, law and order traditions seem to be relatively weak in Russian society, which results in a higher crime rate, a larger shadow economy, widespread corruption, etc. Finally, egalitarian and collectivist feelings are more pronounced in Russia; there is a less tolerant attitude towards income inequality and a much stronger emphasis on the preservation of employment in times of recession.

On the other hand, Russia does not have the same traditions in business and work ethics as East Asian countries. The individual's links to the community are weaker than in East Asia. Even in the Soviet era, labour mobility, for instance, was much higher in Russia than in Japan (or in Western Europe), while the social services provided by enterprises (health care, housing, recreation, etc.), though substantial, were never as extensive as in China.

Pessimists claim that the Russian tragedy has occurred because Asian-type responsibility of the individual to the community has already been destroyed (partly before and partly after the 1917 revolution), whereas the new European-type responsibility to the society (state) has not yet emerged. Optimists see this as a source of Russian strength, claiming that it allows the best of both worlds to be combined. Century-old debates between Westerners and Slavophiles are now being revitalized, as Russia struggles to define its new identity and to find a new role in the world economy and politics. Below, we focus on some likely features of a 'Russian-style' market.

2.4.1. *Asset and Income Distribution*

Though data on the distribution of wealth in Russia in recent years are lacking, there is reason to believe that this distribution has changed dramatically in recent years and is now extremely uneven. The initial accumulation of capital in the late 1980s and early 1990s proceeded under conditions of unbelievable opportunities for enrichment. The first fortunes of the new Russians were built in external trade, in the commodity-exchange business, and in banking and finance; in virtually all cases, it was the arbitrage between state-regulated prices and free market (domestic or foreign) prices that laid the foundations for these fortunes. The share of managers in the total shareholder equity is said to have increased from 8 per cent right after the end of voucher privatization (mid-1994) to about 20 per cent in 1996, whereas in newly established companies managers already controlled over 50 per cent of the shares in 1994.

As a result, the increases in income inequality were much more pronounced in Russia than in the Central and Eastern European countries: the Gini coefficient grew sharply in just four years (Table 2.1), while decile and pentile ratios increased more than threefold. This is an exceptional record for economies in transition and is matched only by Bulgaria and some former Soviet republics (see Cornia, this study).

2.4.2. Corporate Financing and Control

Overall, at least for the time being, Russia seems to be the only country among transition economies that is drifting in the direction of a market-based system of corporate financing and control. The weak and decentralized banking sector was the single most important reason that determined the development of the Russian financial system along the lines of the British–American model. Besides, the distinct character of Russian privatization—large concessions to workers and managers, coupled with the high speed of the process—definitely contributed to the dispersion of shares among millions of individual shareholders (Popov 1999a).

Russia's stock market, extremely undervalued on the eve of the transition, greatly outperfomed other emerging markets: Russian stocks grew eight times in dollar terms from December 1992 to February 1998, whereas Hungarian stocks only grew about threefold, and Polish and Czech stocks about twofold over the same period. By mid-1997 market capitalization was presumably at a level of $100 billion (at par with China), about 25 per cent of GDP, whereas the volume of trading—over 5 per cent of GDP—made Russia one of the leaders of stock market development, together with China and the Central European countries. Following the August 1998 exchange rate, debt and stock market crisis, however, the stock market lost 90 per cent of its value, and the capitalization and volume of trade indicators returned to their early 1990s levels. The institutional framework of the Russian stock market based on the self-governing association of stock market participants (Paufor, later Naufor) had been generally regarded as a success story before the 1998 crisis (Frye 1997).

Nevertheless, the usual advantages of the securities-based system of corporate financing and control were not yet readily noticeable in Russia: shareholders did not seem to exercise an efficient control over management, and, even before the 1998 financial crash, the markets for corporate securities could not compensate for the lack of bank credits. And the situation worsened further in the post-crash paralysis of the years 1999–2000.

The future role of institutional investors is still an open issue. Until 1996 banks were not the major owners of the shares of non-financial companies, not to mention the mutual, pension, and insurance funds that were just starting to emerge. Later, however, there was a lot of speculation in the press that this pattern may have changed after the 'shares for loans' auctions—the sales of the most lucrative pieces of government property to the highest bidder that started in late 1995 and did not involve any concessions to the work collectives. Several major banks received, as collateral for the credits issued to the government, large blocks of shares of non-financial companies. In the largest Russian banks, investment in non-government securities increased from 1 per cent of the total assets in the beginning of 1995 (compared to 3 per cent in US banks and much more in other Western countries) to about 10 per cent in mid-1997 (Dmitriyev et al. 1996; OECD 1997).

In November 1996 the newspapers began writing about the group of five to seven banks that control a good half of the Russian economy.[11] The largest group, Oneximbank, reportedly controls banks with assets of some $5 billion and industrial enterprises with sales of about $9 billion; the second largest, Menatep, has banking assets of about $2 billion and holds control over enterprises with sales of about $6 billion.[12] This was obviously a significant proportion of the national economy (the 1995 GDP was $364 billion).

Moreover, in large privatized state enterprises, financial institutions (holding companies and financial-industrial groups, investment funds and banks) controlled only 10 per cent of all shares. In the 100 largest Russian corporations, the shares of stock owned by financial institutions were somewhat higher, 18 per cent, but the proportion of stocks belonging to outsiders was also higher, so that the share of financial institutions in total outsider ownership is approximately the same for large and the largest companies, about one-third.

After the August 1998 financial and banking crisis the position of banks in general and vis-à-vis non-financial corporations in particular was weakened dramatically. Even before the crisis, the banks acquiring shares of several large non-financial companies were believed to be only transitional investors. Bank-based FIGs were often expected to sell the shares of the industrial enterprises they had acquired at 'shares for loans' auctions after more or less cosmetic 'investmentless' restructuring. Studies of the Oneximbank and Menatep groups by Dun and Bradstreet characterize their activities towards acquired firms as, first and foremost, preparation for resale, while Alfa Bank publicly proclaims this as a primary goal (OECD 1997, p. 103). Nor did banks account for a substantial portion of investment financing or have the funds needed for industrial restructuring. After the crisis, some of the major banks went bankrupt; others sold their industrial property or transferred it into non-bank holding companies not linked to the banks themselves. Though the stock market was dormant in 1999–2000, the prospects for the formation of bank-based financial systems after the crisis definitely looked worse than they had before it.

An additional argument to support this view is that, with large imbalances in the distribution of wealth, Russia is unlikely to develop a system of corporate financing and control that is based on institutional rather than on individual investors. In short, Russian capitalism with regard to wealth and income inequalities and the market for corporate control may resemble more that of the 'robber baron' days in the US, rather than a consensus-based Asian model or state-regulated Western European one. As one Russian parliamentarian has put it, 'this is not the wild West; this is the wild East'.

2.4.3. *The Role of the State*

In the Western European countries the role of the government is extensive in many areas: in creating institutions and regulatory frameworks, in providing public goods (education, health care, infrastructure, etc.), and in carrying out social transfers. In contrast, in East Asian economies, while government regulatory functions are sometimes even stronger than they are in the Western European countries, the size of government, as measured by revenues and expenditure in relation to GDP, is considerably smaller, which means that the state involvement in the provision of public goods and, especially, social transfers is limited.

The model that emerges in Russia seems to be based on minimal government involvement in all areas of economic life. In the FSU not only were government regulations pervasive, but also the financial power of the state was roughly the same as in Western European countries. This allowed the state to supply the bulk of public goods and extensive social transfers.

In post-transition Russia, the state has found itself deprived of its former vast resources and powers. On the one hand, it has turned out that government regulatory activities have only limited efficiency due to difficulties in enforcing regulations, since the authoritarian regime was replaced by a weak democratic one. On the other hand, government revenues plummeted after central planning was dismantled, approaching some 30 per cent of GDP (including off-budget funds) in 1996 (Table 2.1). This is still more than in East Asian countries on average, but much less than needed to finance government commitments—a still very large defence expenditure, mostly free education and health care, and a universal pay-as-you-go system of social insurance.

Cuts in government expenditure thus became the only way of bringing down the deficit and were gradually carried out in 1992–6. However, because a consensus on major reform issues was lacking and the state was not really prepared to reassess its commitments, cuts in budgetary expenditure were carried out without any coherent strategy. The poor administration of shrinking public funds turned into a major problem. As a result, past social responsibilities are currently financially unsustainable, and there is a gap between the obligations of the state and the ability of the state to deliver what it promises.

Unless the government is prepared to reassess radically its commitments, so as to make them financially sustainable, it is safe to predict that many activities in the provision of public goods and social transfers will slowly lose steam. Since they can only partly be replaced by private and semi-private businesses, this would probably be the worst option and a clear-cut case of government failure.

2.4.4. *Industrial Structure and International Specialization*

In the late 1920s, when the New Economic Policy that allowed the existence of a market economy was about to be rolled back, there were debates between two schools of planners—geneticists and teleologists. The former suggested that planning should be indicative rather than directive, that it should conform to trends identified by the market, that industrialization should start from light industry and proceed gradually, as savings generated in a natural way became available. The latter argued that planners should not feel constrained by the objective laws and potentials of the economy, that they should not rely on the slow and obsolete market, but should speed up development by mobilizing savings through price controls and directive planning in order to create quickly a heavy industry that would lead the industrialization process in the country.

It is this latter view which became official policy, with the result that the industrialization of the 1930s and beyond generated a major isolationist import-substitution experiment. From that time on, the share of exports in Soviet GDP stagnated until large-scale fuel sales abroad started in the 1970s. The huge 'perverted' industrial structure created without any regard to world market prices proved to be stillborn and non-viable in 1992, when it finally faced foreign competition after a half-century of isolation.

Today, Russia is choosing once again between export-oriented growth and autarchy. On the one hand, there is the example of the East Asian countries which managed to rely on exports as a locomotive of economic growth: in China, for instance, the share of exports in GDP increased from 5 per cent in 1978 to 23 per cent in 1994, while GDP itself was growing at an average rate of about 10 per cent. On the other hand, there are much less appealing examples of 'the champion of isolationism', North Korea (see Lee, this volume), and other socialist countries and of many developing countries of socialist orientation, which were creating their own heavy industries following the advice and using the assistance of the Soviet Union, of India (where the share of exports in GDP remained frozen at a level of 6 per cent from the 1950s to the 1980s) and many Latin American countries.

The option of promoting export-oriented growth would require massive and rapid industrial restructuring: mostly in favour of resource-based industries, but also in favour of some competitive high-tech sectors (e.g. aerospace) and, perhaps, particular capital- and labour-intensive industries at the expense of agriculture and most secondary manufacturing industries. Similar to the restructuring of government services, it is more efficient to make the needed cuts at once (and to support people through social and manpower programmes, instead of subsidizing non-competitive companies) rather than to stretch them in time, thereby forcing inefficient industries to die gradually. A rapid growth of the resource sector may provide rents (partly appropriated by the resource sector itself, partly by the government) for much-needed investment to restructure a few still promising secondary manufacturing industries and enterprises (Gazprom and major oil companies are already trying to diversify by buying companies which produce mining equipment).

This radical option, however, may prove not entirely feasible politically, since the inefficient sectors suffering from the competition of imported goods (agriculture and machine production) account for a much larger share of total employment than do the efficient sectors and also exercise a good deal of influence in the corridors of power.

The other option—continuing support for major non-competitive industries—is a slower and more costly way of restructuring, implying the preservation of subsidies to and the protection of weak producers. Paradoxically, this option, despite the intentions of those who propagate it to stop the deindustrialization of the country, may lead to exactly the opposite: the poor performance of the resource sector will not generate enough revenues to support all non-competitive industries, with the result that the few still competitive or potentially competitive secondary manufacturing industries will fail to get necessary support and will slowly disintegrate.

In sum, it would be tempting to characterize the emerging Russian market structure as the one that combines the features of both the Western European and the Asian model. A closer look, however, reveals that this kind of description may be no more than a general negative statement: evolving Russian capitalism is going to be compatible neither with the Western European nor with East Asian patterns.

The closest analogue can probably be found in some of the most common Latin American archetypes of the 1970s—very high wealth and income inequalities, strong social tensions and poor consensus in society about reforms, large unreformed latifundia, non-competitive sectors in industry supported by government subsidies, an economically and politically weak government whose commitments stretch beyond its financial abilities, resulting in numerous cases of government failure, populist macroeconomic policies, leading to outbursts of inflation and capital flight, discouraging savings, investment and growth.

This is rather pessimistic, yet it is the most probable scenario based on an extrapolation from the existing trends. To change this scenario into a more favourable one, non-cosmetic reforms will be required: the restructuring of government services (public goods and social transfers) so as to make them smaller, but more efficient and financially sustainable; sound industrial policy supporting competitive export-oriented industries rather than non-competitive inward-looking ones; a strategy to promote savings and investment (maintaining a low exchange rate for the rouble, reforming the pension system and housing subsidies, increasing government investment and attracting foreign direct investment into resource projects (see Sachs and Warner 1996; Schmidt-Hebbel *et al.* 1996)); strong social policy which may be the only chance to build consensus under the conditions of high wealth and income inequalities. The political feasibility of such a scenario does not seem to be great, though some moves in this direction are likely.

NOTES

1. The comparison is based on national statistics. The share of machinery and equipment industries in total value-added in manufacturing in 1992 was higher than 1/3 only in Malaysia, Thailand, Singapore, and Japan (World Bank 1995, pp. 172–3).
2. Commission of the European Communities (1990, p. 173) (data are derived from official Soviet statistics); Goskomstat (1990, p. 638).
3. Capital/labour ratios in the township and village enterprises are only 25 per cent of those in the state sector, while the labour productivity is about 80 per cent of the level in state enterprises. See World Bank (1996*a*, p. 51).
4. A more detailed description of the data and the regressions is in Popov (1998*a,b*, 1999*b*).
5. *Segodnya*, 31 May 1997.
6. *Finansoviye Izvestiya*, 20 June 1996; *Segodnya*, 31 August 1996.
7. *Segodnya*, 31 July 1996.
8. Bruno (1995); Bruno and Easterly (1998); World Bank (1996*a*, p. 37).
9. World Bank (1996*a*, p. 53).
10. EBRD (1995, p. 132).
11. Boris Berezovsky was quoted in the *Financial Times* (1 November 1996) saying that seven bankers control half of the Russian economy. The banks usually named are Oneximbank (headed until recently by V. Potanin), Menatep (headed by M. Khodorkovsky), Stolychniy

Bank (which recently acquired Agroprombank, headed by A. Smolensky), Most Bank (headed by V. Gussinsky), and Alfa Bank (headed by P. Aven and M. Friedman). Another company often mentioned together with these banks (Logovaz, headed until recently by the outspoken B. Berezovsky) is not a bank, but a dealer for the major 'VAZ' autoplant.

12. *Expert*, 2 December 1996, p. 19.

3

Reform Paths in Central Asian Transitional Economies

RICHARD POMFRET

The Central Asian economies offer an interesting comparative study in reform paths of formerly centrally planned economies. From fairly similar starting points they have pursued different policies since the demise of the Soviet Union in December 1991. This study analyses the reform strategies and their outcomes in Kazakhstan, the Kyrgyz Republic, Turkmenistan, and Uzbekistan, omitting Tajikistan whose post-independence history has been dominated by internal conflicts. The study will seek to identify what kind of economic systems are emerging as a result of the differing reform paths in Central Asia.

In analysing outcomes, an attempt will be made to disentangle the influence of natural resource endowment and initial conditions, availability of external financing and other support, and policy-related factors. The four countries are often regarded as similar insofar as they were among the poorest Soviet republics, assigned within the Soviet division of labour to focus on primary products, shut off from the rest of the world, and culturally subordinated. The four Central Asian republics also differed substantially from one another in their income levels, resource endowment, and industrial structure.

The reform paths can be ranked by commitment to the establishment of a market economy based on private ownership; from most to least reformist, the conventional wisdom places the Kyrgyz Republic first followed by Kazakhstan, Uzbekistan, and Turkmenistan.[1] Although there are difficulties in synthesizing the many elements of reform and of measuring informal as well as formal institutional changes, there would be widespread agreement that the two smallest countries lie at the extremes. More interesting are the reform paths of Kazakhstan and Uzbekistan which are moving to differing market models, and which will be analysed in greater detail in this chapter.

3.1. INITIAL CONDITIONS

The Central Asian Republics (CARs) have a geographical, religious and cultural unity and much shared economic history (Pomfret 1995). The defining geographical features of Central Asia are the two major river systems running from the high mountains in the south-east corner of the region into the Aral Sea, which have provided the basis for irrigated agriculture for centuries. A small area of rain-fed agriculture flourishes in the densely populated Fergana Valley, which is divided between Uzbekistan, the Kyrgyz Republic, and Tajikistan. Much of the remainder of the region is desert, which turns into steppe land in Kazakhstan.

The CARs were, together with parts of the Caucasus, the most economically backward areas of the USSR. Huge expanses of desert separated the CARs' main population centres from the Soviet heartland. Differing ethnic, cultural, and religious makeup also kept the CARs' distinctive flavour, despite large-scale voluntary and involuntary migration within the USSR. Public policy tried to repress the differences by imposing Russian as the common official language, promoting atheism, outlawing archaic social customs (especially related to the economic role of women), and encouraging loyalty to the Soviet Union. While this achieved major social changes and brought clear benefits in areas of education and provision of other basic needs, particularism remained in the CARs and discontent with Slavic domination was often not far beneath the surface.

The CARs' role within the Soviet division of labour was as primary producers, with much of the region becoming dependent on cotton. In the 1950s, northern Kazakhstan became an important grain-growing region. Mineral resources were also developed, and Kazakhstan became a major producer of coal, lead, silver, chrome, and other minerals, while Uzbekistan was the USSR's second largest gold producer. In the later decades of Soviet rule, energy production increased in Kazakhstan and Turkmenistan.

Industrial development was prompted by the German invasion in 1941 when whole factories were moved from exposed parts of the western USSR to Tashkent. After the war, the tendency of Soviet planners to seek scale economies by locating new industries in established industrial centres led to the further expansion of Tashkent, which is the only major industrial conurbation in Central Asia (and which was the fourth biggest city in the USSR). Other industrial projects were aimed at promoting regional development in poorer areas, but did not have solid economic foundations. The Soviet space centre and major nuclear testing facilities were located in Kazakhstan.

The CARs suffered some undeniable costs from the Soviet era, of which the most obvious was the extreme environmental degradation. The shrinking of the Aral Sea as a result of the overexpansion of the water-hungry cotton economy led to well-documented health problems and less predictable long-term consequences including climatic changes. Severe radiation in Kazakhstan led to environmental groups being more active than elsewhere in the USSR, especially after the Chernobyl disaster highlighted the safety deficiencies of Soviet nuclear installations.

The Soviet economy was planned as a single unit, which imposed major constraints on the newly independent states' ability to pursue independent economic policies. The railway between the Kyrgyz Republic's two main cities, for example, passes through Uzbekistan, Tajikistan, and Kazakhstan. The individual republics had open economies, but were shut off from buying or selling in world markets; only about a tenth of the CARs' trade was outside the USSR, and most of that was barter trade within Comecon or with third-world clients of the USSR. Thus the dissolution of the USSR and collapse of Comecon led to severe disruption, while the CARs were ill-prepared to participate in international trade in the world marketplace.

The CARs enjoyed large net capital inflows during the Soviet era. It is impossible to reconstruct with any precision pre-1992 balance of payments for the republics, because much of the inter-republican transfers took place within the huge all-Union enterprises which played a major role in the USSR. The consensus estimates for the CARs are of resource transfers in the order of 10–20 per cent of GDP in the late 1980s (e.g. Pomfret 1995, p. 72; Griffin 1996, p. 19). Some of these were already being rolled back in 1991 as the USSR crumbled, and transfers continued at a dwindling rate after the dissolution of the USSR (this was the main carrot to remain in the rouble zone in 1992/3). The cessation of transfers, even if it was spread over three years, was unexpected and exacerbated the problems of transition from central planning. During the first half of the 1990s the CARs suffered a drop in gross national expenditure (GNE) which was substantially larger than the decline in output; among transition economies not suffering from armed conflicts, only Mongolia suffered a larger fall in GNE than the CARs during the early 1990s.

In Central Asia, and in the Caucasus, during the Brezhnev era the political leadership lost much of its ideological basis and developed a neofeudal system. While corruption became endemic all across the USSR, the distinctive feature of the southern republics was the emergence of networks based on family or clan loyalties. The corrupt and often criminal leaders, however, enjoyed strong local support for standing up to Moscow. One consequence of this political development was that after independence the incumbent leaders of Kazakhstan, Turkmenistan, and Uzbekistan remained in office with essentially the same power structure, just changing their labels from communists to nationalists.

3.2. POLICIES

As republics within the USSR, the CARs had similar economic policies, with resources allocated by central planning and assets owned by the state. In the Gorbachev era some Soviet republics did undertake local experiments in economic reform, but the CARs were not among them. During 1992 the CARs were preoccupied with institutional matters associated with independence, and economic policies were largely reactive.

Flexibility was reduced by continued use of the rouble. Thus, all of the CARs followed Russia's price reform in January 1992; not to have done so would have encouraged commodity arbitrage within the rouble zone. Nevertheless, the degree to which individual CARs tried to shelter their economies from key price rises was an early indicator of relative commitment to the establishment of market-determined prices. The ranking, according to closeness to Russian post-reform prices, was Kazakhstan, the Kyrgyz Republic, Uzbekistan, Turkmenistan (Pomfret 1995, pp. 53–6).

Privatization was characterized in 1992–3 by paper commitments but little real movement. Some form of privatization or use-rights was generally introduced for small enterprises, housing and land, but little or no progress was made towards privatizing large state-owned enterprises. Labour market reform also proceeded slowly in practice, as open unemployment remained minimal and new social safety nets were not constructed.

In 1993 the CARs all exited from the rouble zone. The Kyrgyz Republic was one of the first former Soviet republics to establish its own currency in May 1993. Turkmenistan more or less planned its exit for early November, confident in its ability to maintain the national currency's value with the country's natural gas wealth. Kazakhstan and Uzbekistan also left the rouble zone in November 1993, when they finally rebelled against Russia's conditions for continued membership (Pomfret 1995, pp. 140–51). Uzbekistan initially issued a temporary currency (the sum coupon), before the banknotes for the new national currency, the sum, were issued in July 1994.

In 1994–6 differentiation in national economic policies became more apparent. The Kyrgyz Republic has been the most committed reformer, taking the most determined steps. Turkmenistan has been the least committed reformer with a regime concerned more with political stability and distribution of the resource rents, than with creating a market-oriented economy. Kazakhstan and Uzbekistan are both progressing with economic reform, but in Uzbekistan there is more concern with controlling the process and moving gradually.

3.2.1. *Uzbekistan*

Uzbekistan has adopted a gradualist reform strategy; official statements denounce rapid change and promote the need for stability. The gradualism is most apparent in fiscal and monetary policy and in price reform. The government has had some success in containing the budget deficit, but this has been for prudential reasons rather than as part of a macroeconomic policy aimed at containing monetary growth and hence inflation. The government has relied on price controls as its main anti-inflation weapon.

During 1992–3 Uzbekistan gave the impression of being a reluctant follower of Russian price reforms. By retaining a wider range of price controls than neighbours within the rouble zone, Uzbekistan opened the door to commodity arbitrage, and on several occasions the borders with the Kyrgyz Republic and Kazakhstan were closed. Following the introduction of the national currency in July 1994, however, the government has pursued cautious but cumulatively significant price reforms. All subsidies for consumer goods were eliminated and only flour, sugar, and vegetable oil remained subject to rationing; the IMF in its 1996 Staff Country Report (p. 11) concluded that 'the process of price liberalization was essentially completed' by early 1995.

The degree to which prices are market determined remains opaque. Some key commodity prices still remained far below world prices in 1997, although domestic oil and gas prices were brought substantially closer to world prices in 1996. The government announced its intention of eliminating state orders for grain in 1997 and for cotton in 1998, but control over cotton prices is the most important source of government revenue so that the latter would have major negative budgetary implications.[2] State orders for cotton and wheat remain in place. The two most critical sets of prices in a market economy, interest rates and exchange rates, also remain artificial; entrepreneurial banking is discouraged and interest rates controlled, and exchange controls have been tightened in recent years.

In late 1994 Uzbekistan began to pay more attention to macroeconomic stabilization, but actual policy has been cautious. Monetary tightening has been inconsistently implemented.[3] The drop in inflation in 1995 was less dramatic than in the Kyrgyz Republic or in Kazakhstan (Table 3.1), and some of Uzbekistan's cumulative inflation performance is due to repression of price increases by controls rather than success in containing the underlying inflation.

Uzbekistan has an open economy, but restrictive trade and foreign exchange policies. Cotton and gold have proven to be buoyant exports. The government has used the exportables as a tax base,[4] and provides substantial protection for import-competing producers in industry and in agriculture. In the mid-1990s trade policy became more liberal, in that tariffs were simplified and reduced, but less relevant, as by 1996 all foreign exchange earnings had to be turned over to the central bank which then allocated foreign exchange to approved importers and other certified buyers. The exchange rate is market determined at auctions, but access to the official market is controlled. The system simplifies tax collection and permits discretionary control over imports, but leads to substantial resource misallocation. The gap between the official and black market exchange rates has widened, with a premium on foreign currency of over 100 per cent by early 1997.

Privatization and enterprise reform is difficult to assess in Uzbekistan. There has been no sweeping privatization of large enterprises and land remains state owned, but

Table 3.1. *GDP growth and inflation in the Central Asian republics*

A. GDP growth rates (%)

Country	1971–80	1981–9	1990	1991	1992	1993	1994	1995
Kazakhstan	4.4	2.0	−4.6	−6.8	−13.0	−15.6	−25.0	−9.0
Kyrgyz Republic	4.4	4.0	6.9	−9.1	−15.8	−16.3	−26.5	−6.0
Tajikistan	4.9	3.3	−2.4	−8.7	−30.0	−27.6	−15.0	−12.0
Turkmenistan	4.0	4.0	0.8	−5.0	−5.4	NA	NA	−5.0
Uzbekistan	6.2	3.4	2.0	−0.5	−11.1	−2.4	−4.5	−2.0

B. Average annual inflation rates (%)

Country	1990	1991	1992	1993	1994	1995
Kazakhstan	4.2	91.0	1,610.0	1,760.0	1,980.0	180.0
Kyrgyz Republic	3.0	85.0	854.6	1,208.7	280.0	45.0
Tajikistan	4.0	111.6	1,157.0	2,195.0	452.0	635.0
Turkmenistan	4.6	102.5	492.9	3,102.0	2,400.0	1,800.0
Uzbekistan	3.1	82.2	645.0	534.0	746.0	315.0

Source: World Bank (1996, pp. 173–4).

housing was almost completely privatized in 1994. Within both agriculture and industry there is some evidence of improved incentive structures. State enterprises (to some extent in service sectors such as education and health, as well as in industry) have been captured by incumbent managers, which has increased income inequality but may be conducive to greater efficiency now that the managers have claim to residual profits as well as fixed salaries. In agriculture there has been some limited increase in private farms, and state farms have been turned into cooperatives. The potentially most significant step, initiated in 1995, has been the spread of arrangements whereby individual farmers within cooperatives contract to supply a certain quota at a specified price and then retain a larger share of the above-quota production; this resembles China's successful household responsibility system, but its impact in Uzbekistan has yet to be documented.[5]

There has been some formation of new enterprises. After negligible foreign investment in the early years of independence, direct foreign investment accounted for 1 per cent of total investment in 1994 and 17 per cent in 1995 (UNDP 1996a), before slipping back in 1996. The inflows are dominated by a few large investors: Daewoo, BAT, Newmont Mining, Mercedes Benz, and Lonrho. Formation of new small-scale private enterprises has been limited, certainly less than in Kazakhstan or the Kyrgyz Republic, but more than in Turkmenistan. Both foreign investors and indigenous entrepreneurs are deterred by the red tape and corruption in a still heavily regulated economy in which entrepreneurial activity is viewed with official suspicion.

The most distinctive element of government policy has been the steps taken to provide social security. In many transition economies words have been louder than actions, but Uzbekistan's government has produced some innovative actions. Government spending on education and health has been maintained at least as a share of GDP (Table 3.2; see also Klugman and Schieber (1996) and chapters by Hatland and Haycock and by Tibi in Griffin (1996)). Although measures of school

Table 3.2. *Allocation of general government spending in USSR, Kazakhstan, and Uzbekistan (as % of GDP)*

	USSR (1989)	Kazakhstan (1994)	Uzbekistan (1994)
Education and health	7.4	4.7	16.5
Social protection	7.4	5.7	7.4
Support for the economy	14.1	11.4	12.2
Capital and restructuring	7.2	0.2	3.9
Law enforcement	0.9	1.3	0.0
Defence	8.0	0.8	0.0
Administration	0.3	0.7	1.0
Interests	0.7	0.3	0.0
Other	3.5	4.2	7.0
Total	49.5	29.3	48.0

Source: Cheasty and Davis (1996).

maintenance or hospital beds per inhabitant have deteriorated, this appears to be part of a genuine programme of improving efficiency from the capital-intensive Soviet approach to education and health. Since 1994 assistance to low-income families has been channelled through neighbourhood committees or mahallas; one in five households received money from the mahalla fund in 1995 (Klugman 1997). The mahalla programme has reduced administrative costs and appears to have permitted better targetting of the needy, although there have been some concerns about regional variations in the standards of need.

3.2.2. *Kazakhstan*

Since independence, Kazakhstan has followed a more freewheeling approach to economic liberalization than Uzbekistan has. Initially many outside observers interpreted this as showing greater commitment to economic reform, underpinned by more favourable initial conditions in terms of natural endowment and human capital. In 1992–3 Kazakhstan followed Russian price reforms more closely than the other, more cautious, CARs. After Kazakhstan exited the rouble zone in November 1993, its macroeconomic policies were firmer than those of Uzbekistan. In other areas, the Kazak approach has been laxer than that of Uzbekistan, which can be seen either as a greater commitment to market forces or as actions of a weaker central government. The issue of whether lack of law and order inhibits successful transition to a more market-oriented economy has come to the forefront in the mid-1990s, often in explicit comparisons between Kazakhstan's faster liberalization and Uzbekistan's gradualism.

Price liberalization was substantially completed in 1992. By early 1993 the only retail prices still regulated were for transportation and communication services, bread and bakery products, baby food, some energy products, and imported medicines. The signalling function of prices was, however, obscured by hyperinflation within the rouble zone, and this continued after the introduction of the national currency in November 1993 (Table 3.1). The state order system was abolished in 1993, when a 'state needs' system was introduced, by which state procurement for schools, hospitals, etc. and for exports under interstate trade agreements are purchased from voluntary suppliers at negotiated prices.

Foreign trade was controlled in 1992–3, but then substantially liberalized in 1994–5. Licencing and quotas for imports and exports were abolished, and barter transactions prohibited. The average tariff on imports in 1996 was 13 per cent. As in Uzbekistan the effectiveness of price and trade policy reform was undermined by hyperinflation and exchange controls, but on both counts Kazakhstan was more successful, with inflation under reasonable control by 1995 and exchange controls less draconian than in Uzbekistan.

Privatization moved at a slow speed in 1991–2, but was addressed more seriously in March 1993 when the government adopted a three-prong strategy of auctioning small-scale state enterprises for cash, converting medium and large enterprises (employing 500–2,000 workers) to joint stock companies to be managed by investment privatization funds in which citizens would have shares through a voucher scheme, and privatizing very large enterprises on a case-by-case basis. In 1994, the first prong was implemented successfully, the coupons for the second prong were distributed, but little progress was made on the third prong. Land and other natural resources remain state property, although long leases (up to 99 years) are transferable and inheritable. Housing privatization is the responsibility of local authorities, so that the methods and extent of privatization vary; about half of all dwellings had been privatized by mid-1993, i.e. slower progress than in Uzbekistan.

Despite widespread dissatisfaction with the privatization process and many stops and starts on the coupon programme, which was terminated in 1996, the ownership situation has been transformed. By 1996 private, mixed, joint stock, and other non-state forms of ownership accounted for over 70 per cent of all property. Nevertheless, there is concern about the nature of privatization with much of it being privatization from within, as existing managers took control of state enterprises, often making big material gains for themselves. The creation of a new private sector is not well documented, but appears to be proceeding faster in Kazakhstan than in the other CARs, although still at a far more limited rate than in European transition economies.

Effective reform of the financial sector is a necessary prerequisite for successful privatization. In Kazakhstan non-state enterprises still complain of their limited access to capital markets, despite a big increase in the number of banks. By early 1995 there were 280 banks, up from 5 in 1988 and 72 at the end of 1991, but the 3 largest specialized state banks and the state savings bank held 80 per cent of the assets. Most of the other banks were associated with individual enterprises, and acted principally as conduits for state-subsidized credit. An August 1995 presidential decree introduced serious privatization of the banking sector by forbidding enterprises in which the state is a major shareholder from holding stock in banks.

The macroeconomic stabilization programme has been successful in reducing the inflationary effect of government budget deficits. With a declining tax base and difficulties with tax collection, cutting the deficit to less than 5 per cent of GDP by 1996 involved substantial reductions in government expenditure. This process has been threatened by some major projects, such as the removal of the capital from Almaty to Akmola, but has been kept on track. Public spending on health has dropped by over 40 per cent in real terms, with many formerly free services no longer generally available and widening regional disparities in the quality of health care—all at a time when economic and ecological problems are increasing the demand for health services. State spending on education has also dropped, from 7 per cent of GDP in 1990 to 3 per cent of the smaller GDP in 1996. Almost half of all kindergartens and day nurseries were closed between 1991 and 1995, while in grade schools physical facilities deteriorated, teacher shortages increased, and equipment was in short supply (e.g. the number of textbooks issued in 1995 was half that of 1991). As with health services, the provision of education services has become less uniform; private institutions have grown in response to demand, but exacerbate the inequality of access.[6]

3.2.3. The Kyrgyz Republic

The Kyrgyz Republic is often lauded as being among 'the most active reforming countries of the Commonwealth of Independent States'.[7] It was the first CIS country to issue its own national currency with the intention of achieving the macroeconomic stabilization that was impossible within the rouble zone. Trade policy has been liberal and exchange rate policy has been market based, including full convertibility of the som since May 1995. Privatization and enterprise reform have progressed faster than in other CARs but the Kyrgyz Republic is not the CIS leader in these structural reforms; it lags behind Russia on performance-based measures such as the share of private sector output in GDP or institutional development.

The national currency was introduced in May 1993, but monetary control was uneven during that year and the som depreciated substantially (from 4 som/US$ to 8.5/US$ at the year's end). In 1994 the som again depreciated (to 10.66/US$), but then was more or less stabilized (in the range 10.7–11.2) in 1995, which represents a real appreciation. During this period, the Kyrgyz Republic had the best record among the CARs in reducing inflation (Table 3.1).

The Kyrgyz government did not, however, succeed in controlling its budget deficit, which increased to 12.5 per cent of GDP in 1995. The revenue base shrank as a result of reforms and collection difficulties exacerbated the decline in revenue, which was not matched by expenditure cuts. Monetary balance was maintained in part by confidence in the banking system in 1993–5, which kept money demand down, but appears to be more crucially due to success in obtaining foreign aid. Gross official transfers in 1995 amounted to US$103 million (US$71m in bilateral aid and US$32m from multilateral institutions), of which US$45m was technical assistance, US$30m grants in kind, and US$28m counterpart funds for budgetary support.

Price reform is essentially complete. State orders were eliminated in 1993, and practically all prices liberalized by 1994. Export taxes were abolished in 1996. With low import barriers, the relative price structure should be based on world prices (allowing for the high transactions cost in the landlocked republic with poor external transport links).

The Kyrgyz privatization programme has been the most extensive among the CARs. Practically all small-scale state enterprises (less than 100 employees) and state commercial assets had been sold by cash auction by the end of 1994. The 1994–5 programme earmarked 900 medium-sized and large state enterprises for privatization by a mix of coupon and cash auctions, and by the end of 1995 a total of 836 enterprises had been auctioned and the government had fully divested itself of state shares in 434 enterprises. The 1996–7 programme targeted 320 medium-sized and large companies for a similar process, including some of the largest state monopolies. Most state and collective farms have been broken up with individuals holding land-use rights, which were extended to 99 years in November 1995; land leases can be sold or used as collateral, but the land remains state property and must be used for agricultural purposes.

Financial sector reform has aimed at creating appropriate institutions for the conduct of monetary policy and for efficient financial intermediation, but has been hampered by the small market economy and lack of trained personnel. Despite attempts to create market-based financial instruments, the commercial banks ran into serious difficulties in 1995, primarily due to non-performing loans to state enterprises. The government response was to undertake a major restructuring with assistance from the World Bank; two of the four large specialized banks were liquidated in 1996 (the savings bank and the agricultural bank), while the other two large former state banks were recapitalized. Two of the smaller commercial banks had their licences suspended and others were put under direct supervision of the central bank. The outcome, assuming an appropriate regulatory and supervisory framework is developed, should be a sounder financial system than in any other Asian transition economy.

In sum, the Kyrgyz Republic has moved further and faster than any other CAR in the transition to a market economy, although the progress has been slower than in the Central European transition economies and in some respects slower than in Russia. It is the only CAR whose price liberalization has produced market-determined exchange rates and interest rates, although in both areas market thinness has limited allocative efficiency. Enterprise reform has been less dramatic than price reform, but the momentum has been maintained and by the mid-1990s appeared to reflect a more genuine government commitment to relinquishing control over enterprises than in other CARs.

3.2.4. *Turkmenistan*

Turkmenistan is at the opposite end of the CAR reform spectrum to the Kyrgyz Republic. Reform of the economy towards a more market-oriented system was minimal during the first four years following the dissolution of the USSR. A highly personalized government has sought to cement popular support by using the resource rents from Turkmenistan's abundant natural gas to provide free services and subsidized staple products. This strategy proved unsustainable and the first significant reforms were announced at the end of 1995, but they are as yet difficult to assess.

Some prices have been freed, but many key prices remained controlled. The government sets an average wage, and payments above this level are subject to a punitive excess wage tax (set at 50 per cent on all wages over 20,000 manat following the January 1996 wage reform). Interest rates and exchange rates are tightly regulated. Although Turkmenistan anticipated the final dissolution of the rouble zone by introducing the manat at the beginning of 1993, the goal appears to have been to end the restrictions on monetary expansion imposed by membership in the rouble zone rather than to control inflation through monetary policy. Water, gas, and electricity are provided free (up to generous limits), rents on public housing are nominal, and retail prices of sugar, rice, tea, butter, and flour are subsidized. Monetary policy has been based on accommodation to the needs of the social protection system, of state enterprises, and of prestige construction projects; it has been highly inflationary.

Privatization has progressed slowly and has been constrained by the government's unwillingness to cede control. By 1996, 1,652 out of 3,980 small enterprises targeted for privatization had changed ownership structure and four medium-sized and one large state enterprise had been privatized by auction, but the government retained a majority shareholding in many of these enterprises. Urban housing privatization has been suspended. The June 1995 agrarian reform replaced state farms and cooperatives by peasant associations, whose members must fulfil state orders but can retain additional output. Although this arrangement has superficial resemblance to China's household responsibility system and Uzbekistan's agrarian reform, in Turkmenistan all produce in key sectors (including cotton, grains, and livestock) must be sold at official procurement prices rather than market-determined prices, so that the Turkmenistan situation is less favourable to producers.

The IMF staff team diplomatically described the situation in early 1996 as one of 'limited progress' in reform and where 'a heavily subsidized public enterprise sector continued to dominate the economy' (*Country Report 96/30*, April 1996). The no-reform strategy gave no incentive for the development of non-traditional sectors. Apart from a small number of kiosks and restaurants, there has been little new private sector development in Turkmenistan.

3.3. PERFORMANCE

By any measure, the Central Asian republics have suffered an awful economic experience since becoming independent in 1991. Output has fallen substantially, all the CARs experienced hyperinflation in 1992/3, the distribution of income and wealth has become more unequal, and poverty has increased. The output and inflation measures in Table 3.1 overstate the poor performance by underestimating quality improvements and for other reasons (Pomfret 1995, pp. 171–6); greater choice and ability to trade can be welfare increasing even if output declines,[8] and some higher prices are associated with better quality products. Nevertheless, material living standards have declined for the majority of the CARs' inhabitants and economic insecurity has risen.

The measurement issues become more significant in making comparisons among the CARs. There have undoubtedly been variations in economic performance, but there is disagreement even about the CARs' ranking by performance. To some extent such disagreements are due to confounding of performance with policies; the speed with which a market economy is created becomes a measure of economic success. In this section I will consider performance in the narrow sense of satisfying the material needs of a nation's inhabitants.

Uzbekistan had the smallest decline in GDP over the period 1990–5 of any former Soviet republic. Uzbekistan's 1995 GDP was 82 per cent of its 1990 GDP; comparative figures are 45 per cent for Kazakhstan and 50 per cent for the Kyrgyz Republic (UNDP 1996*a*, p. 16). This favourable gap has persisted until 1999 (see Table 1.1). Uzbekistan also had relative success in avoiding hyperinflation, never recording a four-digit annual increase in the consumer price index, although by

Table 3.3. *Demographic change in the CARs and Russia during the first half of the 1990s*

A. Population change, 1989–95 (in thousands)

	Population		Change	Natural increase	Migration
	1989	1995	1989–95		
Kazakhstan	16,536	16,683	147	1,212	−1,065
Kyrgyz Republic	4,290	4,476	186	545	−359
Russia	147,400	148,249	849	−867	1,716
Tajikistan	5,160	5,777	668	903	−235
Turkmenistan	3,534	4,455	921	606	315
Uzbekistan	19,905	22,633	2,728	3,393	−565

Source: *Transition*, No. 6, September–October 1995, World Bank.

B. Birth and death rates, 1990 and 1994

	Crude birth rate		Crude death rate	
	1990	1994	1990	1994
Kazakhstan	21.71	18.2	7.7	9.6
Kyrgyz Republic	29.3	24.6	7.0	8.3
Tajikistan	38.8	28.2	6.2	7.0
Turkmenistan	34.2	32.0	7.0	7.9
Uzbekistan	33.7	29.4	6.1	6.6
Russia	13.4	9.5	11.2	15.7

Source: Falkingham *et al.* (1997, p. 11).

1995 the Kyrgyz Republic and Kazakhstan had made more progress in reducing inflation. The more controlled economy of Uzbekistan may have more repressed inflation and less undercounting of the output of small-scale private sector activities, i.e. a poorer record in reducing inflation and maintaining output than the data in Table 3.1 suggest.

Elsewhere in the former Soviet Union and in Eastern Europe, vital statistics have underlined the decline in living standards; increased death rates and reduced birth rates have been interpreted as evidence of increased insecurity and economic pessimism. Population figures from the 1989 census to 1995 show large natural increases in Uzbekistan, Kazakhstan, Tajikistan, Azerbaijan, Turkmenistan, and the Kyrgyz Republic, while the other former Soviet republics had small natural increases or declines (Table 3.3). To some extent this may be cultural, as the six listed republics are those with predominantly Muslim populations, but it also reflects stable life expectancies, unlike the Russian Federation where the life expectancy for men has fallen dramatically since independence (Cornia and Paniccià, 2000). Crude birth rates fell and death rates increased in the CARs during the first half of the 1990s, but by far less than in Russia (Table 3.3B).

The migration figures in Table 3.3A present a less positive picture, with Kazakhstan, the Kyrgyz Republic, and Uzbekistan all experiencing large emigration. This has a cultural element as the emigration is overwhelmingly of non-titular ethnic groups, mainly Russians or other European groups, but also Uzbeks and Kazaks from the Kyrgyz Republic and so forth. The emphasis placed by the new national governments on matters such as the status of the national language clearly make a difference, but poor economic performance is a reinforcing push factor.

Income inequality has almost certainly increased in all former Soviet republics since 1991 (see Chapter 10), but it is difficult to measure. The same applies to poverty.[9] Unemployment figures are practically meaningless as they reflect the relative attractiveness and specific conditions of unemployment compensation, which tends to be low in all CARs (and hence reported unemployment is low even though many people have lost their jobs and are supported by the extended family or are underemployed in the informal sector). Among those still in the same job as before 1992, there is a widespread phenomenon of workers having assets (unpaid wages accumulated over many months) but living in poverty. There is almost no firm evidence on these phenomena, although the growing frequency of urban riots, often ignited by demands for payment of back-wages, indicates their importance.

Crime has also increased in the 1990s. This is a symptom of economic hardship; in Kazakhstan 45 per cent of arrestees are reported by UNDP (1996*b*, p. 61) as having no permanent source of income, as well as of the decline in social control since the end of communism. The increase in crime appears to be greatest in Kazakhstan and least in Uzbekistan and Turkmenistan, which clearly reflects the tighter central control in the latter two countries, but also raises the question of whether it is a cost of Kazakhstan's economic reform strategy—at least in comparison with Uzbekistan's more gradualist and controlled approach.

Finally, agriculture is still important in the CARs, and even more so given the post-independence decline in industrial output, so that year-to-year performance is susceptible to vagaries of weather. Grain production in Kazakhstan declined sharply from 16.4 million tonnes in 1994 to 9.5 m.t. in 1995, partly due to severe drought in western and central areas, but also ascribed to the deteriorating stock of agricultural machinery. Turkmenistan was also hard hit by harvest failure in 1995, although even more than in Kazakhstan there is a suspicion that economic mismanagement exacerbated the negative impact of adverse weather conditions.

3.4. ANALYSIS

What has been the relationship between policies and performance? I have argued that it is dangerous to seek a simple ranking of the CARs by degree of economic liberalization, although the Kyrgyz Republic has been the most committed to economic reform and Turkmenistan the least committed. Section 3 showed that simple rankings by economic performance are also fraught, although Uzbekistan appears to have done best in both the first five years after independence and the subsequent quinquennium, and Turkmenistan has done worst. Finding a relationship between policies and performance is further complicated, because resource endowment and other initial conditions also play a role. Moreover, during the 1991–6 period other forces have interacted with national policies to determine performance, and some of these forces have been exogenous (e.g. weather conditions) while others (e.g. the amount of external financing) have been related to the policy choices. Finally, although five years is long enough to identify differences in reform paths and their immediate consequences, it is too short to capture the long-term effects of substantial systemic reform, which in most cases only dates from the mid-1990s, rather than from independence.

As with performance evaluation, it is difficult to isolate the analysis from preconceptions or the benefits of hindsight. How, for example, should we rank the CARs with respect to resource endowment? Tarr (1994), in his calculations of the terms of trade impact of moving from Soviet to world prices, found Turkmenistan (+50 per cent) and Kazakhstan (+19 per cent) to be big gainers, while Kyrgyzstan (+1 per cent) and Uzbekistan (−3 per cent) would be hardly affected. This fitted with the common perception that Turkmenistan with its natural gas wealth and Kazakhstan with its oil and mineral wealth had suffered from Soviet pricing policies and would enjoy a large windfall gain after independence. Moreover, these two countries had further energy reserves, including Kazakhstan's Tengiz oilfield which quickly attracted the largest foreign investment in the entire former USSR. In practice, however, realization of economic benefits from the natural gas and oil has been stymied by the pipeline network. Turkmenistan has maintained its gas exports but has experienced payments difficulties, reflected in (notional) capital inflows, while oil flows from Tengiz have been a mere trickle. At the same time, Uzbekistan with its dependence on cotton benefited from buoyant world markets in 1992–3 and some flexibility in transport outlets. Moreover, Uzbekistan has developed its energy sources, on a modest scale but enough to reduce its imports so that it has not suffered from the expected terms of trade loss. In sum, Turkmenistan and to a lesser extent Kazakhstan looked exceptionally fortunate in 1992, but turned out to be not as blessed as they thought, while Uzbekistan's resource endowment turned out to be not as bad as expected in 1992; behind this superficial assessment lurks the question of whether the reversals of fortune might be due at least in part to more or less astute national policy making.

The CARs have had differing amounts of external assistance, but this is not independent of economic policy decisions. All benefited from Russian assistance in 1992 and 1993 when the transfer mechanisms from the Soviet era were wound down rather than abruptly terminated. The most important such mechanisms were currency credits within the rouble zone and Russian products supplied at below world prices. Since 1993 the World Bank and IMF have led in the provision of external assistance, but the international financial institutions' lending has not been evenly distributed (Table 3.4); it is heavily skewed towards those CARs adopting reform strategies favoured by the World Bank and IMF, with the Kyrgyz Republic being the first CAR to receive World Bank funds and consistently receiving the most per capita, while Kazakhstan has received the largest total World Bank assistance.

Table 3.4. *Lending operations of the World Bank in Central Asia (commitments in millions of US dollars by fiscal year)*

	1993	1994	1995	1996	Total	Per capita
Kazakhstan	—	274	283	260	817	49
Kyrgyz Republic	60	78	77	98	313	70
Tajikistan	—	—	—	5	5	1
Turkmenistan	—	—	25	—	25	6
Uzbekistan	—	21	226	—	247	11

Note: The per capita amount in the final column is the total divided by the 1995 population estimate in Table 3.3.
Source: World Bank (1997, 3.1).

3.4.1. *Uzbekistan*

Even allowing for the conceptual and measurement difficulties, there is general agreement that Uzbekistan[10] has been the most successful of the CARs in maintaining output level since independence. While poverty measurement is even more difficult than output measurement, Uzbekistan appears to have done relatively well in restraining increases in poverty. In social areas such as education and health care, Uzbekistan could also claim the best record, which not only helps to avoid widening gaps in income and wealth but lays a firmer foundation for future economic growth. On the other hand, Uzbekistan has lagged behind Kazakhstan and the Kyrgyz Republic in establishing a market-based economy, and the still heavily distorted prices and readiness to use controls over resource allocation may inhibit long-term growth prospects.

Uzbekistan had some favourable initial conditions. The unexpectedly beneficial trade situation in the early 1990s due to buoyant world cotton prices was reinforced by the country's ability to substitute fairly readily (and apparently not at a major cost in resource misallocation) domestic production for some grain and energy imports. The diversified industrial base had grown reasonably organically since 1945, so that although many state enterprises experienced difficulties the industrial sector had some flexibility in adapting to new conditions. In industry and in public service Uzbekistan benefited from high levels of trained personnel, for its national income level, and suffered much less than Kazakhstan or the Kyrgyz Republic from emigration of trained people after independence.[11]

Policy is more clearly responsible for some aspects of performance. Price and exchange controls were the main elements behind the lower peak in hyperinflation, although they had to be reinforced by progress in reducing the budget deficit if the hyperinflation was to be brought down eventually. Uzbekistan's gradualism has helped to maintain the tax base (although so did the strength of cotton earnings), and Uzbekistan has been the most successful of the CARs in controlling the government budget deficit. Doing this while maintaining provision of education and health services better than its neighbours is a major positive achievement. The mahalla system appears to be an efficient method of delivering social security, which has contributed to the relatively good performance with respect to poverty alleviation.

Some of the favourable conditions could be ascribed to good government too. The development of new grain and energy production and even the continued supply of cotton exports presupposes a certain amount of economic stability, and involved some government initiative. The resilience of the industrial sector could likewise be ascribed to an environment which involved neither rapid imposition of a hard budget constraint nor sweeping reforms which might add to the disruption of supply chains associated with the collapse of the USSR. The limited emigration could be due to less fear of economic decline or of political subjugation in Uzbekistan, although the greater ethnic homogeneity of Uzbekistan (relative to Kazakhstan or the Kyrgyz Republic) is surely the dominant factor here.

The doubts about Uzbekistan's policies concern their ability to generate long-term growth. The IMF and the World Bank have been much less well-inclined towards Uzbekistan than towards Kazakhstan or the Kyrgyz Republic (Table 3.4), because they see it as not pursuing economic reforms actively enough or in the right way. Uzbekistan has not placed monetary policy aimed at restraining inflation high on its agenda, even though it has in fact done well in reducing the budget deficit. More fundamentally, the Uzbekistan government has been suspicious of the market mechanism, and has tight controls over both interest rates and exchange rates. Foreign trade policy is superficially liberal, but, with pervasive exchange controls, trade measures are redundant and in practice government officials wield discretionary control over the composition of imports.

Whether World Bank and IMF support is necessarily a good thing is not self-evident; while lack of such support limits access to foreign capital, it has also engendered greater self-reliance among Uzbekistani officials. Moreover, the absence of systemic change can be overstated. Uzbekistan has moved more slowly than other CIS countries, including the Kyrgyz Republic, and has retained tighter economic and social control than Kazakhstan, but it has not followed a no-reform path, as Turkmenistan tried to do. There is no doubt that Uzbekistan is moving towards a more market-oriented system, and that in areas like housing it moved fast and in other areas (such as agriculture or provision of social services) it moved imaginatively in what appear to be desirable directions.

3.4.2. *Kazakhstan*

Kazakhstan is the natural point of comparison with Uzbekistan, given their similarity in economic size (Uzbekistan has the larger population, Kazakhstan the larger GDP), which underlies competition for leadership in the region. Kazakhstan has moved significantly faster than Uzbekistan in price and enterprise reform, reflecting the government's greater willingness to relinquish control over resource allocation. President Nazarbayev of Kazakhstan has also been viewed as more liberal in political and social matters than President Karimov of Uzbekistan, although in 1995 and 1996 the Kazakhstan government appeared to be becoming increasingly authoritarian. As a result of these perceptions, Kazakhstan has enjoyed greater external assistance than Uzbekistan (Table 3.4).

Kazakhstan's performance since independence has been strongly influenced by its resource base. It is the only significant grain exporter among the CARs (it was third in the USSR behind Russia and Ukraine), and a disastrous harvest like that of 1995 has economy-wide impact. The major hope for prosperity after independence lay in oil exports, and Chevron's multi-billion dollar contract to develop the Tengiz oilfield is the largest DFI project in the former USSR, but difficulties with existing pipelines through Russia and Ukraine and in financing new pipeline routes to the Indian Ocean or the Mediterranean have proven far more severe than expected; five years after independence no concrete progress had been made in improving physical outlets. Thus, Kazakhstan's economic record since independence has fallen well short of expectations.

Has government policy alleviated or exacerbated this performance shortfall? In broad outline, Kazakhstan's economic policy has followed Russia's path; Popov's description of Russian reforms as inconsistent shock therapy (Chapter 2) applies to Kazakhstan, but with less shock and more inconsistency. Extensive price liberalization should have improved resource allocation, but there is considerable dissatisfaction over the disposal of state assets and the role of the government, which are both viewed as having enriched an elite while impoverishing the majority. There is evidence of increased crime, and fears that criminal organizations have become overpowerful.

From an economic perspective, a key shortcoming of Kazakhstan's reform path up to the mid-1990s was the failure to create an entrepreneurial financial sector. Banks acted as conduits for state funds to well-connected enterprises, which had often been privatized from within so that the managers became rich at public expense. Whether this will be a long-term feature of Kazakhstan's economy depends upon the implementation of the financial reforms signalled in late 1995. A related shortcoming was the decline in government spending on health care, education, and other social services (Table 3.2), which would have been more beneficial than using public funds to subsidize state or formerly state enterprises.

President Nazarbayev's room for manoeuvre is restricted by the delicate ethnic balance.[12] Inconsistencies in economic policies are often driven by short-term political imperatives, aimed at satisfying Kazak nationalists or retaining support of the large Russian minority. Remaining in the rouble zone through 1992–3 restricted ability to pursue independent monetary policy, and the current enthusiasm for a customs union with Russia will constrain Kazakhstan's trade policy independence (since the customs union's external trade policy will be set by Russia). Economically unjustifiable policies, such as the proposed relocation of the capital city, have their roots in the ethnic problem (in this case attempting to avert secessionist tendencies in the north by placing the capital further north).

Kazakhstan's economic prospects, which were generally regarded as the brightest of the CARs in 1992, now seem less rosy. Outside the IMF and World Bank, there is an increasing sense that Uzbekistan's gradualism may have been more successful than Kazakhstan's more radical but inconsistent reform path, but the jury is really still out. Kazakhstan has gone further in establishing a functioning price system with appropriate relative prices (i.e. domestic prices are closer to world prices with

Kazakhstan's more liberal external economic policies), and the false path in financial sector development is not irrevocable. In practice, much will depend on the future of grain and especially energy exports. If routes can be found for efficient pipeline facilities to tidewater ports, then Kazakhstan's economic prospects will rapidly improve and support for continued marketization will grow. If the economy continues to stagnate, then it could enter a vicious circle in a semi-reformed state characterized by widespread graft and anti-competitive behaviour which inhibits growth and becomes self-sustaining.

3.4.3. *The Kyrgyz Republic*

The Kyrgyz Republic is difficult to assess, because it had the least favourable initial condition in terms of resource endowment but has enjoyed the most external support. It is also controversial because of its espousal of the rapid macro-led reforms advocated by the World Bank and IMF.

One indicator of the Kyrgyz Republic's poor underlying prospects has been the limited response of foreign investors to the opportunities presented in the most reformist CAR. Direct foreign investment (DFI) did rise, from US$10 million in 1993 to US$45 million in 1994 and US$61 million in 1995, and there were 363 registered joint ventures by the end of 1995. This record was, however, dominated by a single project, the Kumtor gold project, in which DFI was US$30 million in 1994 and US$45 million in 1995.

The Kyrgyz Republic has been the most successful CAR in controlling inflation. This has a policy basis in the early decision to introduce a national currency, and after 1994 successfully maintaining the currency's value without resorting to exchange controls or other non-market methods. Yet the success is misleading because it was not achieved by controlling the budget deficit and hence reducing the need for inflationary finance. Generous external support helped the government to finance spending far in excess of domestic revenue. The anti-inflation policies were successful, not because of the direct impact of the policies but because they induced foreign governments and institutions to lend sufficient to cover the budget deficit.

The Kyrgyz Republic has been less successful in maintaining output levels. This may be an inevitable consequence of rapid reform in a former Soviet economy, exacerbated by a poor resource base. Certainly, in comparison to Uzbekistan, which started with lower income levels than the Kyrgyz Republic, the Kyrgyz Republic had a disappointing performance in 1992–6. It could be argued that the Kyrgyz Republic, with its more fundamental reforms of enterprises and the financial system already in place, may have performed less well than Uzbekistan in the short run but has better long-term prospects; only time will tell whether this is true.

3.4.4. *Turkmenistan*

Turkmenistan's economic performance is the easiest to assess. The government's policy of non-reform, trying to retain the pre-existing structure while currying support by giveaways based on the natural resource rents, had collapsed by 1995. Continuing hyperinflation in 1995 and 1996, when it had receded in the other CARs, and the collapse of the currency on the black market are the most evident signs of economic disarray. In the tightly monitored country, reports of opposition to government policies are censored, but news of riots against the economic conditions began to filter out in 1996.

3.5. DIFFERING MARKET MODELS

The various reform paths adopted by the independent governments of the CARs have implications not just for economic performance but also for the nature of the reformed economy. All the governments have abandoned central planning, at least as it operated in the USSR, but they have expressed different ideas of the type of market-oriented economy which they wish to establish. Moreover, there may be gaps between the policy aims and their effect, or between the stated policies and their actual implementation.

This section will analyse the differing market models which are emerging. The most obvious difference is the degree of government involvement, but this can have many dimensions. All the CAR governments profess concern about providing social safety nets, although all lack the resources to match their targets and the approaches differ substantially. Policies towards resource allocation and especially the direction of capital formation are more diverse in theory, with Kazakhstan and the Kyrgyz Republic showing greater adherence to market principles, but in practice all of the CARs' governments have shown reluctance to leave resource allocation to market forces, at least beyond small-scale producers and traders; this is most clearly shown in the limited emergence of entrepreneurial financial institutions. Most officials still have a suspicion of loosening their control, a predilection for administrative solutions to serious economic problems, and a bias towards heavy or hi-tech industries as the defining elements of a modern economy.

3.5.1. *Uzbekistan*

Uzbekistan has developed the most sophisticated managed market model among the CARs. After independence the government had a suspicion of the market mechanism, especially as it affected large industrial enterprises and the key commodity exports, cotton and gold. Government policy has also been characterized by caution.

The government moved quickly to privatize housing, which posed no problem, and moved more slowly to privatize other small-scale productive enterprises and to change the incentive structure in agriculture, which might have more uncertain economic consequences. Despite the differing speeds, by 1996 all of these policies had been implemented. The prices facing agents in these reformed sectors had also been liberalized, although potential housebuyers, farmers, and other small-scale producers were still affected by the regulated interest and exchange rates.

The cotton sector is more complex. There is a tradition of extensive government involvement, which has its basis in the need to manage the irrigation facilities upon which cotton cultivation depends. Cotton exports were marketed through intergovernmental contracts in the Soviet era; this has been changing since independence, but there is a continuing belief that Uzbekistan has market power in world cotton markets and that the government should prevent ruinous competition in selling the nation's cotton. Cotton also provides an important source of government revenue, which is most easily levied by manipulating prices paid to producers through state orders. Both economic theory and empirical evidence suggest that the market power and fiscal motivations for government intervention are unlikely to be valid; propping up Uzbek cotton export prices will lead to loss of market share as there are many alternative cotton-growing locations in the world, and taxing producers directly or indirectly will reduce the incentive to farmers and will encourage illicit marketing. Nevertheless, with respect to both cotton and gold, the government sees these as national resources which require government management.

A similar attitude pervades government policy towards the industrial sector, although in a more selective form. The government has loosened its control over small-scale production units and has allowed direct foreign investment in some sectors. Tight control over capital allocation and imports, however, reflects a concern to ensure that desirable industrial enterprises are sheltered from foreign competition. The danger in such an approach is that it will ossify an inappropriate economic structure. The lesson from developing countries' policies over the last half century is that import-substituting industrialization might stimulate growth in the short run, but is a dead end with respect to sustained growth.

Government intervention is more firmly based in areas of social policy. The government's commitment to limit the reduction in its spending on health and education represents the most promising approach in any CAR to retaining the major benefits from the Soviet era in these areas. The mahalla scheme is an interesting experiment in dealing with the universal problem of transition economies: how to establish an effective social safety net with diminishing resources? By decentralizing decision making into community-based organs, the Uzbekistan government is attempting to reduce costs and ensure effective targeting. The extent to which the mahallas resurrect traditional institutions is debatable, but the Uzbekistan government is making a constructive appeal to tradition, in contrast to many empty such appeals in other CARs.

Thus, Uzbekistan is moving towards a market economy in which the government plays a guiding and paternalistic role. By 1996 the non-state sector had become dominant, unlike in non-reforming countries such as Belarus or Turkmenistan.[13] The government hampers new entrepreneurs by its bureaucratic regulations, but it does provide law and order better than in Kazakhstan. Due to the obvious benefits from cotton and gold exports, the economy is fairly open relative to other CARs, and positive measures such as the mahalla scheme and, for the long term, spending on education and health have undoubtedly given Uzbekistan the best record among the CARs on poverty alleviation.

3.5.2. *Kazakhstan*

Kazakhstan's government has been more willing than that of Uzbekistan to cede economic control at both the micro- and macro-level. The extent to which this represents a commitment to a competitive market model has, however, become increasingly a matter of debate. Alienation of state assets has largely been to the benefit of insiders, and anti-competitive market structures have often remained in place after the change of ownership. Reduced government intervention has exacerbated the increased income and wealth inequality by cutting off social security in the short run and by reducing the capability of disadvantaged people to acquire the human capital which will enable them to improve their economic situation.

Kazakhstan has so far created a market system with concentrated ownership in which rents are accruing to a small elite. The state has supported this development through privatization favouring insiders and other policies, while substantially neglecting its role as provider of public goods such as law and order and of health care and education. The trade and forex regime is more liberal than in Uzbekistan but is manipulated to the benefit of favoured interests. The growth strategy is based on exports of raw materials and protection of domestic industry. Little concern is shown over the increasing income inequality, and the social security system is limited and poorly functioning. In sum, the state apparatus has largely been co-opted to support the interests of the elite rather than operating in a market-friendly way to promote growth with equity.

As with all of the CARs, however, this must be an interim report on the emerging market model, because elements of the current situation are unstable. Large increases in oil revenues will have an unpredictable impact on the political and economic structure. More immediately, the evolution of financial reform will have a critical impact on the ability of producers to compete on a level playing field; if capital markets start to operate impartially with entrepreneurial financial institutions attracting and allocating funds on the basis of price (i.e. interest rates), this will erode the benefits of government and other contacts, increase economic efficiency, and reduce the prospect of ending up with crony capitalism.

3.5.3. *The Kyrgyz Republic*

The Kyrgyz Republic has been the CAR which has most closely followed the World Bank and IMF blueprints for transition. Priority was given to price reform, supported by inflation control and integration into world markets. The Kyrgyz Republic had by 1997 the purest market model among the CARs. The sustainability of this market model depends upon two factors. Price stabilization has been achieved by large injections of foreign financial assistance rather than by internal fiscal control, which raises the spectres of welfare dependence and of loss of sovereignty if advice from Washington DC has to be followed in order to sustain the flows of assistance. The Kyrgyz Republic is the most isolated and resource poor of the four CARs covered in this study. Even with good policies the economic future is unpromising, and this could lead to a backlash against the market model.

3.5.4. *Turkmenistan*

Turkmenistan adopted a populist model based on absolute political power for a leader who would satisfy his people's economic needs. The model was based on abundant resource rents, and implementation broke down when these rents proved to be limited. The economy retains the non-market features of the Soviet era without the benefits of central planners to allocate resources, so that it functions even worse than in the years prior to the dismantlement of central planning in 1987/8. The non-market model of 1992–5 was unsustainable, but it is unclear what will replace it. In some respects Turkmenistan's reform path is starting to resemble that of Uzbekistan, but there appear to be critical differences in commitment.

The absolute power of the president has interfered with the creation of property rights and with institutional development. Industrial policy is a mixture of atavistic Soviet-style desire for autarchy (as in promoting cotton textile production in order to retain value-added on the cotton grown in Turkmenistan) and grandiose third-world nationalism (as in the new Ashgabat airport and the marble-clad presidential palace, which appear to be the two largest post-independence construction projects). Despite the president's assumption of the title 'Turkmenbashi' (Head of the Turkmen) and the initial populist policies, there has been no effort to alleviate poverty comparable to the measures being pursued in Uzbekistan.

3.6. CONCLUSIONS

The Central Asian economies offer a natural experiment in the adoption of differing reform paths. Unfortunately, the conclusions are obscured by significant differences in initial conditions and in external environment, and even more by the drawn-out nature of the transition from central planning. None of the CARs had even contemplated independent economic reform before mid-1991, and even the relatively rapid reformers had not completed their reform programmes by 1997. Thus, any assessment of reform paths and the ensuing market models must be an interim assessment.

Turkmenistan yields the strongest conclusions. It was one of a handful of transition economies in which autocratic governments adopted non-reform strategies. These strategies have all failed, but Turkmenistan is a good test of the unsustainability of the strategy, because at independence Turkmenistan was considered to be very favourably placed in terms of resource endowment and since independence it has not suffered from invasion or civil war. The extremely poor economic performance since independence can be related directly to the chosen reform path.

At the other end of the reform spectrum, the Kyrgyz Republic has been lauded for its purposive moves to a market economy despite poor economic prospects. Although it has benefited from more substantial foreign assistance than any other CAR, the Kyrgyz Republic's economic performance has been poor. Of course, this could be due to its unfavourable resource endowment, but so far the Kyrgyz Republic's record does not lend support to the rapid reform strategy led by price and trade liberalization and macroeconomic stabilization.

The most interesting comparative reform paths are those of Uzbekistan and Kazakhstan. Uzbekistan has adopted a gradual reform strategy with a heavy government hand restraining the pace of change and helping to provide social security. Kazakhstan has had a more freewheeling approach to economic policy, but has not yet created a well-functioning market economy and is in danger of ending up with a market model in which cronyism or criminal organizations play a more significant role than the price mechanism.

NOTES

1. See the summary of alternative progress indicators in *Transition*, No. 7, July–August 1996, World Bank and the much quoted indices in World Bank (1996).
2. State orders for 1996 applied to 40 per cent of the cotton crop and 25 per cent of the grain crop, with procurement prices at 70 per cent and 75 per cent of world prices (Klugman 1997).
3. As a counterpart to the characterization of Russia's transition strategy as 'inconsistent shock therapy' by Popov (1996), Pomfret and Anderson (1997, p. 20) conclude that 'Uzbekistan's macroeconomic policy since 1994 could be characterized as inconsistent gradualism'.
4. Klugman (1997) reports World Bank estimates that the cotton sector provided 13.4 per cent of government revenue in 1993.
5. Craumer (1995) and Khan (in Griffin 1996, pp. 65–92) provide differing assessments of agricultural reform in Uzbekistan.
6. See UNDP (1996*b*, pp. 35–49) and World Bank (1997) for useful discussions on health and education since independence.
7. The quotation is from the opening sentence of IMF *Staff Country Report No. 96/98* (September 1996).
8. The proliferation of kiosks in the major towns has been primarily in response to demand for imported chocolate, cigarettes, alcohol, underwear, condoms, tapes, and other consumer products which were either not supplied or were of poor quality in the Soviet era. Privatization of housing, allowing people to exchange housing more readily than in the past, has permitted a better matching of the housing stock to people's wants, e.g. as family sizes change or jobs in new locations become available.
9. Ackland and Falkingham (in Falkingham *et al.* 1997, pp. 81–99) document this for the Kyrgyz Republic on the basis of a 1993 survey; a comparable survey for Kazakhstan has yet to be processed, and that in Uzbekistan has been halted.
10. This section draws on the more extensive analysis in Pomfret and Anderson (1997).
11. Emigration from Uzbekistan was about half that from Kazakhstan, and relative to population much smaller than that from the Kyrgyz Republic (Table 3.3A). Moreover, part of the emigration from Uzbekistan consisted of movement of Turkic Central Asians across the Turkmenistan border, which was less economically harmful than the mass emigration of ethnic Slavs and Germans (groups with above average education levels) from Kazakhstan.
12. In the 1989 census the population consisted of 39.7 per cent Kazaks, 37.8 per cent Russians, 5.8 per cent Germans and 16.7 per cent other ethnic groups, but by 1995 the estimated ethnic composition was 46.0 per cent Kazaks, 34.8 per cent Russians, 4.9 per cent Germans and 14.3 per cent others; see UNDP (1996*b*, p. 30).
13. Klugman (1997) reports official figures showing employment in the non-public sector to have reached 50 per cent in 1995.

4

The Chinese Road to the Market: Achievements and Long-term Sustainability

FAN GANG

4.1. INITIAL CONDITIONS

China started its economic reforms in 1978 after 30 years, not 70 years, of Soviet-type planning. Measured by the exchange rate of that time, per capita GDP in 1978 was about $220. (Measured by the current rate, it was less than $50.) The 10-year Cultural Revolution, which ended in 1976, had driven the economy to the edge of collapse, but this made it easy to achieve high growth rates in subsequent years because recovery was from a very low base. The shortage of food and other consumer goods was obvious, and the inefficiency of industries was enormous. Dissatisfaction in economic performance led to demand for changes, although complete change or 'radical reform' was never adopted as an official policy. In fact, such a radical change did not seem necessary, given that the economy was still manageable, with a growth rate of more than 10 per cent per year (for 1977 and 1978), in contrast to the negligible or even negative rates experienced by some other socialist countries during the late 1980s.

The transition has therefore been taking place in a so-called gradual or, more accurately, incremental manner. Economic reforms have been implemented without major political change, and the privatization of state-owned enterprises (SOEs) was included among official policies only recently (though still not under the term 'privatization'). The transformation has followed the path of the so-called 'dual-track transition', meaning that the old system (the old track) was not dismantled until the new system (the new track) had developed and become sufficiently strong to take over.

An *ex post* analysis of the initial conditions, however, does explain why some economies can be successful in pursuing incremental changes, while others would fail. China was characterized by a number of special conditions, illustrated hereafter, that made gradual reform more feasible (Tables 4.1 and 4.2).

To begin with, although the state sector accounted for more than 70 per cent of output at the end of the 1970s, it employed less than 20 per cent of the labour force; the rest were working mostly in the poor agricultural sector and surviving on stagnant

Table 4.1. Change in the economic structure of China, 1978–1998

		1978	1995	1998
Level of development	Per capita GDP (RMB)	379	4,754	6,392
	Per capita GDP ($, at current exchange rate)	222	573	773
Economic growth	Growth rate of GDP (%)	11.7	10.5	7.8
	Share of investment in GDP (%)	38.0	40.5	38.1
Economic structure (industrialization)	Structure of GDP (%)			
	Primary sector	28.1	22.9	18.4
	Secondary sector	48.2	49.2	48.7
	Tertiary sector	23.7	31.6	32.9
Labour	Non-farming labour (% of total labour force)	30.7	50.6	54.0
Military expenditure	Defence expenditure (% of total government expenditure)	15.0	9.3	8.7
Economic structure by type of ownership (% of industrial output)				
State sector	State sector	77.6	30.9	28.2
	Collectives	22.4	42.8	38.4
	Private, corporate, joint venture, etc.	0.0	26.3	33.4
Urbanization	Urban population (% of total)*	17.9	29.0	32.0
Government revenue	Budgetary revenue (% GDP)**	30.9	10.7	12.4
	Budgetary deficit (% GDP)	−0.3	2.3	2.6
External balance	Balance of foreign debt ($ billions)	0.0	106.5	146.0
	Debt service ratio (%)	0.0	7.3	10.9
	Liability ratio (%)	0.0	15.5	15.2
	Trade/GDP ratio (%)	9.7	40.3	38.6
Education	Primary school enrolment (%)	95.5	98.5	98.7
	Compulsory education (years)	6.0	9.0	9.0
Health	Life expectancy (years)	56.0	69.0	71.0

Notes: *Not including all unregistered immigrants from rural areas. **Not including extrabudgetary revenue and off-budgetary revenue.
Source: CSSB (various years), *China Statistic Yearbook*.

subsistence incomes. The rural reform and the liberalization of private economic activities in the presence of a huge rural labour surplus could generate growth rapidly enough to outpace the speed at which the need for subsidizing state enterprises increased.

Second, in 1978, only about 18 per cent of the population was registered as urban residents, for whom the state took responsibility for employment. Accordingly, the state had a low burden of social security expenditures, considering that only state employees and the urban population enjoyed various social welfare programmes, while

Table 4.2. *The development of non-state sectors, 1980–1997 (percentages)*

	1980	1985	1986	1987	1988	1989	1990	1991	1992	1993	1994	1995	1996	1997
Output value of industry (OVI), % total OVI	24.0	35.2	37.7	40.3	43.2	43.9	45.4	47.1	51.9	56.9	64.1*	69.1	71.5	73.5
Contribution to the growth of industrial output	—	50.5	54.7	51.2	52.4	47.5	62.2	56.3	67.5	68.7	84.0	77.0	81.1	80.5
Employment, % of total labour force	81.1	82.0	81.8	81.7	81.6	81.7	81.7	81.9	81.8	81.6	81.9	82.0	83.7	85.2
As % of total non-agriculture labour force*	—	—	—	—	—	—	62.4	62.4	63.6	65.0	66.1	66.7	67.0	70.4
State budgetary revenue from non-state sectors, % of total state revenue	18.0	29.6	25.4	28.6	31.6	33.2	33.6	36.1	37.2	39.4	34.3	34.2	—	—
Retail sales, % of social total	48.6	59.6	60.6	61.4	60.5	60.9	60.4	59.8	58.7	60.1	68.1	70.2	72.8	75.7
% of total fixed investment	—	33.9	—	36.9	38.6	38.7	34.4	34.1	32.9	38.5	43.1	45.6	47.5	47.0
% of bank credit	—	18.0	—	—	—	19.8	—	21.1	21.2	19.3	18.8	12.6	—	—

Notes: *The 1994 figure includes output (of 460 billion yuan) by shareholding companies controlled by state-owned.

Source: CSSB (various years), *China Statistical Yearbook*.

rural residents were mostly left to take care of themselves. In some sense, in comparison with the Soviet Union, China has never been more than 20 per cent a socialist economy.

Third, because of the low level of economic development, China possessed greater potential for higher growth and more opportunities to solve structural problems and to gradually converge to the income per capita of the advanced countries. The excessive investment in heavy industry, for instance, could be overcome not so much by a dramatic restructuring, which could cause a sharp fall in national production, but simply by growth in labour-intensive industries and service sectors which could better utilize the advantage of a vast, low-cost, and fairly educated labour force. More importantly, the domination of the state sector could be broken down by the incremental development of the non-state sector during a process of overall growth which did not require the immediate and costly restructuring of the state sector. At the same time, despite the low per capita income, China had the largest population in the world, and therefore this largest of potential markets served as a great attraction to foreign investors, given the political and legal weaknesses of the moment.

Fourth, although during the late 1970s the situation was characterized by a perceptible shortage of consumer goods and a growing monetary overhang, the situation remained still manageable in comparison with that of other transitional countries. During the beginning of the reform, the low government deficit, the low debt, the low subsidies to the industrial sector, and the low trade deficit allowed the government to mobilize fiscal resources in order to exercise effective macroeconomic control in general and control on prices in particular.

Fifth, the wealth of overseas Chinese communities (including Hong Kong and Taiwan) and their special cultural ties with the motherland provided China with a unique and ready access to international markets, to information about new technologies and to the management of know-how, as well as to capital inflows. China also benefited from its close geographic and economic connections with Hong Kong.

Sixth, with its access to the sea and the traditional contacts between the coastal regions and the rest of the world, China was in a good position to benefit from a coastal-led transformation. The geographic factor could not only contribute to further growth, but could definitely make reform easier. The special economic zones along the coastline played a key role as a showcase to the rest of the country and rendered the reform models domestic rather than foreign. This made them more readily acceptable.

Seventh, although in her effort at marketization and modernization China suffered from the lack of a tradition of the rule of law, it benefited from considerable flexibility when having to reconcile the new approaches with the existing socialist principles. Pragmatic economic reforms (especially at the local level) could take place regardless of the rigidity of old doctrines or principles in terms of the regulations, laws, or even the constitution established under previous governments. Economic reform could therefore advance quite far without political change, which in other nations was considered an essential element of the overall reform process.

The situation in 1978 was characterized also by a number of unfavourable initial conditions, however. The main problems in this regard included the following:

1. The situation was characterized by a lack of incentives and social consensus for fundamental changes in institutions. From the beginning, there was therefore no clear and consistent objective model for reform. During the process of transformation, this lack of consensus often led to the introduction of policies unfavourable to the new sectors and of too many steps backwards in favour of the old system.
2. Due to the size of the country, there are vast geographical and cultural differences among regions. Many state enterprises are still concentrated in some interior regions, but these regions can hardly develop thanks to the free play of market forces. This situation has been and still remains a latent source of complex political tensions during the transformation.
3. The large size of the nation means that coordination costs are higher. Decentralization is unavoidable, but it can create situations in which reform efforts cannot

be carried out in a well-coordinated manner. This could therefore have led to a rather long process of chaotic, gradual changes. With the weakening of central planning and coordination soon after the introduction of the reforms, there was a distinct risk that the reform process could lose the momentum desired by the central authorities.

4.2. DUAL-TRACK TRANSITION

4.2.1. *Rural Reform and Market Liberalization*

The crucial part of China's dual-track transition has been the development of a new track, that is the market-oriented non-state sector. Two reforms in the early stages of the transition made this possible. They were the rural reform and the gradual liberalization of prices.

The first step of the whole economic transition was to dismantle the rural collectives—the people's communes—and to replace collective production by *de facto* private household farming. The introduction of the so-called 'household responsibility contract system' did not alter the collective ownership of farmland, but did put the land into the possession of households through 15-year long-term leases (the term of the contract was lengthened to 30 years in the early 1990s). The households had the autonomy for further decision making on matters of production and management, on condition that they would sell a certain amount of their produce to the state at official prices and that they would also make contributions to the local community, all according to terms set out in the contracts. This reform first took place in 1979 and was 95 per cent implemented by the end of 1983.

This single step provided the institutional precondition not only for the stable growth of agricultural production that was so important in the late 1970s and early 1980s, but also created a large low-cost labour force which had the economic freedom to pursue their own interests through private initiatives and market-oriented activities. They were the base from which the non-state sector could rapidly grow.

The market liberalization began with the production and sale of a portion of agricultural output in 1978. Farmers were allowed to sell their products on the free market after meeting the quotas for procurement sales set by state planners. Later, such an arrangement was introduced in many industrial sectors, too. The proportion of planned production in the value of total industrial output was thus reduced from over 90 per cent in 1978 to 5 per cent in 1994 (Table 4.3).

China started to open her economy to the rest of the world at the very beginning of the reform process. Foreign trade has grown at an average annual rate of 16.5 per cent over the past 20 years. Total trade reached $323.9 billion and the trade–GDP ratio was 38.6 per cent in 1998. Exports accounted for 19.2 per cent of GDP. Although trade and current account deficits were registered in most years during the 1980s, in the 1990s there were trade surpluses every year except 1993 (when the country recorded a trade deficit of $12.22 billion).

Table 4.3. *Reduction of planned production and sales, 1978–1994 (% of total industrial output)*

Year	1978	1984	1987	1991	1992	1994
Total planned production (central and provincial)	91.0	80.0	NA	16.2	12.0	5.0
Planned distribution of intermediate goods						
Steel	77.1	NA	NA	42.2	NA	NA
Wood	85.0	NA	NA	22.5	NA	NA
Cement	35.7	NA	NA	10.6	NA	NA
Coal	58.9	NA	NA	49.7	NA	NA

Sources: Fan *et al.* (1994); SSRC (1994).

A total of $265.6 billion of foreign direct investment (FDI) had flowed into China by the end of 1998, and China has been the largest FDI recipient among developing countries since 1993. The capital account balance has been mostly positive. Foreign reserves increased to $154 billion in 1998. At the end of 1998, the balance of foreign debt was $146 billion, with a debt service ratio of 10.9 per cent and a liability ratio of 15.2 per cent (Table 4.4).

After 17 years of openness to FDI, the Chinese manufacturers are now facing competition from 'domestic multinationals' which have been acquiring significant shares in domestic markets. The pressure exerted by industrial groups for the protection of national industries against this 'tariff jumping' triggered by FDI aiming at capturing the Chinese market is now rising fast. Nevertheless, this is unlikely to stop the general trend towards FDI growth, and China will remain the major attraction for FDI in Asia. A recent official statement[1] that encourages, rather than criticizes, FDI shows that the benefits of FDI are overwhelming. The growth of FDI, however, may be below 10 per cent in the next decade.

As in other countries (the US for example), the issue of the Chinese entry into the WTO is a domestic political issue revolving not only around national sovereignty, but also jobs and other vested interests of industrial groups. For China, a developing country undertaking institutional transformations, the entry into the WTO is not only about tariff cuts, but is also about various economic and social changes. China will require a great deal of time to fit into the international division of labour, to develop a legal system, and to create business habits which are compatible with international rules.

4.2.2. *Changes in Economic Structure and SOE Reforms*

4.2.2.1. *Growth of the Non-state Sectors*

The most important dual-track transition has been the change in the ownership structure of the economy (see also Chapter 9). China's progress in the development of the market system and the country's rapid growth have been mainly due to the

Table 4.4. *Trade openness and external balance, 1978–1997*

	1978	1980	1985	1990	1993	1994	1995	1996	1997
Total foreign trade (bil. $)	20,6	38,1	69,6	115,4	195,7	236,6	280,9	289,9	324,9
Total export and import as % of GDP	9.8	12.6	22.9	29.77	32.55	43.62	40.11	35.12	36.04
Current account (bil. $)	NA	NA	−11,417	11,997	−11,902	7,657	1,618	7,243	2,252
Capital account (bil. $)	NA	NA	8,972	3,256	23,472	32,644	38,674	39,967	—
Balance of foreign debt (bil. $)	0	NA	NA	52.5	83.6	92.80	106.6	116.3	139.1
Debt service ratio (%)	0	NA	2.8	8.5	9.7	9.1	7.3	6.7	—
Actually utilized foreign capital	0	2,887	4,647	10,289	38,960	43,213	48,133	54,804	51,900
Accumulated amount of foreign direct investment actually used (FDI)	0	7,219	21,790	68,074	137,790	181,003	229,136	283,940	329,850
FDI as % of total fixed investment	0	4.7	5.3	10.9	17.1	21.8	20.1	21.1	14.0
FDI			1,661	3,487	2,752	3,377	3,752	4,173	4,538
Number of foreign-funded companies (1,000)	0	NA	NA	43.7	147.5	206	233.5	240.4	307.6
Number of employees in foreign-funded companies (mil. persons)	0	NA	0.1	0.7	2.9	4.1	5.1	5.4	6.2
Foreign-funded companies as % of total industrial output	0	NA	NA	4.8	9.8	11.6	11.7	13.3	14.9
Import and export of foreign-funded companies as % of total foreign trade	0	—	—	—	—	37.0	39.1	47.3	51.6
Number of students studying abroad	860	2,124	4,888	2,950	10,742	19,071	20,381	20,905	—
Number of foreign tourists (millions)	NA	570	1,783	2,746	4,153	4,368	4,638	5,113	57,12

Source: China Statistical Yearbook (various years).

dynamic expansion of the non-state sector, which includes private and semi-private enterprises, community-owned rural industrial enterprises, shareholding corporations, foreign joint-venture companies, and individual businesses (Table 4.1). This development is what has made the Chinese economy a dual-track economy.

The rural reform turned the agricultural sector, which accounted only for over 30 per cent of GDP, but employed 80 per cent of the labour force at that time, in a *de facto* private sector little controlled by the state. When farmers became able to decide not only what they wanted to do with the land they held under contract, but also what they wanted to do with their surplus labour, then small private businesses (such as private transportation, retailing, crafts, and so on) and community-owned industrial enterprises, that is, the so-called township and village enterprises (TVEs), started to develop. Although the TVEs may be based on a transitional form of ownership and are still undergoing dramatic institutional changes as they grow,[2] they have already become the major competitor of state enterprises and accounted for over 40 per cent of total industrial output in 1995.

Another important factor underpinning the changes in ownership structures is the increasing capital inflows and the growing number of foreign joint ventures, especially those with overseas Chinese. Overseas Chinese investors have greater and more ready access to Chinese markets and invest mostly in the labour-intensive non-state sectors. From 1979 to the end of 1995, $137 billion in FDI was put into 330,000 projects, and in a single year, 1995, FDI reached $37.8 billion. Of the total FDI, 67.5 per cent comes from Hong Kong, Macao, and Taiwan. A considerable proportion of the investment from the US and Japan (which are the third and fourth largest sources of foreign investment) is also being made by overseas Chinese in these countries. In 1995, companies benefiting from foreign investment produced about 14.6 per cent of the total industrial output and about 50 per cent of the manufactured consumer goods on the domestic market, but they only contributed 39 per cent of international trade.

The non-state sector developed more quickly in those regions where the reforms and the creation of open markets took place relatively earlier and more rapidly (Table 4.5). Four southern coastal cities, including Shenzhen and Xiamen, were

Table 4.5. *Growth in the coastal regions, 1981–1994*

	Nation	Guangdong	Fujian	Zhejiang	Jiangsu	Shandong
Average annual growth of GNP	9.3	19.7	17.3	18.9	16.4	16.3
Growth of SOEs	NA	10.1	9.5	9.0	9.1	9.2
Growth of TVEs	NA	19.5	19.6	24.0	17.8	18.5
Growth of foreign and joint ventures	NA	58.6	50.0	38.6	42.3	37.3
Contribution of non-state sectors to the GDP growth	NA	63.0	60.0	73.0	70.0	69.0

Sources: Fan *et al.* (1994); SSRC (1995).

chosen as special economic zones (SEZs) in 1980, and Hainan province became the fifth in 1988. In addition, another 20 cities were allowed to develop as 'economic and technological development areas' (ETDAs). All these SEZs and ETDAs represent experimental areas for new institutions and reform policies. In most of these regions, the non-state sector was already contributing more than 70 per cent of GDP by the end of 1995.

4.2.2.2. State Enterprises: The Remaining 'Old Track'

After over 20 years of transition, the remaining hard core of the old economy is represented by the problematic state sector, which includes the SOEs, state-owned banks, and the government administration.

The reforms in the state sector have consisted in the decentralization of decision-making power and managerial reform without changes in ownership. These reforms have resulted in decentralized SOEs and more autonomous local governments, which now all play an increasing role in determining the allocation of resources and the distribution of income within an unchanged ownership framework. Despite some improvements in productivity, the profitability of SOEs has been deteriorating continuously (Table 4.6) as competition from non-state sectors has forced monopoly profits downward. Wage payments, bonuses, fringe benefits, and publicly financed consumption (which is often disguised as costs) have increased more rapidly than has output, resulting in declines in the returns on capital (Fan and Woo 1993). By the end of June 1996, the proportion of loss-making SOEs had reached 51 per cent.

Table 4.6. *Financial performance of major state enterprises,*[*] *1978–1997*

	1978	1980	1985	1988	1989	1990	1991	1992	1993	1994	1995	1996	1997
Profit rates[**]	15.5	16.0	13.2	10.4	7.2	3.2	2.9	2.7	2.2	1.2	1.4	0.8	0.8
Profits and taxes as % of total assets value[***]	24.2	24.8	23.5	20.6	17.2	12.4	11.8	9.7	9.7	9.7	6.4	7.1	7.0
Profits and taxes as % of output value	24.9	24.1	21.8	17.8	14.9	12.0	11.6	11.4	11.1	11.4	9.2	8.2	—
Revenues from state sector as % of total revenue	—	—	82.0	70.4	68.4	66.8	66.4	63.9	60.6	65.7	65.8	—	—
Total losses (bil. yuan)	4,2	3,4	3,2	8,1	18,0	34,9	36,7	36,9	45,3	48,2	54,1	79,7	74,4
Total losses as % of total profits	8.2	5.8	4.3	9.1	24.2	89.8	91.3	69.0	55.3	58.1	81.2	191.9	165.1
Subsidies for losses (bil. yuan)	—	—	32,5	44,6	59,9	57,9	51,0	44,4	41,1	36,6	32,8	—	—
Loss subsidies as % of budgetary revenues	—	14.3	17.0	20.3	17.4	14.1	10.7	8.1	7.0	7.0	5.3	—	—

Notes: [*]Large and medium-sized state enterprises with independent accounting. [**]The State Statistic Bureau stopped to provide the 'profit rate' in 1994, and therefore some figures in the table are calculated using other data available. [***]The definition of 'profits and taxes total' is different from 'pre-tax profits' because it includes all sales tax or value-added tax, not only the income tax.

Due to the fiscal and financial reforms of the 1980s, the SOEs now receive fewer subsidies from the state budget (Table 4.6).[3] Nevertheless, they receive quasi-subsidies from state banks in the form of 'policy loans' and the non-reimbursement of overdue debt. The main reason behind the slow reform of the financial sector is the need of the state to mobilize financial resources to support the fledgling industrial SOEs. Because of the easy access to bank credit, the average debt–asset ratio of SOEs has increased to over 80 per cent in recent years.[4] Financial experts have estimated that for 1998 alone bad loans represented 25 per cent of the total. Meanwhile, the inter-enterprise debt (IED, or 'triangle debt') has climbed rapidly in recent years, and the IED–GDP ratio rose to 42.9 per cent, which was among the highest in the world (Fan 1996).

That of the SOEs is now the core challenge of the Chinese economy. This problem is at the basis of many other dysfunctions, including financial underdevelopment, macroeconomic instability, corruption, government inefficiency, and the lack of the rule of law. But what is the basic cause of the deterioration in the SOEs during the last 15 years? The following list includes some of the managerial problems that people usually complain about: political appointment of managers; government interference in the decision-making process in the field of investment, production and wage distribution; public involvement in the decisions on the use of existing assets; excessive bureaucratic regulation and lack of the rule of law.

While all these problems still exist, more and more people have started to realize that they are closely linked to the ownership issue: why should the owner, that is, the state, have no right to choose the managers to administer its assets like a private firm? Why should the owner have no decision-making power over investment and the distribution and uses of assets in order to protect its special interests, which are increasingly vulnerable to insiders (managers and workers)? In such a state-owned economy, all citizens are actually non-owner players. This is the reason, when the talk comes to reform, everyone asks the state to go away and let the managers control the firms autonomously. But the question that is hardly raised is: who should be the stand-in for the current owner?[5]

4.2.2.3. *Changes in the Ownership Structure of the SOEs*

At the present time, there still is no centrally promoted programme of mass privatization, and public ownership remains pivotal in the official approach to the development of a socialist market economy. The ownership reform, however, is already under way, although it is moving at a slow pace.

A first step undertaken by the government was the corporatization of SOEs. Shareholding started to be used as a method to reform SOEs in 1984, and this was accelerated in 1988 when two stock exchanges were set up in Shanghai and Shenzhen. Since then, corporatization into shareholding companies has represented one of the main ways of accomplishing SOE transformation, starting normally with majority shareholding of the state. By the end of 1999, over 1,000 companies, most of which were state controlled, were listed on the stock market. In the same year, the total market value of the stocks was about 26 per cent of GDP, though the market value of the tradable stocks was only about 8 per cent of GDP, since on average 70 per cent of the shares of the listed companies were state owned and not yet tradable. There is no doubt that the government wishes to use the securities market as a means of fundraising for the SOEs, and the high percentage of shares in the hands of the state makes the current shareholding companies more like conventional SOEs.[6] Indeed, as long as society is not in crisis, ownership reform in China will be undertaken in a gradual manner. Yet, when market pressure starts to be felt (because shareholders are 'voting by walking away'), ownership control begins to function to some extent. Nevertheless, it will still take several years before the new patterns of ownership will be able to affect the efficiency of management and enterprise performance. Indeed, how can one expect the performance of a previously state-owned enterprise to change overnight after a halfway corporatization and to resemble that of a true corporation operating in a market system that has been evolving for hundreds of years?

The government has also proceeded to the sale of most small local SOEs. Although it is still trying every means to revive or strengthen the SOEs (this policy is formally announced in every government statement), it has become more and more difficult and expensive for the government to maintain them. This fact explains the recent wave of privatization among small local SOEs.

The sale of the assets of SOEs has been nominally permitted since late 1993,[7] but such a sale had *de facto* been restricted by official policy. However, in 1993, county and city governments started to act the moment they found out that getting rid of the financial and fiscal burden of the SOEs would have been beneficial to the local economy. Besides the establishment of joint ventures, an increasing number of small SOEs were sold to private owners, to TVEs, and to foreign investors. While it is difficult to find investors willing to buy the equities of the existing SOEs, selling the securitized net equities (the total value of assets minus total debt) to the workers of the enterprises concerned and converting the companies into so-called 'cooperative shareholding corporations'[8] became a popular way to achieve the restructuring of local-level SOEs.[9] In some counties of Shandong province, for instance, up to 70 per cent of the small SOEs have been sold in this way. The results of such a restructuring are so far quite encouraging. Most firms have improved their financial situation. Those that turned out to be unprofitable chose to go bankrupt (without much government intervention). The transfer and resale of the shares are already taking place, meaning that the concentration of ownership is now at a preliminary stage.

Since 1996, the central government has been implementing a policy of 'controlling the big ones and letting the others go to the market'. The basic idea is that the government may eventually only keep about 6,000 large SOEs under its control, and the transformation of all the rest should be guided by the market forces. Although the method to be used to liberalize small SOEs remains ambiguous, this policy will definitely encourage a local process of privatization. Up to 80 per cent of small SOEs have been privatized one way or another in many regions in recent years. As far as the large ones are concerned, it seems that conditions are not yet ripe for the real reform.

4.3. LONG-TERM FEATURES OF THE CHINESE ECONOMY IN TRANSITION

4.3.1. *The Moving Target in Objective Models*

When analysing the emerging features of the country's economy, public announcements about the target institutional model towards which China should move may seem a good reference point. Many factors, however, should be kept in mind in this analysis. For instance, the government's objectives may not be coincident with the evolution of the actual situation, and, more importantly, the government agenda itself may change along with the changes in the economy, since the government is constrained by the current situation. In general, the government's objectives are not so much the result of public choice in changing circumstances. Rather, the changes in the official target models reflect changes in the social balance among various interests groups and the changes in the economic structure that result from the process of reform and development. In other words, the changes have been due to endogenous changes in economic conditions and constraints.

This argument may also be proven to be valid in the evolution of China's official reform model. The reforms have actually gone through a long series of readjustments of the final target model being sought, from a planned economy with some market adjustment to a combination of plan and market and to the current socialist market economy (see Table 4.7). The definition of this socialist market economy is constantly changing, too, from the domination of state ownership (not including collectives) to the domination of public ownership (including collectives) and to the leading role of the state sector and then to the leading role of public ownership. Today, it is still changing non-stop. A question often raised, 'What is the current official position on the reforms?' should be rephrased to 'What is the trend or direction in the evolution of the official position on the reforms?'

Ideology is still a constraint in the transition reforms. Yet, compared to other countries which have a long historical tradition of religious beliefs, China may be less

Table 4.7. *Evolution of the official formulation of the reform objectives since 1978*

Periods	Objective formula
1978	Planned economy using the law of market exchange value
1979–84	Planned economy supplemented with market regulations
1984–87	Planned commodity economy
1987–89	State regulating the market and market regulating enterprises
1989–91	Organic integration of planned economy and market regulations
1992	Socialist market economy
1995	Reform of property rights
1997	Development of all kinds of ownership
1998	Amendment of Constitution to include protection of private ownership
1998	Village election

Source: Various official documents of the Central Committee of the Chinese Communist Party.

constrained by ideology over the long run. Many ideological arguments have in fact been called forth to protect existing economic interests. Ultimately, they may grow quiet when the economic structure is changed.

4.3.2. *In Which Direction is China Eventually Going to Go?*

China, like all other countries in transition, is heading towards a market economy. All the main principles of the market system, such as individual incentives and responsibilities, market competition, democratic decision making over the provision of public goods, information sharing, and so on, will eventually prevail also in China.

On the other hand, there may be Chinese characteristics in the market system that may emerge. Nevertheless, even that may only refer to the different ways the Chinese would carry out their institutional changes given their special historical and cultural background. Comprehensive analyses can show that many of the current 'special' arrangements part of the Chinese model are not due to Chinese culture or ideological constraints but due to the *particular stage* of transition and economic development: the market-oriented economic transformation has now been taking place for 20 years in a country with a 2,000-year history of centralized government and 40 years of central planning. The transition to a modern market economy may not require 400 years in China, as it did in Western countries in the past, but 20 or so years are still too few to reach the conclusion that the current picture should lead to stable institutions with Chinese characteristics.

So when we think about the long-term features of the Chinese economy, our thoughts should focus on the meaning of 'long'. China is still far from completing its transition, and it is also far from reaching a stable system. Because there does not appear to be any major difference among nations in their economic rationality and their ability to develop institutional arrangements over a long term that is long enough to allow all changes to take place and work out the constraints, the only meaningful discussion here may not revolve around the eventual features of the Chinese system, but rather around the features of the Chinese economy during the *next phase of transformation*, which may nonetheless be long enough for us to desire to put some effort into discussing it.

4.3.3. *Features of the Economy during the Next Phases of Transformation*

Unlike some other economies in transition, China is undergoing two concurrent processes: the institutional transition (from plan to market) and basic economic development (with the starting point a peasant society and an economy with a per capita income of $200). China benefits from this combination, but at the same time it struggles with the complexity of this dual task. The whole process of economic and societal transformation may take a rather long time (most likely another 20–30 years), and the whole process may pass through many phases before reaching the ultimate goal. Listed below are some predictions of the likely emerging features of the Chinese economy during the next 10 years or so of transformation.

The transition from an economy dominated by the state sector to a market economy not characterized by mass privatization may take a long time. The structure of the economy is constantly moving in the direction of higher shares for the non-state and private sectors. However, state enterprises, especially the large SOEs, will still play an important role, and various collective, semi-collective, or community-owned entities will still account for a large proportion of the economy. Shareholding corporations will continue to be set up, although still with significant shares going to the state or state entities (SOEs, state financial firms, government institutions, etc.). The contribution of pure SOEs to GDP may decrease further to 20 per cent or even to 10 per cent, while mixed ownership may still account for up to 40 per cent or 50 per cent during the next decade. Nevertheless, this may be, or may not be, the optimal way of transition in China, as long as we do not forget all the special conditions and constraints.

The economy will continue to be highly decentralized. Local governments will gain more autonomy in local development. Reforms and development in many areas will continue to be bottom-up, rather than top-down. Although a new mechanism of macroeconomic coordination is starting to emerge, the central government may still not be strong enough to carry through the implementation and coordination of central policies over the next decade. Many observers might consider this to be negative. However, it may also be a phase China needs to pass through before a new type of mechanism of central–local coordination based on more local autonomy is established. Reshaping the central–local relationship will definitely be one of the key issues in China in the near future.

The state will continue to play certain roles in economic development, although a lot of governmental control and intervention may take place at the local and ministry level. When so many kinds of ownership entities and local communities are competing against each other based on various kinds of incentives and constraints, a certain degree of government control (including some kind of industrial policy) may be needed in order to avoid too much chaos. Some kind of industrial policy will still be pursued, although in a somewhat weaker manner, compared to the years of central planning. Local governments at various levels, especially in the underdeveloped interior regions, will be playing an important part in organizing and coordinating economic development.

With membership in the WTO (that may be achieved soon), the Chinese economy will become more involved in international trade. Protection of domestic industries, especially state companies, by means of high tariffs and other barriers to trade and market access, will be reduced as the benefits of internationalization increase. Domestic institutional changes will also be pushed forward because of the need to conform to the international rules, which has already begun to take effect.

Social security will be expanded to cover more workers in the formal sector, as industrialization and urbanization continue. But the majority of the rural labour force will still be left out by such provisions, at least in the near future. The emerging social security system is more individualized and commercialized, though enforced by the government, and with a small social pool.

Income disparity is going to be a hot issue (see Chapter 10). More attention will be drawn to the rising income differentials between the rich and the poor in the process of industrialization. More institutions, such as tax collection on high income and wealth, will be set up, and fiscal transfers will play a more important role. Regional differences will still be an issue, but will become less critical as the migration from the interior, the less developed regions, continues to increase, and this will therefore help narrow the regional disparities in actual per capita income. The regional differences with regard to the level of economic development may be larger than now, but the regional disparities in *per capita income* may be narrowed as a result of migration.

In short, in 10 years time, China will still be in the process of transforming towards a market economy, and it will still be far from completing this process. All the changes taking place then should still be considered *transitional*, rather than as a 'new model of the market economy'. While the uncertainties are still numerous, one thing is sure: the Chinese economy and society will be very complicated and diversified in the next phase of economic development and institutional change.

4.3.4. *Factors that May Lead to Failure*

Financial crises, unemployment among state employees, income disparity, corruption among government officials, macroeconomic instability, and so on, taken individually or all of them together, may cause the current transformations to derail, social unrest, or even a breakdown of the economy and society. When the economy becomes so complicated, and so many different sectors and entities are mixed together and compete against each other during the painful process of transformation, some important elements may go out of control.

One might describe a dozen scenarios of failure and breakdown so as to warn people. But the first question is: How can one possibly imagine that, in the process of transformation in China, things cannot be complicated or problematic? How can one avoid such negative trends, conflicts, limitations, or dangers? Are there any examples of progress in history without problems and risks, especially for big, developing countries? From history, we can learn that the risks should be fully confronted, and better and quicker reform policies should therefore be recommended. Economists should then provide more policy recommendations and urge policy makers to react conveniently. But there are still so many 'shoulds'. And policy makers have their own inherited interests from the previous establishment and the previous phases of transition, no matter how right or wrong they are from the perspective of social welfare. The fundamental transformations of the Chinese society are unavoidably, maybe unfortunately, going forward, although they face many difficult and risky phases. In that sense, there should be no more hope focused on the emergence of the great wisdom of a great leader to light a great miracle of a way to a smooth transition.

However, at least this is now the first time in China's modern history that economic growth and the institutional evolution towards a market economy are on track. And this is also the first time the Chinese people can see a real possibility to overcome the problems.

NOTES

1. See *People's Daily*, 12 August 1996.
2. One of the major advances in this area has been the recent development of the collective shareholding system in TVEs, which involves redistribution or sales, up to 50 per cent, of property rights, in the form of shares, among workers in the firms or members of the community (see Chen *et al.* 1992).
3. The nominal amount of total budgetary subsidies to loss-making enterprises was 36.6 billion yuan in 1994, only slightly more than that in 1985, 32.4 billion yuan (no discount for inflation).
4. It was officially estimated as 79.3 per cent in the first half of 1995 (see *Economic Daily*, 10 October 1995). The recent estimate in a government circular was 82 per cent.
5. The resistance to privatization mainly comes from the managers (see *Asian Wall Street Journal*, 4 March 1994).
6. In the statistics, when an SOE has become a shareholding company, it can no longer be listed among the SOEs. So, any improvement through corporatization will not show up in the statistical performance of the SOE sector and will only be reflected in the overall situation.
7. In October 1993, the Third Plenary of the 14th Central Committee of the CCP adopted a new, comprehensive 'Decisions on Economic Reform' which, for the first time, announced, among other things: (1) the objective of reform is a socialist market economy; (2) the non-state sector should be encouraged to develop along with the state sector; (3) the reform of 'property rights' over SOEs and the sale of state assets should be allowed; (4) the 'corporatization' of SOEs is viewed as the main method to achieve the immediate target of institutional change. This document is regarded as a major breakthrough on the reform agenda of the top leadership.
8. This is a special form of shareholding with more characteristics of public ownership. The shares of the firm are owned by employees individually; but no matter how different the amounts of shares held are, everyone in the firm has equal voting rights, and part of the dividends must be distributed equally among the employees. After a period of time, the shares began to be transferred and traded. Therefore, a concentration in ownership is also expected.
9. Cooperative shareholding (CSH) was first developed in TVEs. By the end of 1995, three million TVEs had been converted into CSH companies and accounted for more than 20 per cent of the total. In some regions like Jiangsu, Shandong, and Zhejiang province, over 50 per cent of TVEs are not CSH (see *China Information Daily*, 13 July 1996).

5

Vietnam: Transition as a Socialist Project in East Asia

MANUEL F. MONTES

5.1. INTRODUCTION

The marketization process in Vietnam has so far been pursued, at least in public declarations, as a socialist project. The very basic question about such socialist experiment concerns its sustainability. At the practical level, it is important not to confuse all shortfalls in economic performance with shortfalls in the marketization effort, and all shortfalls in the marketization effort with the implicit or explicit defence of the overall socialist project (which has admittedly become more amorphous over time). In this context, this study seeks to develop the following propositions on the basis of Vietnam's transition experience:

1. Transition can occur without a period of overall output decline. Though the traditional 'development' industries will suffer, their decline can be made up for, at least temporarily, by growth in other industries. Of particular importance is the growth of non-tradable activity financed by improvements in household incomes engendered by the liberalization of the labour market (see proposition 5).
2. Privatization is not necessary to create efficient markets and to put into place the incentives needed to restructure the economic structure and increasing output.
3. Drastic implementation of the hard budget constraint in the context of party control is possible.
4. The state can continue to play a key role in important economic areas, such as state-owned enterprises and tax reform.
5. Profound labour reallocations and the creation of a liberalized labour market can be facilitated by the granting of generous separation allowances.

The rest of this chapter proceeds as follows: Section 2 addresses the question of characterizing Vietnam's transition problem as one embedded into that of economic development and proposes the manner in which transition can be distinguished from development. Section 3 provides a brief chronology of Vietnam's transition path and strategy. It discusses the macroeconomic and public finance adjustments intervened in the first years of the transition. Section 4 discusses trade and industrial issues. Section 5 discusses the labour market and selected welfare aspects of Vietnam's transition.

5.2. DEVELOPMENT VERSUS TRANSITION

In considering Vietnam's recent experience, it is important to differentiate between 'development' and 'transition'. Transition might be thought of as the process of increasing the market determination of economic outcomes. Development, in turn, might be thought of as a steady increase in the average productivity of an economy, i.e. in the amount of output per labour input or, more appropriately, per unit of total inputs. The 'Washington consensus' suggests that marketization (with a whole barrage of qualifications—including good governance—a formulation necessitated by the narrow reach of neoclassical analysis) is a necessary condition for development. Economies of scale, indivisibilities, and first-mover hesitancies, however, are well-known examples of impediments that do not allow the market to achieve by itself the development goals mentioned above. In other words, marketization, including opening up the economy to foreign goods, may actually retard permanent increases in productivity.

The movement towards the market in Vietnam was launched in the context of disappointing economic performance after the unification of North and South Vietnam and the actual and expected contraction in Soviet assistance. The subsequent spurt in growth seemed to confirm the predictions of the Washington consensus. Indeed, poor incentives and dirigiste institutions have been known to maintain any economy below their production possibility frontier curves. Removing, if in part, these restrictions (Vietnam still retains some) can thus move an economy closer to its long-term potential output. Moving the whole production possibilities curve outward, i.e. engendering 'development', is however a different matter.

In economies characterized by a highly distorted endowment of physical and human capital stock, the rapid shift to international prices entailed by the transition can cause a temporary inward shift of a country's production possibilities frontier curve. But, if the existing production structure is not too distorted in relation to the new set of relative prices, the transition can instead push an economy towards higher output levels. Given the predominance of low capital-intensive agriculture and other relatively favourable initial conditions, Vietnam followed the second path, a path which proved politically taxing but which was less arduous from an economic perspective. The real question now is whether Vietnam can escape the international forces responsible for the divergence in economic performance among open economies and succeed in triggering a broad-based and equitable development.

Figure 5.1 attempts to characterize the main issues of Vietnam's transition making use of the production possibilities frontier diagram. The two axes are labelled T for tradables and N for non-tradables; the main point is that N are goods that were specific to and given great value in the planned socialist economy and could only be exchanged with difficulty elsewhere. Alternatively, N can represent goods that can be produced with the labour skills available in a socialist economy, labour being the last

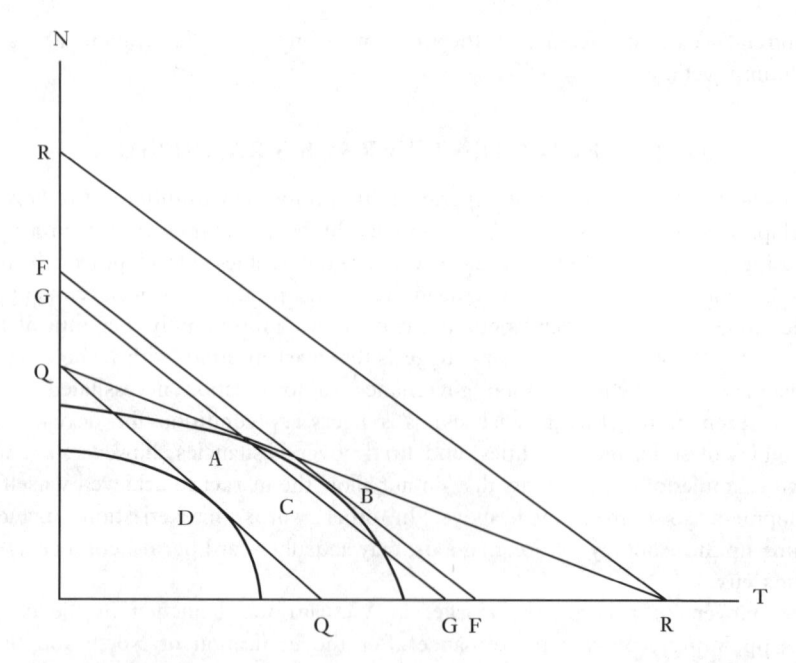

Figure 5.1. *Graphical representation of Vietnam's transition and development paths*
Source: Author's compilation; see text in Section 2.

non-tradable good in today's global economy. Before transition, the economy starts at point A, based on a socialist and trade-protected production possibilities curve and using resources represented by the line QR in which the fact that tradables were underpriced in the socialist economy is represented by the gradient of the slope. RR represents the international trade-off in these two goods, and if only the resources represented at point Q could be easily traded internationally, the country could move to a production possibility frontier tangent to RR.

Instead, the economy either experiences a shrinkage of the production possibility frontier curve to D on QQ or—if its production activities can be adjusted rapidly enough to produce tradables—to a point C or B, the latter representing full employment under the old socialist economic structure. Because we have defined the level Q of goods of type N to be difficult to trade outside the socialist economy, to attain either C or B additional resources to the amount of QG or QF will be required, otherwise the economy can be stranded in C or stuck in low-level equilibrium at D.

The analysis in this chapter underscores that some key transition-related adjustments, such as the introduction of wage flexibility and the liberalization of the planning mechanism, occurred as early as 1981, but identifies the period 1986–91 as that of Vietnam's most intensive transformation. The period from 1992 onwards, in contrast, is regarded as one in which development efforts became more important than the structural transformations, even though transitional issues such as privatization and the development of financial systems continued to be critical.[1] During this period, the investment rate recovered and increasing attention was paid to current account deficits and industrial development issues.

During the high period of transition (1986–91), prices and price-setting mechanisms were reformed and the relationship between the state and the production units deeply modified. As shown in Section 5, this process involved production declines in the traditional sectors (e.g. textiles), an increase in agriculture and non-tradables (especially home remodelling and construction), and a somewhat fortuitous boom in the exports of raw materials. Though there were dramatic reallocations of labour away from the state sector (discussed in Section 6), the unemployment rate rose only modestly due to sustained overall growth, an increase in rural incomes, the granting of generous separation allowances in the declining sector, and the consequent expansion of the construction and other non-tradable sectors.

At the beginning of the transition, Vietnam enjoyed favourable structural conditions that permitted a comparatively easy adjustment to the international prices. Indeed, Chapter 1 of this volume indicates that Vietnam's (as well as China's) initial industrial structure, trade distortions, average number of employees per enterprise, and level of development were likely to lead to a smaller output loss than in other transition economies characterized by less favourable initial structural conditions.[2]

As pointed out in this chapter, many of the transition-driven adjustments in economic variables were temporary, fortuitous, and of conjunctural nature. The institutional changes that accompanied them, however, permanently improved Vietnam's development prospects. Vietnam has dealt with most of the transformations required by the transition to the market economy, but must now face the more complicated challenge of development.

The economic crisis which swept through Asia beginning in July 1997 illustrates well Vietnam's development dilemmas. The 'Asian crisis' was primarily caused by the sudden withdrawal of short-term lines of credit by private investors from the high-growth East Asian economies. Before the onset of the crisis, Vietnam's economic growth had been slowing down due to the completion of the first wave of reforms and the decline in foreign investments brought about by 'disappointment' over the low speed of the country's economic reforms. With the hindsight of the Asian crisis, this 'disappointment' can also be interpreted as the onset of greater realism on the part of all parties about a sustainable and safe speed of reform.

On the one hand, Vietnam was spared the debilitating impact of the sudden withdrawal of short-term capital because its capital account had remained closed and a dependence on short-term capital had not built up. On the other hand, the economy saw its growth rate halved (from about 8 per cent to 4 per cent) as investment flows, especially from neighbouring countries such as Malaysia, disappeared as a result of the crisis, which indicates that a key component of growth has now come to depend on foreign resources. The most difficult reforms that now confront Vietnam are domestic and relate to the reform of state enterprises and their dependence on state credits. In fact, it would be ironical if Vietnam, under the stress of accelerating market reforms, were to liberalize foreign investment rules faster than its domestic financial markets.

5.3. INITIAL CONDITIONS AND *DOI MOI* REFORM PROCESS

The start of Vietnam's transition is normally dated at the Sixth Party Congress of the Communist Party of Vietnam in December 1986 when a contract system was introduced in the agricultural sector and state enterprises were permitted to swap and sell goods on their own to raise money to buy inputs or to increase the salaries of their employees. At the start of its reform process, Vietnam's economy was predominantly agricultural; large enterprises did not dominate its industrial sector and the typical industrial operation was a locally controlled state enterprise or cooperative.

In 1988, Vietnam began developing a two-tier banking system, principally as a means to separate central bank functions from enterprise and trade financing activities. Officially, from that date on, all enterprises were to be able to borrow at the same interest rate; however, state enterprises still continued to soak up the bulk of domestic lending. Until 1990, 90 per cent of outstanding bank credit were claims on state-owned enterprises; in 1994, this had fallen to 63 per cent (World Bank 1995*b*, Table 4.2).

The next turning point of the reform process is 1989 when, in response to the high inflationary pressures set in motion by the initial wave of policy reforms (inflation reached 411 per cent in 1988; Dang 1994, p. 173), the government phased out price controls, set interest rates on deposits above inflation rates and above loan rates (Nguyen 1994), and instituted stricter controls over lending to state enterprises. The reform process accelerated in 1990 with the drastic devaluation of the dong. Money creation to finance the budget was stopped in 1991. When strict rules on lending to state enterprises began to bite, enterprises started to shut down or shed workers. Between 1988 and 1992, the number of state enterprises decreased from 12,000 to 7,000 and a third of the workforce of state enterprises, about 800,000 people, lost their jobs (Dollar and Ljunggren 1995).[3] Meanwhile, inflation was brought down further, from 67 per cent in 1990 to 18 per cent in 1992 (Dang 1994), in a classic devaluation-cum-tight money manoeuvre, but without IMF resources (Vietnam was still under the US embargo).

It is this episode that inspired Sachs and Woo (1994) to declare Vietnam to be a case of shock therapy. Yet, the record of consistently positive growth rates (with slowdowns but still positive growth in 1987 and 1989) while the state share of output paradoxically increases from 33 to 39 per cent (Table 5.1) raises questions about such formulation. What is evident from the accounts of the period (Dang 1994) was that production breakdowns were already evident, part in 1987 and part at the end of 1988, before the shock-therapy-type policies were finally accepted by officials. Indeed, during these years, the state committee on prices was compelled to update prices monthly so as to engender adequate supply of goods (even when considering that rice can be hoarded only for limited periods). In the end, such effort was eventually abandoned and price

Table 5.1. *Gross domestic product by ownership in Vietnam, 1986–1995 (in billions of dongs at constant 1989 prices—and in percentages)*

	Total	Growth rate	Distribution		Growth rate	
			State	Non-state	GDP—excl. oil and state	GDP—excl. oil and rice
1986	24,431	—	33.3	66.7	—	—
1987	25,291	3.5	34.1	65.9	3.3	5.3
1988	26,835	6.1	34.8	65.2	3.1	1.2
1989	28,093	4.6	33.2	66.8	5.3	3.8
1990	29,526	5.1	32.4	67.6	2.7	3.1
1991	31,286	5.9	33.2	66.8	4.3	4.9
1992	33,991	8.6	34.3	65.7	7.2	6.6
1993	36,735	8.0	35.4	64.6	7.5	7.9
1994	39,982	8.8	36.7	63.3	8.3	9.5
1995 (est.)	43,797	9.5	38.8	61.2	NA	NA

Sources of basic data: Central Statistical Office (1996); table 13 and table 2.1 of Dodsworth *et al.* (1996).

controls were removed. A comparison of the columns of total GDP growth rate and GDP excluding rice and oil (Table 5.1) suggests that, in 1987, the GDP growth rate *excluding rice* would have been *higher* than the overall growth rate, unveiling in this way the crisis of the agricultural sector. This comparison also indicates the vigorous recovery of rice production in the subsequent year.

The shock therapy interpretation of the Vietnamese policy reforms is questionable on few counts: first, in many cases there was no clear intention to inflict a shock, meaning simultaneous reforms including price liberalization, devaluation, privatization, and so on; instead, the reform effort was led by the failure of rearguard measures such as the continued updating of prices; second, the 'shock therapy' policies actually permitted production to restart, even though this entailed an acceptance of the shooting up of inflation rates and currency substitution (see below); third, Vietnam's experience suggests that privatization is not a precondition for an increased reliance on price signal to foster production.

As far as the macroeconomy is concerned, Vietnam has managed to maintain positive growth rates throughout the transition period and to engender since 1993 a rising trend in investment/GDP ratio and in savings (Table 5.2). However, current account deficits and fiscal deficits remained large.

Vietnam's authorities implemented deep spending cuts in response to macroeconomic imbalances in the late 1980s in combination with some Israeli-style heterodox approaches, such as acquiescing to currency substitution by permitting the widespread use of the US dollar in domestic transactions (Van Arkadie and Montes 1995).

Even though savings in dollars and gold have a long tradition in the country, official dollarization exploded in 1988 when state banks were permitted on a

Table 5.2. *Recent macroeconomic data, 1991–1995*

	1991	1992	1993	1994	1995
GDP growth rate	6.0	8.6	8.1	8.8	9.5
In per cent of GDP					
Gross domestic investment	15.1	17.0	20.5	24.1	27.6
Gross domestic savings	16.5	19.6	14.9	17.6	19.1
Current account deficit			6.7	6.2	8.9
Merch. exports/GDP	—	—	20.4	23.3	30.7
Merch. imports/GDP	—	—	24.6	29.1	42.0
Central govt budget deficit	—	—	6.2	2.4	5.5
Inflation rate	—	—	5.3	14.4	12.7

Sources of basic data: ADB (1996); table A10 of Dodsworth *et al.* (1996).

'no-questions-asked' basis to open dollar bank accounts as a heterodox means of encouraging state trading enterprises to repatriate their export earnings and soak up balances in the informal sector. In 1994, dollar deposits represented 20 per cent of Vietnam's M2, from a peak of 40 per cent in 1991. This policy has, nevertheless, reduced capital flight and made lending resources available in the formal market. In fact, dollarization has permitted the level of intermediation through the domestic financial system to increase, instead of declining (Dodsworth *et al.* 1996).

Vietnam's recovery, subsequent to the stabilization struggles of 1988–91, has been based on an increase in the investment rate from about 15 per cent in 1991 to over 22 per cent after 1994. Vietnam's continuing struggle to trigger an increase in its growth rate while keeping inflation, current account, and fiscal deficits under control derives from the usual development dilemma of how to finance a higher investment rate.

Vietnam's transition path from a planned economy is particularly well captured in Table 5.3, which traces the evolution of state resources provided to state enterprises from the budget and the banking system. The success of these adjustments raises doubts about the appropriateness of focusing at any cost on creating a private sector during the transition and not on concentrating instead on protecting state capacity and fostering exchange and market activities, irrespective of the ownership of the enterprises engaged in such transactions. In the period 1987–94, transfers to the budget by state enterprises actually increased by a modest 1.3 percentage points of current GDP, from 10.8 to 12.1 per cent. This modest increase saw a substitution away from operating surpluses of state enterprises (which declined from 10.3 per cent in 1987 to zero by 1991) to tax receipts from state enterprises (which reached 9.2 per cent in 1994).

However, a key adjustment occurred in state enterprise receipts from the budget, which fell drastically from 7.9 per cent to 0.5 per cent during the reform years, with the greatest drop occurring in 1988–90, when such transfers declined from 8.5 to 2.6 per cent, not to recover subsequently. Capital transfers were gradually reduced to zero, though there was a small blip in 1989 while depreciation payments

Table 5.3. *Transfers between state enterprises and the state budget, 1987–1994 (% of GDP)*

	1987	1988	1989	1990	1991	1992	1993	1994
Transfers to budget	10.8	7.9	8.4	8.6	8.1	10.8	11.8	12.1
Taxes	—	—	—	—	6.9	8.3	9.3	9.2
Transfers	10.8	7.9	8.4	8.6	1.2	2.5	2.5	2.9
Operating surplus	10.3	7.3	7.6	7.4	—	—	—	—
Depreciating allowance	0.6	0.6	0.8	1.2	0.8	2.1	1.9	2.3
Capital user fee	—	—	—	—	0.3	0.5	0.6	0.7
Transfers from the budget	7.9	8.5	4.8	2.6	1.0	0.9	0.6	0.5
Subsidies	4.8	4.9	0.5	—	0.1	0.2	0.1	0.1
Food	3.1	2.7	—	—	—	—	—	—
Production	0.3	0.4	—	—	—	—	—	—
Exports	1.4	1.9	—	—	—	—	—	—
Working capital	0.5	0.6	0.5	0.3	0.3	0.7	0.5	0.3
Capital transfers	2.5	2.9	3.8	2.3	0.7	—	—	—
Net transfers to the budget	3.0	−0.6	3.6	6.0	7.1	10.8	11.2	11.6
Growth in bank credit to state enterprises	9.6	9.2	7.1	4.0	5.0	3.0	2.3	2.4
Net bank and budget support of state enterprises	6.6	9.7	3.5	−2.0	−2.1	−6.9	−8.9	−9.2

Sources of basic data: Dodsworth et al. (1996, table 3.2).

as a share of transfers began a gentle increase (they reached 2.3 per cent by 1994). The cut in food subsidies between 1987 and 1989 reflects the dismantling of rice allotments in kind to state employees which had become an important component of public wages during a period of rising inflation. Finally, throughout this period, working capital transfers to state enterprises were broadly maintained (there is a large increase in 1992 for example) in view of their critical role in maintaining adequate levels of production in state enterprises. As a whole, the modest increase in net transfers to the state budget and the dramatic decline in claims on the budget resulted from a rise in net transfers from state enterprises from 3 to 11.6 per cent during the reform period.

Table 5.3 shows a huge 15-fold increase in nominal amounts provided to state enterprises. But in per cent of GDP, there was in fact a decline in the total budgetary and bank support to state enterprises (from a positive transfer of 6.6 per cent in 1987 to a negative one of 9.2 per cent in 1994), implying that by the latter year state enterprises had become a significant net contributor to the state budget. Oil-related revenues accounted for 1.1 per cent of GDP in 1989 and peaked at 3.8 per cent in 1992 and 1993 (Dodsworth et al. 1996), and thus might be associated with about one-third of the total contribution of enterprises to the state budget by the end of the period.

In Vietnam, privatization and decentralization have taken specific characteristics as a result of the insistence of the national policy makers on the leading role of state enterprises which—as seen above—witnessed a dramatic shrinkage in government

Table 5.4. *Distribution of gross industrial output by management level, 1985–1995*

	Total	Central	Local
1985	100.0	34.0	66.0
1986	100.0	33.8	66.2
1987	100.0	32.8	67.2
1988	100.0	32.2	67.8
1989	100.0	36.4	63.6
1990	100.0	39.7	60.3
1991	100.0	48.1	51.9
1992	100.0	50.5	49.5
1993	100.0	51.9	48.1
1994	100.0	52.2	47.8
1995 (est.)	100.0	52.5	47.5

Source of basic data: Central Statistical Office (1996, table 134).

Table 5.5. *Distribution and growth rate of gross industrial output by economic sectors, 1985–1995 (per cent growth rates)*

	Output (1989 dong, mill.)	Growth rate	% of total	
			State	Non-state
1985	10,521,403	—	56.3	43.7
1986	11,170,876	6.2	56.3	43.7
1987	12,283,386	10.0	55.9	44.1
1988	14,042,955	14.3	56.5	43.5
1989	13,583,596	−3.3	57.0	43.0
1990	14,011,073	3.1	58.6	41.4
1991	15,471,092	10.4	68.5	31.5
1992	18,116,895	17.1	70.5	29.5
1993	20,412,035	12.7	71.7	28.3
1994	23,214,225	13.7	72.4	27.6
1995 (est.)	26,463,000	14.0	72.4	27.6

Source of basic data: Central Statistical Office (1996, table 135).

subsidies. All this led to a situation in which local-level urban enterprises were fully privatized and the cooperatives basically dismantled, while the state participation in trading and modern industrial sectors increased (the latter trend is lamented by Dollar and Ljunggren 1995). Table 5.4 presents the trend in gross output by management level from 1985 to 1995. In 1985, 66 per cent of industrial output was locally managed; by 1995, only 47.5 per cent of gross industrial output was locally managed and the proportion of output accounted for by centrally managed enterprises had increased from 34 to 52.5 per cent. This trend is echoed in Table 5.5 in which the gross industrial output is broken down into state and non-state sectors. Table 5.6 shows that

Table 5.6. *Number of non-state industrial establishments by types of ownership, 1985–1995*

	Total	In numbers of which			Total	In per cent of total of which		
		Cooperative	Joint venture	Private		Cooperative	Joint venture	Private
1985	242,721	35,629	920	206,172	100	14.68	0.38	84.94
1988	350,909	32,034	318	318,557	100	9.13	0.09	90.78
1989	356,522	21,901	1,284	333,337	100	6.14	0.36	93.50
1990	390,756	13,086	770	376,900	100	3.35	0.20	96.45
1993	457,625	5,287	3,322	449,016	100	1.16	0.73	98.12
1994	499,603	1,648	4,909	493,046	100	0.33	0.98	98.69
1995	524,299	1,729	5,152	517,418	100	0.33	0.98	98.69

Source: Central Statistical Office (1996, table 131, p. 280).

in the 'non-state' sector the proportion of enterprises accounted for by cooperatives shrunk from 14 per cent in 1985 to a negligible level in 1995.

While Vietnam now faces the problems typical of a mixed economy, in terms of its international image, the aspect of the transition which attracted considerable attention was that focusing on the transformation of Vietnam from a war to a peace economy. The economy of North Vietnam functioned rather well as a mix of an overall state planning, an agricultural sector under the control of the cooperatives, and price control. While North Vietnam's economic system was—for years—that of a war economy, many of the key economic sectors of that era continued to perform well after reunification. As for the south, the years 1975 to the early 1980s can be seen as an attempt to carry out a 'transition' towards the northern economic system, though such an attempt met with increasing resistance and was characterized by mounting production failures and shortfalls of essential goods. One way to see the reform process in the 1980s, a view that does not require allegiance to the 'Washington consensus', is as a succession of central government actions to acquiesce to successful local experiments, mostly in the south, to solve production problems (Selden and Turley 1993; Fforde and de Vylder 1996).

5.4. INDUSTRIAL AND TRADE ISSUES

As noted, Vietnam's recent growth has derived from the 'easy' part of industrial adjustment; the identification of a sustainable long-term industrial development path, however, still needs to be faced. Vietnam's avoidance of a transformational recession derives from a combination of factors such as an initial excess capacity in rice production, energy, and steel; the decline in competing imports from CMEA countries (fertilizer and steel); a bit of luck (e.g. the increase in oil production); and a surge in household demand (construction materials and foodstuffs, beer, liquor, and cigarettes).

The main patterns are shown in Fig. 5.2. The rapid growth of agricultural production (included in the category 'foodstuffs' in Fig. 5.2) is due to the surge in rice

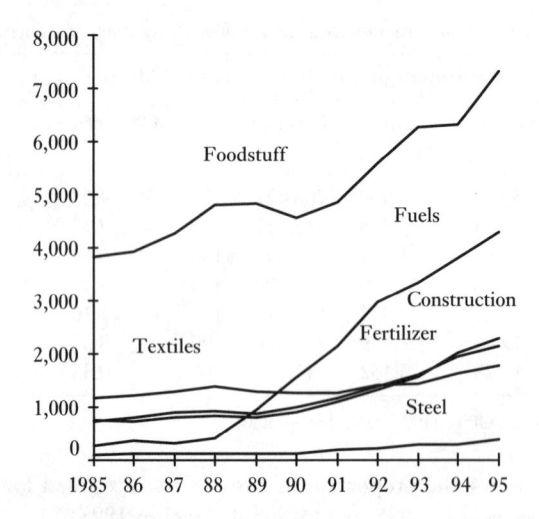

Figure 5.2. *Gross output of selected sectors (value in 1989 million dollars)*
Source of data: Central Statistical Office (1996, table 139).

production following the abandonment of the old rice procurement policies in the south. Thus, rice production grew at 3.8 per cent a year between 1980 and 1987, mainly due to increases in yields per hectare. Over 1987–90, rice output grew by 8.4 per cent a year owing to a growth of 5.7 a year in land yields and to the expansion in the land sown with rice triggered by the commercialization of the foodcrop sector. Over 1990–4 rice production increased by 5.2 per cent a year, with a growth rate of yields of 3.1 per cent a year. This surge in rice production meant that Vietnam moved from a position of rice importer to that of the third largest rice exporter in the world. It also meant rapidly rising incomes in the rural areas. Higher rural incomes in turn boosted household demand for consumer goods such as liquor, beer, and cigarettes, the production of which was being improved thanks to the creation of joint ventures with foreign partners.

The coming on-stream of the Bach Ho oilfield (a joint venture between Vietnam and firms from the old Soviet Union) accounts for the rapid rise in fuels production, which Dodsworth *et al.* estimate to have added 8 percentage points to the industrial value-added in 1988–9 and another 25 points in 1990–1. The new oil production does mask out the negative growth of the industry/construction sector before 1992; however, by 1992, industry/construction began to grow at rates over 10 per cent per year. The data in Table 5.7 illustrate the role played by fuel production in sustaining the overall growth rate of output. In the period where the industrial recession was the deepest, 1988–90, oil production grew by over 96 per cent. Such a large increase did not lift by much the total growth rate of output, as in 1998 and 1999 oil production respectively accounted for only 3 and 7 per cent of industrial output. However, in 1990–1, as industrial restructuring continued, other industrial sectors (notably ferrous metallurgy, equipment and machinery, wood and wood products, glass, earthenware, and porcelain, foodstuffs, and textile products) had begun to recover and the overall growth started to be less dependent on fuel production. Eventually, by 1995, oil production accounted for 16 per cent of gross industrial output. If the fuels sector had grown over the periods 1988–90 and 1990–1 at the same rate as it did in 1985–8, total output would have fallen by 3 percentage points in relation to the levels shown in Table 5.7. This means that, in 1990–1, the growth rate of gross industrial output would still have been of the order of a respectable 7 per cent a year. Moreover, oil also did not add much to employment absorption even though it added a new source of revenue (which by 1993 already accounted for almost 4 per cent of GDP).

Vietnam shared with China the boom in 'private' housing construction as farm households began to upgrade their quarters. The ensuing demand-driven boom in construction materials, especially cement (a commodity for which there was excess capacity), is evident in Fig. 5.2. In the case of cement, the increase in household demand more than made up for the fall in public demand as government construction fell due to the fiscal crisis.

Table 5.7. *Average annual growth rates of gross real industrial output by sector over selected periods*

	1985–8	1988–90	1990–1	1991–5
Total	10.1	−0.1	10.4	14.3
Electricity	7.1	12.8	5.2	13.7
Fuels	14.8	96.3	38.0	19.0
Ferrous metallurgy	12.8	−0.1	57.0	18.9
Non-ferrous metallurgy	19.6	17.1	32.7	8.1
Equipment and machinery	16.9	−11.4	−1.6	13.4
Electric and electronic products	25.4	13.0	1.9	16.6
Other metallic products	15.6	−7.4	−2.5	8.4
Chemical products, fertilizers and rubber	5.0	2.4	21.0	19.8
Construction materials	8.8	3.8	16.4	16.4
Wood and wood products	9.9	−8.0	4.0	10.8
Cellulose and paper	8.0	−6.4	−6.2	18.3
Glass, earthenware, and porcelain	6.3	−9.1	22.0	13.0
Food	10.9	9.6	9.2	14.7
Foodstuffs	7.7	−2.4	6.4	10.7
Textile products	5.8	−4.8	1.4	8.5
Sewing products	22.5	−4.3	8.2	31.0
Tanning and mfrs of leather products	26.7	−4.0	−39.8	45.7
Printing	26.3	0.3	11.3	26.5
Others	14.0	−10.2	−3.5	8.3

Source of basic data: Central Statistical Office (1996, table 139).

The collapse of imports from CMEA thus had a favourable impact in redirecting demand to domestic suppliers, as shown by the growth in domestic production of steel and fertilizers (Fig. 5.2). The domestic small steel sector produced goods of inferior quality in comparison to those imported from the CMEA. Yet, these goods were of adequate quality for housing construction, and domestic production thus experienced a steady increase (Table 5.7). The same was true for fertilizers which earlier on were imported at low prices from the CMEA countries, but whose domestic production grew by 21 per cent over 1990–1 (*ibid.*).

Figure 5.2 also illustrates the changes in the traditional textile sector which fared poorly during the industrial transformation. The production of bicycles, sewing machines, and other products whose imports were liberalized and for which there was an increase in smuggling followed the same patterns. Table 5.7 shows also deep falls in output in 1988–90 in equipment and machinery, other metallic products, wood and wood products, and small household goods.

Figure 5.3 describes the relation between the industrial output shares in 1985 and the subsequent growth rate of each industry over 1985–95. Figure 5.3 shows clearly that the industries which accounted for a large share of output in 1985 grew between 1985 and 1995 at slower rates than the average, while those which accounted for a small share of total output in 1985 grew faster than the average between 1985 and 1995. The increase in oil production was somewhat fortuitous as Vietnam is not an important oil producer. There are some oil reserves in remote mountain areas of the country, but their development would be highly problematic from an environmental perspective. This sectoral spurt is likely therefore to extend only over the medium term.

Food, dominated by rice, grew above average as a result of the reform of the agricultural sector. Especially in the south, agricultural output per hectare and the extent of crop diversification are already high and fairly close to world standards.

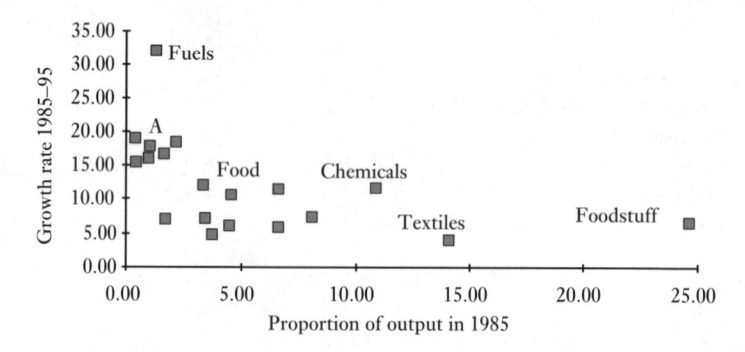

Figure 5.3. *Growth rates and 1985 industrial weight*

Note: A: ferrous metallurgy; non-ferrous metallurgy; electric and electronic products; tanning and leather products; sewing products; printing.

Source of data: Central Statistical Office (1996, table 139).

While the increase in productivity in the foodcrop sector provides a strong basis for industrialization, the actual development of the industrial sector still faces a number of challenges. Textiles and processed food, the traditional industrial sectors of the socialist era, grew below the average during *doi moi* underscoring in this way the limited competitiveness of this state-dominated sector.

The fastest growing industries were in the non-traditional group, marked by the letter A, in Fig. 5.3. Vietnam has a potential international competitiveness in light manufactured goods such as 'sewing products', metallurgy, shoes, and small electric and electronic products. As shown in Fig. 5.2 and Table 5.7, these industries went through a difficult period during the initial years of the transition but subsequently staged a strong recovery in which small-scale foreign investments played an important role.

The main aspects of Vietnam's evolution in the structure of exports during the transition are shown in Fig. 5.4. Fuels, agricultural products, and aquatic products are the fastest growing export sectors. As the economy develops further, however, an increasing proportion of the output of these sectors (whose growth is expected to taper off) will be absorbed by the domestic demand and reliance on export earnings from fuels and these other goods must therefore decline. Other sectors have shown dramatic increases or declines in exports. Beyond crude oil and rice, between 1990 and 1994, Vietnam increased the exports[4] of coal by 2.65 times, chromium by 5.8 times, coffee by 1.96 times, footwear by 8.48 times, and garments by 2.13 times. At the same time, the following items experienced reductions: textile yarn fell by 41.8 per cent, rattan and bamboo products by 60.0 per cent, and embroidery products by 64.2 per cent.

When compared with the agricultural sector, it is clear that light manufactured exports (the mainstay of traditional East Asian export growth) have faced a hard time taking off due to increased competition from imports and smuggling. As an increasing proportion of the labour force moves into industry and the growth of agricultural

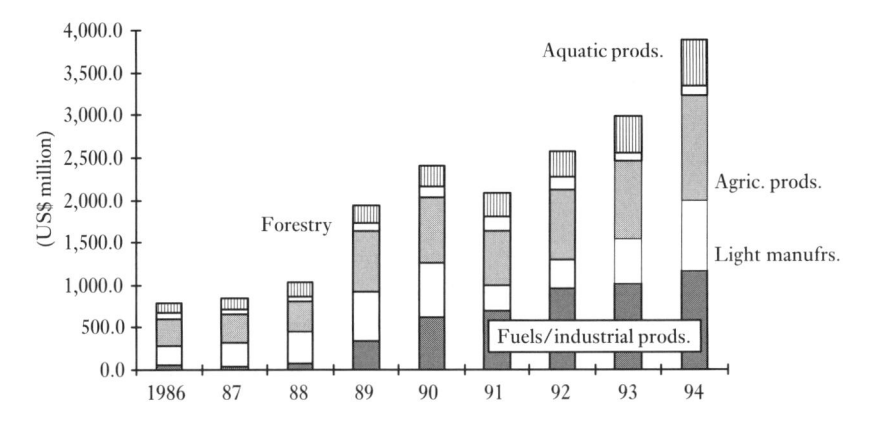

Figure 5.4. *The changing structure of exports*
Source of basic data: Central Statistical Office (1996, table 212).

productivity tapers off, a growing proportion of the exportable agricultural output will be required domestically. Likewise, while cultivated shrimp exports to Japan have provided an important growth impetus, the expansion of this sector might have caused permanent environmental damage (the destruction of mangroves and the coastline) and cannot represent a long-term source of growth for Vietnam.

The problem of international competitiveness is at the heart of the problem of enterprise reform and privatization. As mentioned earlier, the state enterprise sector has seen significant cutbacks in employment, despite an increase in its share of output, which is suggestive of a remarkable improvement in the performance and productivity of state enterprises (Sun 1996, p. 4). Vietnam's definition of state enterprise includes also those enterprises where productivity increases derived from the creation of joint ventures, in which the foreign contribution in terms of technical know-how, machinery, and access to both input and output markets was especially marked. Even where most of the capital is provided by the foreign partner, the joint venture is still counted as state enterprise.

The state enterprise sector thus includes a mix of firms with a variety of ownership structures and performance. In equitized firms, the state typically owns 30 per cent of the shares, employees and management around 50 per cent, and the public or foreign partners 20 per cent. Since 1993, individuals can obtain loans of up to $300 to purchase shares in companies, thus effectively opening a channel for investing in companies and for acquiring greater control by the managerially inclined. There are still fully owned state firms in manufacturing with the same tax obligations to the central budget as other types of companies. In contrast, in the export-oriented areas, especially in garment production, there are many private companies.

Trading, retail, home and equipment repairs are served by many small, often family-based, ventures. These were the first private firms to emerge at the start of the reform process, and it is estimated that in 1995 a total of 300,000 individual businesses or sole proprietorships were either registered under Vietnam's Company Law of 1991 or operated without registration (Thuyet 1995).

5.5. LABOUR MARKET AND SOCIAL SECTOR REFORMS

At over 72 million, Vietnam has a relatively large population on a relatively small territory of 332,000 square kilometres which includes the sparsely populated mountain regions in the east of the country. For long, Vietnam has counted on a relatively high level of human capital compared, for example, with Thailand. Already in 1980, 40 per cent of females and 44 per cent of males of the corresponding age group were enrolled in secondary education in Vietnam; in 1993, the corresponding figures for Thailand were 37 per cent for females and 38 per cent for males (World Development Report 1996).

During the key reform years of 1988–91, overall state sector employment fell from 4.1 to 3.1 million (or by 24 per cent), while employment in state enterprises fell from 2.7 to 1.9 million. The decline was particularly marked in local-level state enterprises (Table 5.8). By any measure, these are significant job losses. These were, however, accompanied by an increase in non-state employment and the voluntary exits from the state sector.

Non-state employment (which includes the cooperatives sector, mostly concentrated in agriculture) increased by 3.5 million between 1988 and 1991, thus more than compensating the losses incurred by the state sector (Table 5.8). Employment in the cooperative sector shrank by 2.8 million, but private sector employment increased by 6.3 million. A significant amount of the job losses in the cooperative sector and in state enterprise consisted of workers already working part-time and moonlighting in other enterprises.

The voluntary nature of job exits from the state sector was made possible by relatively generous separation allowances. On average, the World Bank (1993) estimates that separated workers received the equivalent of one year's salary. The minimum three-month severance scheme was particularly generous for younger workers who already had additional employment opportunities. Also, separated workers living in enterprise housing were permitted to keep their units in exchange of the payment of a rent. Finally, the severance pay package actually included an additional allowance

Table 5.8 *Employment statistics by type of enterprise, 1988–1994 (thousands of persons)*

	1988	1989	1990	1991	1992	1993	1994
In thousands of persons							
Total employment	24,408	28,851	30,294	30,974	31,819	32,718	33,669
Non-state employment	24,357	25,051	26,874	24,830	28,843	29,750	30,735
Cooperatives	20,998	19,674	19,380	18,174	—	—	—
Private	3,359	5,377	7,494	9,656	—	—	—
State sector employment	4,051	3,800	3,420	3,144	2,976	2,968	2,934
Government	1,342	1,295	1,241	1,227	1,193	1,199	1,192
Central	315	282	253	278	264	260	254
Local	1,027	1,013	988	949	929	939	938
State enterprises	2,710	2,506	2,181	1,916	1,782	1,761	1,740
Central	1,255	1,188	1,091	1,018	978	995	996
Local	1,455	1,318	1,090	898	804	766	744
Distribution (per cent of total)							
Total employment	100.0	100.0	100.0	100.0	100.0	100.0	100.0
Non-state employment	99.8	86.8	88.7	80.2	90.6	90.9	91.3
Cooperatives	86.0	68.2	64.0	58.7	—	—	—
Private	13.8	18.6	24.7	31.2	—	—	—
State sector employment	16.6	13.2	11.3	10.2	9.4	9.1	8.7
Government	5.5	4.5	4.1	4.0	3.7	3.7	3.5
Central	1.3	1.0	0.8	0.9	0.8	0.8	0.8
Local	4.2	3.5	3.3	3.1	2.9	2.9	2.8
State enterprises	11.1	8.7	7.2	6.2	5.6	5.4	5.2
Central	5.1	4.1	3.6	3.3	3.1	3.0	3.0
Local	6.0	4.6	3.6	2.9	2.5	2.3	2.2

Source of basic data: Dodsworth *et al.* (1996, table A12).

based on the floor area of the apartment to cover initial expenses for housing repairs, a factor that contributes to explaining the housing boom during the process of industrial restructuring discussed above.

In the rural areas, which traditionally represent the main reservoir of unemployment and underemployment, the labour reallocation was more complex. The rise of incomes triggered by the increase in productivity in agriculture sparked a flourishing of informal sector activities such as home repairs. However, the dismantling of the cooperatives wiped out the implicit social insurance programmes that these provided.

The remuneration systems in state enterprises had been uncharacteristically flexible (even by the standards of state enterprises in market economies) and facilitated the re-emergence of open labour markets in the late 1980s. In 1981, a government decree permitted state enterprises to remunerate workers on a piece-rate basis as an incentive for exceeding production quotas. This pattern of remuneration later took the form of bonuses through which, beyond a guaranteed minimum wage, pay was closely linked to performance. In addition, a major part of employee compensation took the form of new housing and housing maintenance allowances, a fact which permitted enterprises some flexibility on whether to undertake these expenses depending on their financial situation.

Thus, a well-functioning labour market with open unemployment emerged in Vietnam even in the presence of persistence of excess labour in urban-based state enterprises. The compulsory allocation of labour in the planned economy was thus effectively superseded by the easing of unemployment registration in the urban areas, the strong growth of rural incomes, which improved the bargaining power of peasants (Fforde and de Vylder 1996), and the emergence of non-state enterprises that absorbed the labour shed by the state sector (see Table 5.9, which suggests a slow increase in the rate of unemployment).

Table 5.9. *Growth rates of labour force, employment, and unemployment, 1985–1995*

	Growth rate of labour force	Employment	Unemployment	Rate of unemployment
1985				3.1
1986	4.7	5.3	1.5	3.0
1987	2.7	2.1	16.4	3.4
1988	3.2	3.4	−0.6	3.3
1989	4.9	0.1	81.3	5.6
1990	4.2	4.7	−21.1	4.3
1991	3.1	2.3	11.4	4.6
1992	2.6	2.7	29.5	5.8
1993	2.5	2.8	−7.3	5.3
1994	2.8	2.9	−1.0	5.1
1995 (est.)	2.9	3.0	1.0	5.0

Source of basic data: Central Statistical Office (1996, table 4).

All firms employing more than 10 employees have been required to provide social insurance to cover sickness, pregnancy, retirement, death, work accidents, and occupational diseases. Workers contribute 5 per cent of their basic wage, employers contribute 15 per cent of the total wage fund, and the state is supposed to provide additional funds in what is in effect a pay-as-you-go system.

Vietnam experimented with the introduction of user fees in both education and health. In both cases, the total expenditure in these areas increased significantly but a major share of it is now borne by the users. The introduction of user fees in health services and reduction in public subsidies to health facilities implied a reduction in the quality of the services provided and a fall in their utilization rates from 2.1 per 1,000 persons in 1987 to 0.93 in 1993 (World Bank 1995*a*). In contrast, the use of private health services rose very rapidly so that by 1993 virtually all medicines were purchased from private shops and two-thirds of outpatient consultations were carried out by private doctors (Jansen 1997).

The above trends were accompanied by a marked reduction in the participation by the poor in health services. The Vietnamese transition has then seen the retreat of the traditional socialist provisions of basic services in health, education, and income maintenance. For instance, the income transfers targeted to the poor are very small, since most of the social security outlays are earmarked to retired civil servants and military personnel and the state has retreated from health and education subsidies.

5.6. WHAT TYPE OF ECONOMY IS EMERGING?

The East Asian model has been touted as one that Vietnam might take inspiration from in the course of its transition/development effort. Montes and Lee (1996) describe the key elements of these models:

1. Strong state role in the direction of the development process, with a strong subsidiary and supporting role assigned to the private sector.
2. Trade policy is at the service of industrialization. This entails trade protection and state subsidies to industry with potential for growth, overall export orientation, attracting of foreign investment, and obtaining technology for industrialization.

The problem with the East Asian model of development is that the understanding of its functioning and social underpinnings is still rudimentary. For a long time, Anglo-Saxon economics interpreted the East Asian model as a case of private-sector-led industrialization emerging in the context of a neutral trade and industrial policy regime (Krueger *et al.* 1981). Subsequent interpretations of the East Asian miracle (World Bank 1993) have superseded this view. The new analyses emphasize the important role played by the state in industrial policy and overall development, but underscore also that these state interventions were politically neutral and economically efficient.[5] However, by not identifying the bases for state capacity, this interpretation shifts the explanation of the East Asian miracle one step further away, i.e. on the sources of state capacity.[6] If state capacity is closely dependent on economic structure and socio-political configuration, then countries like Vietnam should seriously ponder whether the East Asian approach to the transition should be further pursued.

There are practical and technical reasons suggesting that rapid privatization of state enterprises might be rejected: to start with, privatization will have severe implications for tax revenue (Dodsworth *et al.* 1996). Second, the rapid privatization of the banking system will reduce the capacity of the government to monitor the earnings of both state and non-state enterprises for tax purposes. Third, at the moment, easier access to credit by the state enterprises and the greater bureaucratic restrictions on renting land and other assets and in obtaining business licences faced by non-state enterprises end up favouring state firms. Evaluating whether state enterprises in Vietnam are more efficient or have adjusted better is also made difficult by the fact that the contribution to industrial output by entirely private entities is still insignificant.

At the present juncture, with liberalized price-setting and export-oriented firms freed of most licencing restrictions, Vietnam could be seen as having successfully completed most of the transformation from socialist planning to the market economy (Dollar and Ljunggren 1995). According to this view, the only surviving vestiges of the socialist system are represented by the steady growth of the state sector and by state control of the financial sector.[7]

Yet, the picture is far more complex. There has been a noticeable increase in the incidence of difficulties in the banking sector, continuing losses in state enterprises, and stories of embezzlement by public officials.[8] Also, the government has increasingly asked companies from the thriving and profitable private sector to bail out the loss-making state enterprises, currently estimated to account for 30 per cent of the remaining 6,300 state companies.[9]

Short of privatizing, reforming the manager incentive systems has proven quite effective in the case of China in the mid-1980s (Naughton 1995; see also Chapter 9). Reducing or eliminating party dominance over state enterprises and the independent choice of managers was critical to the success of this approach. In effect, managers were hired and extended on the basis of the amount of enterprise profits they could contribute to local budgets from the operation of their enterprise. Will Vietnam be able to implement a similar policy without severely undermining the authority of the party? The prospects are for continued economic difficulties in the state sector, with episodes of bankruptcies and large losses. If the agricultural sector continues growing steadily and generating adequate savings, the losses due to the bankruptcies of state enterprise can be absorbed and the economic *status quo* maintained. In more general terms, however, it is necessary to note that the nature of the state is endogenous (a point forcefully made in the case of Vietnam by Fforde and de Vylder 1996), and that what happened in the recent past and what might happen in the future are both indications of the various pressures being brought to bear on state organs, which themselves are affected by these events.

Though such a trend has been halted in recent times, the significant retreat of the state from the equitable provision of essential social services may also influence the future course of development in Vietnam. This retreat has caused losses to many rural dwellers and other poor members of society, though economic growth has raised family incomes and increased the variety of consumer choices also for many of them, thus offsetting to an unknown extent the losses due to the retreat of state provision.

Is there a socialist road to the market? If a well-functioning market is what is being sought, if a functioning market requires a state with a strong influence over economic outcomes, and if 'socialism' is characterized by a state with a strong (if indirect) control over economic outcomes,[10] then Vietnam has, so far, illustrated a socialist path to the market. Each of the 'ifs' is obviously subject to severe definitional problems. Can further market development, especially in the field of investment, be consistent with an increasing participation of the state to production? The state of Vietnam stubbornly resists a decline in its economic influence. The impact of this stubborness will not be felt only in terms of the success of the transition, which the Vietnamese authorities consider as completed, but especially on the country's future development.

NOTES

1. Attempting to apply the same periodization for China would be problematical since China has always followed a gradual price reform strategy. While China has had to undertake stabilization episodes, the investment rate in China has never declined drastically as it did in Vietnam's 1988–9 experience.
2. The only initial condition in which Vietnam was disadvantaged was the high share of defence expenditure GDP (19 per cent as compared to 13 per cent in the former Soviet Union).
3. The contrast with China is striking. China's strategy was to open entry for non-state firms while maintaining employment in state firms. Vietnam's rapid price reform undermined employment in state firms and, coupled with the generous separation allowances, this led to the large losses in employment. Vietnam has opened entry only through investment into state firms.
4. Figures are calculated from table 214b of Central Statistical Office (1996).
5. The additional fillip added by this literature is the importance of macroeconomic stability. This permits the exclusion of Latin America and the Philippines, which had highly capable states and strong private sectors, but were unstable macroeconomically.
6. See Montes (1995) for this type of critique.
7. Lee (1996) discusses the system of 'legal person socialism' in China in which profitable state enterprises are being transformed into shareholding corporations.
8. See Murata, *The Nikkei Weekly* (1997).
9. In comparison to China, the proportion of loss-making enterprises seems to be smaller, but Vietnam has a more fragile macroeconomic situation.
10. Socialist projects, while loud about outcomes, have tended to be suspicious and at least deafeningly silent about economic incentives.

6

The Tortuous Road to the Market in North Korea: Problems and Prospects

KEUN LEE

6.1. INTRODUCTION

The communist regime of the former Soviet Union collapsed due to reform failures, whereas in Eastern Europe the reforms began with the fall of the former communist regimes. Faced with a systemic economic crisis, North Korea has launched its own reforms, aiming to avoid either of the two paths followed in Europe. For North Korea, there are better reform examples—China and Vietnam (see Chapters 4 and 5). These communist countries are making steady progress and do not face immediate dangers of political collapse (Than 1996; Lin 1996). It is natural for North Korea to hope the reforms will follow the Asian way and not the European one. For this hope to be realized, North Korea should reform its economic system successfully before the regime has to face a more serious crisis. At the same time, the North Korean leadership would like to control this reform process so as to avoid an unexpected political collapse. This is the fundamental constraint on the speed, scope, and depth of reforms in North Korea. It is with due consideration of this fundamental constraint that this study will analyse the current state and the prospects of the economic reforms in North Korea.

The transition experiences in Europe and Asia reveal increasing differences in economic performance in spite of the increasing uniformity of the liberalization measures adopted (Murrell 1996). This suggests that initial conditions greatly determine the effectiveness of policies (Ickes and Ryterman 1995; Lee 1993a, 1994; see also Chapter 1 of this volume). Somewhat alarmed by the divergence in performance among the transition economies, the North Korean leadership seems to have a more pessimistic view of the reform process. Their reform model focuses on an open-door policy without much import liberalization and on a domestic liberalization (mainly in the consumer sector), which is similar to the so-called 'East Asian growth model' followed by South Korea and Taiwan.

This chapter assesses the current economic situation and past reform efforts, and it investigates possible reform packages and scenarios in North Korea. In doing so, it relies on the reform experiences of other transition economies in Eastern Europe and

Asia. In the next two sections, we begin with a description of the North Korean economic system and then investigate past reform efforts. We conclude with an assessment of the current situation so as to reveal the factors responsible for both the crisis and the continuing survival of the North Korean economic system.

The study also assesses, in Sections 5 and 6, the effectiveness and limits of the current reform measures in North Korea and discusses alternative policy packages. It will be argued that the basic direction of the current North Korean reforms is correct as it focuses on export promotion and foreign direct investment, light industry, and agriculture. However, the problem is that the reform measures introduced so far have not been radical enough. In addition, these measures have exhausted the meagre domestic resources available for this purpose while North Korea's difficulty in accessing external financing has not been lessened.

The chapter concludes with the following arguments. First, even if the regime survives the economic crisis, nothing guarantees its future survival. Although the North Korean leadership survived the crisis of 1997–8, it still needs to rely on a 'big push' from the outside to generate new momentum for the recovery of the economy. Otherwise, collapse or continuing stagnation is almost certain, since the regime does not have an independent ability to revitalize the economy. Second, the success or failure of the current and the future reforms will determine the future of North Korea. Failure could lead to the collapse of the North Korean regime (hard landing), which will bring in radical reforms either by a new North Korean leadership or by a South Korean takeover. Success of the reforms could, in contrast, lead to the widening and deepening of measures to deal with the main domestic economic problems (soft landing). Third, it will also be argued that the sudden collapse of the regime is not a good option, and that a soft landing is a better option for all countries concerned.

6.2. THE NORTH KOREAN ECONOMIC SYSTEM AND PAST REFORM EFFORTS

6.2.1. *Evolution of the Planning System and the Mid-1980s Reforms*

The North Korean economic system is essentially one variant of the centrally planned socialist economy. Following an order of Kim Il-Sung in 1964, the North Korean economy implemented the so-called 'unified and detailed planning' scheme so as to recentralize further the system of material allocation of resources. The aim was to control all economic activity for a more coordinated development of the economy, avoiding the situation where an emphasis on selected priority goods leads to a shortage in the production of non-priority goods which, in turn, affects the production of priority goods (*Economic Dictionary*, p. 334). However, in hindsight, it was obviously wrong to impose additional rigidities on the economy. Since the first seven-year economic planning period, beginning in 1961, chronic shortages and bottlenecks have blocked economic development (Chung 1983, p. 177). Recognizing that the economy was overcentralized, North Korea launched important decentralization measures during the mid-1980s (Kang 1989; Lee 1990; Lee 1987).

Other important reform measures included a new emphasis on the financial accountability and relative autonomy of state enterprises, as well as on material incentives for labour, a reduced scope for central planning through the adoption of the associated enterprise system, and the promotion of foreign direct investment and the non-state sector in consumer goods and the service industry.

6.2.2. Emergence of the Associated Enterprise

At the enterprise level, an important reform decision made in July 1985 was to introduce on a wider scale the associated enterprise model (*yeon-hap gi-eop*, or *lianhe qiye* in Chinese). This was aimed at the 'normalization of production activities', which emerged as an important policy objective due to frequent production stoppages caused by material and energy shortages (Kim 1986, p. 75). Horizontal integration seemed to be designed to overcome the problems of 'enterprise localism' whereby each enterprise or local authority pursues their own partisan or local interests at the expense of global interests (Kim 1986, p. 76; Lee 1986, p. 51).

The vertical or horizontal integration of enterprises was accompanied by the increase in enterprise autonomy at the level of enterprise associations. Associated enterprises are now regarded as independent planning, production and execution units and are allowed to sign purchasing and marketing contracts directly with each other without going through state material allocation agencies (Kim 1986, p. 71). Clearly, the move towards associated enterprises was a retreat from detailed central planning. Kim acknowledged the difficulties of detailed planning, given the increasing complexities of production linkages among enterprises and factories (Kim 1986, p. 75).

However, North Korean associated enterprises are faced with coordination problems among member enterprises due to widespread ambiguities of property rights (both income and control rights) (Kang and Lee 1992). Their vertical or horizontal integration does not resemble marketization. Rather, it appears still to be anti-market and merely a transfer of authority from one tier to another in the overall planning hierarchy. From the centre's perspective, to control directly a small number of big units without going through intermediaries would be easier than controlling a large number of small enterprises. In sum, the North Korean move towards associated enterprises strongly resembled the former DDR's *Kombinaten*, whereby vertical and horizontal integration was used to improve the planning system in lieu of adopting market reforms (Andreff 1989).

6.2.3. State Enterprise Reform

In December 1984, the 10th session of the Sixth Central Committee of the North Korean Worker's Party passed a new draft of the Provision on the Independent Accounting System in state enterprises, thereby giving greater autonomy to enterprises (Kang 1989). The main emphasis in the new provision was the strengthening of the financial accountability and independence of state enterprises, and the reduction of the serious losses these incurred, not least because of heavy enterprise subsidies.

Numerous articles appeared in the North Korean media warning enterprise managers that they were now on their own and would get no sympathy (and more importantly, would be held accountable) if they failed to meet production goals (Merrill 1989, p. 10).

Such efforts to disengage state enterprises financially from the state budget were not new; indeed, they were recurrent in socialist economies. But, unlike in the case of China, in North Korea such measures did not have much effect on hardening the budget constraint of state enterprises and, hence, on economic efficiency. The renewed emphasis on the financial independence of state enterprises indicated that North Korea was starting to deal with the soft budget constraint problem of state enterprise like all other planned economies. As a matter of fact, North Korean managers of firms outside Pyongyang reportedly spent most of their time in Pyongyang dealing with state authorities to obtain stable supplies of needed intermediate goods, preferential tax treatment, or subsidies. One symptom of the soft budget constraint problem is the runaway demand for input. An article by a North Korean scholar indirectly confirmed the existence of a hoarding problem in North Korea. In discussing the efficient use of working capital and how to reduce its circulation period, Hyun (1989) argued that enterprises should always check whether they were holding an optimum level of circulating capital in the form of intermediate inputs.

6.2.4. *Marketization and Privatization in Agriculture and Light Industry*

Up to the mid-1970s, North Korea officially allowed between 30 and 50 pyong (1 pyong = 3.3 square metres) of 'private plot' or 'kitchen plot' (*tut-bat*) for each peasant household; since then, this was reduced to between 15 and 30 pyong (W. Kim 1994). The productivity of private plots is known to be two to three times higher than that of collective fields (W. Kim 1994). More importantly, as the peasants were being left to solve their own food problems, another kind of private plot, called 'petty plots' (*so-to-ji* or *duigi-bat*), started to be tolerated even if it were illegal (Kim 1996*a*). These petty plots were usually found in areas which had previously remained uncultivated because they were in hilly and mountainous locations. It is reported that not only peasants, but also workers, officials, soldiers, and even party cadres cultivate petty plots in order to grow their own food and barter any surplus for other necessities. Running one's own petty plot has been popular since the mid-1980s and has helped to reduce black market food prices by 30 per cent (Kwon 1996).

Such a tendency towards a creeping, if partial, privatization of agriculture meant that there was also a tendency towards spontaneous marketization. For instance, beginning in 1984, peasant markets were allowed not only in rural areas, but also in urban areas, including Pyongyang (Kwon 1996), while collective farms started being run almost like a group of independent peasant household farms (W. Kim 1994).

Recently it has been reported that the so-called 'production team contract system' has been introduced. This is different from the former 'production team management system' (Kim 1996*b*). One of the most important features of this new system is that it establishes the state procurement target based on the last three- (or 10-) year production average, and allows the team to dispose freely of any output in excess of the agreed procurement targets. Given that production was very low during the last couple of years, this new system is expected to generate strong incentive effects. Although it differs from a more radical household contract system, it has strong potential to develop into a radical form like that in China.

Although most light industry is under the tight control of the state, in the mid-1980s some reforms were introduced also in this area. Kim Jong Il himself initiated the so-called 'August Third Campaign' in 1984, which encouraged the spontaneous production by the non-state sector of consumer goods using scraps from state enterprises and locally available resources (Lee 1990). The so-called 'in-household work teams' of factories and collective farms have been encouraged to produce consumer necessities using by-products and waste material (Kwon 1996; KUB 1994, p. 85). The volume of transactions involving these products is estimated to be as much as 10 per cent of the volume of transactions occurring on state-owned retail sales channels (KUB 1994, p. 85).

6.3. THE ESCALATING CRISIS SINCE THE EARLY 1990s

6.3.1. *Overall Economic Performance*

During the late 1980s, the North Korean economy grew at an average annual rate of about 3 per cent. However, between 1990 and 1996, the economy recorded a negative growth and its size shrank by more than 30 per cent.

In 1990 the growth rate turned negative mainly because of a bad harvest and a fall in mining production. However, manufacturing output contracted in 1991 and 1992 when communism in the former Soviet Union and in Eastern Europe collapsed. While in 1990, North Korean trade with the Soviet Union stood at $2.57 billion (accounting for more than half of total trade) it was reduced to a mere $0.46 billion in 1991. Furthermore, trade became hard currency based, and the existing trade agreements became *de facto* ineffective. As a result, Soviet crude oil provisions to North Korea dropped from 440,000 tons in 1991 to 40,000 tons in 1993, less than one-tenth of the previous level. The situation with wood products, textiles, and other intermediate goods was similar.

The impact of the withdrawal of Soviet assistance was very large. For years, the Soviet Union had been exporting strategic materials and intermediate goods to North Korea and had been a key provider of critical technical aid and equipment for several mammoth projects in the country. This sudden decrease in essential inputs and external financing caused a sharp fall in the utilization of installed industrial capacity and transportation vehicles, which caused further damage to the rest of the economy through supply-side multiplier effects.

In 1991 and 1992, the output of heavy industry decreased by 15.8 per cent and 21 per cent, respectively. The decline of heavy industry slowed down in 1993 and 1994 when the overall growth rate of output declined by only 4.2 and 5.2 per cent.

The situation in light industry was much better, with a 5 per cent growth in 1993 and a minus 0.1 per cent in 1994. Two consecutive years of floods in 1995 and 1996 further aggravated the economic performance and had a lasting effect on the production capacity of agriculture (Table 6.1).

All this suggests that the North Korean economy was recovering from the sudden shock caused by the separation with the Soviet Union before it was hit badly by floods in 1995. This does not mean that the current North Korean economic crisis is attributable to external conditions only. As Table 6.2 shows, the long-term trend points to a gradual deterioration in performance. In other words, the sudden external shock described above exacerbated the declining trend in performance that was already underway for structural reasons.

6.3.2. *From Food Crisis to Famine*

Table 6.3 shows the trend in food supply and demand in North Korea. It indicates that food production had been declining from 1989 and that from 1992 annual food shortages amounted to more than two million tons. The North Koreans have responded to this situation in three ways: through imports, the forced reduction of food consumption, and adjustments in food reserves.

Until 1991, North Korea was able to broadly fill the emerging food gap through imports. However, since 1992, even after imports, the estimated food shortage surpassed one million tons and almost approached two million tons. In 1992 and 1993, most of the shortage was filled by reducing food rations and consumption. Through campaigns such as 'eating two meals per day' and '10 per cent confiscation of patriotic food', 1–1.5 million tons of food was saved (Chun and Kim 1996; Lee and Choi 1996). In 1993 and 1994, the forced reduction of food consumption was not enough, and the remaining gap was filled by dipping into reserves (Chun and Kim 1996).

Table 6.3B shows the food situation in the 1996 harvest year (from November 1995 to October 1996) and the 1997 harvest year (November 1996 to October 1997). Assuming that about 1–1.5 million tons of food was imported in the proportion of 3/10 of rice and 7/10 of corn, the import bill would amount to more than $200 million. Indeed, the volume of food imports and the import bill in 1996 was, of course, much bigger than it had been in previous years. However, they seemed to be within a range that North Korea could manage. The country receives every year remittances between $100 million and $800 million from Japanese Koreans. Also, the country reduced the scale of military exercises requiring the consumption of oil, and its annual military budget dropped to about $5 billion. In this way, the 1996 food year passed without a report of large-scale famine or a major political crisis.

During the 1997 food year, the situation worsened (FAO and WFP 1997). First of all, the effects of the comparatively modest 1996 floods were just as devastating because the people had not yet recovered from the floods of 1995. Furthermore, the supply of agricultural inputs was in worse shape, and farmlands were seriously degraded. All of this resulted in much lower grain output in 1996 (for the 1997 food supply) relative to 1995, as shown in Table 6.3B. Supply shortages increased to

Table 6.1. *Overall economic performance by sector in North Korea, 1990–1996 (annual percentage growth rates)*

	1990	1991	1992	1993	1994	1995	1996
Nominal GNP (billion $)	23.1	22.9	21.1	20.5	21.2	22.3	21.4
GNP deflator	80.2	83.9	83.7	84.9	89.4	100	99.83
Real GNP (in 1995 prices, billion $)	28.8	27.3	25.2	24.1	23.7	22.3	21.4
GDP growth (%, annual average)	−3.7	−5.2	−7.6	−4.0	−1.7	−6.0	−4.0
Population I (1,000s)	21,412	—	22,336	—	22,953	23,261	23,558
Population II (1,000s)	21,711	22,062	22,375	22,677	22,953	23,261	—
GNP per capita (in 1995 prices, $)	1,326	1,237	1,127	1,064	1,033	958	911
GNP per capita (in current prices, $)	1,064	1,038	943	904	923	958	910
Growth by sectors (%)							
Agriculture and fishing	−10.2	3.0	−3.0	−8.0	3.0	−11.0	1.0
Mining	−8.5	−7.0	−6.0	−7.0	−6.0	2.0	−12.0
Manufacturing	−1.5	−13.0	−18.0	−2.0	−4.0	−5.0	−9.0
Light	−6.2	−4.0	−7.0	5.0	0.0	−4.0	−7.0
Heavy	−0.4	−16.0	21.0	−4.0	−5.0	−6.0	−10.0
Public utilities	−2.2	−5.0	−6.0	−9.0	4.0	0.0	−8.0
Construction	5.9	−3.0	−2.0	−10.0	−27.0	−3.0	−12.0
Services	0.3	3.0	1.0	1.0	2.0	2.0	1.0
Foreign trade (million $)							
Total	4,720	2,720	2,660	2,641	2,108	2,052	1,980
As % of nominal GNP	20.4	11.9	12.6	12.9	9.9	9.2	9.3
Exports	1,960	1,010	1,020	1,021	839	736	730
Imports	2,760	1,710	1,640	1,620	1,269	1,316	1,250
Trade balance	−800	−700	−620	−599	−430	−580	−520
Gross foreign debt							
Billion $	7.86	9.28	9.72	10.32	—	11.83	12.00
As % of GNP	34	0.41	0.46	0.50	—	0.53	0.56
Exchange rate (won/$)	—	—	—	2.15	—	2.05	—

Source: From 1990 on, GNP growth rates and nominal GNPs are estimates by the Bank of Korea. They are estimated by the SNA method. GNP per capita in current prices are estimates by the Bank of Korea. Before 1990, nominal and constant GNPs are estimated by the Korean Unification Board. Other statistics are estimates by the Bank of Korea, unless otherwise noted. Population: 1990 figure from Eberstadt and Banister (1991); 1989 figure from USCIA (1990). The 1992 figure is estimated by the Korea Unification Board. The 1996, 1995, and 1994 figures are from the Bank of Korea. Population series II are derived by dividing nominal GNP by per capita GNP. Foreign trade figures are estimates by KOTRA (Korea Trade Promotion Agency).

Table 6.2. *Long-term trend of economic growth (annual average, per cent)*

1961–7 (1st 7-year plan)	8.6
1971–5 (6-year plan)	6.0
1978–84 (2nd 7-year plan)	4.5
1987–93 (3rd 7-year plan)	−1.7

Source: Estimates by the Korean Unification Board, the Government of Korea. Based on Lee and Choi (1996).

Table 6.3. *Food grain situation, 1996 and 1997 (1,000s metric tons)*

A. Trend over the 1989–95 period

	1989	1990	1991	1992	1993	1994	1995
Demand	6,000	6,200	6,400	6,500	6,580	6,670	6,720
Food	4,219	4,359	4,500	4,570	4,627	4,690	4,725
Non-food	1,781	1,841	1,900	1,930	1,953	1,980	1,995
Supply	5,901	6,343	6,081	5,347	5,358	4,484	5,018
Output	5,210	5,482	4,812	4,427	4,268	3,884	4,125
Net imports	691	861	1269	920	1,090	600	893
Shortages	99	−143	319	1,153	1,222	2,186	1,702

Note: Output means production of the preceding year.
Sources: Taken from table 1 in Chun and Kim (1996). Original estimates are done by the Korea Agricultural Promotion Authority, except import figures, which are from W. Kim (1994) and UN sources.

B. Estimates for 1996 and 1997

	North Korea Official Report UN, 1996	FAO/WFP, 1996	South Korean Government Estimates, 1996	FAO/WFP, 1997
Demand	7,639	5,988	5,530	5,400
Food	4,869	3,688	—	3,800
Non-food	2,770	2,300	—	1,600
Production	3,764	4,077	3,450	2,840
Original expectation	5,665	4,967	—	4,300
Reductions by flood	1,901	890	—	300
Reductions by early consumption	—	—	—	1,160
Production shortages	3,875	1,911	2,080	2,360
Net import	—	—	1,150	—

Sources: The 1996 figures are taken from table 2 in Chun and Kim (1996). Estimates by the South Korean government take into account forced consumption reductions by North Korean population. Otherwise, normal demand would be 6,730,000 metric tons. Net import figure is an estimate by the National Unification Board of the Korean Government. The 1997 FAO/WFP estimate is based on the actual visits to North Korea in fall 1996, which is reported in FAO and WFP (1997).

2.4 million tons in 1997 compared with two million tons in 1996. Indeed, there were many reports of the increasing seriousness of the food shortage in 1998. It is estimated that roughly seven million people of the total population of 21 million in North Korea were exposed to the risk of starvation; another seven million, the privileged class, did not suffer any deprivation, and yet another seven million were peasants with access to food.

One of the underlying reasons for the survival of the last group has to do with the existence of 'informal institutions', including the second economy in agricultural production and consumer goods, which are usually not recorded in official statistics. The North Korean government either ignores or implicitly allows these illegal 'black plots' to persist, along with the official private plots, because they lessen the economic hardship of the people.

6.3.3. *Between Collapse and Survival*

One could argue that the North Korean regime is near collapse, and that it does not have the ability to recover from the current crisis without external help. Historically, as seen in the case of Eastern Europe, socialist regimes tend to be more vulnerable to political disturbances than to economic decline. Total collapse requires both political and economic shocks. In this sense, North Korea is better situated than its East European counterparts. In contrast to those who thought Kim Jong Il would not last very long, the regime under his *de facto* leadership has survived even after his father's death. Furthermore, the link between economic difficulty and political crisis appears to be weak in North Korea, in comparison to the situation among European socialist regimes. North Korea is more isolated, and in the Korean (or East Asian) context the tradition of civil society is very weak. In other words, it is very difficult to organize a countervailing power or authority against the state. Thus, unless the current leadership disintegrates naturally or is overthrown by a coup, the collapse of the regime is not an immediate possibility.

Finally, an important neighbour, China, which is emerging as a new economic power, would not sit idly by and watch North Korea's economic collapse. Even the US and South Korea have good reasons to want to avoid North Korea's collapse, since this could mean huge economic costs and unwanted political uncertainty. Furthermore, North Korea does not suffer from ethnic tensions as has been the case in Eastern Europe. Nationalism will act not as a state disintegrator, but rather as a powerful cohesive force.

Despite these factors favourable to North Korea, the situation in 1997 worsened. Thus, although the crisis is being overcome with external help, this does not guarantee that the long-term, even medium-term, prospects of the North Korean economy will improve. The country needs to be able to rely on a kind of 'big push' from outside which would give the system a new momentum for recovery. Otherwise, collapse or at least continuing stagnation is certain, since the domestic economy does not have the ability to pick itself up.

6.4. THE LEGACIES OF THE KIM IL-SUNG ERA AND GROWTH POTENTIALS

6.4.1. *Population and Employment Structure*

In 1990, the total population of North Korea was 21.4 million, among which there were 14.4 million people between the ages of 15 and 64 (Eberstadt and Banister 1992; Chun 1996, table 16). The proportion of the population under 15 years old was 29.4 per cent, a relatively large figure. The labour force participation rate was 72.4 per cent in 1985, which is about 10 percentage points higher than that of South Korea (Chun 1996, table 18). According to official North Korean figures, the urbanization ratio measured according to the share of the urban population was 59.6 per cent in 1986 (Chun 1996, table 8).

In 1989, primary industry employed 35 per cent of a total labour force of 12.5 million (Table 6.4). Although official North Korean estimates given by Eberstadt are as low as 25.3 per cent, the method of calculating these estimates is beset by several problems. For instance, it is assumed that the entire population over 16 years of age has jobs. Thus, some of those who are classified as peasants may not really be part of the agricultural labour force (Eberstadt 1995). The following estimate of the balance between light and heavy industries also reveals that the official figures on primary sector employment are too low.

Within industry, the imbalance between light and heavy industries is really serious. First, in terms of value added, light industry accounted for about 6.9 per cent of GNP, whereas heavy industry accounted for 28.1 per cent in 1990. In other words, the ratio is 1 : 4.1 (Table 6.4). In terms of employment, two different estimates are possible. To get the first estimate, we take the official North Korean estimate of the share (57.9 per cent) of secondary industry in total employment and then calculate the absolute number of those employed in heavy industry knowing that total employment in light industry is about 700,000 (UNIDO 1995). This gives a ratio of employment between light industry and heavy industry of 1 : 6.6. The second estimate uses the employment shares of the secondary sector (47 per cent) estimated by KDI researchers. According to this method, the ratio of employment between light and heavy industries turns out to be lower, i.e. 1 : 4.6.

Both estimates reveal an interesting aspect of the North Korean economy: there is a big discrepancy between the relative ratios of employment and value-added shares of light and heavy industries. In other words, although heavy industry hires 4.6–6.6 times more workers than light industry, it produces only 4.1 times more output than light industry. The consequence is much lower labour productivity in heavy industry than in light industry. Given the higher capital–labour ratio of heavy industry (see Table 6.4B), this amounts to a major economic aberration which, if further verified, would require that substantial amounts of labour should be transferred from heavy to light industry, and that the production efficiency of heavy industry should be greatly enhanced.

Anyway, if the ratio of 6.6 is considered too high, this implies that official North Korean figures on primary sector shares are too low and that the figures on the

Table 6.4. *Industrial structure in 1989–1990*

A. Basic estimation

	Production		Employment I		Employment II	
	Shares (1990)	Values (mil. $)	Shares (1989)	1,000 person	Shares (1989)	1,000 person
1. Agriculture, forestry, and fishery	26.8	6,190	35.0	4,381	25.3	3,167
2. Secondary sector	50.6	11,688	47.0	5,883	57.9	7,247
Mining	7.8	1,801	7.8	976	7.8	976
Manufacturing	35.0	8,085	31.4	3,930	42.3	5,295
Light industry	6.9	1,593	5.6	700	5.6	700
Heavy industry	28.1	6,491	25.8	3,230	36.7	4,595
Construction	7.8	1,801	7.8	976	7.8	976
3. Tertiary sector	22.6	5,220	18.0	2,253	16.8	2,103
Total	100.0	23,100	100.0	12,517	100.0	12,517

B. Labour productivity ($/worker)

	Estimate I	Estimate II
Light industry	2,277	2,277
Heavy industry	2,009	1,412

C. Relative ratios

	Production shares	Employment share I	Employment share II
Light industry	1.0	1.0	1.0
Heavy industry	4.1	4.6	6.6

Sources: Estimate I is derived using the employment shares of the three sectors estimated by the KDI and reported in Chun (1996). Also used is the light industry employment number (70,000) provided in UNIDO (1995). Estimate II is derived using the employment shares of the three sectors provided by the North Korean government to the UN and reported in Eberstadt and Banister (1992). Production shares are those given in Chun (1996, table 21). Total employment (12,517) is provided by the North Korean government to the UN and reported in Eberstadt and Banister (1992) and also in Chun (1996). It is assumed that, both in mining and construction, shares in production values are the same as the shares in employment.

secondary sector are too high. This is likely to be the case so that the estimates by KDI appear to be more accurate. This means that there is still room for out-migration from agriculture to manufacturing. A comparison of the shares of primary industry in employment and GNP gives the proportion of 35 : 26.8. If a ratio of 1 : 1 is taken as the balanced one, then in the North Korean case it would still be desirable to move some workers from agriculture to secondary industry.

Finally, according to the estimates of the International Institute for Strategic Studies, the proportion of the military in the total population is 5.2 per cent, one of the highest levels in the world, similar only to the level in Iraq (Chun 1996). The share of military expenditures in the total government budget was also high, at 35 per cent.

6.4.2. Foreign Trade and Debt

Over the last 10 years, North Korea's foreign trade has decreased substantially. Table 6.1 shows that, after hitting a peak in 1988, at a total of $5.24 billion, it dropped to a mere $1.98 billion in 1996. One of the most important reasons for the decrease was the disintegration of the Soviet bloc in the early 1990s. As the former socialist economies underwent systemic changes and a serious recession, and as imports had now to be settled in hard currency and not through barter, North Korean trade with these countries declined significantly, especially in 1990 and 1991.

In 1996, the trade dependency ratio (the ratio of total trade to GNP) was only 9.3 per cent. As North Korea continued to experience trade deficits, its cumulative 1996 foreign debt stood at $12 billion in gross terms (Table 6.1) debt/GNP ratio at 56 per cent.

6.4.3. Any Positive Legacies for Future Growth?

Negative legacies can turn out to be the source of future rapid progress. For instance, features such as an overly small light industry or an excessively large heavy industry, too little foreign trade and investment, and an overgrown defence industry imply that North Korea may enjoy the advantages of a 'latecomer' and ample room for catching up. Correcting these features can indeed generate substantial growth. Of course, such a scenario requires a market-oriented economic system, an open economic environment, and sound policy leadership, i.e. issues which will be dealt with in the next section.

6.5. RESPONDING TO THE CURRENT CRISIS AND OUTLINING LONG-TERM SOLUTIONS

Economic reforms require time to generate visible effects, as shown by the Eastern European experience, and should be understood as a long-term process (Murrell 1996). Since the North Korean economy is in a deep crisis, it should adopt both short-run anti-crisis measures and long-term-oriented reform policies. The current economic crisis in North Korea has two features. One is the problem of feeding the population under conditions of an impending chronic famine, and the other is the general production declines associated with supply-side problems. The latter are related, first of all, with shortages of energy and of fundamental intermediate inputs and, secondly, with low labour morale caused by shortages of food and other basic consumption goods. These shortages which generate negative supply-side multiplier effects are mainly attributable to the lack of hard currency and could be prevented if there were enough foreign exchange to pay for the needed imports.

6.5.1. *Anti-crisis Measures*

Any anti-crisis package aiming at North Korea's survival must deal with these two features of the crisis. An immediate concern is feeding the population. The country needs to be able to earn hard currency by exporting or borrowing internationally to pay for the food import bill. Measures to elicit supply-side responses in agriculture should include more encouragement of official and unofficial private plots in rural areas, as well as liberalization of market transactions for consumer goods. Spontaneous small-scale border trade in consumption goods and foods by individuals should also be explicitly allowed. To secure food supplies, the modernization of production technology and a stable supply of fertilizer should be dealt with urgently, and this will, again, require hard currency.

Securing energy supplies is critical to avoid that shortages in this area are magnified through the play of supply-side multiplier effects. Again, this shows the importance of hard currency to pay for oil imports and the costs of modernizing coal mining production. The current energy crisis, especially the shortages of electricity, is linked to the lack of coal for thermal power plants, and the main problem with coal production facilities is the outdated technology.

6.5.2. *Longer Term Reform Goals and Strategies*

Alongside anti-crisis measures to deal with the more immediate problems, North Korea needs to launch longer term reform policies. Given the initial conditions and the specificities of the current crisis, reform should aim at three goals: (i) the economy should undergo liberalization and marketization in order to generate competition and an efficient allocation of resources; (ii) modernization and industrial restructuring are needed to raise productivity; and (iii) stabilization is required to reduce the costs of transition.

De Melo *et al.* (1995) argue in favour of the liberalization of internal markets, foreign trade, and private sector entry in the economies in transition. These measures and the liberalization of foreign direct investment is what North Korea should focus on at an earlier stage of reform. Concretely the measures should focus on the liberalization of the internal markets for consumer goods, private sector entry, and foreign investment. However, the liberalization of foreign trade should focus on promoting exports while avoiding the early liberalization of imports which would aggravate the trade deficit and the hard currency shortage. Thus, import liberalization should be gradual and dependent on the progress of exports, as the experiences of South Korea, Japan, China, and Vietnam show.

To initiate the marketization of the domestic economy, the choice is between reforming (including privatizing) old economic entities and the entry of new ones (Lee 1994). The author's view is that the liberalization of internal markets should rely primarily on private sector entry (see Chapters 1 and 9). Seeing that marketization has increased the number and share of non-state enterprises, Lee (1993a, 1994) has argued that the entry of new economic entities is always easier than trying to transform the old state-owned enterprises into competitive private entities (see Chapter 1). This pattern is visible in China, but can also be observed during the economic recovery of several economies in transition of Central Europe, where private entries have played a decisive role (Murrell 1996; Gomulka 1994).

Second, modernization and industrial restructuring must first focus on the replacement of outdated production facilities, and this will require hard currency. Regarding industrial restructuring, one important task is to raise efficiency by transferring resources from heavy to light industry. Thus, modernization should also focus on new production facilities in light industry so as to give leverage to international competitiveness and gain hard currency. Meanwhile, economic resources should be transferred from the military to the civilian sector.

Until the new private sector grows enough to be able to absorb much of the labour force, an overly rapid restructuring of the state sector should be avoided. However, rather than undertaking numerous experiments to increase the autonomy of state enterprises (in China these have generally failed; see Lee 1993b), North Korea should from the beginning attempt to transform state enterprises into shareholding companies. Once this is accomplished, it will be much easier to introduce more radical reforms. For example, a feasible option, like the one tried in China, is for state enterprises to invite foreign investors as partners in order to try the so-called 'one factory–two systems' method, which combines old production sites with new management and technology and additional capital. This method has been effective and popular in China, since the establishment of new factories or firms with foreign partners is too costly for a China with little financial resources. By this method, whole companies can be turned into a foreign joint venture or into subsidiaries. Also, once state enterprises are transformed into shareholding companies, it will be much easier to undertake at a later stage their privatization.

Given the two major goals of liberalization and modernization, specific policies consistent with these goals would include: (i) an open-door policy aimed at gaining access to international borrowing, attracting investment, and promoting exports, and (ii) the promotion of light industry and agriculture by allowing private entry. Actually, these policy lines are what North Korea declared as its priorities right after the failure of the third seven-year plan. However, the real issue is the actual implementation of the policies. In other words, progress is very slow in every aspect, including foreign investment and borrowing, exports, and domestic liberalization. The next section will discuss the progress of the open-door policy. This is the highest priority and may prove to be critical for future economic changes in North Korea.

6.6. NORTH KOREA'S OPEN-DOOR STRATEGY
6.6.1. *The North Korean Version of the East Asian Model*

Hard currency shortages and the related multiplier effects have been the direct causes of economic hardship in North Korea. Easing this shortage would be an important element of an overall solution. Top policy makers in North Korea nowadays clearly state that they will pursue an outward-oriented development strategy with exports and foreign direct investments (FDI) as the engines of growth. On the other hand, there is no sign that they will be initiating a reform of the domestic state sector, although they have been allowing the spontaneous marketization of the consumer goods sector. As in the East Asian growth model, such a strategy combines an outward orientation with a marketized consumption goods sector and a protected domestic producer sector.

As a core component of its open-door policy, and in a new effort to attract FDI, on 28 December 1991, the North Korean government designated the Rajin and Sunbong area as a free trade zone (FTZ). While the country promulgated the 'Joint-Venture Law' in 1984, this was the first concrete 'Special Economic Zone' created in the country's history. Rajin and Sunbong is located at the northeastern edge of North Korea, near the Tumen river, where the borders of two other countries—China and Russia—meet. The three main lines of specialization are export processing using North Korean labour, transportation linkages connecting the hinterland, China and Russia, and tourism and the hotel trade. The success or failure of this project will significantly affect the destiny of the North Korean economy.

By the end of 1993, the FDI committed to this initiative amounted to $150 million distributed among 144 projects. Only a few Western firms invested, while more than 90 per cent of the projects were with overseas Korean businessmen living in Japan (S. Kim 1994). Of the 144 projects supposed to receive FDI, only about 60 were reported to have begun production in 1993. Thus, the general perception was that the effort was not successful in attracting foreign investment. Even the investments by overseas Koreans slowed after the initial spurt.

The situation did not change appreciably in the following years and, by June 1996, it was reported that 49 investment projects worth a total of $350 million had been signed, and, among these, 22 projects worth $34 million had already been started. The first major international investment forum was held in the FTZ on 15 September 1996 with the help of UNDP. In attendance at the forum were 439 businessmen representing 110 companies and other persons from 26 countries. These people met with 100 North Korean businessmen representing 59 companies and other local counterparts.

The forum is considered to have achieved only a modest success partially due to the absence of South Korean investors. The total money value of the investment contracts reached was $285 million in eight projects, and the total amounts discussed and agreed through an investment memorandum were $834.5 million in 30 projects. However, of the contracted $285 million, the investments in tourism and services loom heavily, especially because of the $180 million in hotel projects signed by the Emperor Group

A
Brief
Response
to Criticism

Having designed and built the Temple	for the statues sitting in state rather small
of Venus and Roma Hadrian	Venus and Roma might bump
invited professional comment	their heads if they tried to stand
Apollodorus considered the niches	Hadrian had him hanged

OLIVER REYNOLDS

...of hurced and associates it with the language", writes Allen. The fuller "enough d" was first recorded in the seventeenth

uted to the seventeenth century (specifically to *Othello*) – it can more convincingly be traced back to medieval tournaments in which a knight

The Europa Biographical Reference Series

The International Who's Who 2008

Providing hard-to-find biographical details for more than 2... eminent personalities, this outstanding reference work re... women from almost every profession and activity - from h...
June 2007: 285x220mm: 2,100pp
Hb: 978-1-85743-415-6: **£360.00**

International Who's Who in Classical Music 2...

A complete biographical reference work covering all aspe...
- Over 8,000 detailed biographical entries
- Covers the classical and light classical fields
- Includes both up-and-coming musicians and well-establi...

March 2007: 285x220mm: 1,180pp
Hb: 978-1-85743-416-3: **£225.00**

International Who's Who in Popular Music 2...

Comprehensive biographical details on some of the most... and individuals from the world of popular music.
- Over 6,000 alphabetically arranged entries
- Fully revised and updated for this 8th edition
- New for this edition is an index of groups for ease of refere...

March 2007: 285x220mm: 750pp
Hb: 978-1-85743-417-0: **£200.00**

For mo...

Table 6.5. *Foreign investment in the Rajin-Sunbong free trade zone as of June 1996*

A. Contract	
Total number of projects	49 cases
Total amount of investment	$350 million
B. Actual execution	
Total number of projects	22 cases
Total amount of investment: distribution by sectors	$34 million
Manufacturing: $0.53 million (1.6%)	
Infrastructure: $13.50 million (40.0%)	
Commerce and transportation: $11.21 million (33.0%)	
Tourism: $1.00 million (2.9%)	
Banking: $7.60 million (22.3%)	

Note: Contracts made in 1995, 60 per cent of the total; contracts made in the first half of 1996, 30 per cent of the total.
Source: Based on Lee (1996).

of Hong Kong. In manufacturing, one of the biggest contracts was with a Yantai-based Chinese company, which invested in a motorbike factory worth $5 million.

6.6.2. *The Role of South Korea and the United States*

The Rajin-Sungbong FTZ project emerged from North Korea's mid-1980s unsuccessful efforts to attract FDI and the failure of the third seven-year plan which ended in 1990. It seems likely that additional foreign investment will enter the FTZ, especially since the recent investment forum showed some success. For the foreign investors, however, this project presents two basic problems. First, infrastructure remains inadequate, thus discouraging small-scale investments in manufacturing (Lee 1996). Second, political uncertainty makes investment risky.

From a broader perspective, the biggest stumbling blocks ahead are the economic sanctions imposed on North Korea by the US and the persistent political stalemate between South Korea and North Korea (the recent meeting between the leaders of the two Koreas has not yet yielded concrete results). In addition, North Korea does not have diplomatic relations with either the US or Japan. The US played a vital role in helping the East Asian tigers grow by providing export markets and investment capital, and it can do the same for North Korea. The US can also offer political help and assist the country in gaining access to international credit and capital. However, to a certain extent it is South Korea which will determine whether the US gives North Korea help.

Thus, only when the complex problem of the international political economy of the US and both Koreas is solved, can North Korea normalize diplomatic relations with Japan and obtain international aid and loans from international agencies, such as the Asian Development Bank, the World Bank, and the International Monetary Fund. With the normalization of relations with Japan, North Korea might receive monetary compensation (in the form of war reparations) for past Japanese colonial rule and elicit greater investments by Koreans living in Japan. These are critical for the success of North Korea's open-door policy.

6.7. FUTURE SCENARIOS AND CONCLUSIONS

The country's reforms have so far been limited both in scope and depth and are therefore the main cause for the escalation of economic hardship in the country. In response to these limited policy reforms, the economy has been experiencing a limited but highly significant spontaneous marketization and privatization, especially in agriculture and the consumer goods sector. This controlled decentralization of decision making in the light industry and agricultural sector is intended to provide the North Korean population with basic necessities. However, the scope of economic decentralization should be expanded and enlarged decisively if it is to have tangible effects nationwide. The open-door policy is supposed to meet the goal of modernization through the reduction of the foreign exchange gap. Progress is slow due partly to the international political and economic circumstances revolving around the Korean peninsula, and this is beyond the control of North Korea to a certain extent. Nevertheless, these policies are expected to marketize North Korea's economy by inviting new economic entities into the coastal zones, rural areas, and eventually other areas.

The open-door policy, one of the most important elements of this strategy, critically depends on the positions taken by the US and South Korea. If North Korea normalizes relations with the US, joins the international community, and becomes free from economic sanctions, the open-door policy has a greater chance of being successful. The country will also be in an advantageous position then to further reform the domestic economy and improve relations with South Korea.

Success with the open-door policy means that the reforms of the domestic economy can proceed more swiftly. Given the small size of the economy, the tradition of taut planning, relative political stability, and higher administrative capability, radical reforms can be a very feasible and effective option for North Korea's future.

There are several reasons why North Korea has opted for this strategy and is expected to follow it. First, success with the open-door policy will revitalize the economy—given its small size. Second, there is a strong sentiment against radicalism in the current North Korean leadership, based on the comparison between the experiences of the Eastern European countries and Asian socialist countries. Third, relative political stability persists and there are no visible alternative political groups in North Korea. Finally, given the strong legacy of the former leader, Kim Il-Sung, the radical reform of the domestic system would be burdensome to the current leader Kim Jong Il (who is known to have expressed a personal distrust of radical reform).

While the rationality of gradualism is becoming more difficult to accept, time is running out. Depending on the success or failure of the open-door policy, two future scenarios are possible. First, there is an optimistic 'soft landing' scenario. This supposes that the open-door policy will lead to economic success via help from the US and

South Korea, which will usher in international cooperation. This will be followed by radical domestic reforms, which will prepare the ground for a peaceful economic integration with South Korea. Within this scenario, however, if success is obtained without much South Korean help, this could lead the North Korean leadership to take a somewhat hostile position towards South Korea, and then progress in the unification of North and South will be slow or the existing division will continue.

Second, there is a pessimistic 'hard landing' scenario. Here, the open-door policy ends up with a failure and no US and international help. In this case, the current crisis will have deepened into a collapse, which will bring in a change in the internal political leadership or result in a South Korean takeover. In either case, the simultaneous and radical reform of the domestic system and of external economic relations initiated by either a new North Korean leadership or South Koreans will be a natural course. In this case, reforms will proceed simultaneously with rapid economic integration with South Korea, and the German big-bang model will become relevant. Of course, a sudden internal coup is now an ever-present possibility in North Korea. This scenario can be considered as a variant of the hard landing scenario in that it will also lead to a radical reform and an open-door policy.

The general international perception has been that the costs of the hard landing scenario and the uncertainties that would emerge from it would be excessive and too big for neighbouring countries to bear. Although some concern has been raised that it is too late to count on the success of the soft landing or the gradual path scenario, this does not mean that the sudden collapse of the regime is the best option. The author agrees with Eberstadt's (1997) observation that hastening unification is beneficial for every country involved. However, hastening unification does not necessarily mean going along with the hard landing scenario. It is felt that a better and less costly option is to move towards the soft landing scenario with a view to hastening unification.

The soft landing scenario does not mean 'act slowly'. To realize the scenario, we have to act as quickly as possible to improve the situation in North Korea by taking unilateral initiatives and to urge North Koreans to opt for more radical policies.

On the other hand, as is now clear, an important element in the soft landing scenario is a more radical reform package on the side of the North Koreans, including the *de facto* privatization of the agricultural production system and more encouragement for non-state and market-oriented activities in the consumer goods sector, as well as border trade with China and Russia. Then, the question becomes whether we can expect the current leadership to take such a policy line. The nature of the North Korean leadership is therefore a very critical element in the future of North Korea—especially in the soft landing scenario. A big assumption in the soft landing scenario is that the success of the open-door policy will lead to further reform of the domestic economic system with 'reform dividends' materializing as a political force supporting more reform. If the leadership intervenes in this process to check such a tendency, then an emerging pattern would be a typical stop–go-type reform cycle, as has been observed in the past reform waves in the former Eastern European planned economies and, recently, in Cuba.

7

Cuba: The Stalled Transition

MANUEL PASTOR JR

7.1. INTRODUCTION

An attempt to sketch Cuba's future is not for the faint of heart. After all, who would have thought that a communist regime would have been able to survive 40 years in the shadow of a superpower eager to sweep it out of existence? Who could have predicted that a political system would have remained largely intact despite a nearly 50 per cent fall in output and income between 1989 and 1993? Who would have guessed that one of the world's last remaining 'socialist' economies would have come to rely on, ironically enough, tourism, foreign investment, and remittances from political exiles as the key generators of foreign exchange?

This paper takes up the challenge of prediction, albeit in a limited form which offers several possible scenarios. A central point of the analysis is that fundamental change in the economy of Cuba is blocked because regime leaders are not fully committed to reform and are, in fact, generally hostile to forming new political alliances with those who can 'win' from the emerging economic structure. This stymies policy making and, in turn, the economy. Any reform-induced recovery is likely to be followed by a slowdown while Cuban leaders wait to see if they have altered policy just enough to avoid a downward slide. The resulting 'stop-and-go' cycle diminishes confidence in the irreversibility of reform and discourages both investment and growth.

Despite these continuing political economy challenges, Cuba does enjoy a number of longer term factors that could produce a relatively rapid and positive transition, including a high level of human capital, a reasonable degree of initial economic equality, and what may be an eager group of outside investors. Moreover, it has already suffered a large reduction in GDP, further reforms need not trigger the massive recessions typical of other transition economies, and there is a new dynamism taking root in the economy, particularly during 1999. One persistent difficulty is the United States, which continues to pressure Cuba with a trade embargo which closes off access to a large and close market. How all these factors will affect transition depends on the route Cuban authorities choose.

Section 2 begins the analysis by discussing the pre-1989 Cuban economic structure and tracking how the post-1989 external shocks filtered through the Cuban economy. As we will see, the government initially responded with a sectoral approach which retained the central tools and attitudes of socialist planning but sought to redirect resources to sectors which could best alleviate foreign exchange pressures. Section 3 discusses how the reform process in Cuba shifted in 1993–4 to a more profound reworking of the economic rules of the game, including the depenalization of dollar use, increased space for self-employment, and the emergence of new, albeit limited, free markets in agricultural products. Section 4 explains why various political blockages have stymied further systemic reform, leading to a pattern of stop-and-go policy reform.

Section 5 considers the future, beginning with an analysis of the positive and negative factors that could ease a transition to some form of market economy in Cuba. I then sketch some likely scenarios for the future, noting that the most probable is a sort of 'muddling through' which continues the current mix of tight political control and minimalist market reform. I close this section by considering how best to preserve equity in any transition and end the paper by noting the need for modesty in our considerations of Cuba's future: many observers have been wrong before and we should at least acknowledge the need for caution in our analysis and projections.[1]

7.2. EXTERNAL SHOCKS AND STRUCTURAL ADJUSTMENT IN THE CUBAN ECONOMY

The Cuban economy changed drastically in the years after the 1959 revolution that brought Fidel Castro to power. Four trends stand out: (1) Market forces and private property were nearly entirely suppressed; in the late 1980s, Cuba was among the most statist of the socialist economies (rivalling the other non-transition economy analysed in this volume, North Korea). (2) Social spending was high by developing country standards, resulting in tremendous achievements in the fields of education and health and, in turn, a high level of human capital.[2] (3) The economy gained an industrial base, with the share of industry in Cuban gross social product doubling between the early 1960s and the late 1980s.[3] (4) Despite the last trend, the rural area was the recipient of significant governmental development of infrastructure and social support services, leading to a relative rural–urban balance which is also unusual by developing country standards.[4]

What did not change significantly was the dependent role pre-revolution Cuba had occupied in the world economy. Diversification of the domestic economy/non-tradable sector was not matched by changes in the tradable sector: in the 1984–9 period, exports of sugar and sugar products averaged 77 per cent of total exports and nearly 70 per cent of the country's trade was with just the former Soviet Union.[5] Meanwhile, the emerging domestic industry was dependent on intermediate imports to fuel production (quite literally in the case of oil) even as imported foodstuffs rose in pace with improvements in health and the general standard of living.

A unique aspect of this dependence was that it was generally favourable for Cuba: the Soviet Union propped up the terms of trade via preferential agreements, maintained a steady market to absorb export volume, covered any payments deficits with automatic rouble loans, and maintained military and other transfers. In short, Soviet largesse meant that the usual macroeconomic hard budget constraint—that is, the foreign exchange gap—was not binding on the Cuban state. Indeed, the combination of favourable terms of trade and the ability to run a persistent payments deficits with the USSR yielded the Cuban economy a 'subsidy' of over 20 per cent of GDP in the 1980–7 period.[6]

Most important was that the aid was directly used for tradables and hence relieved the foreign exchange constraints on production. Moreover, the Soviet Union supplied 99 per cent of the island's oil imports. The unique nature of the Cuban–Soviet trading relationship also made oil a surprising generator of hard currency: since the sugar–oil terms of trade between Cuba and the Soviet Union were so favourable to Cuba, Cuban authorities found it profitable to re-export unused Soviet oil, use the proceeds to buy sugar on the spot market, and then tranship the purchases to meet their sugar obligations to Russia. By the mid-1980s, as sugar prices fell, re-exports of Soviet oil became Cuba's leading earner of hard currency.[7]

The steady collapse of Cuba's trading relations with the Soviet Union and CMEA after 1989 exposed the island to a harsh new reality. Between 1989 and 1993, export volume and the terms of trade deteriorated; as a result, export revenues fell by nearly 70 per cent. Import capacity fell even more as the 'soft' budget constraint of Soviet balance-of-payments financing was replaced with the 'cash and carry' of the international market. By 1992, the country was forced to keep its trade more or less in balance, a far cry from the beginning of the period (see Fig. 7.1).

The government's initial response to the resulting macroeconomic difficulties was a sectoral strategy that focused on generating new sources of foreign exchange. The goal was to improve import capacity (and hence output) by finding new ways to reduce and/or finance the trade gap. The central elements of the government package that

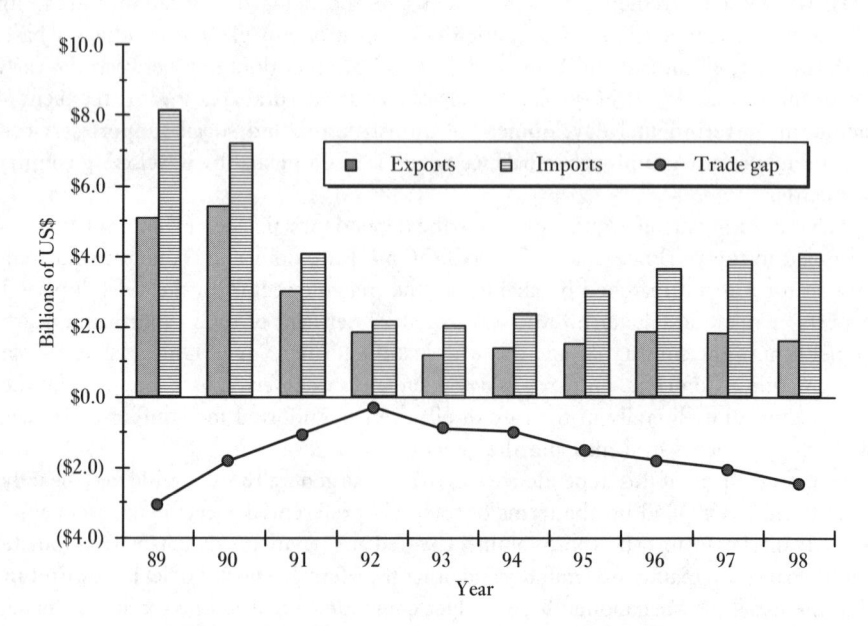

Figure 7.1. *Exports and imports in Cuba, 1989–1998*

emerged involved decreasing food imports, developing new biotechnological and pharmaceutical exports, encouraging foreign investment, and promoting tourism.

This sectoral approach yielded limited results. Progress on the food front was slow, partly because the foreign exchange crisis constrained the ability to import fertilizer and other inputs and partly because local producers had no price incentives to enhance output.[8] Biotechnological and pharmaceutical exports did build on Cuba's comparative advantage (relative to other developing countries) in science and health but such industries faced difficult competition in world markets and were significant consumers of foreign exchange on the input side (see Feinsilver 1992; Cardoso and Helwege 1992). Foreign investment found a new welcome but Cuba's labour rules and insecure property rights (as well as the limits imposed by the US embargo on trade with the island) limited investor enthusiasm. Tourism managed to increase at a healthy pace but this is an import-intensive industry which faces intense competition from other Caribbean islands.

In any case, Cuba's GDP declined between 35 and 45 per cent over the 1989–93 period. While this amounts to a major depression, Cuba avoided Korean-style mass starvation as the rationing system delivered a basic, albeit inadequate, diet and the black market was allowed to fill the rest of consumers' needs.[9] While the government let its fiscal deficit soar (see below), it managed to keep priorities straight, with defence expenditures falling from nearly 10 per cent of GDP in 1985 to less than 3 per cent in 1994 even as education spending more or less retained its share of the steadily shrinking GDP.[10] While an impressive performance in some respects, nonetheless the decline in output had been sizeable and the dawning of 1994 saw an increasingly dismal and stagnant economy.

7.3. CHANGING THE SYSTEM

In the summer of 1994, the economic low point was mirrored in the political realm: riots broke out in Habana on 5 August after a series of confrontations between government authorities and individuals seeking to flee the island, including one incident in which as many as 41 people died when Cuban naval patrols sought to prevent the exodus of a hijacked tugboat (Mesa-Lago 1995, pp. 4–5). The resulting civil unrest, involving 20,000–30,000 people smashing windows and shouting 'Down with Fidel!', had not been experienced in Cuba since the revolutionary triumph of 1959.

The government responded by deciding to grant those wishing to leave the island the right to go. The resulting barrage of 'rafters' leaving Cuban shores led the United States to reverse its previous stance on immigration which, by granting any Cuban leaving the island by any means eligibility for permanent residency, had served as a magnet for Cuban emigration. In subsequent US–Cuban talks, Cuban authorities were asked to once again enforce restrictions against the exodus of their people; US authorities, in turn, agreed to retract the carrot of legality which had provided one incentive for Cubans to head north across the Caribbean (Mesa-Lago 1995).

The government also decided to take a more dramatic approach to reforming the economy. Movement toward systemic reform had actually begun a year earlier, albeit in an extremely cautious fashion. On 26 July 1993, for example, the government depenalized the use of dollars, a move which had the effect of fuelling and regularizing the black market on the island. On 8 September 1993, the government legalized self-employment; by June 1996, there were over 200,000 individuals in business for themselves under official government licence—and some Cuban economists estimated that for every self-employed worker under licence there are another four or five unregistered workers.[11] On 15 September 1993, existing workers on many state farms were given the right to lease their lands, rent free, in permanent usufruct; nearly 60 per cent of state land passed into the hands of 4,000 new cooperatives (called Basic Units of Agricultural Production, or UBPCs).

The events of 1994 drove the government to consider deeper reforms. In October of that year, a decision was made to allow agricultural markets in which neither prices nor production were controlled; this was significant in ideological terms since the previous version of such free agricultural markets had been closed since 1986 by the intervention of President Castro himself.[12] Moreover, in contrast to the earlier farmers' markets in which participation was limited to the very small number of private farmers, state farms and the new cooperatives were also allowed to vend their above-quota output.

An additional significant policy shift came during 1994 with the explicit acknowledgement of a state fiscal crisis. Following a 1993 budget deficit on the order of 30 per cent of GDP (see Fig. 7.2), the government began cutting subsidies to state enterprises, raising prices of state-supplied goods, and implementing new taxes (mostly on non-essential items). Fiscal improvement had two important consequences. First, it began the process of sopping up the monetary overhang (estimated in June 1994 as being nearly 100 per cent of GDP) that threatened hyperinflation in case prices

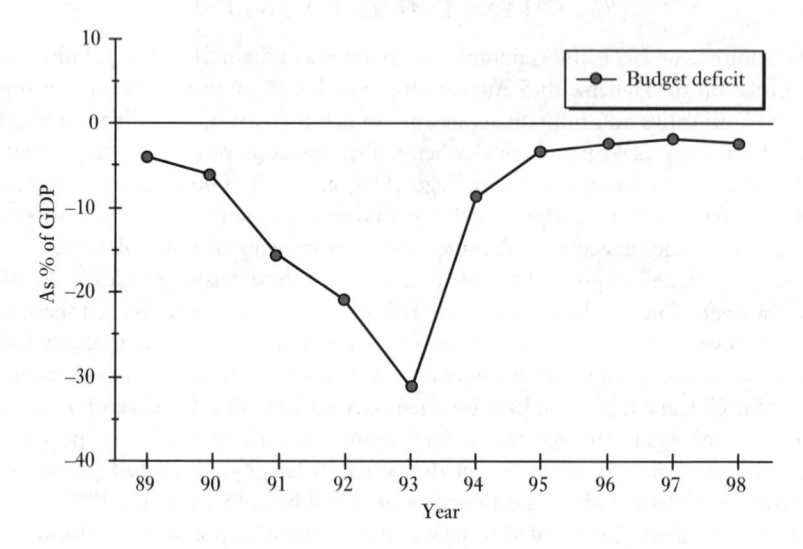

Figure 7.2. *Budget deficit, 1989–1998*

were ever to be freed. Second, the 'hardening' of the budget constraint on state firms signalled an indirect application of market rules on enterprise.

Perhaps because of the systemic changes—and perhaps simply because the economy had reached rock bottom after its 1989–93 decline—GDP took a slight upward tick in 1994 (see Fig. 7.3). Some of that year's increase was probably due to productive activities moving from the 'black' to the 'informal' markets as a result of the reforms in self-employment, dollar use, and agricultural marketing. Still, the economy was definitely beginning to turn the corner. GDP growth in 1995, for example, was 2.4 per cent while growth for 1996 was a torrid 7.8 per cent (although growth subsequently slowed in 1997 and 1998 to 2.5 and 1.2 per cent, respectively, partly because of poor sugar harvests and partly because of a slowed reform process, before returning to above 5 per cent in 1999).[13] Exports and imports began a slow drift upward, with import growth outpacing export growth and producing a widening trade deficit (recall Fig. 7.1); the ability to sustain this deficit suggests an improvement in offsetting service and capital flows (such as remittances, tourism, and foreign investment).[14] Increasing numbers of foreign firms did indeed evidence interest in Cuba (although the actual dollar flows fell far short of the announced intentions).[15] And tourism increased significantly (see Fig. 7.4), although the net earnings ratio fell from around 60 per cent in 1990 to around 30 per cent in 1996 as import content rose in the effort to make the sector more 'international' and competitive. In view of the large external shock suffered by the Cuban economy, such a relatively rapid rebound compares well with most other economies in transition (see Table 1.1, Chapter 1).

In any case, the key point is that the shift to a more systemic approach to reform during 1993–6 was at least temporally correlated with an improvement in economic

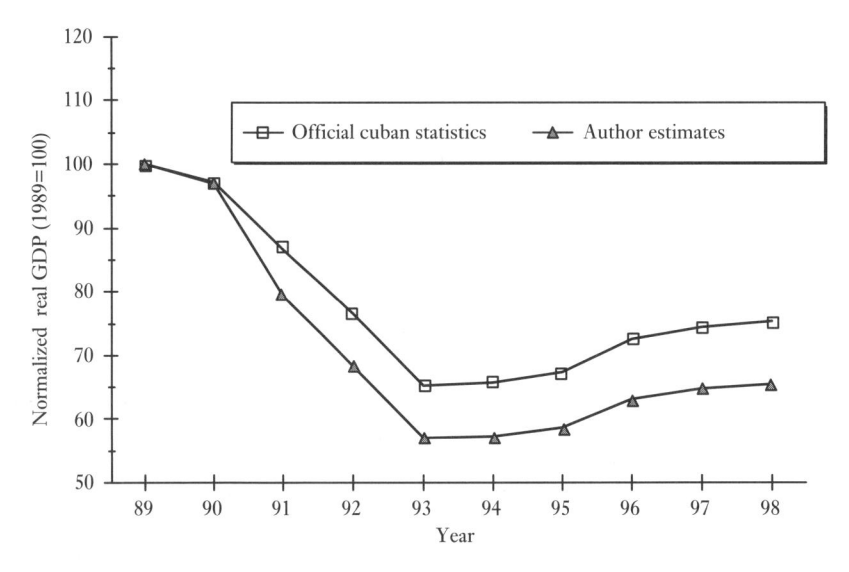

Figure 7.3. *Real GDP index, 1989–1998*

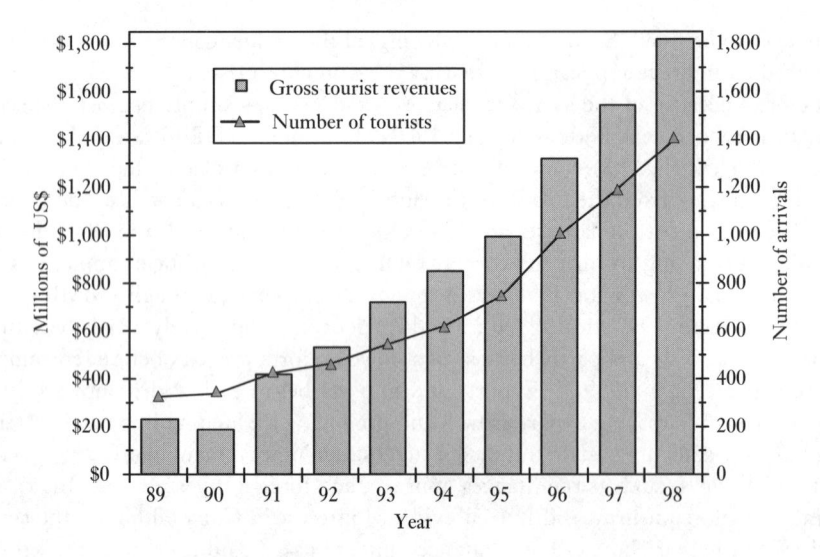

Figure 7.4. *Tourist flows and revenue, 1989–1998*

outcomes. In most countries in the developing and post-socialist worlds, this sort of result would tend to strengthen the hand of reformers and lead the government to stay the course with regard to economic strategy. However, by 1996, the Cuban government seemed to be back-pedalling away from its own success, cracking down politically and economically on those who would have tended to support reform the most. While certain new reforms did move forward, including the creation of a new Central Bank and a revamping of the financial system, 1997 and 1998 did not see a continuation of the sweeping structural moves of 1993–4. Why did this happen and what does it mean for the future of reform in Cuba?

7.4. THE POLITICAL ECONOMY OF REFORM

Reform in any environment is driven by a mix of political and economic factors.[16] Since any change involves upsetting an existing constellation of political actors, policy makers must move ahead of the politics, hoping that: (1) the reforms themselves will weaken contemporary political alignments (as some asset holders find their wealth and political power reduced by new policy) and hence create the space for technocrats to implement new policy; and (2) the eventual 'winners' from the reform will materialize as a political force that can support the reformers and carry the process through the medium term. It is this sort of political economy logic which has led some analysts to justify 'big bang' approaches to post-socialist transitions; slower approaches may have less output costs but delays in reform tend to give political interest groups more time to organize and resist change.

The Cuban approach has certainly been gradual, with timid step following timid step. While this could be viewed as responding to the need to soften the pains of transition, the real difficulty is that the government is not especially committed to reform. Instead, it is seeking to repair the economy sufficiently to maintain power while avoiding steps that would not be at least partially reversible in the future. This imparts a lack of credibility to the reforms—and any winner from the new economic strategy therefore worries about the security of his/her investment.[17]

The government's ambivalence about reform has been quite evident in key public statements. President Castro told the Cuban National Assembly on 26 December 1995 that the ongoing economic changes meant that Cuba has 'to reckon with a new social class, and the more power and influence it has, the bigger will be the challenge to the revolution'.[18] In March 1996, Raúl Castro, the President's brother and head of the armed forces, suggested that the newly emerging class of self-employed individuals is 'creating the basis for organized groupings, associations and actions free of the state' which could 'constitute a test tube for subversive efforts of the enemy'. Thus, while the reforms are generating sectors that might support further policy action to open the economy, this is not the preferred policy sequence of the Cuban government; in fact, the leadership does not really want the winners to win. As a result, when aggregate growth hits a reasonable target—as it did in 1995 and 1996—the government tends to backtrack from reform.

Thus, in 1996, the government began to place new taxes on the self-employed sector, especially on the private 'family' restaurants that sprung up in many urban areas after enabling legislation was adopted in June 1995.[19] This was followed up by a political crackdown on human rights groups as well as on Party members and state bureaucrats who had voiced the most support for pushing further on economic reform.[20] Indeed, some have suggested that it was these internal political problems which gave rise to the government's 1996 decision to shoot down two planes flown by Cuban-American protestors, an event which triggered the passage of the Helms–Burton legislation by the US Congress.[21]

Such political events are crucial to economic policy. While the Cuban government retains strong control over the domestic political scene, neither it nor the Communist Party are monolithic. There are at least three different groupings of power and policy.[22] The first is the top-level leadership, a group which is generally committed to the maintenance of Party power and some form of socialism; for these individuals, reform has been reluctant at best and many still regret the shift from sectoral to systemic strategies. The second grouping is composed of individuals in the top- to mid-level moderate leadership—best typified by Economy Minister, Jose Luis Rodriguez. This group is less powerful but more committed to an 'economy with market mechanisms but within a socialist framework of organization'.[23] A third group is younger and more educated than the political cadres who initially stepped into the political and economic leadership vacuum after the exodus of Cuba's upper and middle classes; these individuals remain loyal to the Cuban state, partly because it provided them with both an education and key roles in economic and political management, but would like to see both political and economic space broaden. This last grouping may contain the key agents for coherent change within Cuba.

Unfortunately, it is exactly this group of policy makers which came under attack in 1996—and in the subsequent years, those who were not explicitly criticized have heard the message and begun to constrain their own vocalization of more radical alternatives. Some hoped that the Pope's visit in 1998 would herald a new era and while it did open up more social space for religion, it did not have the same effect on the politics (Suchlicki 1999). In any case, the political situation remains quite scrambled: those in charge must reform but do not want to; those who want to pursue reform more systematically lack real political power and must push for changes at the margins of policy making. This, then, is the backdrop for considering scenarios for transition in Cuba.

7.5. TRANSITION CONDITIONS AND SCENARIOS

In considering the economics of transition, a key issue is the size of the output loss likely to result from changing economic rules of the game. While any major shift in economic rules is likely to cause reorientation of productive activity and perhaps a decline of investment and output in certain sectors, it should be noted that GDP fell dramatically between 1989 and 1993. Moreover, state investment is already highly curtailed, and the dynamism of the economy, particularly in 1999, is coming from areas that would benefit by further reform (tourism, foreign investment, and the small private sector). In short, Cuba may have already experienced the worst of the usual transition-induced recession.

To explore this issue further, I compare Cuba to a set of other developing countries (see Table 7.1); inclusion in the sample was based on having a similar level of GNP per capita and all the data necessary for the comparison.[24] For several series, the Cuban figures were available for both 1993 and 1989, the year for the reference sample and the year before the recent Cuban recovery began. Not all data are comparable between the reference sample and the island economy: Cuba's socialist accounting in 1989 means that the sectoral and trade shares are of global social product and national income, respectively, and the 1993 sectoral and trade share are themselves estimates and subject to methodological criticisms.

Still, the story is roughly consistent with what might be expected: in 1989, Cuba was, like many socialist countries, over-industrialized in terms of both labour force allocation and sectoral share. By 1993, industry had downsized to a share similar to that of the reference sample—and there had been a sharp flight into services. The trade share has also shrunk considerably but it is not far off the sample average. The latter suggests that trade 'under-openness', which was a cause of transformational recession in other former socialist countries (see Chapter 1), may not be as strong a factor in Cuba's case; at the same time the reduction in openness (and the decline in trade deficit) over the 1989–93 period indicates that Cuba may be less vulnerable to external shock than at the beginning of its crisis.[25] Overall, the pattern suggests that much of the pain has already been experienced and that further large collapses may not be necessary provided that new reforms are sufficiently gradual.[26]

Table 7.1. *Structural indicators: Cuba versus a sample of comparable reference countries*

	GNP per capita, US$ from WDI	*GDP per capita, US$ from HDR*	*Human development index*
Sample, 1993	1,388	3,860	0.678
Cuba, 1993	1,450	3,000	0.727
	Share of labour in agriculture	*Share of labour in industry*	*Share of labour in services*
Sample, 1993	35.9	22.5	41.5
Cuba, 1989	18.0	30.0	51.0
	Agriculture as % of GDP	*Industry as % of GDP*	*Services as % of GDP*
Sample, 1993	15.5	32.3	52.1
Cuba, 1989	14.2	45.5	40.3
Cuba, 1993	7.2	30.7	62.1
	Exports as % of GDP	*Imports as % of GDP*	*Trade as % of GDP*
Sample, 1993	18.3	30.2	48.5
Cuba, 1989	34.8	52.5	87.3
Cuba, 1993	14.2	23.4	37.6

Sources and Notes: Data for reference sample from UNDP's Human Development Report and World Development Indicators. Cuban GNP per capita for 1993 is an estimate; GDP per capita in dollars and the human development indicator from HDR. Cuban data for 1989 from Annuario Estadistico de Cuba, 1989. The 1989 sectoral shares are of global social product; the 1993 shares are of GDP as taken from La Economia Cubana, 1994. Cuban export and import shares from 1989 are of national income; for 1993 are of GDP according to author estimates. Reference sample of countries consists of Algeria, Colombia, Dominican Republic, Ecuador, El Salvador, Guatemala, Jamaica, Jordan, Morocco, Papua New Guinea, Paraguay, Peru, and Tunisia.

An additional positive factor is that the government, after allowing the deficit to grow as the economy recessed, has managed to dramatically cut its own fiscal gap.[27] Partly as a result of the fiscal picture, as well as the depenalization of dollar use and the emergence of the free markets in agriculture and certain urban services, the currency has stabilized. In mid-1994, as the economy bottomed out and policy was shifting, the peso was trading in black markets at over 100 to the dollar; by late 1996, it had fallen below 20 to the dollar and has since hovered around this level all the way through 1999.[28]

A fading positive factor for any transition is the relative equality of Cuban society, a fact which generally reduces social conflict and allows for a more evenly spread base of human capital. Unfortunately, Cuban equality is fading as the piecemeal reform continues.[29] In the context of dollarization and informalization, those with family abroad are able to receive remittances and spend them in new dollar stores while those without such ties remain constrained by peso wages.[30] While professionals are generally prohibited from leaving their positions, bellhops and maids in the tourist industry are able to collect dollar tips, and both they and the newly self-employed have wound up among the highest income receivers on the island; for example, a hotel doorman can pick up in one day's tips the monthly salary of a brain surgeon.[31] The result is a political paradox; those most loyal to the revolution (its professionals and those who cut off relations with family members in exile) are now among the lower income individuals in Cuban society.

Cuba, of course, faces several disadvantageous conditions for any sort of transition. The current state enterprises are very poorly managed; while subsidies to money-losing firms have been cut in order to balance the government budget and there is a government programme to 'modernize' firms, particularly those in the export sector, the government is clearly worried about the political consequences of mass layoffs. Meanwhile, firms have reacted to the subsidy cuts by building up high levels of inter-firm debt (as in other post-socialist economies; see Chapter 2); this latter phenomenon will straightjacket any recovery. Firms in the foreign sector are in better shape as they are expected to be self-financing and to pay for imported inputs with their own hard currency earnings.[32]

The layoff issue is a particular challenge. Enterprise rationalization requires labour shedding, which, given the extremely low productivity of marginal workers in state firms, could likely be done with negligible falls in output. However, state employment is a form of social security and a full restructuring could result in the dismissal of 20–30 per cent of the industrial workforce; not surprisingly, unions have resisted and the government has held off. In China (see Chapter 4), the strategy has been to go slow on the reform of state industrial enterprises, allowing this sector to serve as an absorber of labour. That country, however, has a thriving private sector which has been able to draw in displaced labour over time even as very high and sustained rates of aggregate growth have given China the 'luxury' of maintaining a bloated state sector in the interests of social peace.[33] Cuba does not enjoy such a growth dividend, particularly after the 1997–8 slowdown, and, unless it adopts a more dramatic commitment to privatization and the opening of space for small business, it has limited opportunities for redundant employees.

Another unfavourable factor for Cuba is the implacable hostility of the US, evidenced on the economic front by the ongoing trade embargo and the 1996 Helms–Burton legislation which seeks to punish foreign investors in Cuba through various means. The central element of Helms–Burton is its declaration that US citizens can sue foreign companies in US courts for 'trafficking' in their property. While this initially refers to US nationals whose property was lost as a result of the revolution almost 40 years ago, the legislation also envisions permitting (after a few years) suits by those who since became US citizens: this implies that Cuban exiles in Miami and elsewhere could also hit the US courts for property now held by foreign firms. Since nearly all the property of the state was once in private hands, this had a dampening effect on investment flows.[34]

Finally, foreign exchange remains a central problem for the Cuban economy. In order to step up sugar production in 1996, the government obtained short-term credit from European financiers for key inputs and capital equipment. Interest rates were usurious (reported to be between 14 and 17 per cent), partly because Cuba has a significant stock of Western-held foreign debt (reported to be well over US$10 billion in 1998) that is in arrears. What has provided new breathing room on the foreign exchange side is the growth of tourism and foreign remittances. Tourist growth tapered off in 1997, partly as a result of a rash of bombings in hotels and other tourist sites, but it has since recovered as local security has improved. The US has sought to limit remittance flows and cash transfers made during family visits but inflows from remittances have probably exceeded net tourism revenues since 1995.[35]

Another key factor in any transition consideration is the role of Cuban-Americans. This highly organized interest group has managed to persuade the US to forego dialogue with the communist regime. The dominant political forces in that community seem to be hoping for a post-Castro era in which Miami Cubans would take economic, and likely political, leadership; in the meantime, they refuse to entertain thoughts of investment (in contrast to the relatively eager attitude of the overseas Vietnamese and Chinese, a phenomenon which has helped in the transitions in those countries). Since a Miami-style vision for Habana includes little role for the younger reformers mentioned above, this group is driven back into the arms of the Party leadership and away from the process of social change.

At the same time, Cuban-Americans could constitute a positive factor for reform once it is initiated. Few post-socialist countries have an exile community which is so wealthy and so well versed in international business, the latter deriving from experience in a variety of niches in Miami's role as Latin America's business centre. The challenge for Cuban authorities is how to incorporate this dynamism without losing control.

What sort of transitions could occur in Cuba?[36] The most likely scenario involves 'muddling through' with lukewarm reform and moderate growth, and probably does not constitute what many would label an actual transition. The critical factor here would be the current leadership's hope to maintain power: like China, Cuba hopes to engage in economic reform without having to face political liberalization. Thus, the government will continue some degree of reform, mostly because this will be necessary to keep the aggregate economy on a growth path. However, measures will be quite cautious and the impacts will be correspondingly modest.

In such a muddling-through scenario, the key features are as follows:

1. The government retains its ability to attract some degree of foreign short-term finance and uses this to expand sugar production further (Alvarez 1997). The partnership with the Canadian firm, Sherritt (which has been able to more than double nickel production at the Moa plant since 1994), continues and nickel sales improve.[37] The rest of the export sector increases slowly.
2. Tourism continues to expand, despite some decline in the rate of growth from the striking 16.4 per cent annual increase in the number of tourists between 1990 and 1995 (Alvarez 1997, p. 5). Net revenues rise as Cuba creates more backward linkages to the industry, especially to manufacturers of textiles, tobacco, and other light retail products.
3. The government continues to clean up state firms for restructuring. Layoffs occur but the process is slow and efficiency increases are minimal. Despite efforts to modernize management and instil a new entrepreneurial attitude, few state firms emerge as competitive in international terms; the exception will be those enterprises actively tied to foreign investors.

4. The government expands the realm for self-employment. Under the guise of worker cooperatives, small businesses emerge. Strains are placed on the state input supply system as smaller businesses compete informally (and often illegally) for intermediate goods.[38]
5. Fiscal management continues to be strict. New taxes on income are implemented and collected, yielding slight improvements on the revenue side. The monetary overhang continues its slow decline; however, at the current pace, it could still exceed 50 per cent of GDP at the end of a five-year period.[39] Price liberalization is postponed in formal terms, although there is some effective liberalization as more goods slip out of state distribution networks and the government returns to the parallel market pricing strategies that were common in the early 1980s.[40]

Will this allow for a recovery of the economy? A growth rate of 4–5 per cent under this scenario is possible although we should note that the slowdown of 1997–8 occurred under a similar policy regime. Still, foreign exchange availability will continue to rise slowly, mostly due to tourism and remittances, and this will allow a recovery of even the state-run economy; of course, 1997 and 1998 have also shown that a poor sugar harvest or adverse international prices can strain the supply of foreign currency and knock several points off the growth rate. Under this scenario, the small private sector will grow more rapidly but this will not lift the aggregate growth rate too much as such activity remains a small, albeit growing, share of national output.

Unfortunately, the medium-term picture is less positive. Without substantial change in the domestic political economy, there is not likely to be any change in US policy—and, as a result, most foreign investors will be reluctant to commit to longer term non-tourist projects. Encouraging the domestic private sector could spur growth but the Party will continue to be concerned about creating alternative centres of power. Thus, the Cuban economy will simply simmer; inequality will accelerate in this situation of half-reform, giving an impetus for political unrest (or at least dissatisfaction).

Another scenario includes dramatic market reform including the liberalization of prices and the promotion of private property. However, given the current political configuration, the most probable way that such dramatic change might occur is as a result of either an external crisis—which further shakes up the regime and alters the current constellation of political forces—or some form of external intervention.[41] In either case, there would likely be a new openness to US investors and policy makers. Such a dramatic policy shock could derail any careful sequencing of policy reforms, primarily because the Miami-based and other investors who would gain power, or at least access, would worry that a cautious and logical gradualism would risk a reversibility of the policy change.

As a result:

1. Privatization would occur in an accelerated fashion as Cuban-American investors pressure their way into island opportunities. Small- and medium-sized enterprises would be put on the block early with larger firms scheduled to follow. For reasons noted below, this privatization scheme would quickly bog down.

2. Market liberalization would proceed rapidly, partly because of ideology and partly because of a desire to integrate Cuba with the global economy (i.e. use domestic deregulation to ensure that national relative prices are parallel to those ruling in world markets). To avoid a hyperinflationary price spiral, the government would engage in fiscal policy reform and work to create an independent monetary authority (see Castañeda 1993).
3. Such fiscal policy reform would include the dramatic reduction of state subsidies to money-losing firms and thus induce mass layoffs. While attempts would also be made to raise revenues, Cuba's system of taxation is still in the process of development and there would likely be mass evasion. Social welfare expenditures would then become a target, but these are difficult to cut for reasons discussed below.

What are the consequences of such an approach? First, the rapid adjustment to new pricing would disorient many enterprises and individuals and drive others into very short-term projects (until the churning of relative prices settles down); as a result, output might decline. Second, the fiscal situation would be problematic: the resulting inflation would also contribute to a slowdown. Third, and perhaps uniquely to Cuba, privatization in the context of open internationalism would lead to a temporary collapse of investment.

Why would the fiscal side be problematic? Many authors, including those quite sympathetic to a capitalist transformation, have noted that the social props beneath the populace are one of the achievements held most dear by both the Cuban people and the Cuban state (Dominguez 1993; Maingot 1993; Mesa-Lago 1993). The social safety net has already been shredded by the crisis; further cutbacks could create political problems, particularly when accompanied by a new ideology stressing a reduced role for the state. Resistance to social spending declines could produce continuing inflation, especially as improving tax collection will likely be a slow process.

Why would rapid privatization produce an investment slowdown rather than a boom? While incorporating Cuban-American investors would help secure an ample flow of foreign exchange and management know-how, the presence of Cuban-Americans also raises the problem of property claims (an issue which is avoided because of a lack of contact in the muddling-through scenario above). Claims will be difficult to establish and settle, particularly given the incompleteness of records and the inadequacy of the Cuban legal system.[42] Property will be hung up in court for years; in the interim, eager investors in-waiting will remain just that—eager and in-waiting.

Growth would be uneven but the economy would likely recover at the end of the five-year period examined here. A new private sector with clear rules should be able to animate domestic production, particularly when helped by US investors. However, in the meantime, inequality will worsen because of unequal access to dollars, a shrinking state, and rising unemployment.

Pastor and Zimbalist (1995a) argue for a very different approach, the centrepiece of which is a rapid privatization of most state assets to island-based Cubans. In this vision:

1. The government would first open up more space for private enterprise by further expanding the scope for self-employment. It would then allow for firms to hire

non-family members, perhaps in the form of worker cooperatives (following the model involved in transforming state farms). Input markets would need to be liberalized to allow competition between this sector and state enterprises and a tax system would need to be developed.
2. In a second stage, the government would privatize small- and medium-sized enterprises amounting to about half of the capital stock of Cuba; larger firms would generally remain in state hands, with the government pursuing privatization opportunities with foreign investors. While the various merits of specific voucher schemes can be debated, the key feature here is that asset sales should be limited to Cubans residing on the island—and that some share of the vouchers would automatically accrue to both the workers in the privatized enterprise and Cuban citizens more generally.
3. Price liberalization would take place immediately following privatization. Inflationary impacts would be limited for at least two reasons. First, the sale of assets should absorb most of the monetary overhang, especially if vouchers are allowed to rise in price to clear the market. Second, privatization should shore up the revenue base of the government, both by cutting subsidies to firms and because of direct proceeds from sales.
4. The government would save part of the proceeds to ride out fiscal shortfalls as the tax system matures. Another portion of the proceeds would be used to expand the social safety net, including expansion of education and health and the development of a more extensive financial base for unemployment insurance; the latter would reduce the social costs of rationalizing state enterprises.

This sort of privatization seeks to spur production by delivering both real property rights and therefore real incentives. More significantly, it seeks to give property to island-based Cubans. This would avoid the property rights confusion and investment stagnation of the previous scenario even as it builds a local class which may be both loyal to the state and ready to be the new motors of accumulation.[43]

Such a programme could generate faster and more sustained growth by creating a thriving private sector.[44] The programme also does not rely on any dramatic shift in the political system or a sudden rapprochement with the US; indeed, under this strategy, it is better to hold off warming relations until after privatization has proceeded and local Cuban investors are better able to compete with their Cuban-American counterparts. Of course, one key limit to such a strategy is political; such privatization is not reversible and the government would need to be firmly convinced that the nation is leaving state socialism behind.

But, if properly executed, such a scheme could enhance equity, a key element for a successful transition to the market economy (see Chapter 10). Recall that much of East Asia's success can be attributed to its initial relative equality in the distribution of physical and human capital, a development precondition which was achieved via land reform and a significant public investment in mass education. In a parallel fashion, the strategy above achieves a widespread distribution of productive property and provides a better fiscal basis for Cuba's social welfare and educational expenditures. It would be a shame to erode Cuba's existing equality via a pell-mell rush to the market. It would be an equal tragedy if the current half-hearted reforms continue, worsening distribution and economic potential along the way.

7.6. CONCLUSION

As Jorge Dominiguez so aptly put it in a 1993 article, Cuba has begun a 'transition to somewhere'. No one, not the political leadership nor the opposition-in-waiting (and in-Miami) nor even astute academic observers, can offer a definitive answer with regard to what sort of system will evolve on the island. While dramatic changes are possible, including a full-fledged externally driven transition, what is most likely is more of the same: half-hearted reform, modest growth, and accumulating social contradictions. There are clear limits to this approach and such a path is likely to provoke another economic slowdown within a few short years. Yet the tenacity of the Cuban regime, even in the face of a dysfunctional economy, should not be underestimated.

It has been said that those who know Cuba do not easily predict its future, and those who easily predict the island's future do not really know the political economy of the Cuban state. Modesty is therefore in order, particularly since the gap between the early bold predictions of easy success in Russian and Eastern Europe and the consequent problematic outcomes suggest that we know much less about transition than would be useful. The other chapters in this volume suggest that there is much unsettled about where post-socialist economies can and should head. As Cuba determines its own possibilities, it will need to learn from the experience of others even as others learn from the political economy dynamics of blocked transition on the island.

NOTES

1. A caveat is in order regarding the figures offered in this paper. There has long been debate over the reliability of official Cuban data (see Pérez-López 1991; Zimbalist and Brundenius 1989; Joglekar and Zimbalist 1989); the problem became worse when the government ceased publication of the country's statistical yearbook after the economy slipped into crisis. Limited figures on output and income have been released in recent years. For the purposes of this paper, I have summarized what few series seem to be reliable and offered adjustments as needed.
2. Pastor and Zimbalist (1995*b*) compare Cuba to eight other Latin American countries along various educational and health dimensions, including adult literacy, mean years of school, share of GDP spent on public education, life expectancy, child mortality rates, number of doctors per capita, daily caloric supply, and share of GDP spent on public health. Using a simple average rank for all these indicators, Cuba was first—even though it was dead last against the same eight when ranked by the dollar value of GNP per capita. Cuba's infant mortality is now the twentieth lowest in the world, a startling achievement for a developing country (*Business Tips on Cuba*, March 1997).
3. For a review of structural shifts toward industry in the Cuban economy, see Figueras (1991).

4. To illustrate this, consider a reference group constructed in a process similar to that for Table 7.1: all developing countries with a GNP per capita in 1993 ranging between $1,000 and $2,000 for which we could obtain data on rural–urban disparities from UNDP's *Human Development Report* (given data availability, this yields a slightly different group of countries than that in Table 7.1). With a variable of 100 indicating rural–urban equality and lesser values indicating poorer relative performance in rural areas, Cuba posts values of 97 for health, 89 for safe water, and 72 for sanitation while the reference group posts average values of 64 for health, 60 for safe water, and 68 for sanitation.
5. Moreover, in 1989, Cuba's bilateral deficit with the Soviet Union accounted for 84 per cent of the total trade deficit of the island. Data on composition of trade taken from *Annuario Estadistico de Cuba, 1989*.
6. In the earlier part of the period the subsidy was mostly in the form of terms of trade, while in the latter the Soviets opted for the more transparent mechanism of automatically financing trade deficits. See the estimates in Pastor and Zimbalist (1995*a*); the calculation corrects for Soviet overpricing as in Ritter (1990).
7. Hard currency earnings from exports were around 20 per cent of total export revenues but were critical to paying off Western debt and obtaining certain key inputs not available from the socialist world. For a lengthy discussion of the re-export of Soviet oil, see Turtis (1987).
8. In addition, urban 'volunteers' transplanted to the fields had few incentives; even those that received monetary bonuses for their rural work were hard-pressed to do more than accumulate cash balances in light of the collapse of domestic production.
9. This is not to say that malnutrition was completely avoided. For example, between November 1991 and the summer of 1993, more than 50,000 people suffered from a neurological disorder which generated temporary blindness and nerve damage in legs and feet and which was apparently caused by inadequate diet. The Cuban authorities eventually responded by handing out free vitamin pills and the epidemic was largely eradicated. See Terence Monmaney, 'Politics of an Epidemic', *Los Angeles Times*, 20 November 1995: A-1.
10. Defence expenditures from UNDP's *Human Development Report 1996*; education expenditure from various years of the same.
11. Other estimates are more modest, putting the figure at around 400,000 or around 10 per cent of the labour force (see Mimi Whitefield, 'For Cuba's Self-employed, the Tax Man Comes Calling', *Miami Herald*, 9 June 1996). For an excellent analysis of the 'second economy' both prior to and after the reforms, see Pérez-López (1995). The number of officially registered self-employed has fallen in recent years as the government has sought to tax the sector.
12. On the early period of the farmers' markets, see Rosenberg (1992); for a review of the evolution of recent policy, see Deere *et al.* (1994) and Deere (1996).
13. The 1996 improvement reflected an improvement in commodity prices for both sugar and nickel in the beginning of the year, as well as volume increases in both key products and continuing growth in tourism. The 1997 and 1998 growth rates were lower due to poor sugar harvests and unfavourable world prices for Cuba's products; indeed, the 1998 sugar harvest was the worst in over 50 years.
14. See Pérez-López (1998*b*) for a discussion of the long-term shift from merchandise exports to services such as tourism and remittances over the 1990s.
15. For a detailed and balanced look at foreign investment in Cuba, see Pérez-López (1996).
16. In this section, we draw heavily on the sort of 'positive political economy' framework typified by the works of Alesina and Drazen (1991), Rodrik (1994), and others; see the

review in Rodrik (1996). For a more formal approach to this topic with reference to Cuba, see Pastor and Zimbalist (1997).
17. See Rodrik (1991) on policy reversibility and investment behaviour in a period of reform.
18. Quoted in Ibon Villelabeitia, 'Cuba's Dollarization', AP, 30 January 1996.
19. The legal framework for income and profit taxes has been in place since mid-1994 but the institutional capacity for collection has remained underdeveloped. The sharp increase in the monthly dollar tax on small private restaurants came in June 1996.
20. Two research centres which had been focal points for theorizing a transition strategy were explicitly attacked by the leadership and their members were dispersed to other centres.
21. The government insisted that the incident took place in Cuban waters while the US authorities and others have argued that the shoot down happened in international territory.
22. For another characterization of the power groups in Cuba, see Gonzalez (1996). See also Roca (1993) and Fitzgerald (1995).
23. The quote is attributed to José Luis Rodríguez; see Robert P. Walzer, Eduardo Kaplan, and John Bussey, 'Notes from Havana: Cubans Pursue a Tenuous Balancing Act', *Wall Street Journal*, 27 September 1996.
24. I specifically selected countries whose 1993 GNP per capita in dollars was between $1,000 and $2,000 (and again, which also had the other key variables). Cuba does not report dollar GNP per capita but UNDP's *Human Development Report* does include an estimate of GDP per capita; to translate, I took all countries between $700 and $4,000 in GNP per capita, regressed this on the HDR GDP variable, and used the coefficient to predict Cuban GNP per capita. The result places Cuba near Peru, which is roughly similar to earlier estimates I have made.
25. My thanks to Vladimir Popov for pointing me in this direction of analysis.
26. On the other hand, the Cuban industrial structure was biased toward larger firms, perhaps making downsizing more difficult.
27. Less progress has been made on the monetary overhang, which has fallen only slightly from its 1994 peak of nearly 100 per cent of GDP.
28. In October of 1995, the government created a new currency exchange institution, CADECA, that has also allowed it to better monitor and capture the dollar flow.
29. Distributional data are hard to come by in Cuba. One indicator of the changing distribution of income: while 14 per cent of the account holders held 77 per cent of the balances in December 1994, three years later 13 per cent of the account holders held 85 per cent of the balances (Everleny Perez 1998; p. 10). The same author suggests that over 60 per cent of the Cuban population is living in poverty, even controlling for sources of informal income (Everleny Perez 1998).
30. Up to 60 per cent of the population has some access to dollars. By 1998, the new dollar shops were doing $800 million in sales, largely to domestic residents. See Economist Intelligence Unit, *Country Report*, 1st quarter 1999, p. 19.
31. See Andrew Cawthorne, 'Tourism Boom Shakes Up Cuban Society', Reuters, 31 August 1999.
32. See Economist Intelligence Unit, *Country Profile 1995–96*, p. 10. There are also a number of independent trading companies.
33. For more on the Chinese reforms and a comparison to Cuba, see Pérez-López (1998*a*).
34. Although implementation of key provisions of Helms-Burton has been held up by the executive decree of US President Bill Clinton, partly to avoid conflicts with Europeans and

others who object to the 'extraterritoriality' of this US law, there does seem to have been a decline in the investor enthusiasm that was evidenced for Cuba after 1994.

35. Remittances are currently estimated to be between $600 and $800 million a year, with some reason to believe that the number is closer to the top end of the band (Pérez-López 1998*b*). If we assume a net import coefficient in tourism of about 60 per cent, earnings from that sector were about $725 million. The US imposed a ban on remittances to Cuban from US-based relatives and restricted travel to visit relatives in the wake of the rafting crisis of 1994. These regulations were liberalized slightly in October 1995, tightened again after the February 1996 shootdown, and liberalized once again in 1999. In the interim period, Cuban-Americans have found alternative, third-country routes to transfer cash to needy relatives on the island.
36. For an earlier attempt at forecasting scenarios, see Mesa-Lago and Fabian (1993).
37. The increase in the Moa plant's production is detailed in 'Castro's Capitalist: Canada's Sherritt Cleans Up in Cuba', *Business Week*, 17 March 1997: pp. 48–9. There was a 150 per cent increase in the production of nickel and cobalt between 1994 and 1998, and almost half of Cuban nickel production comes from the Moa joint venture.
38. Such competition has not been a serious problem yet since most of the self-employed are involved in services, such as home repair, or family restaurants which tend to buy their inputs on the free agricultural markets.
39. According to Economy Minister Rodriguez, for example, there was no significant decline of the overhang in 1996 after a nearly 20 per cent fall over the previous two years (see Economist Intelligence Unit, *Country Report*, 1st quarter 1997, p. 13). Indeed, in absolute terms, there was a 5 per cent increase in the overhang between 1995 and 1998 which, given GDP growth, did produce a modest decline in the relative overhang.
40. Parallel markets, used in many socialist states, charged higher prices for goods not officially rationed (or for a quantity of goods beyond the rationed amount).
41. When such a dramatic collapse of the Cuban regime seemed more imminent, the US State Department commissioned a study, 'Transition in Cuban: New Challenges for US Policy', which carefully laid out this sort of transition (as well as others). Cardoso and Helwege (1992) also explicitly consider transition but their discussion is much less detailed.
42. The Cubans do have pre-1959 property registers preserved in 82 municipal archives. This could help with clarifying property rights and authorities have announced that the archives are open, partly as a way to reassure foreign investors anxious in the wake of Helms-Burton. Moreover, the government could honour former property rights by providing vouchers which could be used for investment anywhere in Cuba rather than tying compensation to particular properties.
43. Sanguinetty (1993, p. 474) notes that both Hungary and Czechoslovakia were able to forbid or limit the return of privatized property to former owners; the thought here is to follow the same strategy (and international precedent) by privatizing to locals before Cuban-Americans return and confuse the situation.
44. Several analysts have pointed to the potential strength of current entrepreneurs, including in the informal sector. See Peters and Scarpaci (1998) and Pérez-López (1995).

PART III
CHANGES IN KEY INSTITUTIONS

8

Economic Performance in Transitional Economies: The Role of Ownership, Incentives, and Restructuring

DEREK C. JONES

8.1. INTRODUCTION

This chapter surveys theoretical and empirical evidence for key microeconomic determinants of economic performance which theorists in comparative systems have long pointed to as being of crucial importance—organizations and policies that influence structures of ownership and control as well as the motivation of economic agents.[1] To organize the discussion, in the next section a conceptual framework that distinguishes participation in economic returns and participation in control is used. However, the bulk of the chapter is of empirical nature.

In Section 3 evidence on the nature and economic impacts of ownership and control is surveyed. Particular attention is paid to the introduction of privatization and the productivity effects of different property forms, especially employee ownership. By giving special emphasis to findings that are derived from panel data sets for several countries, in general we find that: (i) substantial insider ownership prevails, though majority ownership by non-managerial employees is eroding fast; (ii) the links between employee influence and employee ownership are weak and privatization often does not produce fundamental changes in inherited patterns of corporate governance; and (iii) there is substantial variation within countries at any time as well as over time in patterns of employee participation and employee ownership; (iv) there is no persuasive evidence that a single form of private ownership is most efficient or that the key obstacle to enhanced performance is employee participation in economic returns; (v) there is some evidence that employee participation enhances business productivity; (vi) there is limited evidence that employee participation also acts to boost the effect of employee ownership and employee participation in profits; and (vii) in accounting for the determinants of differences in labour productivity, there is a role for ownership dynamics as well as changes in patterns of influence. In Section 4 we turn to incentive systems. For both managers and other employees flexible pay systems are becoming more prevalent. Econometric evidence for compensation systems for both executives and non-managerial workers points to the beneficial effects of performance-related incentives.

8.2. CONCEPTUAL ISSUES

8.2.1. *The Preferred Form of Privatization*

The theoretical case for privatization rests on several arguments (e.g. Boycko *et al.* 1996) including an alleged need for depoliticization and the view that it is only non-state forms of ownership that will produce an environment conducive to nurturing financial discipline in firms.[2] While not everyone accepts these views and there is also empirical evidence, both for China and for state-owned firms in former communist countries transition (e.g. Pinto *et al.* (1993) for Poland), which suggests that the issue is not as clear cut as proponents believe, in this section we accept the need for a large non-state sector and instead discuss the arguments for the preferred form of private ownership.

To consider these issues, the dominant approach in the corporate governance literature classifies firms by ownership (see e.g. Bim *et al.* 1993). For reasons including allegedly superior solutions to agency problems, it is argued that ownership by outsiders is preferred and that when insiders dominate, the most efficient form of insider ownership is manager (rather than worker) ownership (e.g. Aghion and Blanchard 1998). However, there are several reasons why these conclusions may not always be appropriate for transition economies.

Critics question whether stock markets actually perform their intended functions effectively, especially in the context of formerly centrally planned economies with underdeveloped capital market institutions. Aoki and Kim (1995) note that much of the traditional analysis assumes an idealized view of advanced market economies and that the argument for the promotion of outside ownership and efficient securities markets ignores crucial matters such as inherited factors and assumes competitive product and labour markets. Especially in the context of transition economies Earle and Estrin (1998) argue that the effects of employee ownership may be dependent on a host of factors such as market conditions and that, in particular cases, some forms of employee ownership may be the best feasible solution to the choice of ownership structure.

Moreover, arguably the mainstream view uses a framework that in its conception of organizational processes is quite narrow. There is a tendency to identify ownership with control and to take an overly static view. To illustrate these points, Ben-Ner and Jones (1995) have noted that ownership of an asset consists of two central rights—the right to control its use and to enjoy its returns. This distinction is used to develop a typology of western firms in which diverse allocations of control and return rights between two major groups in organizations, employees and owners of capital who are not employees, are identified.

This alternative conceptual framework may also be used to examine the expected economic effects of different ownership structures. While the argument is developed more fully elsewhere (e.g. Ben-Ner and Jones 1995), contrary to the conventional wisdom, it is argued that some types of insider-owned structures can be justified on several grounds. This is shown to be especially the case when insider-owned structures exist in combination with participatory human resource management policies. Insider ownership and control is arguably more conducive to enterprise stability and long-term employment relationships and thus may contribute to better economic performance in a number of ways. The closer alignment of the goals of the different economic agents within firms may better motivate workers to join in restructuring efforts and to better use their accumulated experience and firm-specific knowledge. Goal alignment effects of employee participation via information sharing (e.g. small group activities) are more subtle (but not necessarily weaker) than effects through ownership. Small group activities may provide valuable opportunities for both management and workers to learn about each other in a more cooperative atmosphere than traditional collective bargaining settings, and thus develop stronger trust. With stronger trust, sharing vital business information with workers will help convince them that it is in their interest to improve productivity and firm performance. Various forms of employee participation may play an important role of providing employees a voice in the firm and thus reduce the costs of exit from the firm, saving specific human capital.

At the same time, the relationship between alternative ownership arrangements and individual motivation, individual performance, organizational structural variables, and ultimately organizational performance is expected to be quite complex. In particular, while in general we expect to see a strong and mainly positive interaction between control and return rights, the relationship between employee ownership with balanced control and return rights on the one hand and productivity on the other hand is not monotonic.

8.2.2. *The Preferred Forms of Compensation*

The conventional wisdom is that market-based arrangements are needed to replace payment systems that existed under planning. For non-managerial workers, reflecting a preference for what are understood to be the dominant schemes in the west, orthodoxy argues for time wages (or possibly individual piece rates). However, based on the framework considered above, more favourable effects on enterprise performance can be expected from alternative compensation systems, especially those that provide for participation in economic returns. Moreover, recent theoretical work on compensation suggests that to motivate employees to work harder and smarter when it is difficult to monitor their effort, various compensation practices may be appropriate, with the effectiveness of a practice varying with firm characteristics (e.g. Jones and Pliskin 1997). Since average firm sizes in former state-owned firms are typically quite large and given the legacy of group-based (rather than individual) schemes of compensation in former planned economies, this suggests that group-based incentive schemes may be expected to be especially appropriate (and effective) for the case of transition economies.

Also it is believed that arrangements in Soviet-type economies (STEs) resulted in acute managerial incentive and motivational problems (e.g. Bonin 1976); reforms of the managerial labour market might be expected to produce success in overall reform during transition (e.g. Aghion *et al.* 1994). Managers in STEs were posited to have much more limited autonomy or scope for discretionary power than top executives in western firms. The main component of managerial reward systems in STEs was a base wage, with limited variation with respect to success indicators such as plan fulfilment. Consistent with egalitarian values, the pay of top managers was a low multiple of the average wage. Indeed in the past chief executives were not even amongst the highest paid.

To try to overcome the tendencies for managerial slack, risk aversion and the pursuit of a quiet life (Kornai 1992) that these arrangements would be expected to produce, the conventional wisdom is to argue for guaranteed pay for top executives. In part this reflects a view derived from agency theory. In addition, the empirical evidence for western firms is believed to find a link between executive pay and firm performance that is very weak, and also that efficient wages for top managers require very high wage differentials between managers and the average worker. Yet, in order to facilitate successful overall reform during early transition, the case for performance-based pay for managers seems to be strong.

During early transition, downsizing of overstaffed state-owned firms and productivity increases appear to be key ingredients of successful reform. Arguably such adjustments will be facilitated when executive compensation rewards managers for rational downsizing, productivity increases, and corporate investment. Moreover a growing body of theoretical and empirical evidence finds that executive compensation is highly responsive to firm performance, that wage differentials between executives and others need not be huge, and that executive compensation tends to be lower in firms that belong to corporate groups (e.g. see Kato and Rockel (1992) for evidence for Japan and the US). Such attributes of executive compensation may have special relevance given the egalitarian legacies in many former command economies and the possibilities of banks playing a monitoring role concerning corporate governance.

8.3. OWNERSHIP AND CONTROL: INCIDENCE AND PRODUCTIVITY EFFECTS

8.3.1. *Ownership*

Perhaps the most significant change that has occurred in transition economies, and which bears on the potential for employee participation in control and in economic returns, is the introduction of widespread employee ownership. As many have remarked, this was a surprising and for many economists an unwelcome development. While there are many excellent accounts of the privatization processes (which have typically led to the emergence of employee ownership, e.g. Estrin 1994), the important case of the new Russia is worthy of review, in part because of its influence in other transition countries.

Initially Russian officials such as Chubais were strongly opposed to introduce legislative provisions that favoured insiders as part of a voucher privatization scheme.[3]

However, already under the provisions of legislation introduced in 1989 (i.e. during the Gorbachev regime), insiders in some enterprises were exercising their options to buyout. And since officials of the new Yeltsin government perceived that the key task was to facilitate depoliticization, the legislation that in fact was adopted allowed employees in medium- and large-scale Russian enterprises, voting as members of their worker collective, to choose from among three privatization options, and all the options provided for insiders to purchase blocks of shares (although not always voting shares) at concessional rates.[4] Moreover, in fact it was the option enabling workers and managers to buy as much as 51 per cent of voting shares which was chosen overwhelmingly by the enterprises being privatized.

By now there have been several studies which have examined the patterns of ownership which have emerged in the new Russia.[5] The data show that while immediately after privatization very different patterns of ownership emerged in the bulk of medium- and large-scale privatized Russian enterprises, initially privatization predominantly led to insider ownership. Also, as time has passed since initial privatization, substantial additional changes have occurred in the structure of ownership in privatized Russian firms. One key trend is the rise in the extent of *outside* ownership. Thus by using panel data, during the period 1992–6, Jones (1998) finds that non-state outsiders were close to gaining parity ownership with insiders. A second key trend is an increase in the *share of ownership held by managers*. For Russia, Jones (1998) finds that while in April 1994 on average managers held about one-seventh of insider equity, by July 1996 the share of managers in insider ownership was almost one-third. Also Aukutsionek *et al.* (1998) find that managers forecast that their share will continue to grow.

It is also instructive to examine changes to the ownership stake of the top manager for firms in which the dominant owner differs. Unsurprisingly, the average stake of a manager is highest in firms in which managers are the dominant group; by 1996 the average CEO owned 7.4 per cent of total equity (Jones 1999). The comparable figure in employee-dominated firms averages 6.3 per cent, having grown from less than one-third of 1 per cent in four years. In firms with outsiders as dominant owners, the stake of top managers was rather less, and lowest of all (averaging 2.5 per cent) in firms owned by non-banking outsiders. Ownership by top managers in state-dominated firms was higher on average than in outsider-owned firms.

Elsewhere too there have been schemes which have led to the development of employee ownership often through the introduction of concessional shares for employees (e.g. Fitzroy *et al.* 1998; Wright and Estrin 1999). While it is clear that there are enormous differences across countries in the incidence of employee ownership, in the main it is also apparent that there is much insider ownership and that some of the trends in the changing structure of ownership identified for Russia are, in fact, more general.

For example, for the Ukraine, several studies indicate that soon after privatization insider ownership was very high, often around 80 per cent (e.g. Buck *et al.* (1996) report figures of 80 per cent for 1995). Subsequently, however, insider ownership apparently has fallen, with recent data suggesting an acceleration in this process—for example, Estrin and Rosevear (1999) report that in 1997, on average, insiders owned only 51 per cent of voting equity, and that it changed only slowly.

For the Baltic States, Jones and Mygind (1998) draw on large panels of new survey data.[6] The Lithuanian data reveal that in 1994 insider ownership averaged between 34 and 37 per cent of the available shares and that in 24 per cent of privatized firms insiders owned a *majority* of shares. In Latvia too, soon after privatization, about 69 per cent of an average firm was owned by insiders, with the state owning an average of 21 per cent and foreigners the balance of about 10 per cent.

The data on ownership in Estonia are particularly rich and reveal that, despite much reliance being placed on a Treuhand-like form of privatization, there is extensive insider ownership (Jones and Mygind 1999). Thus in 1995 some ownership by insiders existed in about two in three firms. In addition, often insider ownership was quite extensive—in about one in seven cases insiders were a majority of stockholders. However, the pattern of insider ownership is rather different than in Lithuania and Russia and, on average, managerial ownership is more pronounced than is non-managerial ownership. While the Estonian data indicate a great deal of path dependence, they also indicate that not all ownership configurations are equally stable. When a change in majority ownership has occurred, it has been especially likely to happen in firms which began by being owned by employees. Consequently, firms in which employees have majority ownership are becoming less frequent. Relative to other types of firms, this diminishing importance of majority employee-owned firms reflects a poorer ability both of existing employee-owned firms to remain employee owned and also of firms which formerly were not majority owned by employees to become employee owned.

Whereas in the countries of the former USSR and Central and Eastern Europe, the most unorthodox form of ownership that has assumed greatest significance is employee ownership, in China diverse forms of ownership have emerged (Sun, this volume). Many of these clearly differ in key ways from traditional state or private ownership; sometimes the labels attached to these new forms of ownership are familiar (including employee ownership). However, attempts to *precisely* specify many of these new kinds of property rights (and the implications for corporate governance) have sparked much controversy (e.g. Weitzman and Xu 1994; Li 1996). The difficulties are perhaps largest for township and village enterprises. For these, as Sun (1996) notes, a broad range of ownership forms are encompassed by this label including collective ownership by township and village communities and joint ownership by individual domestic shareholders.

8.3.2. *Control*

The foregoing makes it very clear that in most transition countries, though to widely varying degrees, there are opportunities for employee participation through individual share ownership.[7] And a small number of studies have tried to assess the degree of employee involvement that flows from privatization. Inevitably, such studies vary in key respects such as coverage, the nature of respondents, sample size, and design. Nevertheless, some general patterns seem apparent.

Most work on this matter appears to have been undertaken for Russia. Some of the earliest findings were based on survey evidence for Russian firms by Blasi (1994) and Blasi et al. (1997) and indicate that the extensive development of insider ownership typically facilitated managerial rather than worker control. The surveys (for both privatized and non-privatized firms) reported by Jones and Weisskopf (1996) also find that levels of employee influence typically were perceived as quite modest.[8] Also, data on board composition show that, on average, insiders accounted for a much smaller fraction of the board of directors than the average share of insider ownership.[9] By contrast, about one in six members on the board was a manager—about twice as high as the average level of managerial ownership. In addition, evidence suggests that, in 1993, typically, there were no statistically significant differences in the average level of perceived employee participation between privatized firms (in which employees typically own many shares) and non-privatized firms.[10] Similar findings emerge from other studies including Commander et al. (1996) and Filatotchev et al. (1996), who report that while employees in Russian firms may own large blocks of equity, they do not have equivalent degrees of involvement in structures of control such as boards of directors.

However, since these findings of low levels of employee influence and growing managerial power are derived from studies which report cross-section data for changing samples of firms, to pin down more reliably these changing patterns of influence it is necessary to use panel data. When this approach is adopted for Russia (Jones 1998), the finding that privatization has created significantly enhanced control of decision making by managers is confirmed. This is found to be especially the case on strategic issues such as basic business strategies, sales, and production plans. In addition the relationship between the form and dynamics of ownership and patterns of control was examined. The distribution of influence between managers and employees was never found to be statistically significantly different in firms that are owned by non-managerial employees, compared to firms in which either banks or outside individuals dominate. These analyses confirm that the evidence for a link between ownership and managerial/employee influence is very weak.

Some of the most reliable participation data are for Bulgaria for which Jones and Ilayperuma (1998) report evidence drawn from a survey of 4,600 workers in a sample of 371 firms that was representative of the Bulgarian economy during both fading communism and early transition, though in both cases before ownership changes had taken place on a significant scale. From worker responses it is clear that, on key issues, employees had typically little influence in decision making. Also, in three of four firms, patterns of influence did not change, though in remaining cases there is some evidence that employee influence usually increased.

The available data on the situation in other transition countries tends to be more limited than for Russia and Bulgaria. In the main the conclusion is that, on average, employee influence is quite limited. For example, a survey of 220 CEOs in Estonian firms found this to be the case on a variety of topics. In addition, in more than half of firms, employees as shareholders (including some instances when employees were the majority group) were judged to be irrelevant in their influence on company decisions while for trade unions the corresponding fraction was about three-quarters. However, the data also indicate that there was substantial heterogeneity amongst respondents in managers' perceptions of the importance of employees on various issues. On non-strategic issues such as safety and health at the workplace, about 30 per cent of respondents judged employee influence to be quite high. In terms of which channel of influence mattered most, employees as shareholders were judged to be most relevant three times as often as were trade unions.

Vaughan-Whitehead (1998) provides evidence for Albania. In about 8 in 10 cases, the introduction of profit sharing helped foster the spread of employee participation in decision making. The synergy was especially apparent in firms that had cooperative ownership structures.

8.3.3. *Effects of Ownership and Control*

In this subsection we selectively review studies of key determinants of business performance in transition economies. While several other reviews have appeared (e.g. Carlin and Landesmann 1997; Bevan *et al.* 1998), ours differs in important respects. First, our survey draws on an alternative conceptual framework and, where possible, examines linkages between employee participation in control and/or in economic returns and economic outcomes.[11] Second, our review covers a broader range of countries than typically found in most reviews. Third, in part because of space constraints, we must be highly selective in reviewing studies which are of various kinds. Of the various possible outcome variables, we focus on productivity both because this is a better measure of social welfare than many other measures (e.g. profitability) and also because its central importance as a direct measure of economic restructuring is recognized in its increasing use in recent work (e.g. Pohl *et al.* 1997; Bevan *et al.* 1998). Also, of the basic categories of study, we choose to concentrate on empirical work which uses standard econometric methods. Finally, because of greater likely reliability, we report findings from studies which use panel data and large samples of firms.

Broadly speaking, econometric studies can be distinguished according to whether they have adopted one of three different approaches. In what is perhaps the most widely used empirical strategy, the essential feature is to estimate regressions in which the dependent variable is a measure of performance (e.g. a quantitative indicator such as labour productivity) and ownership and other controls are the regressors (e.g. Earle *et al.* 1996; Filatotchev *et al.* 1999). Typically ownership is measured either by a privatization dummy or by a set of dummy variables for different ownership structures in which either the dominant or the majority ownership group is identified. Most often cross-sectional regressions are estimated by using OLS though, to deal with potential problems of endogeneity, sometimes instrumental variable methods are used (e.g. Earle and Estrin 1996).[12] Illustrative studies of this first type include the several studies which draw on a representative sample of 394 Russian manufacturing firms (e.g. Earle *et al.* 1996). This paper provided evidence on the propositions that firms with outside ownership are expected to be more efficient than firms with insider ownership and that the most efficient form of insider ownership is manager (rather than worker) ownership. The empirical strategy used was to categorize firms by dominant ownership and estimate a variety of regression models to examine relationships between indicators of restructuring (e.g. labour productivity) and ownership. However, at best the authors find only weak evidence of such links, especially for privatized firms with different dominant owners.

One attraction of this approach is its straightforwardness. Also, by including a lagged value of the dependent variable in the estimated models, it also has the advantage of attempting to take into account the influence of key dynamics on current performance. However, models of this ilk are somewhat *ad hoc*, seldom include controls for capital, and also usually omit variables which our theoretical framework suggests are important in accounting for variation in business success. In particular, the failure to find evidence of an impact of ownership *per se* might imply that ownership does not really matter or instead that firms in some ownership categories have a variety of corporate governance or decision-making structures which are omitted from the regression models with resulting biased regression coefficients. One indication of the sensitivity of results to alternative specifications which incorporate variables which our alternative conceptual framework suggests are important is contained in Standing (1995). After operationalizing a measure of 'human development' (HD) in the enterprise, the impact of differences in HD for enterprise performance is then evaluated by using data for 384 Russian firms. Preliminary empirical work suggests an inverse association between measures of performance, such as labour productivity, and values of HD.

A second approach, first used by Frydman *et al.* (1997), is to estimate growth equations. By using a single indicator of performance, such as labour productivity, this method is broadly comparable to the first approach; however, their work makes significant innovations. Potentially most important, an attempt is made to measure all key variables in privatization (rather than in calendar) time. Moreover, to deal with noisy data, usually they measure the change in average performance over a period of time rather than for a single year. In addition, to focus on the post-privatization performance of firms (and to distinguish privatization from transition effects), a control for inherited pre-privatization differences in performance is included. In their pioneering study that uses this method, Frydman *et al.* (1997) estimate growth equations by using pooled data for 1990–3 for a sample of 185 firms in Poland, Hungary, and the Czech Republic. By using a variety of indicators, including labour productivity, strong evidence is found of privatization effects (when the coefficient on a privatization dummy measures the incremental performance effect specific to privatized firms). To examine the impact of the form of privatization, specifications are estimated in which there is a set of dummies for the largest owner (different forms of privatization) instead of a privatization dummy variable. Relative to state-owned firms, they find that performance is enhanced in outsider-owned firms, while there is no statistically significant effect for firms in which the main group of owners are insiders. Also the performance of firms in which ownership by managers is dominant have far higher rates of productivity growth than do enterprises in which non-managerial employees are the biggest group of owners.

This approach has considerable appeal. Yet, as it is not derived from a well-developed conceptual framework, it too suffers from being somewhat *ad hoc* and also omits variables which our conceptual framework suggests need to be included. In particular, the finding that ownership matters might reflect that what is really happening is that changes in ownership are being accompanied by other changes (which are not being captured by the particular regressions) and that it is these changes that are really driving the productivity gains.

Two other published studies include specifications comparable to those in Frydman *et al.* (1997). Jones (1998) examines the effects of privatization for a sample of Russian firms during 1992–6. By using a single privatization dummy, no evidence was found that privatization affected firm performance. But when a set of dummy variables (reflecting different dominant owners) was used, then the regression analysis provided evidence that ownership sometimes has performance effects. However, only bank-dominated firms were able to increase labour productivity better than the state. In a second study, Jones and Mygind (1998) use panel data for Estonian firms. From regressions where the dummy variable for privatization measures the effect of privatization on labour productivity, it was found that privatization had a statistically insignificant effect. When regressions were estimated in which a set of dummies for the majority owner (different forms of privatization) was included, usually the ownership coefficients again were statistically insignificant. Thus, unlike findings in other transition countries, there is little support for the view that privatization of previously state-owned firms has comparable performance effects in Russia and the Baltics. There is mixed evidence that firms with outside ownership grew faster than those with insider ownership, and that the best-performing form of insider ownership is manager rather than worker ownership.

Moreover, to respond to some of the concerns raised in our theoretical discussion, in Jones (1998) and Jones and Mygind (1998) models are estimated which involve substantial augmentation of the basic 'growth equations' approach. In Jones (1998) the basic specification was augmented by at least one of three sets of other variables which are arguably of importance to the determinants of economic performance: (i) a vector of variables for changes in ownership; (ii) a vector of variables measuring the level of control; and (iii) measures of the dynamics of corporate governance. When diverse specifications along these lines were estimated for Russia, and F-tests were used to select which specification from these augmented approaches best fits the data on productivity growth, evidence was found that ownership dynamics (and not just the current ownership configuration) must be taken into account. Moreover, there is no strong evidence that particular ownership configurations have consistently different impacts on productivity. In addition evidence was found that the effects of variation in decision-making power must be considered in accounting for differences in economic performance. Firms with low or medium levels of employee influence recorded faster growth of labour productivity.[13] For Estonia, where information on employee participation was not available, Jones and Mygind (1998) augment the basic specification by at least one of two sets of other variables which are arguably of importance to economic performance: (i) a vector of variables for *changes* in ownership; and

(ii) a vector of variables to measure the influence of a large minority ownership. The findings do not change dramatically when these alternative specifications are estimated. When performance is measured by labour productivity, F-tests accept the null hypothesis that the joint effect on performance of majority and minority variables is zero.

The third approach follows the dominant econometric approaches in comparative economic systems. Either conventional production functions or stochastic frontier functions are estimated. According to the proponents of the frontier approach, by assuming a non-normal asymmetric disturbance, the strength of the stochastic frontier specification is that it allows the error in standard production functions to be partitioned into an inefficiency component and an error which may represent a number of random effects beyond the control of the firm.[14] A main distinguishing feature of these studies flows from the nature of the available data, including for example whether the researcher is able to use panel data. In addition, studies differ according to whether or not a proxy is used for the measure of the capital stock and in the range of the policy variables besides ownership that are included. Since all of these studies use an econometric approach that is based on a solid conceptual framework and, in attempting to account for differences in business performance, include variables other than just ownership (and in particular proxies for participation in control as well as for participation in economic returns), it is these studies to which we give most attention.

One of the first studies of this type for transition economies is that of Smith *et al.* (1997). A large data set for Slovenian firms is used to examine the impact of ownership by employees and by foreigners on firm performance during a period when much 'spontaneous privatization' had already occurred. Importantly, by using a two-stage Tobit least-squares procedure, they control for simultaneity between privatization and enterprise performance. Based on their second-stage translog production function estimates and the use of continuous measures of ownership, they calculate that both foreign and employee ownership enhance business performance though there is evidence of diminishing marginal productivity gains for both forms of ownership. The elasticity of value added with respect to foreign ownership is estimated to be 3.9 per cent while the corresponding estimate for employee ownership is 1.4 per cent.

A second study of this type is by Jones *et al.* (1998) who use Bulgarian panel data to provide econometric evidence on the productivity effects of diverse variables which our conceptual framework indicates will likely be of importance in accounting for differences in organizational importance, including different forms of compensation for non-managerial workers, employee participation, and non-state forms of ownership during the period 1989–92. While their estimates fail to uncover any effect of labour management relations alone, a joint exclusion test on the vector of proxies for participation in economic returns and participation in control, often leads to rejection of the hypothesis that these factors considered together do not affect productivity. As such, this supports predictions derived from the conceptual framework discussed above in which we typically expect corporate performance to be enhanced from combinations of measures that provide for participation in economic returns and in control, even though individual effects may not always be in evidence.

One of the few econometric studies which examines the impact on output, not only of participation in economic returns (in the sense of profit sharing) but also of employee participation control (proxied by a scalar for employees' perceptions of their involvement in decision making), is that by Vaughan-Whitehead (1998). The author uses Albanian data to estimate cross-sectional OLS translog production functions when these variables are included in an augmented production function and the dependent variable is either sales or value added. In all reported estimates the estimated models account for much of the variation in output and coefficients on the capital and labour inputs are typically estimated at reasonable levels. The effects both of employee participation and different forms of ownership are found to be not significantly different than zero.

Woodward uses data from a panel of 110 Polish companies that were randomly selected from the population of companies that were privatized by the lease method to examine the effects of different aspects of employee participation in economic returns and in control. A production function estimating framework is used to estimate OLS production functions for six separate industries, and models are estimated that specify different forms of technology. The estimates include proxies for different measures of unionization, the percentage of workers that owned shares, the degree of concentration of share ownership, and the proportion of the supervisory board that were non-managerial workers. In the reported estimates, it does not appear that any of the proxies for different aspects of employee participation in economic returns and in control had effects on productivity that were statistically significant.

The impact of privatization on enterprise performance is also investigated by Pohl *et al.* (1997) who, in an ambitious study, use data for about 6,000 industrial firms in seven transition countries—Bulgaria, Czech Republic, Hungary, Poland, Romania, Slovak Republic, and Slovenia. While diverse indicators of restructuring are employed, these include the growth in labour productivity as well as the growth of total factor productivity. To examine the impact of privatization, random effect regression models are estimated using large panels of data for each country, when firms are divided into cohorts according to the number of years that have elapsed since privatization. Also, energy consumption is used as a proxy for capacity utilization. The authors find, as typically have others who have examined these countries, that the impact of privatization on restructuring is typically positive.[15] However, the size of the effects is often larger than has been found in other studies—for example, in Bulgaria, during 1992–5 the growth of labour productivity is found to be 12.4 per cent in privatized firms compared to −1.4 per cent in state firms.[16] Unfortunately, the effect of different forms of private ownership is not examined.

While the Baltic Republics began transition from substantially similar starting points, diverse patterns of enterprise ownership soon emerged. This provides an unusual context in which to test competing theories on the productivity effects of alternative ownership structures. In Jones and Mygind (1999) the strategy is to use large samples of firms from Estonia, Latvia, and Lithuania to enable identical production function specifications to be estimated for all three countries for varying years during the period 1993–6. Specifically a vector of five majority ownership variables—whether the majority owners are employees, managers, domestic outsiders, or foreigners or whether there is no majority (the omitted case is state majority ownership)—is always included. For all countries, and unlike many other studies of transition economies, the measure of enterprise production used is the conceptually preferable value added. For control variables, the data allow inclusion of industry dummies, and one or more dummies that capture important regional dimensions (e.g. in Estonia, location in Tallinn or otherwise). The main findings are: (i) the effects of majority ownership vary over time within a country; (ii) the effects of majority ownership vary across countries; and (iii) majority employee ownership has either positive or zero effects upon productivity. Findings thus provide only weak support for the conventional wisdom.

Finally, Jones and Mygind (1999a) investigate the Estonian case alone. As has been indicated, the emergence of varied ownership configurations enables rigorous evidence on conflicting hypotheses on the effects of different types of private ownership on enterprise performance to be provided. Findings based on a unique enterprise panel and fixed effects production function models indicate that: (i) private ownership is 13–15 per cent more efficient than state ownership; and (ii) majority ownership by foreigners, managers, and employees are, respectively, 19–21 per cent, 15–31 per cent, and 13–24 per cent more productive than state ownership. Findings are robust with respect to choice of technology, the use of instrumental variable estimates to control for potential endogeneity of capital and labour, and the use of different proxies for key variables. As such these results provide only partial support for the standard theory of privatization and stronger support for theorists who argue that insider ownership may be preferred in some circumstances in transition economies. However, the authors were unable to examine for the impact of dimensions of participation other than ownership.

8.4. NEW FORMS OF COMPENSATION

8.4.1. *Incidence*

In the main, much less attention has been directed towards new forms of compensation than to employee ownership. Again, while the available evidence is not as robust as one would wish, nevertheless the data are suggestive that apparently important changes are underway in the forms of compensation received by all types of workers (e.g. Vaughan-Whitehead 1998). From the perspective of our conceptual framework, it is of particular interest to determine what is happening to schemes which provide for employee participation in profits and bonuses.

Some evidence on this is beginning to appear from various sources including ILO labour market surveys. Vaughan-Whitehead (1998) discusses the relevant legal changes introduced in Albania, notably by a 1992 law, to encourage firms to make payments to workers beyond their base wage linked to enterprise profits. The success of the law is revealed in findings based on an initial survey of 335 Albanian firms. Of these, 53 per cent of firms in the state sector and 23 per cent of firms in the private sector had introduced a profit-sharing scheme.

For Bulgaria, the large panel of more than 450 firms that was used in the past in several studies (e.g. Jones *et al.* 1998) was utilized to examine the use of flexible pay methods for non-managerial workers in firms that were formerly in the state sector. Early rounds of the survey indicate that, compared to the late stages of the command economy, the use of profit sharing apparently fell—from 4.9 per cent of sample firms in 1989 to 2.8 per cent in 1992. The use of incentive pay also fell—in 1989 it was present in 38 per cent of firms, compared to 17 per cent in 1992. But more recent data for 1995 show a changing picture. By then, profit sharing was evident in 9 per cent of firms and incentive schemes in 44 per cent of cases.

For Russia, the panel data for St Petersburg previously discussed contain information on the form of compensation for non-managerial employees. These data show that the incidence of flexible forms of payment, such as profit sharing, which covers the largest group of non-managerial workers, has increased markedly during 1992–6. In some cases the data (which are responses from trade union leaders) indicate that the incidence of each of these forms grew by more than 30 per cent during this interval.

Also, the use of bonus payments apparently is widespread in Chinese TVEs (Jefferson and Rawski 1994). Finally, initial examination of preliminary data for each of the Baltic Republics also suggests a tendency for particular forms of flexible pay to grow since the introduction of privatization.

Until recently there was very little detail on what was actually happening in managerial labour markets during transition.[17] However, by using Bulgarian data that are representative of the former state-owned firms, Jones and Kato (1996) report how the pattern of executive pay during early transition suggested substantial inertia compared to arrangements that existed during the fading days of communism. Top managers' reported pay averaged only twice the average workers wage compared to comparable ratios of 13 for Japan and 32 for the US (Kato and Rockel 1992). Fewer than half of the managers had a contract which included a performance-related bonus and typically this amounted to less than 30 per cent of total pay. However, more recent data for 1995 suggest that the incidence of executive contracts with a performance-based compensation component had grown to about 68 per cent of respondents, though in only about one-third of the cases is enterprise profits the criterion to which business success is related.

8.4.2. *Effects of New Forms of Compensation*

Evidence on the effects of incentive systems for managers is quite limited. For China, the most important exception is Groves *et al.* (1994, 1995), who find that greater autonomy for managers in state-owned firms together with contingent contracts has resulted in substantial improvements in enterprise productivity. A study of Polish firms (Pinto *et al.* 1993) argues for the potentially important role of differences in management behaviour (and presumably, by extension, differences in management quality and in the structure of executive compensation) in accounting for some of the differences in firm adjustment during early transition.

Jones and Kato (1996) use Bulgarian panel data to obtain some of the first econometric evidence on the determinants of chief executive compensation. In fixed effects model estimates, chief executive compensation is found to be positively related to size and productivity. The estimated pay elasticities of size of around 0.3 are comparable to what has been found for firms in advanced market economies. The estimated pay elasticities of productivity are equal or slightly greater in size than the estimated pay elasticities of size, pointing to the importance of productivity as a prime determinant of chief executive compensation in transitional economies. On the other hand, the authors do not find a significant relationship between pay and profitability. Another interesting finding is that the link of CEO pay to productivity is stronger for privatized firms than for state-owned firms.

The strong pay–size relationships, coupled with the absence of pay–profitability relationships, suggest that in 1992 executive compensation was still largely structured so as to provide incentives for managers to increase size (or resist downsizing) and pay no attention to profitability. Finally, the stronger pay–productivity relationship for privatized firms suggests that management may become more productivity oriented as privatization progresses.

Overall these findings suggest that significant changes in the determinants of executive compensation are apparent even without widespread privatization. Moreover, the pay–productivity relationships in Bulgaria point to the existence of incentives for managers to increase productivity (or slow down the deterioration of productivity) even when executive pay is a low multiple of average earnings and when incentive pay systems for executives are still rudimentary. As such these findings are consistent with evidence for China where managerial compensation is also a low multiple of average employee pay, though executive bonuses are an important component of overall compensation.

Turning to the effects on firm performance of flexible pay systems for non-managerial employees, the available cross-sectional evidence in transitional economies points to the beneficial effects of payment schemes that provide for more flexible forms of pay (e.g. for Russia see Standing 1997). Also, in his study of Albanian firms, Vaughan-Whitehead (1998) finds that profit sharing has a positive and statistically significant effect on labour productivity.

In addition, Jones *et al.* (1998) use Bulgarian data to provide the first econometric evidence using panel data on the productivity effects of different forms of compensation for non-managerial workers. They find that there are beneficial effects both of profit sharing and incentive pay; cross-sectional results suggest that the size of these individual effects often becomes larger as the transition progresses. Moreover, a joint exclusion test on the vector of proxies for participation in economic returns and participation in control, leads to rejection of the hypothesis that these factors considered together do not affect productivity. As such, this supports predictions derived from the conceptual framework discussed above in which we typically expect corporate performance to be enhanced from combinations of measures that provide for participation in economic returns and in control, even though individual effects may not always be evident.

8.5. CONCLUSIONS AND IMPLICATIONS

A conceptual framework that distinguishes participation in ownership and in economic returns is used to review evidence for diverse transition countries on the nature and effects of key microeconomic determinants of business performance. Particular attention is paid to evidence that uses new panel data for large samples of firms that were formerly (or are currently) state owned in each of the Baltic Republics, Bulgaria and Russia.

A growing body of evidence is appearing on the incidence of schemes which provide for varying degrees of employee participation in economic returns and control. While much additional empirical work is needed to more accurately map the landscape, equally the available evidence indicates that important changes are underway in this area in many transition economies. Specifically it appears that: (i) substantial insider ownership is often prevalent, though majority ownership by non-managerial employees often is eroding fast; (ii) increased employee influence based on individual share ownership is also apparent; however, the links between employee influence and employee ownership are very weak and privatization often does not produce fundamental changes in inherited patterns of corporate governance but rather has served to strengthen *managerial* control; and (iii) there is substantial heterogeneity within countries at any time as well as over time in patterns of ownership and influence.

A growing number of studies have also begun to appear which examine the economic effects of organizational innovations such as changes in ownership. While studies which attempt to isolate the determinants of economic performance always face formidable challenges, in the context of the special conditions facing transition economies, many of these difficulties may be even more demanding. Nevertheless, some studies have reached fairly strong conclusions including support for the propositions that privatization has led to sizeable improvements in firm performance and that, from the standpoint of economic performance, the least preferred form of private ownership is employee ownership (e.g. Aghion and Blanchard 1998).

Our review focuses on the productivity effects of participation and examines evidence for a broader range of empirical strategies than typically have been included in other reviews. It concentrates on econometric evidence and methods that have proven their usefulness in other contexts, paying particular attention to findings from studies which attempt to uncover the effects of a broader range of forms of employee participation than simply participation in ownership. Mindful that much evidence is necessarily preliminary (in part because of dynamic contexts), in general we find: (i) there is no persuasive evidence that a single form of private ownership is most efficient or that the key obstacle to enhanced performance is employee participation in economic returns; (ii) there is some evidence that employee participation enhances business productivity; (iii) there is limited evidence that employee participation also acts to boost the effect of employee ownership and employee participation in profits; and (iv) in accounting for the determinants of differences in labour productivity, there is a role for ownership dynamics as well as for changes in patterns of influence. More generally, it would appear that widely differing ownership structures may be most appropriate when institutional contexts vary. Equally, the existence of considerable variation in productivity across samples of firms in different countries which are substantially similar in respects to policy environment, sector, and size points to the crucial role of institutional and organizational change in determining economic outcomes.

A major policy implication of our findings concerns the recommendation that the main obstacle to economic restructuring is the persistence of employee ownership and that what is needed are policies to undo this practice (e.g. Aghion and Blanchard 1998). Our findings suggest that such conclusions are premature. Indeed, in some cases, our findings imply that what may be most appropriate are policies that enhance employees involvement and also provide for sustained employee ownership. Equally, the strategic rejection of workers' participation by many influential analysts (e.g. Hinds 1990) is striking because, both during the command era and early transition, most forms of 'self-management' were never really tried in most communist economies. Hence it seems reasonable to conclude that, in those transition countries where notions of participation and workers' management were discredited, in part this probably reflects their association with a (non-capitalist) third way that amounted to little more than propaganda from discredited regimes.

On incentive systems, evidence is found of flexible pay systems becoming more prevalent. For managerial pay, there is evidence for both China and Bulgaria of a link between CEO pay and firm productivity. For Bulgaria this link was stronger for privatized and corporatized firms than for firms that are still state owned. In both countries base pay of managers is, by international standards, a low multiple of average pay. In addition, for compensation schemes for other workers, we find evidence of the beneficial effects of schemes which provide for earnings related to firm performance. Our findings imply that introducing performance-based compensation systems right is a policy that potentially will have big payoffs for enterprise performance. At the same time, given the heritage, care must be taken to avoid the development of executive pay systems which lead to managerial pay that is too high relative to average pay—this would be expected to undermine the benefits which flow from the introduction of performance-based pay schemes for non-managerial workers.

NOTES

1. The paper has benefited from comments from participants at a WIDER workshop, notably V. Popov. Support from NSF SES 9511465 and the National Council on Soviet and Eastern European Studies is gratefully acknowledged.
2. In this paper the focus is on factors within the firm. Space prevents consideration of the role of other potentially important determinants of business performance such as competition.
3. For references, see Nuti (1996, p. 5).
4. For accounts of privatization in former communist countries, see Estrin (ed.) (1994).
5. A good review of these studies is reported in Estrin and Wright (1999).
6. These ownership surveys were designed primarily by Mygind in collaboration with teams of social scientists in each of the Baltic Republics. For further information, see Mygind (1995) and Jones and Mygind (1998).

7. Various other channels exist for employee participation. However, much less evidence is available on the significance of structures such as membership in trade unions and other bodies providing for collective representation (such as works councils).
8. Thus the bulk of respondents felt that in four issue areas—method of privatization, choice of supervisors, wage policy, and employment policy—there was either no employee influence (management decides) or a modest amount of employee influence (falling well short of management and workers jointly deciding). For both samples, there is some evidence that employee influence was relatively weakest concerning issues of employment and wage determination and relatively strongest concerning choice of supervisors.
9. Moreover, a simple regression accepts the hypothesis that there is no correlation between employee ownership and employee membership on the board.
10. Finally, there is evidence that in 1993 and 1994, compared to the situation that prevailed before mass privatization, there was a slight fall in the perceived degree of employee influence on particular issues. This reduction in employee perceptions of influence is especially pronounced in privatized firms.
11. Most researchers agree that productivity is a key concern for firms in transitional economies. However, some believe that a battery of indicators are needed to gauge performance (e.g. Frydman *et al.* 1997), while others believe that the poor quality of the data may require an approach that focuses on qualitative indicators (e.g. Buck *et al.* 1998).
12. While other approaches have been used, thus far such studies are less common. These include the use of restructuring indexes and the modelling of equity prices as leading indicators of differences in firm performance.
13. However, since these data are from one region in Russia, the findings are not necessarily representative for the entire country; as well, the sample is relatively small and some potentially important econometric matters have not been addressed.
14. By contrast, production functions estimate *average* practice production processes. However, critics of frontier techniques argue that such methods are potentially unduly sensitive to outliers.
15. Recall the findings of, for example, Frydman *et al.* (1999) for Poland, Hungary, and the Czech Republic, Jones *et al.* (1998) for Bulgaria, and Smith *et al.* (1997) for Slovenia.
16. Also during this period there were relatively few private industrial firms in existence in Bulgaria.
17. For China see Bolton (1995), for Russia Linz (1995), and for Bulgaria Jones *et al.* (1995).

9

Unorthodox Ownership and Governance Structures in Transitional East Asia

LAIXIANG SUN

9.1. INTRODUCTION: THE OWNERSHIP PUZZLE IN THE TRANSITION ECONOMIES

This chapter examines the nature of the unorthodox ownership and governance structures which have emerged in the transitional economies of East Asia and the way in which these structures have supported the remarkable economic growth in the region. These economies are embarked on a distinctive process of property rights reform that resists widespread privatization and favours instead an evolutionary transformation of the pre-existing property rights regimes.

Privatization has been one of the earliest consensus views on the post-communist transition and has been a central feature of the transition in Eastern Europe and the former Soviet Union. In theoretical terms, the supposed strength of privatization is derived from the orthodox property rights theory which purports that the existence of well-defined private property rights is a basic precondition for the proper functioning of a market economy. As a corollary, the creation of clear and legally enforceable private property rights for firms is seen as the only way to remedy the problems associated with the soft-budget constraint, the bureaucratic bargaining prevailing in the state sector, and the long-lasting inefficiency of state-owned enterprises (SOEs). By creating property owners who are liable for the consequences of bad decisions, but who are entitled to the rewards of good ones and who are willing to offer better incentives to both managers and workers, privatization is thus perceived as the most direct avenue for unlocking gains in economic efficiency.

After a painful decade of reforms, it is now widely acknowledged in the former socialist economies of Europe that privatization has turned out to be much more difficult and costly than expected. Furthermore, the key outcome of this process, the emerging post-privatization ownership structure, is quite complex, and—with few exceptions—its evolution has not been accompanied by the development of clear and legally enforceable private property rights. On the one hand, the privatization of former SOEs has led to a complex web of cross ownerships involving banks, investment funds, other enterprises, state asset management agencies, and local governments. In addition, in nearly all these countries, the resultant governance structure is characterized by strong insider control, especially by the old managerial class (see Chapters 8 and 11). On the other hand, many of the new private firms still turn to the state for all kinds of financial rents. Subsidies, tariff protection, legal monopolies, and regulations entailing redistributions favouring the enterprise sector still prevail even where direct state ownership has become rare (see, for instance, Brada 1996; Frydman et al. 1996; Gurkov 1997; Stark 1996). Taken together, these developments indicate that the steering of post-privatization ownership and governance structures and the introduction of incentives which promote economic efficiency rather than rent-seeking behaviour remain a great challenge in most European post-communist countries (Havrylyshyn and McGettigan 1999).

The property rights reform followed in the East Asian economies in transition contrasts markedly with the privatization approach adopted in Eastern Europe and Russia. Although it has been officially stated that the industrial reform in East Asia involves management reform, but not ownership reform, there is much evidence demonstrating that the clarification and reassignment of various property rights among different levels of governments, between government and enterprise, and among parties within the enterprises, have progressed substantially if in a piecemeal, incremental and indirect fashion. While reformers at the national level have established the broad parameters of enterprise reform, the actual outcomes have to a large extent depended on the specific degree of competition at the local and enterprise levels. Within an increasingly competitive environment, poor performance results in immediate financial distress, which gives rise to pressures for reform.

In contrast to the unprecedented fall in output, employment and incomes witnessed during the transition in Eastern Europe and Russia, the SOE sector of the East Asian transition economies has done well relative to international standards. In China, the real output of industrial SOEs grew by 7.5 per cent per year from 1978 to 1997 despite increasing competition (SSB 1998, p. 433). The share of medium and large SOEs (over 500 employees) in total industrial output remained approximately constant at about 41 per cent between 1978 and 1994 (Naughton 1995, pp. 164–7, 330–1; SSB 1995, p. 377). Yet, the financial situation of the SOE sector has been worsening in parallel with the steady growth of its output (Bai et al. 1997).

In the case of Vietnam, industrial SOEs have maintained a dominant role in the economy, as their contribution to GDP climbed from 22.7 per cent in 1990 to 36.5 per cent in 1994, and have maintained this level ever since (IMF 1999a, table 2), despite the liquidation of several thousand loss-making SOEs, the elimination of government subsidies, the substantial reduction of the implicit subsidies provided through the banking system, and the institution of the principle of equal taxation between state and private firms (see Chapter 5). Given the average GDP growth rate of 7 per cent recorded over the period 1990–8, these data are indicative of a remarkable improvement in the performance of SOEs (Dodsworth et al. 1996; IMF 1999b, table 3).

Fixed-term asset leasing, prevalent in Laos and Cambodia after 1990, did not change the structure of ownership, but was a practical way to change the governance structure, to effectively harden the budget constraint of the SOEs, to provide much greater incentives to improve performance to the managers of state enterprises, and to prepare the ground for a smooth privatization of state assets in the future (Otani and Pham 1996; World Bank 1994*a*; IMF 1998, pp. 60–2; 1999*c*, table 29).

The greatest achievement of the Chinese economic reforms is probably the emergence of the township and village enterprises (TVEs). The TVEs realized a real average output growth of 21 per cent per annum between 1978 and 1995 and of over 18 per cent in 1996 and 1997. In 1993, the TVE sector exceeded the state sector in terms of industrial production and employment generation. It produced 44.5 per cent of total industrial output and provided employment to 123 million people, whereas the state sector accounted for 43 per cent of total industrial output and employed 109 million people (SSB 1996, pp. 87, 388–9, 403; *People's Daily*, 28 February 1998). The emergence of rural enterprises on such a large scale and at such a rapid rate has never been experienced in any other developed or developing country. Moreover, the TVEs seem to possess features that are unparalleled in any economic organizations in the West or other socialist economies. Understanding the driving forces behind the TVE growth is thus of great importance to policy makers in both transitional and developing economies.

Private enterprises in transitional East Asia tend to need the support of community authorities. However, this support comes at a price, that is, the sharing in both residual benefits rights and residual control rights. As a result, such firms are far from representative of private ownership as this is commonly understood. Instead, they exhibit ambiguous property rights arrangements that involve sharing between private entrepreneurs and community authorities (Li 1996). Although such arrangements rely on the existence of a particular community spirit and a set of ambiguous and personalized relationships that may undermine the long-term development of these enterprises, it has certainly been mutually beneficial during the transition.

The different transition experiences reviewed in this volume suggest that our thinking about property rights needs to depart from the Marxist practice of assuming that an 'owner' is an individual or a homogeneous monolithic group (e.g. a group of capitalist-minded shareholders). More generally, a comparison of different transitional experiences suggests that the process of change in this area should be treated not as the immediate replacement of the old property regimes with new institutions and organizations, but as a gradual process involving the disassembly and reassembly of existing institutional configurations. To stimulate an incentive-based institutional transformation, it is desirable to adopt a dual-track strategy focusing on the introduction of supply incentives and the development of new market institutions that combine the benefits of market principles with the organizational and social capital inherited from the socialist era. In this process, it is critical to provide incentives to governments to transform their role from that of a rent grabber to that of a promoter of the development of market intermediaries and institutions and dispute–settling mechanisms.

9.2. INNOVATIVE TRANSFORMATION AND PROPERTY RIGHTS REFORM: THEORETICAL ISSUES

9.2.1. *Market Transition as a Process of Innovative Adaptation*

As James Buchanan (1979, p. 29) emphasizes, 'a market is not competitive by assumption or by construction', but 'becomes competitive, and competitive rules come to be established as institutions emerge' to shape behaviour. Such a 'process of becoming' is bound to go far beyond any kind of rationalist design or central planning, because the process evolves from sequences of economizing behaviour, market-learning institutional evolution, technical innovation, and, particularly, a multitude of cumulative and mutually reinforcing choices by numerous actors who have diverse interests and constantly evaluate alternatives and reconsider their previous views.

In the West, the market economy did not originate from a given blueprint, but developed through a long evolutionary process. The concrete institutions now operating in the West are rooted in capitalist structures and grew up through adaptive evolution. They cannot be directly replicated in the East. A key lesson from the failure of central planning—i.e. that one cannot organize all economic processes into a grand design—suggests that attempting to replicate market institutions by following a rationalist design is also doomed to failure.

The transition to the market is bound to be path dependent. The transition is not a simple shift between two social orders in a situation of equilibrium. In Eastern Europe and Russia, the collapse of the communist regime did not occur in an institutional vacuum and most of the organizational structures and social relations of the socialist era are still in existence. During the 1980s, market-like transactions and relations were common also in the socialist sector of the economy and in the 'second economy' (Kornai 1980; Laky 1979; Sabel and Stark 1982). During the transition, existing informal structures and networks have played an important role in the enterprises struggle for survival. The interaction of market structures and earlier types of organization has favoured and will continue to favour the emergence of hybrid forms of economic organization.

According to Williamson (1991), between the polar modes of the market and hierarchy, hybrid governance structures generally possess their own institutional advantages. In the transition economies, hybrid governance structures may have greater significance, because they 'use resources and/or governance structures from more than one existing organization' (Borys and Jemison 1989, p. 235) and thus are capable of reducing uncertainty in inter-organizational relationships involving bilateral or multilateral dependence and of supplying a flexible contract mechanism to facilitate continuity and efficient adaptation. In comparison with hybrids in advanced capitalist economies, hybrids in transition economies lack a well-specified structure of property rights. Therefore, they also lack sufficient autonomy and are faced with rapid changes and institutional uncertainty. For this reason, transitional hybrids of superior adaptive capacity are bound to be more flexible, informal, and open to entrepreneurship. They must rely more on social capital such as personal ties and local contacts rather than on legal contracts to provide assurances that the terms of a transaction will be met by both parties (Nee 1992; Carroll *et al.* 1988).

9.2.2. Ownership as a Bundle of Rights

Property rights are relationships among people or organizations that arise from the existence of scarce goods, pertain to the use of these goods, and are sanctioned by norms, custom and law. An owner of property rights holds the consent of others to act in particular ways without interference by the community, provided that the ways are not prohibited in the specification of the rights. This definition of property rights is consistent with Roman law, common law, Karl Marx's writings, and the new institutional economics (Demsetz 1967; Pejovich 1990, chapter 4). Within the general concept of property rights, the ownership right is the most well-known category consisting of a bundle of rights. The core bundle of rights includes the following three elements:

1. The right to utilize an asset, that is, the 'utilization right' or the 'control right'. This is also a collection of numerous specific rights, including management, decision making, and the supervision of utilization. There is a widespread division between ownership and control in modern corporations and in SOEs. Thus, the daily control of the asset is delegated by the owners to their agents or professional managers. For this reason, a residual control right, usually involving the right to appoint and remove managers and other rights beyond the content of contracts, is assumed to be the crucial dimension of ownership. Nonetheless, the separation of ownership from control is definitely a delegation of selected property rights to management. It requires the owner to create a variety of incentive schemes to assure that the management team satisfactorily performs the control functions.
2. The right to capture benefits from the utilization specified under case 1 above and the responsibility for negative outcomes such as debts and damages, namely, the 'return right'. This involves the right to establish rules concerning the distribution of earnings. As an alternative to the notion that residual control rights should be treated as the crucial dimension of ownership, the right to collect residual returns is proposed as the key feature of ownership by Milgrom and Robert (1990) and others (for example Zou 1992). Because of the fact that state socialist economies are commonly recognized as 'redistributive', distribution rights may be more relevant to the reform of property rights in the transition economies.

    In order to clarify further the significance of the right to residual returns in the process of property rights reform in East Asia, let us consider the position of the insider entity of an SOE under the 'contract responsibility system' accepted by the entity (quanyuan chengbao). Taking the simplest case, the entity pays a fixed amount of taxes and profits to the government in exchange for the use of government-owned assets and keeps the residual. Thus, all the employees of the SOE, rather than the principal government, possess the right to the residual returns.
3. The right to change the form or substance of the asset and the right to transfer all or some of the rights specified above to others at a mutually agreed price or as a gift.

This right is usually referred to as the 'alienation right'. It involves the decision to buy or sell the asset and defines the owner's right to effect changes in the value of the specified asset.

Theoretically, an infinite number of configurations of property rights is possible. The historical configurations of property rights are, nonetheless, created by social actors, shaped by struggles among various interests, and subject to changes over time and within different institutional environments. In recent years, the problems encountered in the enforcement of property rights are central in the literature of contracts, industrial organization, and bureaucracies in the West, because the 'attenuation' of property rights has become increasingly significant. An attenuation of property rights is usually induced by the restrictions imposed by government regulations on asset use, on the income flows from the asset, and on the freedom of an owner to transfer some portion of property rights to others (Campbell and Lindberg 1990; Walder 1994).

In contrast to the trend whereby many of the restrictions established by the state through legal provisions are attenuating property rights in the West, the process of economic reform in the transition economies of East Asia is characterized by the downward devolution of property rights in political and administrative hierarchies or the reassignment and clarification of property rights among institutions, communities, and households. Economic reform in East Asia has been dominated by the devolution of selected property rights over assets—particularly a large share of utilization rights and residual claim rights—from higher to lower levels of government administration or from government authorities to enterprises, households, and individuals. These specific reassignments have significantly altered the incentives for economic behaviour, the distributional pattern of subsequent income flows, the structure of political power and interests, and thus the ownership and governance structures of SOEs (see for example Lin *et al.* 1996; Naughton 1995; Walder 1994, 1995).

9.3. PROPERTY RIGHTS REFORM IN THE SOE SECTOR: PROCESSES AND CONSEQUENCES

9.3.1. *Understanding Local Government Property Rights Over SOEs in East Asia*

The existence of local government property rights over SOEs and the substantial downward devolution of financial power over residual revenues have played a leading role in the initiation of reforms of property rights. A description of the features and functions of local government property rights would thus help the understanding of the process of reassignment of property rights between SOEs and their supervisory government bodies.

As argued in Granick (1990, pp. 39–44), the property rights of regional governments over SOEs in China have existed at least since the early 1970s. However, before reform, monetary income was of lesser importance, and thus the financial interests of local governments were weak. The ownership rights of local governments over their SOEs were exercised through control over the distribution of marginal output at the regional level, the management of SOE operations, material allocation within the constraint of delivery quotas for the central government, and the use of depreciation funds.

The fiscal reform of the 1980s fundamentally altered the situation through the devolution of financial property rights from higher to lower levels of government and from supervisory government bodies to enterprises. First, instead of governments appropriating all profits from their own SOEs automatically, the SOEs were to be taxed according to fixed rates. The residual income left to the SOEs served to supply spontaneous incentives to managers and workers. Second, from the tax revenue collected from their own enterprises, each level of government turned over a contractually specified amount to the next higher level of government, while retaining the residual.

This system has given local governments the incentive to exercise financial property rights more effectively over the assets they administer. The better the financial performance of the local enterprises and the more rapid the economic growth of the region, the greater the annual increase in the revenues available to government control (see, e.g. Wong 1992; World Bank 1994*b*; Walder 1995). Such direct causality has pushed local governments to initiate experimental reform programmes far ahead of the central government (Zhang and Yi 1995).

The greater control over residual revenues has been accompanied by more expenditure responsibility. Local governments must strain to meet the expenditure obligations imposed by the policies of higher level governments. They must take direct responsibility for the solution of the large range of social problems arising from unemployment, housing shortages, infrastructure deficiencies, growing dissatisfaction among consumers, and so on. They must also promote rapid local economic growth so as to enhance their own negotiating position within the hierarchy.

Because they have the smallest revenue base and are confronted with the strongest pressure from rising living standards and growing competition, township and village governments have shown the most motivation to develop TVEs and private enterprises (Oi 1996). In turn, as the relevant political restrictions set by the central government have become more flexible, county and prefectural governments have been the most interested in the restructuring of their own most inefficient small-scale SOEs through a great diversity of bold methods, including the establishment of joint ventures with foreign investors, the introduction of employee stock ownership plans, the sale or lease of SOE assets to management and employees, the sale of SOEs to outside investors, liquidation, and equitization (Sun 1997).[1]

In the case of Vietnam, provincial and local governments historically enjoyed considerable economic autonomy from the central government (Probert and Young 1995). During the years of the Democratic Republic of Vietnam (1954–75), the efforts to strengthen central control were in fact reversed because of the war in the south. Most of the SOEs already established in urban areas were forced to move into the mountainous regions. Local self-sufficiency in supply was clearly a critical factor for survival. This primacy of self-sufficiency led in turn to the establishment of more locally run SOEs.

The record of economic changes in Vietnam since unification has shown a cyclical pattern. The cycle begins with the efforts of the government to impose central planning. An economic crisis follows. Meanwhile, local governments and their SOEs start to resist the central planning by 'fence breaking' and expanding market-oriented activities. These activities are tolerated by the central government to a certain extent, and, as a result, the crisis is overcome. Ironically, the economic recovery may lead to new support for the central planning model, as occurred in 1982–3. The readoption of this model induces a new economic crisis and, as a consequence, a new round of reform (Fforde and de Vylder 1996; Probert and Young 1995).

In the Lao People's Democratic Republic, 'the local level is a constant objective structure of the Lao society' (Kaysone Phomvihane, the secretary general of the Lao Communist Party, cited in Evans (1988, pp. 31–2)). Laos does not possess a unified national economy. Rather, it has a combination of a central economy and local economies. In most cases, the governments at each level are organized like sovereign entities, since there is no telecommunications between the capital and most provincial centres, and more than half the road network is impassable in the rainy season. Local administrations are under the sole authority of the presidents of the local administrative committees. The modern sector, which plays only a marginal role in the economy, is likewise extremely fragmented. Each sectoral administration at each level of government supervises those SOEs located on its territory and in its sector. As a consequence, the Lao experience indicates that there is no scope for building socialism in a subsistence economy, and this has finally been admitted by the party (see for instance Bourdet 1995; Evans 1988; Funck 1993).

9.3.2. *The Reassignment of Property Rights in the SOE Sector*

9.3.2.1. *The Case of China*

Prior to the reform, the ownership rights of the different levels of government over their SOEs were far more extensive than those exercised by the owner of a firm in a market economy. The governments exerted direct control over all factors of production within the SOE sector. Customers, suppliers, managers, technicians, and workers all had only very limited freedom to exercise autonomous choice, because of the absence of product and factor markets and legal guarantees. The absence of choice in fact precluded the right of production factors to enter into voluntary contracts that specified rewards and obligations. If one views this causality from the opposite perspective, it can be seen that the creation of product and factor markets and the choice enjoyed by market participants would undermine government control and coercion. Markets disperse effective ownership and favour voluntary contracts to specify rewards and obligations. This means that in the transition economies competitive markets have an additional function: to induce and promote property rights reform (Jefferson *et al.* 1998).

Three sets of SOE property rights reforms have been successively implemented along with 'stop–go' cycles in China. The first two have been characterized by the reassignment of selected control rights and claim rights to residual returns, whereas the third one has involved the reassignment of alienation rights as well.

The first reform effort, undertaken between 1979 and 1983, consisted of tentative steps towards an expansion of the role of financial incentives through a moderate margin of profit retention and towards improved performance through greater enterprise autonomy. The SOEs selected for the reform experiments had the right to retain a share of profits, enjoyed a relatively higher depreciation rate, and had the right to sell any above-plan output. Although the programme as initially proposed applied only to a small number of SOEs, officials at various levels of government quickly saw the benefits of profit retention by their own SOEs. As a result, the programme was extended nationwide (Lin *et al.* 1996, pp. 138–40; Naughton 1995, pp. 99–100).

The second round of SOE property rights reforms was implemented between 1984 and 1988 and remained in force between 1989 and 1992. It centred on two innovations: a dual-track pricing system and the enterprise contract responsibility system. The dual-track pricing system effectively partitioned SOE inputs and outputs into planned and marketed components. Actively responding to this system, most SOEs steadily boosted their marginal sales and purchases on the markets so as to catch the benefits arising from market transactions. Under the contract responsibility system, SOE managers and employees agreed to fulfil specific obligations. These typically involved targets for profits and productivity, as well as other profit-sharing rules. The targets were negotiated individually for each enterprise. In return, the SOEs obtained greater control over business operations, such as drafting output plans, pricing, marketing, fixing wage and bonus differentials, and making decisions on the use of retained profits and depreciation funds (Jefferson *et al.* 1998).

The contract responsibility system and dual-track price system had greatly enhanced entrepreneurial responses to market-determined supply and demand signals. However, because of the rapidly changing environment, profit targets had to be renegotiated annually. As a consequence, managers had to be concerned with 'ratchet' effects, that is, an increase in the coming year's profit targets imposed on successful performers. Government entities continued to be involved in the determination of every aspect of a firm's compensation schedule. More negatively, in order to assure growth in wages and bonuses, SOE managers would boost profits in the short term by cutting depreciation allowances, under-reporting operation costs, postponing necessary investment, and neglecting asset maintenance (Sun 1992).

The third round of property rights reform was initiated in 1992, following the decisive push for renewed reform by Deng Xiaoping. Since then, the international media have paid a great deal of attention to the two new stock exchanges in Shanghai and Shenzhen. The establishment of stock exchanges in a socialist country like China does indicate a fundamental change. In terms of property rights reform, however, the change is more ideological than practical. The stock exchanges are still considered a government experiment. Substantial limitations have been imposed on their development. The number of companies listed on the stock markets is tightly controlled, and there is no guarantee that all firms satisfying the strict requirements can be listed (Sun 1997).

The most radical reform was once again initiated by local governments. Taking advantage of the renewed impulse for reform, local governments obtained a more flexible commitment from the centre to allow experimentation with local firms. Seeing an opportunity, a number of cities and provinces took the bold, radical step of reassigning ownership rights over SOEs. The most impressive reform was implemented by cities, particularly county- and prefectural-level cities. County and prefectural SOEs have typically been the most inefficient ones. These SOEs are often too small to rely on economies of scale, but overly weighed down by bureaucracies to be able to exploit their small size as TVEs usually can. Finding ways to offset the rising losses of local SOEs has been the number one headache for most county and prefectural governments. The reform measures adopted by local governments have included the sale of SOEs to insiders and outside investors, the lease of SOE assets to management and employees, and permission for foreign companies and other non-state institutions to take over local SOEs (for details, see Sun 1997).

Although there was a heated debate over these measures among central government officials and the ideological authorities of the party until the Fifteenth Party Congress held in September 1997, the majority of the reactions have since been relatively much more positive. This round of reform has garnered remarkable benefits in efficiency, without, meanwhile, generating any substantial social costs such as notable unemployment or temporary cuts in production. This is mainly because the local governments have promoted local revenue creation, assured social stability, and been able to play the leading role in the design and implementation of the reform process. The significant efficiency benefits and limited social costs of these reforms induced the party to finally accept them in the documents of the Fifteenth Congress (Jiang 1997; Sun 1997).

It should be pointed out that the third set of property rights reforms has been initiated in only a relatively small number of cities, which are located in coastal areas. The great majority of SOEs still suffer from the unresolved problems accompanying the second round of reform. Particularly due to the less favourable structural conditions and the greater fiscal dependence on the central government, the pace of reform in the vast interior regions has lagged far behind that along the coast (Raiser 1996). The SOE sector is still characterized by excessive production capacity, the insufficient use of facilities, redundant workers, outdated technologies, low energy efficiency, high production costs, and poor competitiveness. The reform of SOEs in the structurally weaker interior regions of the country will continue to be a major dilemma for economic policy makers (Gui 1999).

9.3.2.2. *The Case of Vietnam*
Similar to the reform process in China, in Vietnam three sets of SOE property rights reforms can be identified. The first set of reforms was undertaken between 1979 and 1982 and, in a somewhat altered fashion, between 1982 and 1985. It was characterized by spontaneous 'fence breaking' at the grassroots.

By the end of the 1970s, material shortages, the threat of widespread famine, and the near isolation of Vietnam from the outside world had essentially wrecked the system of state allocations for subsidized inputs and of state procurements of consumer goods for rationing. SOEs had to establish horizontal contacts with each other and, more importantly, to participate in free market activities in order to solve the most acute shortages of food, inputs, and spare parts. Consequently, SOEs began to swap or sell their products on the free market in order to earn cash so that they could fulfil their needs, likewise on the free market.

These spontaneous steps to maintain and stimulate production received some political support during the VI Party Plenum in August 1979. A government decree recognized the fence-breaking activities and announced the launch of a 'three-plan' system. Under Plan A, SOEs were to use the subsidized inputs supplied by the state to reach output quotas, which were set by the state. The output was also to be procured by the state. In return, Plan-A SOEs were permitted to keep 50 per cent of their profits. Plan B, which could only be initiated if additional inputs were required for the production of 'list' goods subject to the state monopoly, permitted SOEs to acquire materials from non-state sources. In this case, the share of the profits that could be retained by an SOE increased to 60 per cent. Under Plan C, SOEs were permitted to produce items not in the state plan, sell them freely at negotiated prices, and keep 90 per cent of the profit.

It is widely accepted that the three-plan system contributed to the recovery in state industrial output in the early 1980s. The annual industrial growth rate averaged about 9 per cent during those years. Nevertheless, the most clearly marked recovery occurred in areas sensitive to market demand and in which domestic raw materials were readily available (see, e.g. Fforde and de Vylder 1996, pp. 138–9; McCarty 1993; Probert and Young 1995).

The second round of reform, undertaken during 1986–9, focused initially on macroeconomic issues such as further price liberalization, the elimination of local trade barriers, and the shift away from the heavy-industry-oriented development strategy. It was a bold response to the spiralling inflation and other compelling economic problems caused by the reassertion of the command-economy model and rural collectivization during 1982–5.

The SOE reform was renewed through two principal pieces of legislation issued in 1988. The SOEs which were officially included in a 'new statute' could make a 'single contribution to the state budget' that took the form of taxes rather than planned output quotas. These SOEs were also given greater autonomy and were encouraged to establish market-like linkages with other enterprises and among different sectors. However, most large SOEs were excluded from the reform (Fforde and de Vylder 1996; Probert and Young 1995).

Along with the substantial marketization, structural readjustment, and increasing openness to the world market, the market share of SOEs was reduced by a large amount, even as government orders continued to fall significantly. The result was a twofold growth in inventories by 1990. At the end of 1989, fully 40 per cent of all SOEs were recording heavy losses, and only about 20 per cent seemed to be operating at a profit (Thanh 1995; Probert and Young 1995). Moreover, the urgency of the SOE reform was sharpened by a new external shock, the withdrawal of Soviet aid, which in various forms had accounted for about 40 per cent of the government budget.

Under such conditions, budgetary considerations alone could force the government to cut its fiscal subsidies to SOEs and to seek to eliminate loss-making SOEs. Thus, the third set of SOE reforms, initiated in 1989, consisted of cuts in budget subsidies for SOEs, the establishment of positive real interest rates, the shutdown of hopelessly loss-making SOEs, and the transfer of the management and financial responsibilities for SOEs to SOE managers, including full autonomy in determining prices, the formulation of production plans, and investment decisions.

This round of reform led to substantial changes in the SOE sector. Over 2,800 SOEs were liquidated, and another 3,000 were merged with viable SOEs, so that by early 1994, only about 6,500–7,000 SOEs remained registered with the State Planning Commission. The 800,000 layoffs which resulted were mainly absorbed by the rapidly developing non-state sector.

The economic benefits of these reforms were also significant. Budget deficits were substantially reduced. The SOE sector showed a strong growth trend and maintained its GDP share despite the remarkable GDP growth rates. The profitability of SOEs was improved as well, although soft bank credit and protective entry barriers were introduced once again for some SOEs in essential industries, and there is still a considerable degree of management weakness in SOEs (see, e.g. Dollar 1994; Irvin 1995; Probert and Young 1995).

Since the second round of reform, SOEs in Vietnam have benefited greatly from foreign investment in the form of joint ventures. Between 1988 and 1994, foreign investment accounted for a combined total of about 10 percentage points (one-fifth) of cumulative growth. Foreign investment has also played an important role in the transfer of technology and in the introduction of modern organization and management techniques. Owing to their established links with policy makers, their preferential access to quotas, land and bank credits, and their relatively larger size, SOEs have been a more attractive domestic partner in joint ventures (Dodsworth *et al.* 1996; IMF 1999*a*). Because official statistics record the output of these joint ventures as SOE output, the development of SOE joint ventures partly explains the relatively strong performance of the SOE sector (see Chapter 5).

9.3.2.3. *The Case of Laos*
By the end of the 1980s, the SOE sector in Laos comprised about 640 enterprises and accounted for virtually all of the modern industrial sector. SOEs employed about 16,000 workers, or around 10 per cent of the non-agricultural labour force. Roughly one-third of the SOEs were centrally managed, while the rest, which were usually smaller, were managed by provincial and district governments. Three-quarters of the SOEs were engaged in manufacturing, and the others in construction, electricity, and mining (Otani and Pham 1996).

Before 1990, the SOE reforms in Laos appeared no different from those in Vietnam (Rana 1995, table 2). The emphasis was on the granting of greater managerial autonomy to SOEs. By March 1988, almost full operating autonomy had been delegated to SOE management. SOEs were free to determine their output levels and mix, their wages and prices, and their investment plans. In the meantime, subsidies and capital transfers to SOEs had been terminated. Responding to the changes, some SOEs strategically transformed their financial obligations into overdue debts to the banking system and used their autonomy to raise the cash wages of their employees.

In response to such strategic behaviour and the weak performance of SOEs, a privatization programme was implemented in March 1991. By December 1994, 64 of the 200 or so centrally managed SOEs existing in 1989 had been privatized. Data available on 58 of these privatizations show that 78 per cent of the relevant SOEs were leased for fixed terms (15 years on average), 19 per cent were sold outright, and 3 per cent were hire-purchased (i.e. the sale price was paid in instalments). The average value of the SOEs which were leased (about $40,000) was higher than that of the SOEs which were sold (around $23,000) or that of the SOEs which were hire-purchased (about $3,000). At the provincial level, the sale of SOEs, rather than leasing, seemed to play a more important role. Between 1988 and mid-1993, more than 52 provincially managed SOEs were sold, and more than 29 were leased.

Why did fixed-term leasing become prevalent in the initial stage of privatization? The answer certainly cannot be limited to the government's reluctance to do more. Several reasons are listed by Otani and Pham (1996, p. 47). Leasing may have been more politically acceptable than outright sales because of a concern among the public that the nation's property might be entirely sold off. Because of uncertainty about the value of SOEs and about the effectiveness of the economic reforms, the private sector may have preferred the less risky option of leasing. When alternative modes of privatization are too costly, contracting out or leasing to employee collectives becomes practical. If SOEs are relatively large or require technology that is more sophisticated than the technology domestic sources are able to provide, joint ventures become more attractive.

Although fixed-term leasing has benefits over the medium run, it can cause problems in the long run. Leasing does not involve the transfer of residual control rights, and management structures are shifted only for a limited period. These two characteristics represent disincentives for long-term investment and even encourage decapitalization because, with an average lease period of 15 years, leaseholders may have only a limited horizon. From the government perspective, monitoring the leased SOEs is difficult and costly. Largely due to the experience with these disadvantages, Lao privatization programmes since 1995 have become increasingly dominated by sales (IMF 1998, pp. 60–6).

9.4. OWNERSHIP AND GOVERNANCE STRUCTURES OF TVEs IN CHINA

In official statistics in China 'township and village enterprise' (TVE) covers a wide range of ownership categories, including collective ownership by township and village communities, private ownership by households and groups of households, joint ownership by domestic and foreign investors, and joint ownership by domestic shareholders (Table 9.1). The sector does not include SOEs and enterprises owned by

Table 9.1. *The output, employment, and number of rural enterprises in China, 1995*

	Total	Township	Village	Joint	Household
Business revenue (yuan, billions)	5,729.9	1,598.8	1,615.4	424.4	2,091.3
Share (%)	100.0	27.9	28.1	7.4	36.5
Employment (millions)	128.6	30.3	30.3	8.7	59.2
Share (%)	100.0	23.5	23.5	6.8	46.0
Number of firms (1,000s)	22,030.0	420.0	1,200.0	960.0	19,450.0
Share (%)	100.0	1.9	5.4	4.4	88.2

Source: Yearbook of China's Township and Village Enterprises (1996, p. 99).

urban collectives, although it does include enterprises owned jointly by urban and rural enterprises.

In 1995, enterprises owned by townships and villages accounted for 47 per cent of employment in the TVE sector and produced the dominant portion (56 per cent) of total business revenue. The individual household-run enterprises accounted for 53 per cent of employment and 44 per cent of revenue. The shares of jointly owned private enterprises in both employment and output were relatively small.

In the discussion which follows, TVEs are understood in the narrower sense of collective ownership only. The ownership characteristics of household-run enterprises and other private enterprises, as well as the close links between them and TVEs, will be analysed in the next section.

The range of activities undertaken by TVEs is much broader than their name implies. These activities include all 40 industrial categories appearing in Chinese statistics, as well as agriculture, construction, transportation and communications, and commerce and services. Some TVEs have reached beyond China to set up joint ventures in Eastern Europe, Russia, Southeast Asia, and the US (Wong *et al*. 1995). Forty TVEs are traded on domestic stock exchanges, and one is traded on the Hong Kong Stock Exchange (*People's Daily*, 16 October 1999).

The annual growth rate of the exports of TVEs has been above 30 per cent since the mid-1980s. Since 1993, TVE exports have accounted for over 41 per cent of the national total. They include textiles, garments, arts and crafts, chemicals, machinery, and electronics and communications equipment (Perotti *et al*. 1999). TVEs also vary in size. For example, by the end of 1995, there were 5,824 large TVE corporations, each of which had an annual business revenue of over $12 million (CTVEs Net, 4 August 1997).

There is an obvious contradiction between the outstanding performance of TVEs and the outcome predicted by traditional property rights theory. As pointed out by Weitzman and Xu (1994), first, a typical TVE has no owner in the sense of traditional property rights theory. Nominally, TVEs are collectively owned by all the members of a community, but these collective owners usually do not have clearly defined shares. Second, there are no residual control rights in the traditional sense. 'Owners' must wait passively to enjoy the ownership benefits, which mainly take the form of communal social investments. The 'owners' of a TVE do not have full rights to use the after-tax income, a majority of which, by law, must be used for reinvestment or for social purposes. Third, until recently at least and in most cases, the 'owners' could not sell, inherit, or otherwise transfer TVE assets. According to traditional property rights theory, TVEs should therefore be relatively inefficient and should thus be privatized.

However, in reality, not only has the growth rate of TVE output been impressive in both absolute and relative terms, but the productivity of TVEs has also been extraordinary. Although capital–labour ratios among TVEs are only about 25 per cent of those in the SOE sector, output–labour ratios among TVEs are about 80 per cent of those in the state sector.[2] Various estimates place the annual growth rate of the total factor productivity of TVEs at between 5 per cent and 12 per cent over more than a decade. This is outstanding relative to world standards (see for instance World Bank 1996, p. 51; Weitzman and Xu 1994; Jefferson and Rawski 1994, p. 56; Woo *et al.* 1994). Likewise, TVEs have exhibited comparative advantages over private firms in China, and their average performance seems to be at least as effective as that of private enterprises (Nee 1992; Svejnar 1990; Dong and Putterman 1997).

Why is this so? First, community members do possess the right to derive significant short-run and long-run benefits from TVE ownership, if, rather than merely short-run financial advantages such as dividends, 'benefits' are understood in the larger sense of job opportunities, job security, pension funds, and communal welfare programmes in housing, health care, irrigation, road construction, and other infrastructure.[3]

Second, although the residual control rights exercised by a community government may imply a certain amount of risk due to bureaucratization, the control by government over the internal reorganization or over the takeover process does sidestep the social and economic costs of bankruptcy through court action or of takeover by outsiders. This control is quite similar to that exercised by the main bank in a Japanese Keiretsu.

Third, because it is a fixed economic entity, the community, unlike a specific TVE, can shoulder an almost unlimited liability. Under the pressure of intense competition, this ability can facilitate a consensus among community members, the community government, and TVE management and workers to maximize profits even by means of the sacrifice of all or part of wage income. Moreover, because a community is diversified in an economic sense, it can diversify the business risk. A township or village can rather easily create several small-scale TVEs in different sectors and then expand the size of these TVEs.

Fourth, because the community is a small society, the citizenry can fully or partially vote by hands in the semi-competitive elections for community officials in wealthier villages and in those with a large TVE economy (O'Brien 1994, pp. 47, 51).[4] The citizens can also participate quite directly in discussions with community leaders. These two avenues clearly contribute to the solution of the problem of monitoring the monitors and help reduce the cost of organization.

Finally, because the community is the corporation, the responsibility contract and subcontract system can be easily arranged between the community representative assemblies and the community government, between the government and the TVEs, and within the TVEs. These contracts and subcontracts have facilitated the solution of monitoring problems within the community and within the TVEs (Lin 1995; O'Brien 1994, p. 45; Wong et al. 1995).

The advantages of the TVE ownership and governance structure are only relative. Many problems exist that may be linked to this structure. Among them, two are often pointed out. First, because township and village governments seem to be shifting the responsibility for the overall development of rural communities onto TVEs and to exercise unfavourable interference in TVE management, many TVEs are now also experiencing redundant employment and increasingly heavy social burdens.[5] Second, because TVE development has been so closely tied to local initiative, rural industrialization has not yet been accompanied by urbanization. As a result, many TVEs have already been restricted by the lack of infrastructure, market information and social services and by poor transportation and communication networks. The existence of such problems means that there is a need for further reform in the TVE sector. The reform would involve more than further clarification in TVE property rights.

9.5. PROPERTY RIGHTS AND PRIVATE ENTERPRISES IN EAST ASIA

The private and household enterprise sector has experienced very dramatic growth during the reform years in China and Vietnam. For example, in industry in Vietnam the share of private and household enterprises in the total industrial output rose from 14.5 per cent in 1987 to 23.3 per cent in 1990 and 26.1 per cent in 1993, while in China the corresponding share climbed from 1.8 per cent in 1985 to 5.4 per cent in 1990 and 12.9 per cent in 1995 (Table 9.2).

Three types of enterprise can be distinguished in the sector: household enterprises, rural private enterprises, and urban private enterprises. Household enterprises

Table 9.2. *Private and household industrial establishments in Vietnam and China, 1985–1995*

	1985	1987	1989	1991	1993	1995
Vietnam						
Number (units)	—	—	334,621	447,730	456,188	611,884
Private enterprises	—	490	1,284	959	3,322	5,327
Household enterprises	—	—	333,337	446,771	452,866	606,557
Share in industrial output (%)	—	14.5	22.0	26.7	26.1	24.0
China						
Number (1,000s)	10,650	—	17,270	17,650	22,850	20,410
Share in industrial output (%)	1.8	3.6	4.8	6.0	8.4	12.9

Sources: Vietnam: Dodsworth *et al.* (1996, p. 45); General Statistics Office (1996); IMF (1999*b*, table 9); China: SSB (1991, p. 391), (1995, p. 375), (1996, p. 401), *Yearbook of China's Township and Village Enterprises* (1996, pp. 108–9).

make up over 95 per cent of the total. Most of these do piece work for SOEs, TVEs, and other 'corporate' organizations. This integration of public enterprises (SOEs and TVEs) and household 'workshops' on the basis of strict contracts has benefited both sides.

Private enterprises which have grown beyond family-based entities nearly always require local government support in order to obtain raw materials, land, equipment, funds, contacts, and access to regional and national markets. This support is typically supplied partly in exchange for a share in both residual benefits rights and residual control rights. The difference between these private enterprises and the typical private enterprise in a capitalist economy was well understood by the Central Committee of the Communist Party of China in the early years of the reform (State Bureau of Industrial and Commercial Administration and Theoretical Department of Beijing Daily, 1984).

The rural private enterprises appear more like the wider community enterprises in which township and village governments have established informal, but effective, proprietary interests (Young 1994). On the other hand, the ties between the urban entrepreneurs who operate private enterprises and the officials staffing state administrative, distributive and production entities appear more like patron–client relationships (Wank 1996). This arrangement raises two very attractive, but quite general, questions: (i) How might one favour stable expectations for long-term investment and the development of private enterprises rather than the uncertainty which can arise from the haphazard enforcement of laws and regulations by agents of the state? (ii) How can social trust and morality be used to facilitate resource allocation, stable expectations, and information flows? While a functioning market economy is popularly understood as a system of well-defined property rights and legal structures, an understanding of the ways in which social trust can institutionally undergird market activity would certainly generate new insights into institutional plurality in market economies.[6]

In China and Vietnam, the bureaucracy is the dominant integrative structure in the social order, and the social trust embodied in a community or a patron–client relationship is not readily transferable by one actor to another community entity or relationship. This fact enhances the likelihood of ongoing future cooperation and an orientation towards mutual benefit. As a consequence, social trust in this form, like property rights, is productive. It enables actors to calculate risks and likely returns, encourages business activity by creating the reasonable expectation that others involved in the relationship will behave in a fairly predictable way, and tends to foster much more business activity than alternative forms, including the absence of this type of social trust.

This social trust links entrepreneurs with the overarching bureaucratic structure. The connection cannot be viewed simply as a localized exchange of commercial wealth for bureaucratic power. Its contribution to productivity and marketization may be much more significant. From the perspective of private entrepreneurs, the connection provides local stability in an environment characterized by central policy instabilities and ideological hostility. At the same time, it offers private entrepreneurs institutionalized access to crucial resources such as bank credits, land, and key raw materials, many of which are directly or indirectly controlled by government. From the perspective of local officials, the connection institutionalizes new sources of revenue to cope with the increasing expenditure and development pressure (Li 1996; Wank 1996; Wong 1995).

The major contribution of patron–client ties is stylized as the stimulation of competition, support for innovation, the reduction of uncertainty, and the easing of market linkages (Leff 1964; Wank 1996). This stylized contribution may be more suited for the ties between rural private enterprises and community governments.

Private entrepreneurs compete against each other for bureaucratic favours that are in short supply. The licences and dispensations are usually renewed on an annual basis, enabling annual cost adjustments. This assures that in the long run only the most productive entities can meet the payment requirements (including bribes). Competition takes place among bureaucratic actors because bureaucratic resources are generally abundant, inducing better service and even reform from below. For example, according to the 'individual business family' policy implemented in China in the late 1970s, a private firm could not expand its business beyond seven employees and beyond the use of vehicle transport. Many local governments circumvented this policy by allowing private firms to register as collectives. Without such a practice, the significance of private business in job creation, in the generation of fiscal revenue, and in the elimination of gaps in supply and demand might not have been recognized by the state and the public as early as 1984 (Liu 1992; Parris 1993; Wank 1996).

The ties between private entrepreneurs and local government entities and officials have reduced the political uncertainties that used to follow policy cycles. They have thereby encouraged investment and diversification away from speculative trade and towards services and industrial production. Because private firms can use these ties to obtain the officially mediated resources that enhance profits and security, they are motivated to develop these ties as new market channels. As a result, private firms have sometimes helped public units market their products, provided production inputs for them, and infused capital through public–private partnerships. They have thus helped public enterprises 'grow out of the plan' (Naughton 1995; Probert and Young 1995; Wank 1996).

9.6. CONCLUDING REMARKS

This chapter has illuminated the dynamic processes of SOE property rights reform in China, Vietnam and Laos, the comparative advantages of China's TVE ownership, governance and liability structures, and the way in which private enterprises in China and Vietnam expand business through social trust because of their participation in community enterprises or their patron–client ties with government entities and officials. Table 9.3 summarizes the approach of this chapter in three panels. Panel 1 outlines the ownership features of major types of firms in East Asia relative to the corresponding features of large Japanese firms (J-firms) and large American corporations (A-firms). Panel 2 compares the liability and governance features of these

Table 9.3. *The features of heterodox ownership and governance structures versus the J-firm and the A-firm**

	SOEs in the reform				TVEs	Private firm in East Asia	J-firm	A-firm
	Management contract	Leasing contract	Employee stock ownership	Joint ventures				
Nominal owner	All citizens	All citizens	All employees	Citizens and partners	Community members	Private owner(s)	Shareholders	Shareholders
Control right	Government	Government	Shareholder assembly	Government and partners	TVG	Owners and local government	Workers and managers	Managers
Major beneficiaries	Government and citizens	Government and citizens	All employees	All the three parts	Citizens and TVG	Owners and community	Workers and managers	Shareholders
Alienation right	Government	Government	Employees and government	Government and partners	Citizen assembly and TVG	Owners and local government	All the three groups	Shareholders and managers
Budget constraint	Soft	Relatively hard	Hard	Relatively hard	Hard for whole community	Hard	Relatively hard	Relatively hard
Subject to bankruptcy	No	Yes	Yes	Not certain	Yes, but not by court	Yes	Yes	Yes
Who monitors the monitors	Nobody	Nobody	Shareholder assembly	Not clear	Citizen rep. assembly	Owners	Shareholders	Shareholders
Agency problem	Most serious	Less serious	Moderate	Less serious	Moderate	Not present	Moderate	Less serious
Average performance (relative efficiency)	Poor	Good	Excellent	Very good	Excellent	Excellent	Very good	Very good

Notes: *TVG = township and village government.

Source: Author's compilation.

firms. Panel 3 presents a brief remark on the performance of these firms wherein performance is valued in relative terms only.

The ownership structure may shape fundamental features of the liability and governance structure of a firm. However, it cannot fully determine the liability and governance structure. For example, SOEs with management contracts and SOEs with leasing contracts show quite similar ownership structures, but the latter experience a relatively hard budget constraint and a less serious agency problem than the former, and as a consequence the latter usually perform more effectively.

The relative efficiency of different types of firms seems to be more directly and closely linked with the liability and governance structures, in which the hardness of the budget constraint, the genuine fear of bankruptcy, the effective monitoring of the monitors, and the existence of compatible incentives for management to reduce agency problems are key dimensions. Within the same general type of state ownership, the management contract system resulted in a performance which was better than that of the SOEs directly controlled by government entities. Meanwhile, the leasing contract system and joint ventures, particularly with foreign investors, have exhibited improved performance. City-run SOEs transformed into full employee stock-ownership enterprises have had impressive success in China, and the approach may be implemented nationwide, especially among medium-size SOEs, in the near future.

The excellent performance of TVEs may be attributed to factors such as the compatible interests and incentives among community members, township and village governments and TVE management, the almost unlimited liability borne by the community as a whole, the intense competitive pressure, and the fact that community governments are effectively monitored by community representative assemblies and by community members. These liability and governance features of TVEs are mainly due to the TVE ownership structure and the marketization of the economy. The ownership features of TVEs appear to stand between the J-firms and the A-firms. While TVEs show more common features with J-firms in terms of the major beneficiaries, the powerful role of community (township and village) government makes TVEs more similar to A-firms in terms of the allocation of control rights and alienation rights. Private enterprises in East Asia show hybrid features of the TVE type (the support and intervention of township and village governments) and of classical private firms (private owners).

The plurality of ownership and governance structures in East Asia may indicate that the actual allocation of residual control rights and residual benefits rights among diverse owners of financial, human, institutional, and social capital could be dependent or contingent on the state rather than unique or deterministic. The basic logic behind this state-contingent ownership is the value-maximization principle of the firm, according to which the optimal ownership arrangement of the firm should match the right to residual benefits with the residual control rights. In other words, the risk makers should be the risk takers (Blair 1995; Hart 1995; Milgrom and Robert 1992). Given the monitoring and agency problems which exist under conditions of asymmetric information, the allocation of partial or full ownership rights in a firm to the most important actors in the development of the firm can effectively reduce the cost of monitoring and the problem of moral hazard and thus maximize the match between the residual control rights and the right to the residual benefits.

One may conclude that, on condition that there is a supportive political, economic, and social environment, the value-maximization principle and increasing competition will push SOEs with management contracts to seek arrangements involving leasing, joint ventures, employee stock ownership, and other hybrid forms of the shareholding company. The evolution of TVE ownership and governance structures will continue and will be increasingly influenced by international competition. The comparative advantages of the TVE in terms of the match of residual control rights and residual benefits rights will be strengthened during this process of evolution. The evolution of private enterprise in East Asia will also retain unique features and will continue to follow the path of mutual benefits, although private enterprises in East Asia may begin to resemble private firms in the West. In the process of evolution, available material, human, institutional, and social capital will continue to look for transaction-cost savings combinations. The pace of evolution will continue to be largely determined by the development level of these types of capital, particularly the rising level of 'know-how'.

NOTES

1. *Chinese Youth*, No. 2, January 1996, pp. 14–20.
2. *People's Daily*, 19 February 1997.
3. For a detailed discussion about the characteristics of TVE ownership and governance structures based on a broader perspective than the notion of property rights, see Sun (1997) and Perotti *et al.* (1999).
4. *The Economist*, 2 November 1996, pp. 81–3.
5. *China Information Daily*, 2 August 1993, p. 2.
6. The institutional plurality in market economies like Japan and the US has attracted the attention of social economists. For instance, because they are considered more easily adaptable to volatile markets, personal contracts are popularly employed in Japan, despite the availability of legal contracts and a legal system (Dore 1983). In the US, for the sake of saving time and costs, sales representatives often settle deals with a handshake rather than by contract (Macaulay 1963).

10

Transition Approaches, Institutions, and Income Inequality

GIOVANNI ANDREA CORNIA

10.1. INTRODUCTION

One of the main distinguishing features of the transition to the market economy has been a widespread rise in earnings, income, and asset inequality. This trend has, however, varied considerably from country to country. On the one hand, the economies of Central Europe have broadly caught up with the level of inequality typical of the Western European market economies. On the other hand, the countries of Southern-Eastern Europe and the former Soviet Union have experienced increases in Gini coefficients two to three times as large. And in the slow reforming Asian countries, the extent and, in particular, the pattern of inequality rises differed markedly from those observed in the European economies in transition.

In view of the steady decline in inequality observed in the first three decades of rapid growth after the end of World War II in the majority of developing and industrialized countries, these trends, particularly those in the states of the former Soviet Union, are perplexing. While the socialist experiment underscored that excessively low income spreads may cause serious disincentive effects and affect negatively economic performance, and that moderate increases in income inequality from low starting points can accelerate growth, there is now concern that the rises in income concentration observed over the last decade may lead to slow growth and persistent poverty.

In light of the above, this chapter examines the trends in the distribution of income observed since 1989 in the European economies in transition (with the exclusion of most countries of the former Yugoslavia and the Caucasus) and in China, and the factors responsible for the changes observed. In line with the main argument of this volume, the chapter emphasizes that differences in the pace and pattern of institutional development explain in part the variation in inequality trends and growth performance of the transitional economies over the last decade.

10.2. INITIAL CONDITIONS: THE DISTRIBUTION OF INCOME PRIOR TO THE TRANSITION

Contrary to a widespread belief, prior to the transition, income distribution in the former centrally planned economies of Europe varied substantially across countries and over time. Over the 1960–89 period, earnings dispersion remained broadly constant in Czechoslovakia and Hungary, and declined substantially in Russia and Poland following the introduction of consecutive wage reforms and increases in minimum wages (Atkinson and Micklewright 1992). In turn, the inequality of the distribution of net disposable income somewhat narrowed up to the mid–late 1970s, but increased moderately during the mid–late 1980s in Hungary, Poland, and Russia. The increase in income differentials during this period has often been put into relation with the spread of the 'second (or informal) economy' in Hungary and Poland (Boltho 1992) or to the introduction of the wage reform aiming at introducing greater incentives during the Gorbachev era in the USSR (Atkinson and Micklewright 1992). In the immediate pre-transition period, one could, therefore, observe non-negligible differences in income concentration. The Soviet Union, for instance, had consistently higher income dispersion than the countries of Central Europe (Table 10.1).

With the possible exception of the former USSR and Yugoslavia, during the pre-transition period, the socialist economies of Europe exhibited a distribution of final incomes which was less skewed than that of the Western market economies. Using data for the end of the 1960s and early 1970s, Pryor (1973) estimated that the Gini coefficients of the distribution of net disposable income were on average 6 percentage points lower in Eastern Europe. In view of the widespread increases in inequality during the 1980s observed in both market and centrally planned economies, such difference remained likely unaltered until 1989, the year that is used in this chapter

Table 10.1. *Income inequality indexes in Eastern and Western Europe, 1986–1987*

Country	Gross earnings[a]		Net disposable income	
	Gini coefficient	Decile ratio	Gini coefficient	Decile ratio
Czechoslovakia	19.7	2.45	19.9	2.41
Hungary	22.1	2.64	20.9	2.61
Poland	24.2	2.77	25.3	3.04
USSR	27.6	3.28	25.6	3.30
UK	26.7	3.23	29.7	3.86
USA	—	—	31.7[b]	—
Germany	—	—	25.2[c]	—
Australia	—	—	28.7	—

Notes: [a]Gross earnings includes all money incomes (including overtime, bonuses, and piece-rate payments) before tax and other deductions of all males and females of all ages employed in all sectors (agriculture included). [b]1979. [c]1981.

Sources: Atkinson and Micklewright (1992); Milanovic (1993).

Table 10.2. *Changes in Gini coefficients due to redistribution, in Eastern and Western Europe, 1986–1987*

	CSFR	Hungary	Poland	UK	Sweden	Germany
Original income	26.0	31.9	34.5	39.3	41.7	40.7
Gross income	19.5	24.8	26.0	29.3	24.1	30.4
Disposable income	19.9[a]	23.1	25.3	26.4	19.7	25.2
Shifts in Gini coefficients due to						
Transfers	−6.5	−7.1	−8.5	−10.0	−17.6	−10.3
Direct taxes	0.4	−1.7	−0.7	−2.9	−4.4	−5.2

Note: [a]From Table 10.1.
Source: Elaboration on data in Milanovic (1993).

as the transition's baseline of the former centrally planned economies of Europe. The lower income dispersion of the European centrally planned economies, however, tended to fade when the comparison was made with the advanced 'welfare market economies', such as the Scandinavian countries or with Germany (Table 10.2). While also in this group of market economies the distribution of gross earnings was substantially more skewed than in the socialist countries, the distribution of net disposable income per capita was rather similar.

Prior to the gradual introduction of the market reforms, which began in 1978 with the introduction of the Household Responsibility System in Agriculture, also in China income inequality was very low. While in 1953, the nationwide Gini coefficient of the distribution of disposable household incomes was 56, reflecting a situation of profound inequality in the access to land, education and social welfare, the creation of the agricultural communes, the socialization of industrial assets, and the development of an embryo of social security led to considerable redistribution and rapid and egalitarian growth. Despite marked regional differences in soil fertility and endowments of other natural resources, by 1975 the national Gini coefficient had fallen to 26 (Hussain *et al.* 1991). Around 1978, the rural Gini index of income concentration was 21 and even lower values were observed in the urban sector. This egalitarian income distribution proved to be an asset for the success of the reforms introduced in 1978, as greater initial equity increased the feasibility of the reform process which, even in the best cases, tends to cause some income polarization.

Four broad sets of factors were at the basis of this systemic difference in income distribution between the socialist and capitalist economies:

1. *Centralized wage regulation*: In all socialist economies, industrial wages were set centrally. The relationship between wage rate on the one hand and skill levels and prior investments of each worker in human capital on the other was weak. In addition, minimum wages were generally set (particularly in Central Europe) at substantially higher levels than in the market economies. The resulting earnings distribution was thus more compressed than in the market economies. As noted by Phelps-Brown,

'... the [lower wage dispersion of socialist economies]... arises mainly from a lower rise of income above the median, that is, broadly: the more skilled manual occupations and still more the higher clerical, the professional and the administrative, are paid less than in the West relatively to the bulk of the manual workers. Allowance for 'perks' reduces the contrast, but is unlikely to remove it.' (1977, pp. 303–4). In the Chinese agriculture, in contrast, the remuneration was set at the commune level on the basis of a work-point system and of other consideration. While the resulting local earning distributions were characterized by a high degree of egalitarianism, average earnings varied visibly between poor and rich communes.

2. *Collective ownership of means of production and 'barriers to entry'*: Prior to the transition, only Poland and Hungary comprised a non-negligible private sector (contributing about a third of GDP in the latter country). Even in these countries, however, 'barriers to entry' did not allow private entrepreneurs to start production in most manufacturing sectors. The dominance of state ownership in the economy reduced drastically the share of profits, rents, dividends, and other capital incomes accruing to households. In addition, the underdevelopment of the banking and financial sector sharply reduced the share of interests in total family income. All these incomes—profits, interests, dividends, and rents—are generally distributed in a more skewed way than labour income and, therefore, the greater their share in the total, the more skewed the distribution of total income.

3. *Subsidies on basic goods and services*: In the European socialist economies, rural and urban consumers alike benefited from substantial subsidies on a wide range of basic goods and services (in China and Vietnam subsidies were provided predominantly to the urban dwellers). In 1980, for instance, in Poland consumer subsidies accounted for around 10 per cent of the total national product (Cornia and Sipos 1991). Most of these subsidies were provided for goods with low income elasticity and therefore benefited the low income households the most. If this factor is taken into consideration, the inequality of the distribution of welfare was even lower than revealed by data on the distribution of monetary incomes.

4. *Redistribution through the tax and transfer system*: With the exception of Asian transitional economies, social transfers (pensions, family allowances, sickness benefits, and other social transfers) accounted for a remarkable 22–25 per cent of total gross household income, i.e. values comparable to those observed in the advanced 'welfare market economies' of Northern and Central Europe (29 per cent in Sweden and 17 per cent in Germany) and substantially larger than the 8–9 per cent observed in the USA and Canada. Pensions accounted for about two-thirds of total transfers. These large transfers helped keep down poverty rates, but had only a limited effect in terms of altering income concentration (Table 10.2). The only exception were family allowance, which were proportionately greater than in all Western market economies and which were strongly pro-poor. Transfers were basically granted on the basis of the demographic characteristics of the beneficiaries, were most commonly unrelated to the income level of the recipients, and their incidence by income decile was generally quasi-proportional.

Taxes generally took the form of payroll taxes borne by the enterprises. Except for Hungary—which had introduced an income tax in the late 1980s—direct taxes amounted to no more than 1–2 per cent of the workers' gross earnings and played almost no role in reducing income dispersion. As a result of this situation, taxes and transfers played a lesser role in shaping the distribution of net disposable income than in the Western market economies. Indeed, it is interesting to note that the same distributive objectives, e.g. a final distribution of net disposable income per capita with a Gini coefficient of, say, 23.0, were obtained through the compression of distribution of gross earnings and the control of the share of capital income accruing to the household sector in the socialist economies, and through redistribution in the Western market economies (Table 10.2).

The above data refer to monetary incomes and do not therefore fully reflect the distribution of real consumption and welfare. Indeed, in economies suffering from chronic rationing of consumer goods and 'shortageflation' (Kolodko 1986), the real distribution of welfare was less favourable than suggested by the above statistics, which disregarded the influence of dual distribution systems, parallel markets, involuntary savings, growing regional differences in the supply of consumer goods, and the rising intensity of shortages over time, i.e. factors that have had a large (though poorly documented) disequalizing impact on the distribution of private consumption and welfare (Kornai 1980; Braithwaite and Heleniak 1989). Sometimes, factual access to scarce goods had greater significance than money income. For instance, though in the USSR the official measures show that income distribution became more egalitarian between 1970 and 1986, private consumption became less equally distributed. By and large, growing differences in the distribution of 'real' private consumption emerged between Moscow and other important cities, the supply centres along the Baikal-Amur railroad on the one hand, and the rural areas and remote cities on the other.

10.3. POLICY REFORM AND EXPECTED CHANGES IN INCOME DISTRIBUTION

10.3.1. *Main Reforms with Large Distributional Implications*

The transition to the market economy has been carried out through a number of structural reforms. Those with the most important distributive implications are discussed hereafter. In the European economies in transition, the re-establishment of macroeconomic balance aimed at eliminating the repressed inflation and fiscal imbalances inherited from the socialist era. Macroeconomic measures inevitably involved fiscal and monetary austerity, with simultaneous trade and price liberalization, the removal of consumer and most producer subsidies, the unification and sharp devaluation of the exchange rate, and an increase in the interest rate. Price liberalization (and the inflationary repercussions of devaluation) were expected to generate a large but short-lived 'corrective inflation' which was to be reduced rapidly through restrictive monetary and fiscal policies and through the stability of money wages or/and of the nominal exchange rate. In most countries, however, these measures led to much higher inflation rates and much greater falls in wage rates and GDP than expected. China, in contrast, avoided major adjustments as at the beginning of the reform process it enjoyed broadly balanced macroeconomic conditions and broadly followed a macroeconomic policy which could be defined as 'prudent' or even 'conservative'.

In the European economies in transition, privatization moved in three different directions: 'small privatization' of shops, service units, etc.; 'big privatization' of large state-owned enterprises (SOEs), land and other large assets by means of auctions, direct sales to foreign companies, restitution to the former owners, insider or workers privatization, and voucher privatization; and the removal of 'barriers to entry'.

This last approach—removing barriers to entry and encouraging the autonomous development of new non-state enterprises—is that which was actively pursued in China. In this country, SOEs started to be commercialized with the introduction of the Enterprise Responsibility System, while their full-fledged privatization and liquidation began only in the late 1990s. After 1984, the reforms were extended to the liberalization of foreign direct investment, the establishment of special economic zones, and fiscal decentralization (Harrold 1992). The commercialization of the industrial sector was preceded in 1978 by deep agricultural reforms which replaced the rural communes with an egalitarian family-based agriculture which generated strong work incentives for the farmers. In Vietnam, in contrast, the reform of SOEs was mainly carried out through the creation of joint ventures with multinational corporations (Montes, this volume).

While in China wage setting has remained fairly centralized, most European economies in transition liberalized labour markets and wage setting. With the exception of the Central European countries, minimum wages—an important tool in the determination of the overall earnings distribution—were left to fall in relation to the average wage. Meanwhile, wages in the budgetary sector were negatively affected by the inability to collect taxes and the ensuing revenue shortage. Finally, a highly progressive tax on the portion of the wage bill that surpassed a pre-established ceiling was temporarily imposed on state companies in order to avoid the inflationary pressures which could have derived from an increase in aggregate demand. This often led to an increase in wage dispersion, as companies depressed average wages in order to increase the wages of qualified workers with skills in short supply.

During the initial phase of the reforms, the coverage of most pre-existing social transfers was enlarged, while new types of benefits (unemployment compensation and social assistance) were introduced (UNICEF 1995). Because of the growing fiscal difficulties faced by all economies in transition, in the subsequent years, the generosity, coverage, and duration of most benefits was reduced. With few exceptions (the Czech Republic and Slovakia), despite the many proposals about targeting, child allowances remained mainly universal though, as noted, with sharply declining real values. In turn, the Chinese social security system remained very underdeveloped and lopsided and it still covers only the formal sector.

Tax reform in the European economies in transition was generally inspired by the West European taxation model and focused on indirect taxes (mainly built around a VAT), corporate income tax, and personal income tax. Progress in the establishment of an adequate tax administration, and in particular in the introduction of presumptive taxation, has however generally lagged behind. Considerable income originating from a growing 'informal sector' often remains untaxed. Tax evasion and avoidance have been widespread in the transition economies, due also to the limited priority attached by some governments (as in Russia) to the development of a sound tax administration and to the low ethical standards of most new capitalists. As noted in Chapter 1, the larger the shadow economy, the higher the horizontal and vertical inequality and the less satisfactory the performance of the economy.

10.3.2. Ex ante *Expectations about Shifts in Income Distribution*

In the case of China, the reforms deliberately proceeded on a pragmatic, trial-and-error basis without determining *ex ante* a specific model of economy towards which to converge. While some policy changes (such as the land reform and introduction of the Household Responsibility System in agriculture and industry) were designed to generate widespread benefits, other reforms (including fiscal decentralization, the concentration of subsidies in urban areas, and selective support to export processing zones) were expected to entail some distributive trade-offs. In contrast, in most European economies in transition, the economic reforms openly aimed at creating a full-fledged market economy, i.e. an economy inherently characterized by higher income inequality.

To start with, with the privatization of state-owned assets and the removal of 'barriers to entry', a sharp increase in the share of private sector activities was expected together with a rise in the share of profits (and mixed capital and labour income) accruing to the household sector. It was also expected that the share of profits and other capital income in total household incomes would rise in line with the pace of privatization and the growth of the 'new' private sector. Experience has shown that the dispersion of the distribution of profits and similar incomes varies with the degree of concentration in the distribution of assets and, therefore, with the privatization models followed. The dispersion of profits is likely to be most pronounced in the case of reprivatization, the least in that of voucher privatization and auctions, and somewhere in the middle in that of workers' privatization.

Second, the abandonment of the centralized wage regulation was expected to lead to growing earnings differentials due to the emergence of a closer relationship between (past) investments in human capital and earnings levels. In particular, the right tail of the distribution was expected to 'explode' because of rises in the wages of managers, professionals, and other workers with high levels of education. In addition, price and wage liberalization (in particular, with the rise of the energy and raw material prices which were set before at levels substantially lower than international prices), productivity differentials across industries could be expected to rise and to be translated in growing intersectoral wage differentials. Finally, with the removal of 'barriers to entry', overall wage dispersion was to be influenced by the spread of the small and informal sector, where wage differentials are generally greater than in the formal one.

Third, the shift to the market economy was also likely to be accompanied by changes in the redistributive role of the tax-and-transfer system. Firm speculations about the direction and extent of these changes were not possible as several regimes of social security (with different kinds of generosity, progressivity, and financing) can be adopted in a market economy. Yet, a few generalizations can be ventured. Shifts in the provision of pensions towards an insurance-based system entail that greater attention is paid to the contributory history and last wage level of the insured worker and that thus the degree of redistributiveness of the overall system will decrease. This shift is therefore likely to increase the inequality of the distribution of pensions. In contrast, the introduction of unemployment compensation and social assistance—which are generally targeted on the poor—and a tighter targeting of family allowances are likely to cause a fall in inequality.

Unlike that of the socialist countries (characterized by modest progressivity or outright proportionality), the tax system of the market economies is generally characterized by medium-to-high progressivity. A tax reform along these lines would therefore have had, if properly implemented, an important impact on the distribution of the net per capita household income. This equalizing effect was expected to emerge gradually with the concrete implementation of these reforms—which normally take several years to become fully operational. In turn, except for possible hypothetical (positive) 'second-round effects', the removal of subsidies is very likely to have a negative impact on the distribution of welfare.

In conclusion, the *ex ante* expectations about the effects of the transition policies that were introduced in the former centrally planned economies of Europe are summarized in Table 10.3. However, while the above analysis suggests that it is possible to determine *ex ante* the direction of the expected changes in income distribution, much less can be said about their extent and speed. Much depends on the model of market economy aimed at.

Table 10.3. Ex ante *expectations about the impact of the transition on income inequality*

	Greater inequality	Lower inequality
Privatization	+++	
Wage liberalization	+++	
Transfer reform		
Pensions	++	
Other transfers		−−
Tax reform		−
Subsidy removal	+	

Source: Compiled by the author.

10.4. EVIDENCE ABOUT CHANGES IN INCOME DISTRIBUTION, 1989–1997

10.4.1. *Data Sources and Caveats*

The data analysis included in this chapter relies heavily on the statistical material generated by the Central Statistical Offices of the economies in transition. Among this material, a key source of information is represented by the Household Budget Surveys (HBS). These surveys—which are normally taken with yearly periodicity—allow one to compute changes in: income structure by type of income (both on average and by income decile); the distribution of income pre-tax/pre-transfers and post-tax/post-transfers; and the distribution of gross earnings and of other incomes and the incidence by decile of income transfers.

According to Atkinson and Micklewright (1992), prior to the transition, the data on the distribution of earnings and disposable incomes generated by the HBS of Hungary, Poland, and Czechoslovakia were of a quality comparable to those generated by the British HBS. The same authors indicate, however, that the situation was less satisfactory in the USSR. Until 1992, the HBS in this country involved no less than 47.3 thousand families, of whom 36.4 thousand were state employees and the remainder *kolkhozni* (McAuley 1994). The survey suffered however from a considerable sampling error as it excluded some of the poorest groups, such as families headed by students and pensioners, and, later on, the families of the unemployed. Since 1992, the sample size of the Russian HBS has declined to around 16,000 families, thus reducing its representativeness at the subnational level. At the same time, the sampling error should have been substantially reduced.

While in most countries (including many of those part of the former USSR) the last few years have witnessed a general—if slow—improvement in sampling procedures, the sharp increase in the number of small firms which are often excluded from employer earnings surveys, growing informalization of the economy, falling response rates, and the introduction of direct taxation (which discourages the declaration of incomes for fear of having them taxed) are very likely to have led to growing under-reporting. The accuracy of reporting—and the precision of the measurement of inequality—appears to be particularly low in the case of informal sector incomes. There is some evidence also that the people being undersampled or whose incomes are measured inaccurately belong to the two tails of the distribution—a fact that substantially reduces the overall 'measured' income inequality.

These problems have in part been corrected by new positive developments in data collection, often resulting from the technical assistance provided by international organizations. A good example of such new development is the Russian Longitudinal Monitoring Study, a survey of several thousand households, of which seven rounds had been held between 1992 and 1996 alone. Such a survey, for instance, complements the inequality data provided by the official HBS sources. In 1996, for instance, the former generated a Gini coefficient of 0.38 while the Russian Longitudinal Monitoring Study showed a value of 0.48 (Flemming and Micklewright 1999).

In a number of countries, the quality of data has been affected also by rampant inflation and large arrears in the payment of wages and social security benefits. High inflation—which has been common in several parts of the former Soviet Union but not in the transitional economies of Central Europe and Asia—renders annual income data meaningless as errors are common when aggregating monetary monthly incomes during periods of high inflation. The picture is complicated further when high inflation is accompanied by large wages and social benefits arrears (Flemming and Micklewright 1999), the real value of which is thus severely eroded. It must be noted also that most surveys of gross earnings make reference to the 'accounting wages' (those that should have been paid) and not to those effectively paid. Arrears are not randomly distributed; for instance, in Russia wage arrears affected on average 40 per cent of the workforce, 92 per cent of the agricultural workers, and 50 per cent of the industrial workers (Lehmann *et al.* 1999). This means that the distribution of the 'accounting wages' in surveys underestimates the real distribution of earnings by between 3 and 17 percentage Gini points, depending on the size and structure of the sample concerned (ibid.).

While it is impossible to assess precisely the net effect of all these changes on the measurement of inequality, the limited evidence available (from targeted surveys, bank accounts, etc.) suggests that capital and informal sector incomes and private sector earnings are systematically underestimated and overall inequality is higher than that estimated on the basis of the HBS. A second conclusion is that the data on income inequality are, at times, not strictly comparable over time as sample size, sampling procedures, and statistical concepts have at times been changed.

10.4.2. *Changes in the Distribution of Net Per Capita Household Income: Three Emerging Patterns*

As expected, income inequality showed a clear tendency to rise during the transition to the market economy. However, the intensity, timing, and causes of such a rise have been far from uniform. Three broad patterns can be distinguished.

10.4.2.1. *The Central European Pattern: A Clear but Moderate Increase in Inequality*

The increase in the inequality ranged from 2.9 (Hungary) to 5.9 (Poland) percentage points of the Gini coefficient (Table 10.4), an amount surprisingly similar to the six points average difference between the market and socialist economies of Europe during the pre-transition period (see above). Income dispersion surged mainly between 1989 and 1994, and since then seems to have broadly stabilized. At present, these economies have levels of inequality close to that of the medium–high inequality countries of the OECD group, i.e. countries such as Italy, France and Canada, and already higher than those of the Scandinavian countries, the Benelux and Germany (Atkinson *et al.* 1994).

In a sense, for these economies one could speak of a physiological adaptation of income inequality to the levels typical of a Western market economy. However, this

Table 10.4. *Gini coefficients of the distribution of net per capita disposable household income in 16 countries in transition of Eastern and Central Europe and the former Soviet Union, 1989–1997*

	1989	1990	1991	1992	1993	1994	1995	1996	1997	Difference between first and peak year	Difference between first and last year
Czech R.	19.8	19.0	—	21.5	21.4	23.0	21.6	23.0	23.9	4.1	4.1
Hungary	22.5	—	20.9	—	23.1	23.4	24.2	24.6	25.4	2.9	2.9
Poland	27.5	26.8	26.5	27.4	31.7	32.3	32.1	32.8	33.4	5.9	5.9
Slovenia	—	—	26.5	25.9	32.0	24.6	26.4	25.2	—	5.5	−1.3
Bulgaria	23.3*	—	—	33.1	33.5	37.4	38.4	35.7	36.6	15.1	13.3
Romania	23.7	22.7	25.8	25.9	26.7	26.4	30.6	30.2	30.5	6.9	6.8
Estonia	23.0*	—	—	—	—	—	39.8	37.0	36.1	16.7	13.1
Latvia*	22.5[(a)]	—	—	—	—	—	31.0	—	—	—	8.5
Lithuania	22.5*	—	—	—	—	37.0*	—	34.7	30.9	10.8	4.7
Moldova*	24.1	—	—	—	—	36.5	—	—	—	—	13.3
Russia (HBS)	26.5	23.6	25.7	36.3	38.1	40.5	38.5	38.0	—	14.0	11.5
Russia (RLMS)	—	—	—	42.0	43.5	45.0	44.0	48.0	—	—	—
Ukraine*	23.3[(a)]	—	—	—	—	—	47.4	—	—	—	24.1
Azerbaijan	30.7	—	—	—	—	—	—	—	—	—	—
Georgia	28.0	—	—	—	—	—	—	—	—	—	—
Kyrgyzstan*	26.0[(a)]	—	—	—	55.3	—	—	—	—	—	29.3

Notes: [(a)]Refers to 1988. The data are not always directly comparable over time due to changes in the sampling framework. For a few countries and years the data refer to gross household income per capita.

Sources: UNICEF's TransMONEE 2000 Database (www.unicef-icdc.org), except for the data for Kyrgyzstan, Latvia, Moldova, Ukraine and for data with * for other countries which are taken from Milanovic (1998), and for the Russia (RLMS) data which are taken from Flemming and Micklewright (1999).

hypothesis needs further probing as the structure of inequality in the economies in transition is quite different from that of the developed market economies.

10.4.2.2. *A Large Rise in Inequality in the Former Soviet Union and South Eastern Europe*

In most successor states of the former Soviet Union and in South Eastern Europe, income inequality rose rapidly over the 1989–94/5 period and broadly stabilized thereafter. On average, the Gini coefficient of the distribution of net income rose by 10–20 percentage points (Table 10.4), i.e. three to four times faster than in Central Europe. In this group of countries, income inequality is now substantially greater than in most OECD countries and is gradually approaching that prevailing in the high-inequality developing countries. In Russia, between 1991 and 1994 the income share of the bottom 60 per cent of the population declined by 15.8 percentage points, and that of the top quintile increased by exactly the same amount (Table 10.5). In March 1994,

Table 10.5. *Income shares of population quintiles, Russia, 1970–1995*

	1970	1980	1990	1991	1992	1993	1994	1995
1st quintile	7.8	10.1	9.8	11.9	6.0	5.8	5.3	5.5
2nd quintile	14.8	14.8	14.9	15.8	11.6	11.1	10.2	10.2
3rd quintile	18.0	18.6	18.8	18.8	17.6	16.7	15.2	15.0
4th quintile	22.6	23.1	23.8	22.8	26.5	24.8	23.0	22.4
5th quintile	36.8	33.4	32.7	30.7	38.3	41.6	46.3	46.9
Quintile ratio[a]	4.71	3.27	3.34	2.58	6.38	7.17	8.73	8.53

Note: [a] Ratio of the 5th to the 1st income quintile.
Source: Goskomstat (1995, 1996).

the richest 5 per cent of the population controlled a share of total income similar to that of the bottom 60 per cent. In view of the under-reporting of income affecting official surveys, it is likely that even these data give only a partial idea of the distributional earthquake underway in this part of the region.

The factors explaining these sharp regional differences can be summarized as follows. To start with, the transitional recession has been far more pronounced in the countries of the former Soviet Union than in those of Central Europe (see Table 1.1 of Chapter 1). Recessions worsen income distribution because the 'wage share' tends to fall in line with the rise in unemployment and with the more than proportional decline of wages in relation to average incomes. While over 1989 and 1994, real output fell by up to 20 per cent in Central Europe, it contracted by over 40 per cent in most countries of the former Soviet Union and Romania, and by an unprecedented 70 per cent in Moldova and Ukraine (UNICEF 1995). As noted above, in these countries, the drop of the wage share in total income is underestimated due to the widespread late payment or non-payment of wages. This problem intensified since 1993 as macroeconomic policy tightened the overall amount of credit granted to the enterprise sector. Enterprises reacted not with bankruptcy or layoffs, but by building up arrears.

Second, the inequality of the distribution of earnings has increased far less rapidly in Central Europe than in the other economies in transition of Europe (Russia, Ukraine, and Moldova) (see Section 5). In Central Europe earnings inequality rose slower than anticipated. While this could have been expected in Hungary that by 1989–90 Gini coefficients of the earnings distribution were already in the 26–29 range, it is more difficult to explain for the Czech Republic, Slovakia, and Slovenia. Also, in Central Europe privatization generally proceeded slower than in Russia, at least during the phase of the transition (this is certainly the case in Poland, Slovakia, and Slovenia), or followed a more egalitarian approach (as in the Czech Republic). In Russia, capital and self-employment incomes provide now a greater share of total income than wages and salaries (Table 10.6). In Bulgaria, inequality of private sector income, already higher than that of other sources, shot up at the same time as its share in the total rose steadily (Milanovic 1995).

Third, the income transfer policy followed in Central Europe was substantially more progressive than that implemented in South Eastern Europe and the former

Table 10.6. *Structure of personal income by income types, Russia, 1990–1995 (percentages)*

	1990	1991	1992	1993	1994	1995
Wages	74.1	59.7	69.9	58.0	46.4	39.5
Transfers	13.0	15.5	14.0	17.2	17.4	16.7
Entrepreneurial incomes	12.9	24.8	16.1	24.8	31.9	38.6
Capital incomes	—(a)	—(a)	—(a)	—(a)	4.3	5.2

Note: (a) Included in entrepreneurial income.
Source: Goskomstat (1996).

Table 10.7. *Share of income transfers in total household income in selected countries of Eastern and Central Europe and the former Soviet Union, 1989–1993/1994*

	1989	1991–2	1993–4
Hungary	26.1	28.2	26.7
Poland	21.2	34.4	—
Slovenia	10.9	—	20.4
Bulgaria	21.9	21.6	19.0
Estonia	—	12.9	12.8
Moldova	11.3	—	8.3
Russia	12.8	12.4	15.6
Ukraine	16.3	11.2	—

Source: UNICEF (1994, 1995).

Soviet Union. Overall transfers to households on account of pensions, unemployment benefits, and child allowances as a share of total household income increased or remained broadly constant at high levels in Central Europe, but fell or stagnated at lower levels in Southern Eastern Europe and the former Soviet Union (Table 10.7). In this way, while in countries such as Hungary and Slovenia the rise in earnings dispersion was offset by adequate income transfers, in the Slavonic and Baltic countries of the former Soviet Union the inadequacies of the tax and transfer system did not allow one to offset huge rises in the distribution of earnings which, as will be shown in the rest of this chapter, are themselves the reflection of severe institutional biases in the labour market (compare the data in Table 10.9 with those of Table 10.4).

The increase of the inequality of net disposable income was influenced also by the composition and targeting of income transfers, and not only by their overall volume. *Ceteris paribus*, pensions tend to be distributed in a less progressive manner than unemployment compensation and family allowances. Though it is not possible to provide here a satisfactory analysis of changes in the targeting efficiency of transfers in Central versus South Eastern Europe and the former Soviet Union over the last 9–10 years, there are indications that, with the exception of Poland, the composition and targeting of transfers in Central Europe were more favourable than in the former Soviet Union and South Eastern Europe (Milanovic 1995). In Bulgaria, for instance, the bottom three deciles of the income distribution received only 40 per cent of unemployment benefits as opposed to the case of Chile where almost half of the benefits from public works and unemployment compensation accrue to the lowest income decile (ibid.). In Russia, social assistance accrued proportionately more to the upper than to the lower income deciles (World Bank 1994).

10.4.2.3. *The Chinese Experience: Stable and Then Rising Regional and Rural–Urban Disparity*

The 1978 reforms induced a sharp acceleration of growth which averaged 9–10 per cent a year over 1978–95. Between 1978 and 1984, such a growth spurt was accompanied by only a minimal upsurge in inequality. During the first period, the interprovincial income gap narrowed (last column of Table 10.8), while the urban Gini coefficient stagnated at a low level, as the introduction of performance-related bonuses in urban-based state enterprises did not lead to a surge of urban income disparity (Hussain *et al.* 1991). Social policy played an important role in containing inequality in urban areas. Transfer payments rose from 4.8 to 5.5 per cent of national income between 1979 and 1985, while the welfare of urban industrial workers was further safeguarded by an increase in consumer and industrial subsidies, which came to represent a kind of invisible transfer payment. In rural areas such transfers were negligible as welfare payments and social relief declined from 0.5 to 0.3 per cent of GDP over the 1980s. As a result of the moderate rise of urban and rural inequality, and of the reduction in the rural–urban income gap, overall inequality dropped somewhat during this period (Table 10.8).

Income disparity grew somewhat faster during the second part of the 1980s mainly owing to the rapid expansion of non-farm activities which exacerbated regional income differentials among rural areas (Ping 1997). The increase in non-agricultural incomes—and particularly in the incomes of the mostly rural-based Town and Village Enterprises (TVEs)—correlates with the rise in income disparity in both urban and rural areas (Hussain *et al.* 1991; Ping 1997), as shown by the increase between 1984 and 1990 of the rural Gini coefficient and, even more so, by that of the

Table 10.8. *Evolution of the Gini coefficients and income gap in China, 1978–1995*

Year	Overall Gini	Urban Gini	Rural Gini	Income gap, U/R[a]	Regional income gap (rural)[b]	Regional income gap (urban)[b]	Regional income gap (total)[b]
1978	0.32	0.16	0.21	2.37	—	—	—
1981	—	0.15	0.24	2.05	2.80	1.81	2.62
1984	0.28[c]	0.16	0.26	1.71	3.16[d]	1.59[d]	9.22[d]
1988	0.38	0.23	0.30	2.05	—	—	—
1990	—	0.23	0.31	2.02	4.17	2.03	7.50
1995	0.43	0.28	0.34	2.47	4.82	2.34	9.79

Notes: [a]Ratio between the average urban and rural average income. [b]Ratio between the average income of the highest to the lowest province, by rural, urban, and total area. [c]Refers to 1983. [d]Refers to 1985.
Source: SBS.

interprovincial rural income gap. Despite this polarization, until 1990 there was convergence among provincial incomes, possibly due to changes in the urban–rural mix of the provincial economies.

Inequality rose much faster in the 1990s, and by 1995 the national Gini coefficient reached 43. A first important component in the 1990–5 surge in overall inequality was the widening of the urban–rural income gap which had risen only moderately until 1990. Between 1990 and 1995 the gap rose rapidly, as most of the new industrial and commercial development were concentrated in the urban sector. Second, in view of the unequal spread of non-agricultural activities across provinces, interprovincial inequality also became an important component of overall inequality, as indicated by the widening of the distance between mean incomes per capita of poor and rich provinces (last column of Table 10.8). Though incomes have grown also in less well-endowed provinces, the 1990s witnessed a visible divergence between the relatively rich coastal provinces and the poor interior regions. Public policy accentuated this process: fiscal decentralization substantially reduced the possibility of the central Government to control regional inequality by means of transfers to poorer provinces. Industrial policy played an even more disequalizing role, as it favoured explicitly the urban areas in the coastal provinces through the establishment of Special Economic Zones which were granted special administrative and economic privileges which facilitated the development of export industries and the inflow of foreign direct investment. Finally, a comparison of the 1988 and 1995 surveys of rural incomes suggests that spreading interprovincial inequality has been accompanied by rising income concentration within each province due to a surge in wage inequality (McKinley and Brenner 1998), particularly in the TVE sector.

10.5. DECOMPOSING THE INCREASE IN OVERALL INEQUALITY: AN APPLICATION TO SELECTED EUROPEAN ECONOMIES IN TRANSITION

Kakwani (1980) has shown that at any point in time, t, the Gini coefficient of the total income distribution can be decomposed as follows:

$$G_t = \frac{1}{m_t} \sum m_{jt} C_{jt},$$

where C_{jt} is the concentration coefficient of the jth income component and m_j is its mean; m is in turn the overall mean of total income. The ratio of the former to the latter is equal to the share of the jth income component in the total. The concentration coefficient C_{jt} is similar to the Gini index except that the ranking of individuals is by the total income and not by the jth income components. As a result C_{jt} can be negative. The above expression can be rewritten as $G_t = \Sigma s_{jt} C_{jt}$, where $s_{jt} = m_{jt}/m_t$. The increase in total inequality between time t and $t+n$ (measured by the difference by the Gini coefficients of the two times) can thus be decomposed as follows:

$$\Delta G = G_{t+n} - G_t = \sum \Delta s_j C_j + \sum \Delta C_j s_j + \sum \Delta s_j \Delta C_j,$$

where the Δs_j and ΔC_j refer to changes of the income shares and concentration coefficients over the period $t - t+n$. In practice this decomposition of the overall increase in income inequality requires the knowledge of the shares of each type of income and the concentration coefficients for both the initial and final year. Hereafter, we discuss the changes in the C_j and s_j for a few European transitional economies.

10.5.1. Changes in Income Structure

Changes in income structure affect overall inequality whenever the share of those incomes that are distributed in a more skewed way (such as capital, entrepreneurial, and self-employment income) rises and that of those incomes that have lower dispersion (such as transfers and gross earnings) drops. The available information (UNICEF 1995, table F.2) shows that during the transition the following changes have been observed.

The share of wages and salaries in total income steadily declined as a result of the recession of 1989–92/3, the progressive liberalization of wage negotiations, the imposition of a tax-based income policy (which heavily taxed increases in nominal wages), the emergence of unemployment, and—particularly in countries of the former Soviet Union—the unwillingness to sustain the minimum wage and the wages in the budgetary sector. The wage share continued to drop even after the recovery of output had started. While in the countries of Central Europe the wage share appears to have lost less ground, it still fell by between 10 and 15 percentage points (even this is most likely an underestimate).

The share of transfers (on account of pensions, unemployment benefits, family allowances, and social assistance) does not follow a universal pattern. As seen in Table 10.7, this share shows an increase (or persistence at a fairly high level) in most countries of Central Europe, but some falls in the countries of the former Soviet Union and of South Eastern Europe. Much of these differences reflect variations in social policy choices. In most countries of the former Soviet Union, the inability to sustain the volume of transfers is not the result of the choice of a 'neoliberal-residualist' welfare state, but rather of inadequate institutional developments, i.e. of the inability to collect the taxes needed to finance an appropriate level of transfers. The evidence points, in fact, to an erosion of the value of the benefits distributed to a large—and often increasing—number of beneficiaries, and not to a sharp fall in their number.

The share of capital incomes (dividends, interests, rents, financial rents, and capital gains) in the total appears to have increased moderately, and less rapidly than expected *a priori*, in most countries. While this might be in part the result of measurement problems (as noted, the HBS grossly under-report these sources of income), it could also be due to the slow pace of privatization (Honkkila 1997), particularly of 'big privatization' (only Russia and the Czech Republic divested a substantial part of SOEs), to the slow creation of joint-stock companies, and to the slow development of the banking and financial sector.

Finally, the share of entrepreneurial and mixed incomes rose sharply with the informalization of the economy, the removal of barriers to entry and privatization.

While also in this case measurement problems cloud the picture, in all countries the share of these incomes rose in particular in those countries where the wage economy and social transfers had contracted sharply. While not much is known about the distribution of such incomes, an increase in their share certainly entails a rise in inequality.

10.5.2. Changes in the Dispersion of the Main Income Components

10.5.2.1. Gross Earnings

There is unambiguous evidence that the dispersion of the distribution of gross earnings rose rapidly in the region over 1989–97 (Table 10.9). Also in this case it is possible to observe two fairly distinct patterns. In Russia, Ukraine, and the other states of the former Soviet Union, earnings dispersion almost doubled and is now much greater than in the Western market economies. In contrast, in Hungary, the Czech Republic, and the other countries of Central Europe, the rise in earnings dispersion was more contained (6–8 Gini percentage points). Data on changes in the decile ratio (not shown) confirm the two patterns of changes in earnings inequality identified on the basis of the Gini coefficient: while the decile ratio rose from 2.5–3.0 to about 3.0–4.2 between 1989 and 1997 in Hungary, Poland, and the Czech Republic, in

Table 10.9. *Gini coefficients of the distribution of gross monthly earnings, in 16 countries in transition of Eastern and Central Europe and the former Soviet Union, 1989–1997*

	1989	1990	1991	1992	1993	1994	1995	1996	1997	Difference between initial and peak year	Difference between initial and last year
Czech R.	20.4	—	21.2	21.4	25.8	26.0	28.2	25.4	25.9	7.8	5.5
Hungary	29.3	—	—	30.5	32.0	32.4	—	—	34.8	5.5	5.5
Poland	20.7	—	23.9	24.7	25.6	28.1	29.0	30.2	30.0	9.5	9.3
Slovenia	21.9	23.2	27.3	26.0	27.6	27.5	35.8	29.8	30.7	13.9	8.8
Bulgaria	—	21.2	26.2	—	25.1	—	—	29.1	—	7.9	7.9
Romania	15.5	—	20.4	—	22.6	27.6	27.8	30.3	42.2	26.7	26.7
Estonia	—	—	—	—	—	—	—	—	—	—	—
Latvia	24.4	—	24.7	33.3	28.3	32.5	34.6	34.9	33.6	12.5	11.2
Lithuania	26.0	—	—	37.2	—	34.9	34.1	35.0	34.5	11.2	8.5
Moldova	25.0	—	—	41.1	43.7	37.9	39.0	—	—	18.7	14.0
Russia	27.1	26.9	32.5	37.1	46.1	44.6	47.1	48.3	—	21.2	21.2
Ukraine	24.9	—	—	25.1	36.4	—	—	41.3	—	—	16.1
Azerbaijan	27.5	—	—	—	—	—	—	45.8	—	18.3	18.3
Georgia	30.1	—	—	36.9	—	40.0	—	—	49.8	19.7	19.7
Kyrgyzstan	26.0	—	—	30.0	44.5	44.3	39.5	42.8	43.1	18.5	17.1

Source: UNICEF's TransMONEE 2000 database (www.unicef-icdc.org).

Russia and Ukraine it surged from 3 to 15 between 1990 and 1994, to stabilize at around 10 over the 1994–7 period. A similar—if less pronounced—pattern was observed in the Ukraine where the decile ratio rose from 3.0 to about 5.5 over the same period. In the economies characterized by a marked decline in labour institutions (Russia and other members of the former Soviet Union), the increase in the relative pay position of managers and white-collar workers arose not only from premia on skills and abilities but also from distributional failures arising, for instance, from privatization. As an example, asset stripping of privatized SOEs often took the form of higher wages (Lehmann *et al.* 1999).

Interestingly, the data indicate that the widening of the earnings distribution has been driven by almost proportional changes in both tails of the distribution. Changes in the ratios 'P10/median' and 'P90/median' broadly suggest that the relative wage position of low-paid workers has deteriorated while that of high-paid workers has improved. Yet, while the position of high-paid workers has improved everywhere, that of low-paid workers has fallen everywhere except in countries (such as Poland, the Czech Republic, and Slovenia) characterized by strong 'labour institutions' such as unionization, collective bargaining, and minimum wages (Rutkowski 1999).

What explains the observed rise in wage inequality? With the progressive liberalization of wage negotiations, a new pattern of job remuneration more closely linked to skill levels has emerged. In some cases, job demand for new skills (computer specialists, accountants, people with knowledge of foreign languages, bankers, and so on) has not found an adequate supply of skilled workers, thus leading to sharp rises in their wages. In addition, returns to education appear to have risen (though less evidently so in the public sector). Vecernik (1994) found that in the Czech Republic the rate of return to one additional year of education rose, on average, from 3.5 to 6.2 per cent. A World Bank (1994) study on Poland found the increase to be from 6.4 per cent in 1989 to 7.5 per cent in 1992. In contrast, returns to experience were found to be declining in East Germany, the Czech Republic, Poland, and Slovakia (but not in Slovenia), as the experience acquired during the previous regime became less valuable under the new market conditions (Milanovic 1995). Be as it may, empirical analyses of the proportion of the inequality surge explained by increasing returns to education indicate that these explain a comparatively modest part of the total rise, and that therefore other observed or unobserved factors must be brought into the picture. In an analysis covering Hungary, Bulgaria, Macedonia, and Poland, Rutkowski (1999, table 11) found that with the exception of Hungary (where they explained 26 per cent of the increase in earnings inequality) in the other three countries higher returns to education explained only 10 per cent of the increase in earnings dispersion, an amount similar to that attributable to factors such as inter-industrial and urban–rural wage dispersion. These findings are corroborated by an analysis based on the November 1997 Russian Longitudinal Monitoring Study carried out by Lehmann *et al.* (1999, p. 11), who conclude that '... only a tiny share of the overall inequality *and a small fraction of the change in inequality* can be explained with raising returns to education'. Inter-industrial wage variations, location, and wage arrears were found to explain a bigger share of the variation in earnings inequality.

Indeed, in Russia, Romania, and most other transitional economies of South Eastern Europe and the former Soviet Union, wage dispersion appears to have risen even more sharply across industries than by skill level (after controlling for skill intensity). What are the reasons for this increased inter-industrial wage inequality? The case of Russia is symptomatic and illustrates a pattern observed elsewhere in the region (Table 10.10). The sectors that have gained relative to the average are mining and extraction, power generation, water and gas, banking, finance, and insurance. On the other hand, sectors depending on the state budget, like health, education, research, and culture, have suffered quite significantly from this increase in wage dispersion. Wages in the agricultural sector also have slipped significantly.

The most plausible explanation for this phenomenon could be a widening of productivity differentials across sectors. This, however, appears to account for only a small part of the story. Often '... workers in enterprises operating as natural monopolies, notably in energy extraction and supply [where output is now traded at world market prices], saw big rises in their wages' (Flemming and Micklewright 1999, p. 61). In Romania, for instance, the mining and power generation have shown wage raises greater than the parallel increases in productivity (Zamfir 1995), possibly owing to the monopolistic nature of these sectors and their ability to exert strong political pressure during wage negotiations. This is particularly true for strategic industries and vital sectors such as mining, oil, transport, and power generation. Workers have much less sway in the agricultural or manufacturing sectors, where competition is growing due to privatization, industrial restructuring and import liberalization, and where the risk of layoffs is much greater than in other industries. Second, wages in several branches of the public administration (education, health, and research) have been affected by the poor

Table 10.10. *Average wage by sector in relation to the national average wage, Russia, 1990–1995*

	1990	1991	1992	1993	1994	1995*
Average	100	100	100	100	100	100
Industry	103	111	118	108	104	111
Agriculture	95	84	66	61	50	43
Construction	124	127	134	133	129	131
Transport	115	120	146	151	150	152
Commerce	85	91	91	107	123	117
Health care, sports, social insurance	67	76	66	76	76	84
Education	67	71	61	68	69	77
Culture and arts	62	67	52	62	62	67
Science, R&D	113	90	64	68	78	78
Credit, finance, and insurance	135	180	204	243	208	—
Government ministries	120	99	94	115	117	119
Public utilities	74	80	82	92	96	110

Note: *Figures for November.
Source: Goskomstat (1995, 1996).

performance in tax collection and the ensuing budgetary difficulties of the last few years. And finally, the relative wage increases in the areas of finance and banking reflect the growing importance of these sectors in the market economy and, as opposed to all other sectors, significant productivity gains resulting from the restructuring process.

By and large, real wages in the 'strong sectors' stopped declining in 1993 and have often increased in real terms since 1994 or 1995. In contrast, wages in agriculture and, in particular, in public social services and agriculture continued their decline (Table 10.10).

Particularly in the states part of the former Soviet Union, wage dispersion was also influenced by the policy towards the minimum wage. The latter have indeed experienced a generalized fall in relation to the average wage (Standing and Vaughan-Whitehead 1995). Indeed, the countries experiencing the largest increases in wage dispersion are generally the same ones in which the minimum wage has fallen most relative to the average wage (Table 10.11). Except in Poland, where the minimum wage rose substantially from its artificially low 1989 level, and in Hungary and Slovenia, where the ratio of minimum to average wage rose moderately from a fairly high level, minimum wages fell in all countries by between 30 and 60 per cent in relation to the wage rate. The sharpest falls were recorded in Moldova and Russia.

Finally, earnings dispersion has also been influenced by the tax-based income policy adopted for macroeconomic reasons in several transitional economies. According to this policy, many workers who have *de facto* been laid off are kept on the books because of the tax benefits available to firms which maintain low average wages. The 'excess wage tax', calculated on the average wage paid out by a firm, provides a substantial

Table 10.11. *Minimum wage as a proportion of the average wage in selected countries, in transition, 1989–1994*

	1989	1990	1991	1992	1993	1994	Difference between 1989–1994	Difference between max/min
Czech R.	—	—	52.8	45.9	37.8	33.3	−19.5	19.5
Slovakia	—	61.0	58.2	54.7	46.5	39.8	−21.2	21.2
Hungary	44.6	48.7	51.9	51.3	48.5	—	3.9	7.3
Poland	11.6	21.4	34.9	37.5	41.0	40.4	28.8	29.4
Slovenia	24.2	37.9	39.1	35.2	32.3	29.0	4.8	14.9
Albania	68.0	66.0	65.0	40.0	27.2	50.0	−18.0	40.8
Bulgaria	51.1	45.7	68.0	41.5	38.2	36.7	−14.4	31.3
Romania	65.3	59.1	61.6	45.8	37.2	—	−28.1	28.1
Latvia	—	—	37.4	25.6	24.1	28.5	−8.9	13.3
Lithuania	31.5	26.6	38.6	33.1	25.6	22.8	−8.7	15.8
Belarus	30.3	26.1	21.3	19.4	14.1	9.1	−21.2	21.2
Moldova	35.0	30.0	31.0	25.0	23.0	15.0	−20.0	20.0
Russia	26.6	23.6	25.3	11.8	10.1	8.3	−18.3	18.3
Ukraine	32.2	28.1	42.6	—	—	—	10.4	14.5

Source: UNICEF (1995).

incentive to firms to keep unneeded workers on extremely low (or zero) salary, rather than laying them off, so as to keep down their total per capita wage bill (Roxborough and Shapiro 1994).

10.5.2.2. Changes in the Concentration of Transfers

A thorough reform of the tax and transfer system could have mitigated the rise in inequality caused by the economic reform. The information compiled in Table 10.12 indicates that such opportunity has been used to some extent in Hungary and Poland in the case of social assistance transfers. The same is true for the family allowances which remained moderately progressive and whose targeting generally improved during the reforms (with the exception of Poland). Improvements in transfer progressivity, however, remained well below those that can be achieved under 'best practice conditions'. In contrast, the move to a new pension regime has considerably increased inequality, as indicated in both the case of Hungary and, particularly, Poland (Table 10.12).

10.5.2.3. Changes in the Concentration of Capital and Self-employment Income

Limited systematic information is available about the dispersion of capital, entrepreneurial, and self-employment incomes. As noted, while these incomes are included in the HBS, their values are often grossly misreported. Despite this, the information compiled below (Table 10.13) supports the view of a sharp rise in concentration in property incomes and of a more moderate one in self-employment income. The surge in income concentration incomes was likely larger in the economies of the former Soviet Union, where the tax and regulatory role of the state (to ensure, for instance, genuine market competition) is less developed.

Table 10.12. *Changes in the concentration coefficients of social transfers in selected countries, in transition, 1989–1993*

		Social assistance, unemployment benefit and sick pay	Pensions	Family allowances
Bulgaria	1992	6.1	—	−4.1
	1993	10.6	—	−5.0
Slovakia	1989	10.8	—	−21.9
	1993	—	17.7	−25.1
Hungary	1989	19.8	7.7	−13.4
	1993	−11.3	19.9	−15.2
Poland	1990	14.7	13.7	−16.2
	1993	−8.6	33.6	−11.8

Source: Author's calculations on the TransMONEE database (November 1995 version), UNICEF-ICDC, Florence.

Table 10.13. *Changes in the concentration coefficients of property and self-employment incomes in selected countries in transition, 1989–1993*

		Self-employment	Property
Bulgaria	1992	55.7	33.8
	1993	53.2	74.4
Slovakia	1989	21.7	—
	1993	28.6	—
Hungary	1989	28.5	35.5
	1993	28.9	67.5
Poland	1990	33.2	—
	1993	41.8	78.6

Source: Author's calculations on the TransMONEE database (November 1995 version), UNICEF-ICDC, Florence.

Table 10.14. *Decomposition of the increase in the Gini coefficients of the distribution of household incomes between the pre-transition period and the years 1993–1996 for selected countries in transition*

Country	Due to							
		Change in concentration of:						
					Out of which			
	Change in income structure	Wages	Social transfers	Pensions	Non-pension transfers	Non-wage private sector	Interaction term	Overall Gini change
Hungary (1989–93)	−1.3	+5.9	−0.6	+1.4	−0.2	−0.6	−1.3	+2.2
Slovenia (1987–95)	−0.2	+3.6	−0.6	−0.1	−0.4	+0.4	−3.8	+2.6
Poland (1987–95)	−1.7	+3.4	+3.5	+3.2	−0.1	+0.8	+0.9	+7.0
Bulgaria (1989–95)	+1.4	+7.8	+0.9	+0.4	+0.4	−0.4	+0.3	+10.0
Latvia (1989–96)	−1.6	+15.0	−1.5	−2.0	+0.5	+1.4	−3.3	+10.0
Russia (1989–94)	−3.4	+17.8	+5.1	+3.9	+0.4	+3.0	+1.2	+23.6

Source: Milanovic (1998, table 4.2).

10.5.3. *In Conclusion*

Where does all this lead to? While lack of data prevents to formally decompose the overall increase in inequality for the countries under examination, the evidence provided in this chapter and in the literature (Milanovic 1998; Flemming and

Micklewright 1999) suggests that the main factor in the increase in overall inequality was the sharp rise observed in earnings inequality (Table 10.14). Changes in income structure have played a less important (or even equalizing) role, as the considerable rise in the share of income transfers in the countries of Central Europe more than offset the increase in that of capital and entrepreneurial incomes. Similarly, non-wage private incomes (including capital incomes and incomes from self-employment) have become somewhat more concentrated but do not appear so far to be the major source of the observed rise in overall income inequality. And as shown by the case of Russia and Poland, the growing concentration of pensions has contributed perceptibly to the increase in overall inequality, while changes in non-pension transfers had a negligible impact on the overall distribution.

10.6. CONCLUSIONS: UNEVEN INSTITUTIONAL DEVELOPMENTS, INEQUALITY, AND GROWTH

Ten years after the onset of the transition (20 in the case of China), there is unambiguous evidence that earnings, income, and asset inequality have risen throughout the former centrally planned economies. The received economic theory which emphasizes market-driven changes poorly explains the extent and pattern of the observed increases in inequality. According to this view, inequality was expected to surge moderately in all economies in transition due to the disequalizing effects of greater returns to education, the privatization of profits, and the removal of subsidies. Yet, this chapter has shown that the extent and pattern of inequality changes during the transition has varied among the main groups of countries depending on their ability to develop adequate institutions in the markets for assets and labour, and in the field of taxes and transfers.

In the transitional countries of Europe, the surge in inequality followed two distinct patterns, juxtaposing Central Europe to South Eastern Europe and the countries of the former Soviet Union. Central Europe has broadly 'caught up' with the levels of inequality observed in the medium-inequality economies of the OECD. This comparatively modest increase was made possible by the preservation of an extensive and fairly efficient welfare state capable of targeting sizeable income transfers to the low-income groups. Even more important, in these countries, earnings inequality rose only moderately despite a full liberalization of the labour market owing to the preservation or creation of adequate 'labour institutions' including a network of labour exchanges, unemployment compensation, adequate minimum wages and public sector wages, collective bargaining, and so on. In addition, in these countries, the measured impact of privatization on inequality has so far been less pronounced than expected.

In contrast, in the collapsed economies of South Eastern Europe and, in particular, the former Soviet Union, Gini coefficients of both earnings and disposable income rose by 10–20 points (despite an even greater under-registration of high incomes), i.e. two to three times faster than in Central and Eastern Europe. Such upsurges were triggered by a much sharper transitional recession and by an inadequate institutional development. On the one side, the volume of social transfers collapsed and their composition and targeting deteriorated (Milanovic 1995). Second, the new labour market emerging in this group of countries has been characterized by huge institutional distortions, as reflected by the sharp rise in jobs without written contracts and legal protection, large wage gaps between sectors and locations unexplained by differences in human capital or experience, the spread of wage arrears (which in 1999 concerned about half of the Russian labour fource; Lehmann et al. 1999), the decline of absolute and relative wages in the budgetary sector, the collapse of minimum wages, the slow development of a network of labour exchanges unable to match vacancies with job applications, and so on. Finally, though most official surveys do not capture a large increase in non-wage, non-transfer incomes, the pattern of privatization followed in this group of countries was much less egalitarian than in Central Europe (Honkkila 1997) and gave rise to a pronounced, if undeserved, asset concentration.

Income inequality rose also in the Asian economies in transition, though the pattern it followed is less likely to have affected incentives, social cohesion, and productivity. In China, the rise in regional inequality which began in 1985–90 can be traced to the lopsided expansion of industrial and commercial activities between the urban centres and coastal regions on the one side and the interior regions and rural areas on the other. The fast rise in inter-regional inequality in the 1990s, however, was accompanied by less pronounced increases in intra-regional inequality and was, to a good extent, driven by market factors (greater incentives, investments, and use of qualified labour) rather than non-market factors (ascription, political rent-seeking, and inadequate institutional development). The growth impact of such kind of inequality is likely to be less pronounced than that of a surge in income stratification which affects most locations of a country, as observed in the former Soviet Union. Indeed, in view of the comparatively modest domestic migration, low local-level inequality in China has had a limited effect on local-level work incentives and social cohesion. This more favourable situation, however, is unlikely to last as many interior regions are now affected by the restructuring and privatization of SOEs, a fact that—in the absence of a regionally balanced industrial policy—will aggravate both intra- and inter-regional gaps in unemployment, inequality, and social tensions. Also, persistence of marked regional gaps over the long term is also likely to lead to further migration to the coastal area, where economic stratification, social marginalization, and instability might therefore increase.

These different patterns of inequality rises—which already emerged after four to five years of transition in Europe and after a decade in China—contributed in an important manner to the huge variation in performance among the economies in transition (Table 1.1 in Chapter 1). In Central and Eastern Europe, the catching up with the inequality levels of the European Union has helped remove the disincentives, labour-shirking and free-riding behaviours typical of the artificial egalitarianism dominating the state enterprises of the centrally planned economies and recording a better than average growth performance among the European economies in transition. In the countries of the former Soviet Union and of South Eastern Europe, in contrast, the pattern of inequality increase observed up to 1994 contributed to the poor economic performance and mounting instability of the years 1994–9. As noted by Doyle (1993, p. 19; cited in McAuley 1994), '... Russia has experienced a widening of its income distribution over one year [1992] equivalent in scale to that which occurred in the UK over ten years'. Such a huge increase in inequality has now taken root and it will be difficult to undo. Because of its level and undeserved nature, it will continue to exert a negative influence on social cohesion, work incentives, and productivity. Indeed, the historical and theoretical evidence suggests that high levels of income concentration cause slow growth and social instability. There are four sets of arguments supporting this contention.

To start with, high inequality (particularly if it arises from undeserved accumulation of assets and opportunities, large wage differentials not justified by differences in human capital endowments and personal ability, the erosion of labour institutions, rent-seeking and predatory activities) can erode work incentives, increase labour-shirking and supervision costs and reduce efficiency. Several empirical studies document such a relation in rural settings and in several industrial branches. In addition, high asset and income concentration augment social tensions which, in turn, erode the security of property rights, increase the cost of business security and contract enforcement, augment the threat of expropriation, and drive away domestic and foreign investment (Benabou 1996).

Second, high levels of income inequality—especially when this derives from ascription—create socio-political instability and social tensions which reduce the financial savings, increase the hoarding of precious metals, stones and foreign currency, drive away domestic and foreign investment and thus depress the rate of growth (Venieris and Gupta 1986). Socio-political instability introduces an additional element of uncertainty in the decision-making calculus of the economic agents since it is usually perceived as a precursor of changes in the govermental regime which, in turn, may affect one's own future level of accumulated wealth and income.

Third, as suggested by the 'median voter theory', under democratic rule, countries characterized by a high degree of asset and income inequality are, *ceteris paribus*, expected to grow less rapidly than countries with lower income concentration. Indeed, high initial levels of inequality are likely to lead to the election of governments which favour redistribution through high marginal tax rates which, in turn, reduce private investment and economic growth (Alesina and Rodrik 1994; Alesina and Perotti 1996). Should this option be resisted, governments may revert to populist monetary and fiscal policies—such as inflationary financing, excessive borrowing from domestic capital markets which crowds out private investment, or accumulating international debts—which tend to destabilize the economy.

Finally, high income inequality leads to a consumption pattern which is more import intensive than that inherent to a more egalitarian society. The tendency by the wealthy to have a higher propensity to consume imported goods than the poor and the middle class exacerbates international payment crises and affects growth. Second, the domestic consumption of the high-income groups tends to be addressed to sectors which have higher capital/output ratios than those producing for the poor, a fact that diminishes the growth potential of countries affected by capital shortage. Third, it is now evident that high inequality does not increase the saving rate, and that in fact the middle class has a higher propensity to save than the wealthy (Venieris and Gupta 1986). The saving constraint may therefore be more severe under unequal growth than under more egalitarian conditions.

11

Informal Institutions, Social Capital, and Economic Transition: Reflections on a Neglected Dimension

MARTIN RAISER

One of the most promising terrains for an application of institutional economics is the current transition process in Central and Eastern Europe, the former Soviet Union (FSU), and parts of Asia. What distinguishes the reforms implemented in all of these countries from earlier stabilization and structural adjustment policies in developing countries is their systemic character. In the transitional economies, policy reform aims not only at changing relative prices but also the entire set of economic, legal, and social incentive structures governing human economic behaviour (for an early recognition of this task and a rebuttal of partial reforms on that basis, see Kornai (1980); similar ideas are expressed in Balcerowicz (1995)). Thus, Chapter 1 of this volume correctly emphasizes that the success of the overall reform effort depends to a considerable extent on the existence of adequate institutions. One might go one step further and state that what transition is all about is a redesign of the institutional framework of formerly centrally planned economies. A transition theory therefore will necessarily be a theory of institutional change.

This chapter focuses on one particular aspect of institutional change, namely the role of informal institutions in economic transition. Thereby, I will adopt Douglass North's definition of institutions as 'humanly devised constraints that structure political and social interaction' (North 1991) or, more specifically, economic exchange. Informal institutions may then be understood as the collection of social norms, conventions, and moral values that constrain individuals and organizations in pursuit of their goals. Section 1 of this study focuses on the interrelationship between informal institutions and economic development. It argues that informal institutions complement formal institutions in reducing the costs of transactions and examines the conditions needed for an efficient set of both types of institutions to emerge. This leads to the formulation of a stylized model of institutional change. Section 2 applies this model to the transition economies by contrasting reform patterns according to the strength of the state, the level of trust in society, and the nature of inherited informal institutions. Conclusions are offered in Section 3.

11.1. INFORMAL INSTITUTIONS: BRINGING ECONOMICS BACK INTO THE SOCIAL SCIENCES

11.1.1. *Informal Institutions and Economic Development*

Informal institutions are usually understood as the set of social and moral norms, which coordinate peoples' expectations of one another. 'It is not done, because...' or 'one ought to...' are typical beginnings of sentences expressing social or moral norms. Since human beings are social animals and have the desire to be accepted by others, informal institutions exert a powerful influence on human behaviour. In the analytical framework of economics, informal institutions may be conceptualized as constraints on individual choice.

Because they limit the number of feasible alternatives, informal institutions (as formal ones) can greatly enhance economic efficiency by reducing transaction costs in the presence of imperfect information and uncertainty. Hence, it has been argued that many social norms arise naturally in the process of social evolution because of their ability to solve collective choice problems by allowing individuals to signal their behaviour to others (Sugden 1989). However, not all social norms serve the purpose of increasing efficiency (Elster 1989). For instance, the social norm against buying one's place in a queue clearly runs counter to economic intuition, which suggests that differences in the value people attach to time spent queuing would present ample opportunities for arbitrage.

A social norm may be distinguished from a moral norm in that it is non-consequentialist. While social norms may be sustained out of selfish motivations alone, moral norms pay explicit attention to the effect of one's behaviour on the others. Moral norms may, however, be important in supporting social norms and sustaining cooperative equilibria. Informal institutions are self-enforcing, in that they become internalized through socialization and need only the threat of social exclusion as a sanctioning mechanism. This property distinguishes social and moral norms from legal norms and regulations that are typically enforced by professionals, such as judges and the police. This does not imply that social norms may not be manipulated to one's individual advantage. However, as an integrated system, informal institutions reinforce each other and limit one's ability to pick the most advantageous norm in each situation.

Social norms, like the norm of reciprocity, play a prominent role in coordinating economic activity in small, 'face-to-face' communities. When the probability of repeated interactions is high, social sanctions against cheating are extremely powerful. Failing to abide by a given rule would trigger one's exclusion from the existing network of social relations. One's access to important information would be restricted, one's credibility as a partner to economic exchange undermined and the transaction costs of participating in intra-community exchange could become prohibitively high.

As the division of labour expands across the border of a small community, individuals acquire increasing exit options and the threat of social exclusion loses in importance. More formal institutional arrangements are sought that may substitute for reputational mechanisms in face-to-face communities. Adherence to a specific religion and command of a certain language might be taken as a signal of trustworthiness and members of periphic ethnic groups would be forced to join the persuasions of the host society.

Hence, in the course of economic development, informal institutions are partly replaced by more formal arrangements, first within a closed social group but ultimately within the structure of a codified system of laws and regulations at the level of the nation state. It should be emphasized, however, that this process of substitution is far from automatic and far from complete. With respect to the first, traditional societies have differed greatly in their ability to enforce informal institutions through a system of collective attitudes that urged members to sanction deviant behaviour even if they were not directly affected. The more successful and persistent such collective attitudes, the less the perceived need to adopt more formal rules of conduct (Platteau 1994).[1]

The replacement of informal institutions by more formal coordinating mechanisms is far from complete even in advanced market economies. Institutional performance continues to be influenced by informal institutions long after economic coordination takes place predominantly through formal rules. On the one hand, transactions costs of economic exchange would become prohibitive if all contingencies were to be fully covered by contract covenants and their breach enforced in court. According to Wallis and North (1986), transaction costs in the United States are already as high as 40 per cent of GDP. A certain amount of mutual trust and goodwill is thus essential for the full potential of the division of labour to be realized. On the other hand, public expectations and existing social and moral norms also influence the behaviour of those agents entrusted with the formulation, implementation, and enforcement of a new set of rules. When economic agents do not trust each other and the readiness to cooperate is low, the pressures on government officials to provide efficient third-party enforcement are weakened.[2] Following this reasoning, the level of 'social capital' (Coleman 1988) in a society is an important factor in facilitating contract enforcement and promoting economic development.

11.1.2. *The Evolution of Informal Institutions: The role of Generalized Morality*

Many of the most effective informal institutions are those that promote cooperative solutions to problems of collective choice. How do they come about? Game theory provides one possibility to analyse the evolution and stability of cooperative equilibria (Platteau 1994). In a variety of the classical prisoners' dilemma, the so-called assurance game, honesty is allowed to directly influence the payoffs of the individual players. In this game, a cooperative solution will emerge if (a) there are a sufficiently large number of honest players and (b) these players believe that they are a majority, i.e. their subjective probability of dealing with another honest person is high. The likelihood of cooperation is also increased by the strength of the moral predisposition to cooperate.

What is the dynamic stability of a cooperative equilibrium? When the experiences of all players are common knowledge, an honest majority will be stable, because meeting a cheater does not change the subjective probability of an honest player of meeting another honest player on occasion of the next encounter. However, when information is imperfect and honest players get discouraged from meeting a series of cheaters and decide to turn cheaters themselves, the cooperative equilibrium may disentangle. In the presence of a sufficient number of cheaters, a fully non-cooperative equilibrium is the only stable solution. Further generalizations allow for detection technologies that help to identify the disposition of another player, guilt feelings on part of the cheaters, and sanctioning of cheaters by third parties, even if these are not directly affected by their action. A conclusion from all these models is that the emergence of cooperation through an evolutionary process where players constantly re-evaluate their strategies depends on the initial distribution of moral propensities and the prevailing technology for disseminating information about other players. Platteau (1994, p. 765) argues that the fulfilment of these conditions 'largely depends on the prevalence of moral norms (concerned about the effects of one's actions on others) in the society'.

Moral norms have to be sustained and reinforced just as other social norms. However, the ability to apply sanctions for disregard towards others is limited, because such moral behaviour is typically not verifiable. Rather, moral predispositions are instilled by socialization.[3] While a charismatic leadership and ideological persuasion through the state may supply a framework of generalized morality, this is unlikely to be sustained. Reinforcement of moral norms is primarily effected through demonstration effects of role model behaviour and through ongoing communication (Platteau 1994).[4] Hence, institutions of a civil society such as the Church, the local football club, or an active media are important elements of a society that allow the reproduction of a generalized morality and sustain a society's stock of social capital. By the same token, the absence of such reinforcing institutions may preserve a non-cooperative social equilibrium adverse to economic development.

11.1.3. *Informal Institutions and Institutional Reforms*

Let me summarize the previous discussion in the form of a graphical model of social interaction and institutional change. In Fig. 11.1, the various formal and informal institutions are presented in boxes, the formal ones on the right and the informal ones on the left, and their interrelationships are represented by arrows. The top and bottom of the figure are taken as exogenous. On the top, one finds exogenous conditions such as history, ideology, and leadership, which determine what particular set of institutions is present in a given society at any one point in time.[5] At the bottom of the figure are represented preferences and technologies. These are factors typically considered as exogenous by economists—although new growth theory attempts to endogenize at least the latter (e.g. Aghion and Howitt 1992). Technologies and preferences also influence the institutional framework, because they determine the costs and benefits of compliance with a set of formal and informal rules (North 1981). In the figure, preferences and technologies are allowed to influence institutions only indirectly through the process of social and economic interaction. Note that the feedback arrows to formal and informal institutions are broken, to express the idea of path dependence.[6]

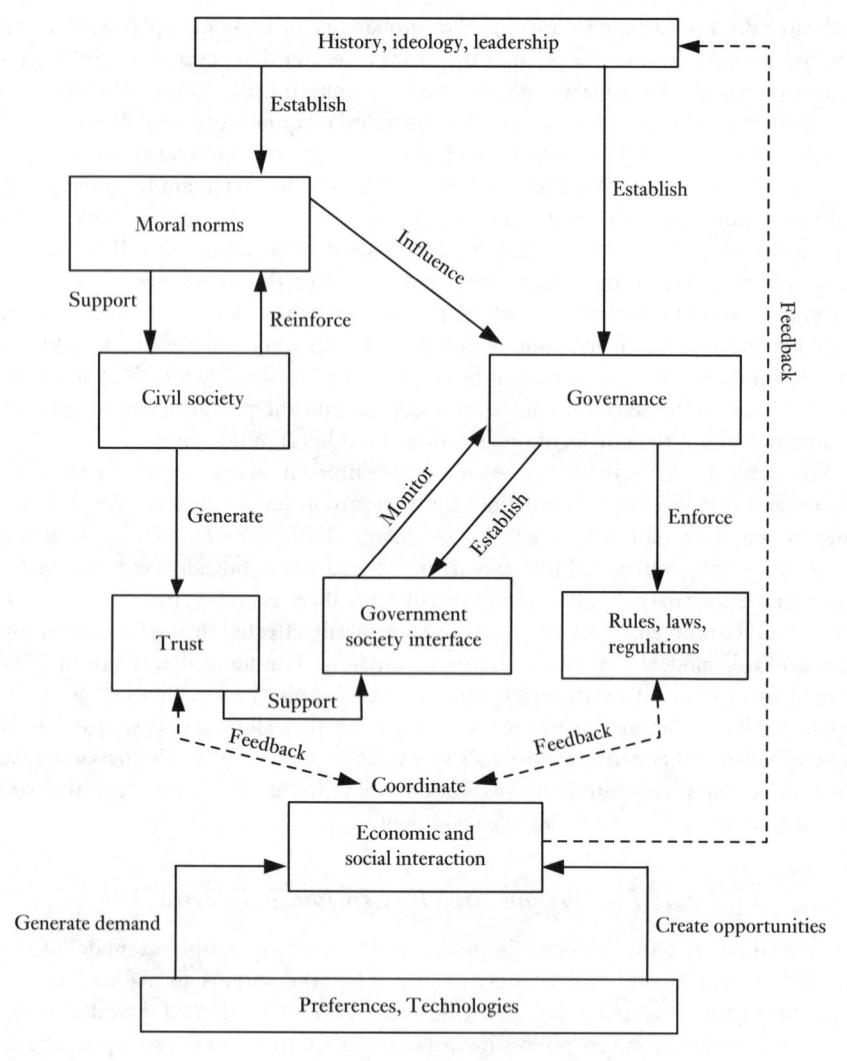

Figure 11.1. *Representation of the interrelationships between formal and informal institutions*

The main body of the figure is filled with six boxes, standing for the broad sets of formal and informal institutions that are to some extent present in all societies. The box at the top left is the set of moral norms. The presence of a specific type of moral norms (i.e. generalized morality as opposed to kinship solidarity) feeds into the emergence of a civil society, understood as comprising all non-governmental organizations such as the press, leisure clubs, churches, neighbourhood associations, and so on. The existence of a working civil society in turn tends to reinforce the moral predispositions of individuals, as noted in the previous section. It also creates 'trust' among economic actors, thereby facilitating economic exchange under imperfect information. The sequence of boxes on the left-hand side of Fig. 11.1 represents a stylized model of how social capital is accumulated.

On the right-hand side of the figure is represented the sequence that leads to a set of formal institutions and a particular form of governance. Again, the form of governance that evolves is the result of both exogenous factors and the existing set of moral norms. The form of governance impacts on the enforcement of a system of laws and regulations which formally structure social interaction and economic exchange. The sixth box is placed in the middle and represents the interface between government and society. What role is accorded to this interface is partly a function of the government's willingness to engage in policy dialogue, but also crucially contingent on the existing level of trust in government institutions. The socio-political interface may involve formal arrangements, such as the East Asian 'deliberation councils' (Campos and Root 1996) or the German *konzertierte Aktion* (Boswell 1990). However, it could also take more informal forms, for instance, when politicians become active members of social clubs and are thus exposed to monitoring by their constituencies.

The above model identifies several levels of action in bringing about institutional change. First of all, institutional change is brought about by exogenous shocks, coming either from the polity (i.e. a change in ideology or political leadership) or from the economic sphere (a change in technologies or preferences). Second, institutional change may occur from inside the institutional framework. Governments can change the formal rules, either in response to an exogenous shock or in anticipation of future changes, or, less benevolently, in maximizing their own returns from a position of power. Governments can also improve incentives for better governance by public officials, by reducing the scope for policy discretion, increasing job competition and raising public sector pay (Rose-Ackerman 1996). Third, governments can attempt to positively influence the interaction between formal and informal institutions by engaging civil society into a policy dialogue. However, the effectiveness of such a policy dialogue will depend on the given level of trust in government and its formal institutions. While a predisposition to engage in policy dialogue is an important ingredient in efficiently using what social capital there exists, the limitations of governments in accumulating social capital have to be recognized.

What does this suggest for the challenge of systemic reform faced by the transition economies? Most evidently, exogenous shocks have varied from case to case. In much of Eastern Europe, the shock caused by the opening of the economy to the world markets was accompanied by the shock induced by the shift to democratic politics (Nelson et al. 1994).[7] Political changes have been much less marked in China and most of Central Asia. Furthermore, the impact of economic shocks has to some extent depended on the initial conditions (Sachs and Woo 1994). Meanwhile, the nature of the exogenous shocks has obviously influenced the choice of reform strategies in transition economies (Fan 1994; Friedman and Johnson 1996). Bearing such constraints in mind, I propose three possible reform strategies which form the basis for the typology of patterns of institutional change in transition economies to be developed in this chapter.

A first reform strategy emphasizes the stability of the formal institutional framework and the only gradual change of laws and regulations. This strategy attempts to reform the formal institutional framework in step with changes in informal institutions so as to minimize the potential for friction. However, when exogenous shocks are large, the resulting inefficiencies from failing to rapidly adapt the set of formal rules may outweigh the costs of friction with a slow changing set of informal institutions. The institutional stability—which is the aim of this strategy—could in fact be undermined from within, as compliance with formal rules gets too costly and attempts to budge the law increase.[8] A second strategy, diametrically opposed to the first, consists in changing at one stroke the formal institutional framework to fully conform to the basic requirements of a new economic system. Lipton and Sachs (1990) are among the early proponents of this strategy. The risks faced by this approach are that the enforcement costs of the new rules are substantial for quite some time, because these are not matched by a set of self-enforcing informal rules. Both the first and second strategies presuppose the existence of an effective government able either to maintain institutional stability or to implement rapid institutional change. A third strategy accepts the limited capability of government in most transition economies. Institutional design in this strategy is guided by political feasibility. This implies that institutional reforms will be more rapid in areas where the costs of adapting to new rules are lower, because of their simplicity, ease of implementation, and limited demands in terms of changes in people's behaviour.[9] Political economy considerations often force the adoption of the third strategy. However, this approach runs the danger that institutional reforms remain blocked by powerful insiders or become bogged down in conflicts between interest groups. Arguably, focusing attention on the socio-political interface (see Fig. 11.1) is of particular importance in this third case and varying degrees of success may be attributed to varying degrees of existing social capital.

The second part of this study argues that only China and East Germany fulfilled the condition of a strong state necessary for the adoption of the first or the second reform strategy. Most other transition economies fall into the third category, albeit with important differences regarding state capacity and the inheritance of a set of complementary informal institutions.

11.2. INFORMAL INSTITUTIONS AND TRANSITION

11.2.1. *Institutional Reforms under a Strong State: Top-down versus Bottom-up*

The Chinese economy has been booming for the past 20 years. By contrast, East Germany has experienced one of the largest industrial recessions in Eastern Europe and average growth rates such as those achieved by neighbouring Poland and the Czech Republic still elude the five new German Laender. On the face of this evidence, one might easily conclude that the strategy of gradual institutional reforms in China is vastly superior to the shock approach chosen on occasion of the German reunification. This section attempts to put these claims into perspective. On the one hand, it argues

Informal Institutions, Social Capital, Economic Transition

that the Chinese success relied to a considerable extent on informal institutions which were already present during the socialist era. Without this 'institutional inheritance' gradualism might not have worked in China. At the same time, there is little evidence that a mismatch between the pace of change in formal and informal institutions is at the heart of the East German recession. A more important cause of the poor performance of the former East Germany is to be found most probably in the widely criticized wage and exchange rate policies adopted during and after the reunification (Sinn and Sinn 1993). On the other hand, this section stresses the communality between these two polar cases, as in both instances there was a strong state able to control the pace of formal institutional change. Arguably, the dichotomy between shock and gradualism breaks down in countries where this condition is no longer met.

11.2.1.1. Invigorating the Local Economy: The Roots of China's success

One of the central elements of economic reforms in China has been a progressive administrative and fiscal decentralization (Qian and Roland 1994). Local government authorities have taken responsibility over a wide range of economic decisions, and with fiscal decentralization have had increasing access to funds for financing local development. The process of decentralization has thus created strong incentives at the local level to implement policies that would favour the prosperity of the locality.

To a large extent, decentralization has been remarkably successful in China. At the root of China's impressive growth performance are the dynamic town and village enterprises (TVEs) (Table 11.1). The notable feature of this sector is that it is collectively owned but it is managed to maximize profits rather than worker incomes. Further, because the resources at the disposal of local governments are limited, TVEs

Table 11.1. *Selected performance indicators in state-owned enterprises, community-owned enterprises, and town and village enterprises, China, 1983–1993*

	1983	1984	1985	1986	1987	1988	1989	1990	1991	1992	1993	1994	1995
Output growth[a]													
SOEs	9.4	8.9	12.9	6.2	11.3	12.6	3.9	2.9	8.6	12.4	5.7	6.5	8.2
COEs	15.5	34.9	32.7	17.9	23.2	28.2	10.5	9.0	18.4	39.3	35.9	29.8	15.2
TVEs	31.5	61.7	38.9	28.0	27.7	28.0	2.8	14.5	27.8	51.6	54.9	11.0	41.0
Profit rate[b]													
SOEs	—	—	23.5	20.7	20.3	20.6	17.2	12.4	11.8	9.7	9.7	8.0	6.5
COEs	—	—	24.6	19.4	18.2	19.8	15.4	11.5	11.9	10.1	—	9.2	7.7
Other[c]	—	—	28.2	23.3	24.9	24.7	16.2	11.3	12.9	11.1	11.3	14.8	14.1
Share of enterprises making losses													
SOEs	—	—	9.5	13.1	13.0	10.9	16.0	27.6	25.8	23.4	30.3	—	—
COEs	—	—	11.7	13.2	15.7	11.7	15.7	19.4	16.7	13.7	—	—	—
Other[c]	—	—	10.2	15.8	15.5	17.2	26.7	32.6	31.7	27.9	—	—	—

Note: [a] In per cent per annum, calculated from SSB (1994); [b] Profits/total value of capital (net fixed assets + working capital). [c] Other include TVEs, joint ventures, and individual business.

Source: Raiser (1997, p. 144).

have typically faced a hard budget constraint (Byrd and Qingsong 1990). The local government has effectively acted as a holding company with majority shareholdings in each TVE, maximizing the extraction of residual profits to further the development of the local economy as a whole (Sun 1996).

What is often not recognized in accounts of China's successful decentralization is that Chinese socialism also differed significantly from the Soviet central planning. Since the 'Great Leap Forward' of the late 1950s, China has experienced several waves of decentralization; the most coherent and permanent one was in the early 1970s (Riskin 1987). During this time, local governments already acquired 'quasi' property rights in local state-owned enterprises (SOEs). The fiscal incentives provided by the formal decentralization process of the 1980s were thus introduced into a local economy used to advance its collective interest in a variety of bargaining relationships both with the centre and with other localities (Granick 1990). The process of learning to live without central subsidies was thereby considerably eased.

At the village level, moreover, discontent with the previous system of collective farming within the commune was rife when agricultural reforms started in 1978 (Watson 1992). Hence, the de-collectivization and introduction of the household responsibility system met with an enthusiastic response by local farmers, in contrast to the muted reaction of workers on the Soviet Kolchozes and Sovchozes, unsure what to do with their newly found responsibilities. With 70 per cent of employment in agriculture in 1978, the fact that existing informal institutions supported de-collectivization must be regarded as a central ingredient of the overall reform success at least until the mid-1980s (see Chapter 1).

One of the central elements of institutional continuity in rural China has been the extended family (Whyte 1996). The Chinese family has been one of the sources for entrepreneurial activity across East Asia. Apart from the reduction of transaction costs achieved through relations of trust among family members, Whyte notes the following advantages of family businesses in the Chinese context. Family businesses face lower employee monitoring costs as turnover is low. Moreover, they allow for risk pooling among different branches of family business interests while at the same time promoting competition amongst junior family members. Finally, the Chinese family encourages social mobility by investing their resources in family members with the highest career prospects. Thereby they mobilize and channel rural savings into productive uses.

Moreover, Confucian family values interacted with changing rural institutions during pre-communist and Maoist time in a way that was more favourable to the development of rural entrepreneurship than for instance in Russia. The underlying historical tradition of the Chinese rural family prior to 1949 was that of a competitive society with considerable social and geographical mobility (Greenlagh 1990). By contrast, the Russia peasantry was trapped in serfdom until 1860. Incentives for social mobility thereafter did hardly improve, as Russia remained an essentially aristocratic society and rural property rights were subject to constant shifts and confiscations. Arguably thus, when agriculture was collectivized in the two countries, already very different modes of behaviour were enshrined in the peasantries of China and Russia. Moreover, according to Whyte, the impact of socialism was to reinforce these differences by respecting and possibly even reinforcing family ties among rural Chinese families, while disrupting most existing family ties in the Soviet Union.[10]

The discussion so far has emphasized the importance of institutional continuities in China's gradual institutional reforms. The central government initiative often merely legalized given practices on the ground, thus greatly reducing enforcement costs of new regulations. However, the central government's role was far from passive. At several instances, the central authority was reasserted, as Beijing attempted to reconcile regional autonomy with the national interest. The traditional policy measure used to this effect has been the central credit plan (Naughton 1996) but occasionally, such as during the 1989–91 rectification programme, direct interventions in pricing decisions and material allocation were also used. While institutional design in the Chinese context thus emerged from below and institutional reforms may duly be characterized as bottom-up, the reform process has also been tightly controlled by the top and experiments deemed unsuccessful have been reversed. The strength and credibility of the central government's reform commitment have thus been of crucial importance for China's success so far.

11.2.1.2. *Legislated Shock Therapy: German Unification*

With the implementation of the German Monetary Union in July 1990, the existing formal institutional framework of West Germany was essentially extended to the five new Laender. The contract on unification specified minor exemptions in the applicability of West German laws, and the regional governments themselves were entrusted with legislative responsibility in a number of areas just as their West German counterparts. Nonetheless, the body of national laws and regulations was to be applied in the East as in the West, from traffic rules to insolvency law.[11]

This legislated shock therapy in East Germany provides an interesting test for the assertion that informal institutions change more slowly than formal institutionals and that the resulting friction may substantially increase transaction costs during the transitory phase. One supporting piece of evidence comes from the prevalence of payment arrears even in circumstances where Western bankruptcy rules are in place and the judicial system is arguably already equipped to handle complaints. In an enterprise survey of 1995 still 60 per cent of all firms reported a low payment morality among customers as one of the major causes of financial problems (DIW *et al.* 1996).

Mummert (1997) has made a recent attempt to find empirical evidence of differences in behaviour of economic agents between East and West that might be attributed to differences in informal institutions. The evidence he analyses is that discounted bills of exchange account for a much smaller share of short-term bank credits in the new than in the old Laender. Mummert has conducted interviews with company managers to find out how they evaluated their external environment and what their specific attitudes were towards discounted bills of exchange, a non-existent means of finance under socialism. The interesting conclusion emerging from his study is that monetary union fundamentally changed the external environment as perceived by East German entrepreneurs and made their expectations statistically indistinguishable from their

West German counterparts. At the same time, significant differences persisted with respect to attitudes to bills of exchange, with East German managers generally expressing a more sceptical attitude regarding its value to their company (Table 11.2). Mummert explains his findings by reference to competitive pressures. While a correct perception of the external environment is crucial for enterprise survival, the use of bills of exchange is not. Hence, argues Mummert, one is likely to observe more path dependence in areas less central to enterprise competitiveness.

The evidence in this area remains, however, scarce. Overall, the adjustment by East German enterprises to changes in the formal institutional framework appears to have been relatively rapid. Thereby, existing social networks have often supported rather than hindered new business formations (Grabher and Stark 1996). Hence, institutional friction due to the sudden replacement of one incentive structure by another is probably not at the root of the disappointing East German performance so far.

Table 11.2. *Perceptions about external environment and attitudes towards means of financing: East versus West German entrepreneurs*[a]

	E. Germ.[a]	W. Germ.[a]	Test statistics for difference	
	Mean	Mean	Wilcoson z	Error probability
Perceptions of external environment				
How probable do you think it is, that you are able to repay your loans?	1.591	1.875	1.25	0.2127
If you had bad luck and would have to close your enterprise—what do you think would happen with the loans you have taken?				
You would have to repay the full loan	1.806	0.375	1.73	0.0833
The federal or state government will take a part of the debt	−1.776	−2.250	−1.06	0.2876
The federal or state government will release you from the loans by the European recovery programme	−1.677	−2.250	−1.18	0.2385
The banks will at least partially grant a debt release	−2.149	−2.125	0.09	0.9280
Attitudes towards means of financing				
Attitude toward taking a loan	1.022	1.196	0.83	0.4088
Attitude toward banks	0.406	0.214	−0.86	0.3906
Attitude toward the bill of exchange	−0.264	0.944	3.24	0.0012

Note: [a]E. Germ.: East German respondents; W. Germ.: West German respondents.
Source: Mummert (1997, pp. 145, 147).

More than in the Chinese case, the East German top-down approach to institutional reform relied on the credibility and strength of the German state. It is arguably precisely the trust in West Germany's institutions that has led to a rapid convergence of expectations among East and West Germans. The challenge for German politics at present is to maintain this credibility in the face of mounting disillusionment among the East German population. Moreover, while beneficial for the reconstruction of a dilapidated local economy, the strength of the former communist *Seilschaften* may prevent the growth of East German businesses beyond the local market by supporting informal enforcement mechanisms unsuited to transactions out of the local context. This institutional inheritance of the new Laender may still negatively affect their economic performance.

11.2.2. Institutional Reforms under a Weak State: The Role of Social Capital

In most countries of Central and Eastern Europe and the FSU, institutional reforms have proceeded in a sequential manner, moving from the easy to the more complex and administratively demanding ones in line with the advancement of the transition (EBRD 1996). This sequence corresponds to what would be expected under the third strategy outlined in Section 1.3, which contended that in the context of a weak state, institutional reforms are highly contingent on existing informal institutions and the way in which these constrain rule enforcement.

The first part of this section will focus on Russia and Ukraine as cases where a legacy of distrust in the state and of corruption within official distribution networks has blocked institutional change and erected considerable barriers to private sector development. Poland will serve as an example for a country where entrepreneurial initiative was kept partly alive during the late communist period and where this asset was capitalized upon by a government that quickly established a firm reform commitment.

11.2.2.1. From the Black Market to the Unofficial Economy: Distortions and Institutional Performance in Russia and Ukraine

Also the Soviet Union instituted a decentralization of power during the 1980s. However, in contrast to China, this did not create incentives for local entrepreneurial initiative but rather undermined the authority of the state (EBRD 1997, chapter 5). By the late 1980s, the Soviet economic system was permeated by bargaining and black market trading both within and outside the official distribution networks. At the eve of its dissolution, the Soviet state had lost control over the final allocation of resources and was concerned more with the allocation of rents among public servants.

The legacy of a weak state and the use of public office for personal gains retains a strong impact on institutional performance in many of the successor countries of the Soviet Union today. There are two aspects to this predicament. The first relates to the continuing discrimination against private businesses caused by remaining bureaucratic distortions and the absence of efficient third-party enforcement across the FSU. The second concerns the transformation of former black marketers into outright criminals acquiring substantial domestic business interests.

While under socialist rule the public servants used their discretion over material allocation to extract rents, now businesses in countries of the FSU are highly taxed through a variety of official taxes and unofficial fees for government services. Table 11.3, reproduced from Kaufmann (1997, p. 7), gives an indication of the extent of unofficial fees in Russia and Ukraine and their development over time. While there

Table 11.3. *'Unofficial' payments by enterprises for official permits, Ukraine and Russia survey results, 1996 (for Ukraine, mid-1994 survey results are in parentheses)*

No.	'Unofficial fee': type of licence/ 'favour'	Ukraine				Russia	
		Average 'unofficial' fee required for 'favour'*		% of enterprises admitting need to pay 'unofficially'		Average 'unofficial' fee required for 'favour'*	% of enterprises admitting need to pay 'unofficially'
		1996	1994	1996	1994	1996	1994
1	Enterprise registration	$176	($186)	66	(64)	$288	44
2	Each visit by fire/health inspector	$42	($40)	81	(72)	$67	23
3	Tax inspector (each regular visit)	$87	($91)	51	(56)	$250	21
4	Each phone line installation	$894	($550)	78	(95)	$1,071	100
5	Lease in state space (sq. metre per month)	$7	(NA)	66	(88)	$26	39
6	Each export licence/registration	$123	($217)	61	(96)	$643	43
7	Each import licence/registration	$278	($108)	71	(93)	$133	50
8	Each border crossing (lump sum)	$211	($194)	100	(90)	(NA)	(NA)
9	Each border crossing (% of value)	3	(NA)	57	(NA)	5	48
10	Domestic currency loan from bank (preferential terms)	4%	(NA)	81	(NA)	8%	38
11	Hard currency loan (preferential terms)	4%	(NA)	85	(NA)	23%	53

Notes: *Average among those that admit making unofficial payments.
Preliminary data based on March 1996 Survey of 150 state/private enterprises in five large Ukrainian cities and of 50 enterprises in three large Russian cities. Caution should be exercised in interpretation of the data, which are not representative of the whole country (particularly in Russia, where the sample is small). The mid-1994 survey results for Ukraine (in parentheses) are based on a similar survey instrument.
Source: Kaufmann (1997, p. 7).

is some evidence that the share of enterprises covered by these fees has been declining in Ukraine (no evidence is given for Russia), the amounts paid remain substantial, particularly for small businesses. Kaufmann estimates that unofficial taxes may add up to 9 percentage points to the total tax bill expressed as a share of turnover. New private businesses are particularly affected, as, unlike established enterprises, they cannot rely on existing contacts to reduce the bribes necessary to evade state regulation. Kaufmann's (1997, p. 18) survey results for Ukrainian enterprises indicate that new private enterprises pay an average US$400 per year an employee in bribes against US$40 in privatized firms and only US$3 in state enterprises. Last but not least, a high level of taxes and bribes has the effect of driving a substantial amount of economic activity into the unofficial economy. This discourages investment in new enterprises and hampers economic recovery as the costs of detection tend to increase with size. High taxation and discriminatory government behaviour is thus a primary obstacle against private sector development and thereby sustained economic growth.

How can this situation be altered? The problem is one of collective choice. First, the rents available to government officials typically result from the survival of old regulations which leave substantial room for discretionary decision making to the government officials. Though the government as a whole would gain in the medium term from higher economic growth and enhanced tax revenues, the latter have no incentives to surrender their discretionary power. Second, were the government to announce a reform to lower tax rates and abolish remaining regulatory distortions, this move might not be credible, as the private sector would discount a later return to higher tax rates once it had joined the official economy (Borner *et al.* 1995). The point here is to show that unless the government can set up a third party that oversees the enforcement of its own commitment, or enhance its credibility by some other means, the needed institutional reforms might not be forthcoming.[12]

The second aspect of the institutional predicament of many countries of the FSU is the transformation of black marketers into modern-day Mafiosi. Black markets under Soviet times were supported by networks of business groups, which ensured contract enforcement amongst one another as the legal system was unreliable. These existing networks could be easily adapted to new economic opportunities (Greif and Kandel 1995; Prior 1997). As black market trading in the past involved considerable access to government favours and protection, the new criminal entrepreneurs could often count on influential contacts to protect their businesses. In Russia, a number of former criminal groups have transformed themselves into legal conglomerates by acquiring substantial business stakes in the process of privatization, while retaining their close links to government. At the same time, the continuing absence of reliable and cost-efficient third-party enforcement from the state has provided huge profit opportunities for so-called 'security firms', often linked to former KGB officers and military officials. Again, these activities discriminate against the new private sector that cannot rely on previous contacts with such security firms and may be forced to pay substantial premiums to benefit from their services.

In sum, bureaucratic red tape, corrupt public officials and the preponderance of private and legally unaccountable security firms that substitute for third-party enforcement by the state continue to present serious obstacles to private sector development and ultimately to economic recovery in the FSU.[13] Reinvigorating the region's economy will have to involve both further economic and administrative liberalization and the rebuilding of trust in the state's institutions. Unfortunately, the path dependence of informal institutions and the considerable private business interests associated with the present predatory system are likely to mean that the accumulation of social capital in support of the transition may take a considerable amount of time.

11.2.2.2. *Establishing Reform Credibility: Poland*

So far, Poland has been the most successful of all Eastern European transition economies. This success seems due in large measure to the rapid expansion of new private businesses, in contrast to experiences further East. As Frye and Shleifer (1997) have shown, Polish businesses face less governmental restrictions and are also less subject to demands for unofficial fees and bribes. How has the Polish state escaped the collective choice dilemmas outlined above?

First of all, Poland arguably did not face the same predicament of a state devoid of any authority. The political revolution that brought the Solidarity government into power in 1989 ensured it with a high initial level of support, while the new government could vest its authority in an existing national tradition that was merely interrupted during the 40 years of imposed communist rule. An additional factor may have been the early turnover of local political elites (Shleifer 1996).[14]

In our model, the political revolution of 1989 must be considered an exogenous factor and is, hence, not part of the reform strategy. Yet, the implementation of Poland's radical reforms and their success arguably relied on beneficial institutional legacies. One beneficial legacy was the existence under communist rule of a substantial number of private businesses. Even excluding agriculture (which was never collectivized), at the start of the reforms the private sector share in GDP was as high as 35 per cent, a fact which provided a strong basis for the rapid expansion of the new private sector. Poland's entrepreneurial talent was, thus, not exclusively concentrated on the black market and showed the ability to seize quickly the legal opportunities which opened after 1990.

Possibly of even greater importance was the strength of the civil opposition to the communist government represented by Solidarity and the Catholic Church. When this opposition movement seized power, the new government was *ab initio* endowed with a high degree of trust. The implementation of policy measures providing for a substantial real wage decline by a government that grew out of the trade union movement testifies to the presence of a generalized morality that was identified as one of the factors contributing to trust in government institutions. As shown below, differences exist among the transition economies with respect to the level of trust, although they are not overwhelming.

Therefore, Poland inherited a stock of social capital that could be harnessed for the success of the transition, while the political revolution at the start of the reforms encouraged the new government to draw on this resource to a larger extent than elsewhere in the region. As described by Kolodko and Nuti (1997), the government coalition that took office after the general elections of 1993 attempted to steer a reform path in which consultation with the main social groups was a central element. It is suggestive of the relative success of this strategy that the Polish government could boast during this period the highest increase in approval rates (from 52 per cent at the end of 1991 to 76 per cent in 1995) among all Eastern European countries (Rose and Haerpfer 1996).

11.2.3. *Social Capital and Economic Performance: Cross-country Evidence*

Governments that can build on trust in public institutions tend to have higher credibility. In turn, higher credibility contributes to better economic performance which further increases confidence in a given institutional setup. This section reviews evidence on the determinants of trust in public institutions and relates cross-country differences to economic performance.

In the New Democracies Barometer (Rose and Haerpfer 1996; Rose *et al.* 1997), respondents were asked a range of questions regarding their approval of the existing political and economic system, the previous regime, and specific public and civil institutions. Survey responses were collected from a total of 10,087 individuals in 1993 in nine Eastern European countries (Bulgaria, the Czech Republic, Slovakia, Hungary, Poland, Romania, Slovenia, Belarus, and Ukraine). The ratings of 15 political and civil institutions in the nine countries are reproduced in Table 11.4. In general, Eastern Europeans are 'skeptics', with a majority of respondents expressing neither fundamental trust nor distrust in the set of institutions. What is particularly striking is that skepticism concerns not just political institutions such as government, parliament, political parties, civil servants, or the police, but generally applies to civil institutions as well. This suggests that the region has inherited a relatively low level of social capital. Moreover, in spite of the substantial differences in economic policies that had been implemented in the various countries by 1993, the variation in the ratings is higher among individuals than among countries. This might be taken as evidence for the argument that social capital changes only slowly. However, whatever country differences there are, they confirm with the arguments made so far, i.e. that trust is lower in the countries of the FSU and Bulgaria and highest among the more advanced transition economies.

Rose *et al.* (1997) use the above ratings to form an overall index of social trust, which they correlate with a variety of potential determinants. The most important conclusions from this exercise are the following. First, personal evaluations of the past play virtually no role in determining the level of trust. Nostalgics are just as likely as dissidents to distrust present institutions. Hence trust has little to do with political affiliation. Also, trust is (surprisingly) hardly affected by demographic and sociological factors such as age, educational level, gender, town size, or church attendance. Second, individual perceptions of the current institutional performance are the main factor explaining variations in social trust. Thereby, political and economic performance have a roughly equal impact, each explaining around 8–9 per cent of the total variation. Political performance includes increases in political freedoms (significant impact),

Table 11.4. *Mean trust in political and civil institutions in selected countries (standard deviations in parentheses)*

Trust in	BUL	CZE	SLK	HUN	POL	ROM	SLE	BEL	UKR	Mean
Government	2.7 (1.6)	4.6 (1.6)	3.7 (1.7)	3.2 (1.7)	3.5 (1.6)	3.3 (1.7)	3.7 (1.8)	3.0 (1.6)	2.4 (1.6)	3.4 (1.8)
Parliament	2.2 (1.4)	3.6 (1.5)	3.4 (1.5)	3.2 (1.6)	3.5 (1.5)	3.2 (1.6)	3.5 (1.6)	2.9 (1.6)	2.6 (1.7)	3.1 (1.6)
President	4.0 (1.9)	5.1 (1.8)	4.8 (1.7)	5.0 (1.8)	3.1 (1.7)	4.0 (2.1)	4.2 (2.0)	3.3 (1.7)	2.6 (1.8)	4.0 (2.0)
Civil servants	2.9 (1.6)	3.7 (1.3)	3.7 (1.5)	3.8 (1.6)	3.5 (1.4)	3.4 (1.7)	4.1 (1.6)	3.2 (1.6)	3.0 (1.6)	3.5 (1.6)
Courts	2.8 (1.7)	4.0 (1.5)	3.8 (1.6)	4.3 (1.7)	3.9 (1.5)	4.1 (1.8)	4.1 (1.8)	3.5 (1.6)	3.2 (1.8)	3.7 (1.7)
Parties	2.5 (1.6)	3.7 (1.3)	3.2 (1.6)	2.8 (1.5)	2.6 (1.3)	3.0 (1.6)	2.8 (1.5)	2.7 (1.7)	2.4 (1.5)	2.8 (1.6)
Army	4.6 (1.9)	4.1 (1.5)	4.4 (1.6)	4.3 (1.7)	4.8 (1.6)	5.5 (1.6)	3.9 (1.9)	4.0 (1.8)	3.8 (1.9)	4.4 (1.8)
Police	2.9 (1.7)	3.9 (1.5)	3.7 (1.6)	4.2 (1.7)	4.1 (1.6)	3.8 (1.8)	4.0 (1.7)	3.2 (1.7)	2.8 (1.7)	3.6 (1.7)
Media	3.7 (1.8)	4.2 (1.4)	4.0 (1.5)	3.7 (1.6)	3.9 (1.5)	3.2 (1.6)	3.8 (1.6)	3.7 (1.7)	3.7 (1.8)	3.8 (1.6)
Churches	3.4 (2.0)	3.5 (1.8)	4.2 (2.0)	4.1 (1.9)	4.0 (1.9)	5.4 (1.8)	3.5 (2.0)	4.6 (2.0)	4.2 (2.1)	4.1 (2.0)
Patriotic societies	2.7 (1.8)	4.0 (1.4)	3.8 (1.6)	3.3 (1.6)	3.2 (1.4)	3.3 (1.8)	4.1 (1.7)	3.0 (1.7)	3.0 (1.8)	3.4 (1.7)
Farm organizations	3.1 (1.8)	4.0 (1.3)	3.8 (1.4)	3.9 (1.6)	3.6 (1.5)	4.0 (1.9)	NA	3.7 (1.7)	3.3 (1.8)	3.7 (1.6)
Unions	2.5 (1.5)	3.4 (1.2)	3.4 (1.2)	3.5 (1.3)	3.0 (1.3)	3.4 (1.9)	3.2 (1.7)	3.0 (1.4)	2.7 (1.4)	3.1 (1.5)
Private enterprise	2.7 (1.8)	4.2 (1.4)	3.5 (1.7)	3.9 (1.6)	3.1 (1.5)	4.1 (1.9)	3.4 (1.7)	2.9 (1.8)	3.4 (1.9)	3.5 (1.8)
Foreign experts	2.5 (1.7)	3.6 (1.6)	3.2 (1.5)	3.3 (1.7)	2.9 (1.6)	3.4 (1.9)	3.5 (1.7)	3.1 (1.7)	3.2 (1.8)	3.2 (1.7)

Notes: Trust is scored on a 7-point scale with 7 = maximum trust and 1 = maximum distrust. BUL = Bulgaria; CZE = the Czech Republic; SLK = Slovakia; HUN = Hungary; POL = Poland; ROM = Romania; SLE = Slovenia; BEL = Belarus; UKR = Ukraine; Mean = average for all nine countries.

Sources: Paul Lazarsfeld Society, Vienna. New Democracies Barometer III, 1994. Rose et al. (1997, p. 17).

increased political fairness (significant impact), and increased personal influence (insignificant impact). Economic performance is measured by evaluations of the current and future macroeconomic situation and current and future family finances. An independent influence is also assigned to perceptions about current economic deprivation. Future economic prospects dominate evaluations of current outcomes in their impact on social trust. This entails the possibility of creating trust through a credible reform commitment at the start of transition, such as described for the case of Poland above. In general, this second result gives strong empirical support for the indirect feedback effect from institutional performance to trust and the accumulation of social capital.

What impact does social capital have on economic performance? As contended in Section 1.3, social trust tends to increase public pressures for efficient governance which in turn positively influences economic growth. Government officials under public scrutiny have lower incentives to become corrupt, as the costs they case in case of detection increase. Social trust will also increase the flow of information from the economic to the political sphere, making policy changes more predictable. Trust in government institutions will increase the reliability of formal institutional arrangements such as property rights and a given set of laws. In the 1997 World Development Report, the World Bank conducted a survey of 3,685 private business people across industrialized, developing and transition economies. Business people were asked to rate their institutional environment for predictability of laws and policies, stability of government, security of property, reliability of judiciary, and the extent of corruption. All five scores were combined into an index of 'political credibility'. This index varies between a high score of over 4 for the OECD and a score below 3 for the CIS, which thereby comes below Sub-Saharan Africa in terms of government credibility. Central and Eastern Europe has a higher average index, placing the region on a level above Latin America but below South and South East Asia.[15] In general, political credibility is positively correlated with growth and investment. Moreover, the low scores for the CIS in comparison to Eastern Europe suggest that political credibility is positively related to the level of trust and social capital in a society.

11.2.4. *Informal Institutions and the Design of Institutional Reforms: The Case of Privatization*

While there is general agreement on the importance of privatization in the economies in transition, the actual privatization paths chosen have differed substantially across countries. I argue that this is another manifestation of the impact of informal institutions on the design of economic reforms, rather than the outcome of different government opinions as to the best privatization method. The relative power of insiders in SOEs will determine whether sales to an outside investor or the distribution of state assets among the population are feasible. When such power is large, insider privatization is much more likely. Moreover, the longer privatization is delayed, the more likely insider privatization becomes, because SOE managers and workers have meanwhile acquired implicit rights in 'their' enterprises, not least by taking some painful adjustment measures in order to ensure survival. What implications this has for the long-run performance of the enterprises concerned is as yet unclear (see Chapter 8). What is clear is that first best solutions to privatization have had little empirical relevance so far.

My argument is largely based on Heinrich's (1993) comparative analysis of privatization methods in the Czech Republic, Poland, and Hungary. I choose the former two to demonstrate my point. The Czech Republic has chosen voucher privatization as the main method of mass privatization. It has been applied in 50 per cent of all large privatizations, although this accounts for only a quarter of all state property which has switched to private or municipal ownership, the remainder being small privatizations, restitution, and free transfer to municipalities (Marcincin and Wijnbergen 1997). Nevertheless, with large-scale privatization more or less completed by 1995, privatization in the Czech Republic has been very fast, rivalled only by the East German and to some extent the Russian experience. By contrast, Poland has experienced repeated delays on the way to mass privatization. Of the total of 3,349 enterprises in the process of privatization by December 1995, only 834 (25 per cent) were included in the so-called capital path which involves direct sales to outside investors and mass privatization through holding companies. By far, the largest proportion was privatized through 'liquidation' involving either the dissolution of the firm and sale of its assets to other owners (Article 19) or the transfer of assets to a different owner, usually a collective of SOE managers and/or workers (Article 37). The latter most closely approximates insider privatization and has had a far higher completion rate than either of the other two paths. In 1996, a mass privatization programme involving several hundred large SOEs was finally started. Nevertheless, so far it has been the new private sector rather than privatized SOEs that has contributed most to Poland's economic growth.

The main difference in the privatization methods chosen lies with the existence of customary property rights by SOE workers and managers in Poland in contrast to Czechoslovakia, where the relative power of the central government *vis-à-vis* SOE insiders was far greater prior to 1989. The evolution of such customary rights in Poland resulted from the partial reform attempts during the 1980s. This led to a considerable role for worker councils in enterprise decision making. With the legitimacy of the state impaired by the imposition of martial law in 1982, and with the ensuing increasing loss of control over government agents at various levels of the bureaucracy, insiders were able to take control of enterprise decisions while being largely shielded from the resulting consequences. Consequently, Polish reform efforts concentrated first and foremost on introducing financial discipline into the state sector. One positive surprise was that given a hard budget constraint, Polish SOEs would display considerable adjustment efforts, at least when they were financially viable (Pinto *et al.* 1993). With performance improving, it became even more difficult to introduce outside ownership into SOEs. Insiders feared redundancy from more vigorous externally imposed adjustment measures, while claiming legitimate rights over state enterprises, which they had helped to preserve by initiating adjustment. The policy reaction to the establishment and strengthening of customary rights was to give them legal protection through Article 37.

The voucher privatization method adopted for mass privatization in the Czech Republic relies on public bidding for SOEs and leaves only a small role for insiders after privatization is completed.[16] In practice, the Czech government has allowed SOE managers to come forward with privatization proposals during the first round of voucher privatization, which shows respect for insider interests even in a country where tight hierarchical control persisted all the way until the Velvet Revolution of 1989. Nonetheless, the weakness of the Czechoslovak labour movement after 1968 has been reflected in the virtual silence over worker concerns during the process of privatization, an achievement which has certainly contributed to the speed of the process, but would have been unthinkable in the Polish socio-political setting.[17]

The above analysis might easily be extended to the case of privatization in Russia. Although Russia nominally followed a voucher privatization method, managers of SOEs more often than not have been its main beneficiaries (see Chapter 2). Even where they do not hold controlling stakes, cross ownership within large industrial conglomerates has meant that property rights are vested in networks of insiders with close connections to the government. As explained above, this pattern reflects a degree of institutional continuity, as it recognizes the implicit property rights that were gained by an alliance of directors and bureaucrats during the late Soviet era. Any privatization programme that had not respected these implicit rights would have met with strong insider resistance.

11.3. CONCLUSIONS

This chapter has made three major points. First, the transition is eminently a process of institutional change. As such, the outcomes of the transition are substantially influenced by the set of informal institutions inherited from the socialist era as these shape people's expectations and limit the enforcement of new market-based incentive structures. History matters for transition outcomes and the assets on which reformers can build in this respect differ between the various economies of the region. This implies that there cannot be one optimal strategy for institutional reform, but that the given strength and legitimacy of the state has to be taken into account in designing policies for institutional reform.

Second, theoretical, historical, and cross-country evidence suggests that a crucial role for informal institutions in all societies is to facilitate economic exchange both by supporting self-enforcing rules of the game and by fostering trust in third-party enforcement through the state. Such trust will grow out of an articulated civil society and depends positively on the level of social capital, including the existence of a universal morality at the level of the nation state.

Third, trust in government institutions is promoted by good political and economic performance. While governments cannot directly influence trust in public institutions, they can do so indirectly through formal institutional reforms that limit the scope for predatory behaviour by public officials and improve political and economic performance. Advance signalling of reform commitment through packaging of individual measures may increase trust by enhancing public perceptions of future economic prospects.

The outlook for transition economies based on the analysis in this chapter is mixed. In the most advanced Central European nations, growing integration with Western Europe will firmly root democratic and market-based institutions in their societies. For the Czech Republic, Hungary, Poland, and Slovenia at least, a rapid return to the group of prosperous industrial nations seems probable in the early part of the new millennium. Further East, the prospects look much bleaker. As a result of a persistent fiscal crisis, state capacity has been eroded to an extent which may have transferred institutional power and control of the reform process from government agencies to criminal organizations. These countries are in danger of reverting to an archaic situation of institutional competition among 'roving bandits' (Borner *et al.* 1995) which is likely to drive the economy underground for a considerable amount of time. In China, finally, administrative capacity has remained intact, albeit it is more regionally fragmented than 20 years ago. The major challenge in this country will be the buildup of a popular legitimacy once the population will start demanding from the government more than economic prosperity. The fragility of an autocratic regime that has few institutionalized channels for participation of the various emerging groups in society remains a danger for China's institutional development in the future.

NOTES

1. According to Greif (1994), the collectivist attitudes of the Maghribi traders in the Mediterranean led to their demise in the face of the superior institutional arrangement of the Merchant Guild formed in the individualistic tradition of the Italian City States.
2. This argument is illustrated by Putnam's (1993) account of the differences in the efficiency of government in Northern and Southern Italy, arguably an important factor in the sustained gap in living standards between these two regions. According to Putnam, Northern Italy benefits from a tradition of social cooperation evidenced in a substantial degree of participation in social affairs.
3. Coleman (1988) similarly argues that social capital is accumulated in the family through the time that parents spend with their children.
4. See also Habermas' (1988) theory of communicative action.
5. Boswell (1990) discusses a number of exogenous factors such as size, experience of war, and ideological tradition, which have influenced the development of corporatist versus conflictual social models in Europe and the United States.
6. Path dependence also exists in the formal institutional framework, mainly because implementation costs are high and the stability of rules as much as their quality is what contributes to lowering transaction costs.
7. That political developments during 1989–90 qualify as exogenous shocks is demonstrated by the East German case, with which I am most familiar. The Monday demonstrations in Leipzig set the tone for rapid unification long before it became official government policy in January 1990. Similarly, political developments in Poland and Hungary urged for rapid responses by economic policy makers suddenly confronted with the task of taking over. In Czechoslovakia, by contrast, the economic reform programme was internally debated for a full year before coming into effect in January 1991.

8. I have formulated the reform strategy just outlined as one emphasizing institutional stability, although it is closely related to proposals for evolutionary institutional reforms (Murrell 1992). To be feasible, such proposals implicitly assume that the existing institutional framework has not fully disintegrated.
9. The latest Transition Report Update of the EBRD (1997, Introduction, p. 2), for instance, notes that 'progress in transition has been particularly obvious in fields where the necessary development of institutions and behaviour, be they in government or in the private sector, is less demanding. Accordingly, it has been most rapid in the areas of price and trade liberalization and small-scale privatization. Progress has been slower in large enterprise privatization and restructuring, competition policy, financial sector reform and development, and legal reform.'
10. Specifically, in China rural collectivization was combined with a policy that inhibited migration, thus tending to keep family members together in the same rural collective. In Russia, the forced industrialization drive transferred entire generations from agriculture into industry often involving large geographical distances as well.
11. East Germany had an interesting traffic rule idiosyncrasy in that a green right arrow allowed right turns even at a red traffic light. Although it enjoyed vast support amongst East Germans, the rule did not survive unification.
12. One means of external enforcement is of course political competition in a working democracy. Shleifer (1996) emphasizes that the replacement of corrupt local officials by new blood would be one way to strengthen bureaucratic efficiency in Russia.
13. Johnson et al. (1997) have calculated the share of the new private sector in GDP in a sample of transition economies. For instance, in Poland it was 50 per cent in 1995, in Hungary 45 per cent against only 20 per cent in Russia and 30 per cent in Ukraine. The latter countries also score far worse in the same authors' indicators of progress in legal reform or of corruption of public officials.
14. According to Shleifer (1996), by 1993 only 30 per cent of local political elites in Poland were former communist party members against 83 per cent in Russia.
15. In an analysis based on a similar methodology, Borner et al. (1996) compute an index of credibility across Eastern Europe and the Baltics which broadly supports the regional ranking presented by the World Bank.
16. I am not touching here the issues of corporate governance involved in judging the ultimate efficiency of new property rights arrangements. It is now widely recognized that the Czech voucher privatization has only partially resulted in strong corporate governance through external owners.
17. That government policy retains some degree of freedom is evidenced by the contrast of the Czech and Slovak privatization methods. In Slovakia, voucher privatization was discontinued after the separation in favour of distribution of state assets to government employees and political allies. The lack of worker resistance ensured that this 'crony' privatization (Marcincin 1996) was completed almost as rapidly as in the Czech case.

References

Chapter 1

Alesina, Alberto and Roberto Perotti (1996). Income distribution, political instability, and investment. *European Economic Review* 40: 1203–28.

—— and Dani Rodrik (1994). Distributive politics and economic growth. *Quarterly Journal of Economics* 109: 465–90.

Asian Development Bank (1997). *Asian Development Outlook 1997 and 1998*. Hong Kong: Oxford University Press.

Åslund, Anders, Peter Boone, and Simon Johnson (1996). How to stabilize: Lessons from post-communist countries. *Brookings Papers: Economic Activity* 1: 217–313.

Benabou, Roland (1996), Inequality and Growth in NBER Macroeconomics Annual 1996. Cambridge, Massachusetts: The MIT Press.

Blasi, Joseph R. (1997). *Russian Research Project*. New Brunswick, NJ: Rutgers University.

——, Maya Kroumova, and Douglas Kruse (1996). *Kremlin Capitalism: Privatizing the Russian Economy*. Ithaca, NY: Cornell University Press.

Bofinger, Peter, Heiner Flassbeck, and Lutz Hoffmann (1997). Orthodox money-based stabilization (OMBS) versus heterodox exchange rate-based stabilization (HERBS): The case of Russia, the Ukraine and Kazakhstan, *Economic Systems* 21 (1): 1–33.

Bokros, Lajos (1996). Stabilization without Recession: The Success of a Long-Awaited Financial Adjustment in Hungary, Paper presented at the UNU/WIDER Conference on Transition Strategies, Alternatives and Outcomes, November 1996, Helsinki.

Bruno, Michael (1995). Does inflation really lower growth? *Finance & Development*, September 1995.

—— and William Easterly (1995). *Inflation Crisis and Long-Run Growth*. Washington, DC: NBER Working Paper Series, No. 2509 (August).

Campos, Nauro F. (1999a). Back to the Future: The Growth Prospects of Transition Economies Reconsidered. William Davidson Institute Working Paper No. 229, Ann Arbor, April 1999.

—— (1999b). Context is Everything: Measuring Institutional Change in Transition Economies. Prague, August 1999.

Cornia, Giovanni Andrea (1997). Discussion note on UNU/WIDER project on Rising Income Inequality and Poverty Reduction: Are They Compatible? Helsinki: UNU/WIDER.

—— and Vladimir Popov (1998). Transition and long-term growth: Conventional versus non-conventional determinants. *Moct-Most*, No. 8, pp. 7–32.

——, Juha Honkkila, Renato Paniccià, and Vladimir Popov (1997). Long-term Growth and Welfare in Transitional Economies: The Impact of Demographic, Investment and Social Policy Changes, *WIDER Working Papers*, No. 122. Helsinki: UNU/WIDER.

De Melo, Martha, Denizer Cevdet, Alan Gelb, and Stoyan Tenev (1997). Circumstance and Choice: The Role of Initial Conditions and Policies in Transitions Economies. The World Bank, International Financial Corporation, October 1997.

Economic Commission for Europe (1997). *Economic Survey of Europe in 1996–1997*. Geneva: United Nations.

References

European Bank for Reconstruction and Development (1995). *Transition Report 1995*. London: EBRD.
European Bank for Reconstruction and Development (1997). *Transition Report 1997*. London: EBRD.
European Bank for Reconstruction and Development (1999). *Transition Report 1997*. London: EBRD.
Holmes, Steven (1997). What Russia teaches us now. *The American Prospect*, July–August, pp. 30–9.
Honkkila, Juha (1997). Privatization, Asset Distribution and Equity in Transitional economies, *WIDER Working Papers*, No. 125. Helsinki: UNU/WIDER.
Mayer, Georg (1997). Is Having a Rich Natural-Resource Endowment Detrimental to Export Diversification?, *UNCTAD Discussion Papers*, No. 124. Geneva: UNCTAD.
Milanovic, Branko (1995). Poverty, Inequality and Social Policy in Transition Economies, World Bank Policy Research Paper Series, No. 9. Washington DC: World Bank.
—— (1998). *Income, Inequality and Poverty During Transition*. Washington DC: World Bank.
Naughton, Barry (1997). Economic reform in China: Macroeconomic and overall performance. In *The System Transformation of the Transition Economies: Europe, Asia and North Korea*, edited by D. Lee. Seoul: Yonsei University Press.
Nesporova, Alena (1997). The Role of Labour Market Policies in Combating Unemployment in Transition Countries. Paper presented at the UNU/WIDER project meeting on Economic Shocks, Social Stress and the Demographic Impact, April 1997, Helsinki.
North, Douglass (1990). *Institutions, Institutional Change and Economic Performance*. Cambridge, Massachusetts: Cambridge University Press.
Ping, Zhan (1997). Income Distribution During the Transition in China, *UNU/WIDER Working Papers*, No. 138. Helsinki: UNU/WIDER.
Polterovich, Victor (1998). Institutional Traps and Economic Reforms. Working Paper 98/004, Moscow: New Economic School.
Popov, Vladimir (1998). Investment in transition economies: Factors of Change and Implications for Performance, *Journal of East-West Business*, 4 (1/2): 47–98.
—— (1999*a*). The financial system in Russia as compared to other transition economies: The Anglo-American versus The German–Japanese model *Comparative Economic Studies*, No. 1.
—— (1999*b*). Investment, restructuring and performance in transition economies. *Post-Communist Economies*, No. 3.
—— (1999*c*). Reform strategies and economic performance of Russia's regions. Mimeographed.
Poznanski, Kazimierz (1996). *Poland's Protracted Transition: Institutional Change and Economic Growth*. Cambridge, UK: Cambridge University Press.
Rodrik, Dani (1996*a*). Understanding economic policy reform. *Journal of Economic Literature* XXXIV: 9–41.
—— (1996*b*). Institutions and Economic Performance in East and South East Asia. In *Round Table Conference: The Institutional Foundations of Economic Development in East Asia*. Tokyo, December 1996, pp. 391–429.
Schmidt-Hebbel, Klaus, Luis Serven, and Andres Solimano (1996). Saving and investment: paradigms, puzzles, policies. *The World Bank Research Observer* 11 (1): 87–117.
Shmelev, Nickolai and Vladimir Popov (1990). *The Turning Point: Revitalizing the Soviet Economy*. New York: Doubleday.

Stewart, Frances (1987). Supporting productive employment among vulnerable groups. In *Adjustment with a Human Face*, edited by G. A. Cornia, R. Jolly, and F. Stewart. New York: Oxford University Press.

Stiglitz, Joseph (1994). *Whither Socialism?* Cambridge, Massachusetts: The MIT Press.

—— (1998). More Instruments and Broader Goals: Moving Toward the Post-Washington Consensus, *WIDER Annual Lecture Series*, No. 2. Helsinki: UNU/WIDER.

Suutela, Pekka (1997). Privatization in the Countries of Eastern and Central Europe and the Former Soviet Union. Mimeo.

Venieris, Yannis and Dipak Gupta (1986). Income distribution and socio-political instability as determinants of savings: A cross-sectional model. *Journal of Political Economy* 94 (4): 873–83.

World Bank (1996*a*). *From Plan to Market: World Development Report 1996*. Washington DC: World Bank.

World Bank (1996*b*). *The Chinese Economy. Fighting Inflation, Deepening Reforms*. Washington DC: World Bank.

World Bank (1997). *The State in a Changing World: World Development Report 1997*. Washington DC: World Bank.

Zakharia, Fareed (1997). The rise of illiberal democracies. *Foreign Affairs* 76 (6) (November/December 1997): 22–43.

Zettelmeyer, Jeromin and Daniel Citrin (1995). Stabilization: Fixed versus flexible exchange rates. In *Policy Experiences and Issues in the Baltics, Russia, and Other Countries of the Former Soviet Union*, edited by D. A. Citrin and A. K. Lahiri. Washington DC: IMF.

Zhang, Ping (1997). Income Distribution during the Transition in China, *WIDER Working Papers*, No. 138. Helsinki: UNU/WIDER.

Chapter 2

ADB (1997). *Asian Development Outlook 1997 and 1998*. Manila: Asian Development Bank.

Åslund, Anders (1994). The case for radical reform. *Journal of Democracy* 5 (4) (October).

—— (1999*a*). Why has Russia's Economic Transformation been so Arduous? Annual Bank Conference on Development Economics, World Bank, 28–30 April, Washington, DC.

—— (1999*b*). Russia's collapse. *Foreign Affairs* September/October.

——, Peter Boone, and Simon Johnson (1996). How to stabilize: Lessons from post-communist countries. *Brookings Papers on Economic Activity* 1: 217–313.

Blasi, Joseph, Maya Kroumova, and Douglas Kruse (1996). Kremlin Capitalism: Privatizing the Russian Economy, ILR Press, an imprint of Cornell University Press, Ithaca and London.

Breton, Paul, Daniel Gros, and Guy Vandille (1997). Output decline and recovery in the transition economies: Causes and social consequences. *Economics of Transition* 5 (1): 113–30.

Bruno, Michael (1995). Does inflation really lower growth? *Finance & Development*, September.

—— and William Easterly (1998). Inflation crisis and long-run growth. *Journal of Monetary Economics* 41: 3–26.

China Statistical Yearbook (various years). Beijing: China Statistical Publishing House.

Commission of the European Communities (1990). *Stabilization, Liberalization and Devolution: Assessment of the Economic Situation and the Reform Process in the Soviet Union*. Brussels: Commission of the European Communities.

Cornia, Giovanni Andrea and Vladimir Popov (1998). Transition and long-term growth: Conventional versus non-conventional determinants. *Moct-Most* 8 (1): 7–32.

References

De Melo, Martha, Cevdet Denizer, and Alan Gelb (1995). *From Plan to the Market: Patterns of Transition.* Washington, DC: World Bank.

—— —— —— (1996). Patterns of transition from plan to market. *World Bank Economic Review* 3: 397–424.

—— —— —— and Stoyan Tenev (1997). Circumstance and Choice: The Role of Initial Conditions and Policies in Transitions Economies. World Bank, International Financial Corporation.

Desai, Padma (1994). Aftershock in Russia's economy. *Current History* 93 (585) (October): 320–3.

—— (1998). Macroeconomic fragility and exchange rate vulnerability: A cautionary record of transition economies. *Journal of Comparative Economics* 26 (4): 621–41.

Dmitriyev, M., M. Matovnikov, L. Mikhailov, L. Sycheva, Ye. Timofeev, and A. Warner (1996). Russian banks on the eve of financial stabilization. *Norma* (St Petersburg) [in Russian].

Dornbush, Rudiger and Sebastian Edwards (1989). The Economic Populism Paradigm. *NBER Working Papers*, No. 2,986.

Earle, J., S. Estrin, and L. Leschenko (1995). Ownership structures, patterns of control and enterprise behavior in Russia. In *Enterprise Restructuring and Economic Policy in Russia*, edited by S. Commander, Q. Fan and M. Schaffer. Washington, DC: World Bank.

EBRD (1995). *Transition Report 1995.* London: European Bank for Reconstruction and Development.

EBRD (1996). *Transition Report 1996.* London: European Bank for Reconstruction and Development.

EBRD (1997). *Transition Report 1997.* London: European Bank for Reconstruction and Development.

EBRD (1998). *Transition Report 1998.* London: European Bank for Reconstruction and Development.

Economic Commission for Europe (ECE) (1996). *Economic Survey of Europe in 1995–1996.* New York and Geneva: Economic Commission for Europe.

Fish, M. Steven (1998*a*). The determinants of economic reform in the post-communist world. *East European Politics and Societies* 12 (1): 31–78.

—— (1998*b*). Democratization requisites: The postcommunist experience. *Post-Soviet Affairs* 14 (3): 212–47.

Friedman, E. J. and S. Johnson (1995). Complementarities and Optimal Reform. *Working Papers*, No. 109 (December). Stockholm: Stockholm Institute of East European Economics.

Frye, T. (1997). Governing the Russian equities market. *Post Soviet Affairs* 13 (4): 366–95.

Fyodorov, B. (1994). Russian finances in 1993. *Voprosy Ekonomiky*, No. 1, pp. 4–85 [in Russian].

Gaidar, Y. (1995). Post-Communist economic reforms: Five years passed. *Voprosy Ekonomiky*, No. 12, pp. 4–11 [in Russian].

Gardner, Stephen (1988). *Comparative Economic Systems.* New York: The Dryden Press.

Goskomstat (various years). *Narodnoye Khozyaistvo SSSR (National Economy of the USSR), Rossiysky Statistichesky Yezhegodnik (Russian Statistical Yearbook)* and monthly publications for various years. Moscow: Goskomstat.

—— (1990). *Narodnoye Khozyaistvo SSSR v 1989 Godu (National Economy of the USSR in 1989).* Moscow: Goskomstat.

Hernandez-Cata, Ernesto (1997). Liberalization and the behaviour of output during the transition from plan to market. *IMF Staff Papers* 44 (4) (December): 405–29.

—— (1999). Price liberalization, money growth and inflation during the transition to the market economy. *IMF Working Papers*, June.

Heybey, Berta and Peter Murrell (1999). The relationship between economic growth and the speed of liberalization during transition. *Journal of Policy Reform* 3 (2): 121–37.

Ickes, Barry (1996). How to stabilize: Lessons from post-communist countries, comment. *Brookings Papers on Economic Activity* 1: 298–305.

Illarionov, A. (1995). The nature of Russian inflation. *Voprosy Ekonomiky*, No. 3, pp. 4–21 [in Russian].

Kaufman, Robert R. and Barbara Stallings (1991). The political economy of Latin American populism. In *Macroeconomics of Populism in Latin America*, edited by R. Dornbush and S. Edwards. Chicago and London: University of Chicago Press.

Koen, V. and M. Marrese (1995). Stabilization and structural change in Russia, 1992–4. In *Road Maps of the Transition: The Baltics, the Czech Republic, Hungary, and Russia*, September, pp. 53–67. Washington, DC: IMF.

Kruger, Gary and Marek Ciolko (1998). A note on initial conditions and liberalization during transition. *Journal of Comparative Economics* 26 (4): 618–34.

Lahiri, A. K. and D. A. Citrin (1995). Interenterprise arrears. In *Policy Experiences and Issues in the Baltics, Russia and Other Countries of the Former Soviet Union*, edited by D. A. Citrin and A. K. Lahiri. Washington, DC: IMF.

Montes, M. and V. Popov (1999). *The Asian Crisis Turns Global*. Singapore: Institute of Southeast Asian Studies.

Naughton, B. (1997). Economic reform in China: Macroeconomic and overall performance. In *The System Transformation of the Transition Economies: Europe, Asia and North Korea*, edited by D. Lee, pp. 27–64. Seoul: Yonsei University Press.

OECD (1997). Russian Federation 1997. *OECD Economic Surveys 1997–98*.

PlanEcon (various issues). Washington, DC.

Popov, Vladimir (1996). A Russian puzzle: What makes Russian economic transformation a special case. *Research for Action*, No. 29. Helsinki: WIDER/UNU.

—— (1998a). Investment in transition economies: Factors of change and implications for performance. *Journal of East-West Business* 4 (1/2), 47–98.

—— (1998b). Will Russia achieve fast economic growth?. *Communist Economies and Economic Transformation* 10 (4): 421–49.

—— (1999a). The financial system in Russia as compared to other transition Economies: The Anglo-American versus the German–Japanese Model. *Comparative Economic Studies* 41 (1): 1–42.

—— (1999b). Investment, restructuring and performance in transition economies. *Post-Communist Economies*, No. 3.

Rostowski, J. (1993). The interenterprise debt explosion in the former Soviet Union: Causes, consequences, cures. *Communist Economies & Economic Transformation* 5 (2): 131–59.

Sachs, Jeffrey D. (1989). Social Conflict and Populist Policies in Latin America. *NBER Working Papers*, No. 2,897.

—— (1994). Russia's Struggle with Stabilization: Conceptual Issues and Evidence, Annual Bank Conference on Development Economics, World Bank, 28–30 April, Washington, DC.

—— (1995). Why Russia has Failed to Stabilize. *Working Papers*, No. 103. Stockholm: Stockholm Institute of East European Economics.

—— and A. Warner (1996). *Achieving Rapid Growth in the Transition Economies of Central Europe*. Cambridge, MA: Harvard Institute for International Development.

—— and W. T. Woo (1994). Reform in Russia and China. *Economic Policy*, April: 101–45.

Schmidt-Hebbel, K., L. Serven, and A. Solimano (1996). Saving and investment: Paradigms, puzzles, policies. *World Bank Research Observer* 11 (1): 87–117.
Shmelev, N. and V. Popov (1989). *The Turning Point: Revitalizing the Soviet Economy.* New York: Doubleday.
UNDP (1997). *Human Development Report 1997.* New York: Oxford University Press.
Warner, Andrew (1997). *Is Economic Reform Popular at the Polls?* Cambridge, MA: Harvard Institute for International Development.
World Bank (1995). *Workers in an Integrating World: World Development Report.* New York: Oxford University Press.
World Bank (1996a). *From Plan to Market: World Development Report.* New York: Oxford University Press.
World Bank (1996b). *The Chinese Economy: Fighting Inflation, Deepening Reforms.* Washington, DC: World Bank.
World Bank (1997a). *The State in a Changing World: World Development Report.* New York: Oxford University Press.
World Bank (1997b). *World Development Indicators 1997.* New York: Oxford University Press.
Zettermeyer, J. and D. Citrin (1995). Stabilization: Fixed versus flexible exchange rates. *Policy Experiences and Issues in the Baltics, Russia and Other Countries of the Former Soviet Union.* Washington, DC: IMF.

Chapter 3

The study draws heavily on the IMF Staff Country Reports which since 1995 have been appearing annually. Unless otherwise noted, general statements about national trends are based on the IMF reports; specific statements from individual reports are cited in endnotes. The UNDP national *Human Development Reports* for Kazakhstan and Uzbekistan in 1995 and 1996 and Chapter 4 of the ECE's *Economic Survey of Europe in 1996–1997* (prepared by Michael Kaser) were also useful general background sources.

Cheasty, Adrienne and Jeffrey Davis (1996). Fiscal Transition in Countries of the Former Soviet Union: An Interim Assessment, *IMF Working Paper WP/96/61.* Washington, DC: IMF (also forthcoming in *MOCT-MOST: Economic Policy in Transitional Economies*).
Cornia, Giovanni Andrea and Renato Paniccià (2000). *The Mortality Crisis in Transitional Economies.* Oxford: Oxford University Press.
Craumer, Peter (1995). *Rural and Agricultural Development in Uzbekistan.* London: Royal Institute of International Affairs.
Falkingham, Jane, Jeni Klugman, Sheila Marnie, and John Micklewright (1997). *Household Welfare in Central Asia.* Basingstoke: Macmillan.
Griffin, Keith (ed.) (1996). *Social Policy and Economic Transformation in Uzbekistan.* Geneva: ILO.
Klugman, Jeni (1997). Uzbekistan: A Cautious Approach to Reform, Paper prepared for a Conference on transition strategies at the World Institute for Development Economics Research. Helsinki (May): UNU/WIDER.
—— and George Schieber (1996). A Survey of Health Reform in Central Asia, *World Bank: Europe and Central Asia Region Internal Discussion Paper* No. IDP-162. Washington DC: World Bank.
Pomfret, Richard (1995). *The Economies of Central Asia.* New Jersey: Princeton University Press.

Pomfret, Richard and Kathryn Anderson (1997). Uzbekistan: Welfare Impact of Slow Transition, *WIDER Working Paper* No. 135. Helsinki: UNU/WIDER.
Popov, Vladimir (1996). A Russian Puzzle: What Makes the Russian Economic Transformation a Special Case? *WIDER Research for Action*, No. 29 Helsinki: UNU/WIDER.
Tarr, David (1994). How moving to world prices affects the terms of trade of 15 countries of the former Soviet Union. *Journal of Comparative Economics*. 18: 1–24.
UNDP (1996a). *Human Development Report: Uzbekistan 1996*. New York: UNDP.
UNDP (1996b). *Human Development Report: Kazakhstan 1996*. New York: UNDP.
World Bank (1996). *World Development Report: From Plan to Market*. New York: Oxford University Press.
World Bank (1997). *Kazakhstan: Transition of the State*. Washington DC: World Bank.

Chapter 4

Chen, Kang, Gary Jefferson, and Inderjit Singh (1992). Lessons from China's economic reform. *Journal of Comparative Economics* 16 (2) (June): 201–25.
CSSB (China State Statistical Bureau) (various years). *China Statistical Yearbook*. Beijing: China State Statistical Press.
CSSB (China State Statistical Bureau) (various years). *China Statistics of Fixed Investment*. Beijing: China State Statistical Press.
CSSB (China State Statistical Bureau) (various years). *China Statistics of Industrial Economy*. Beijing: China State Statistical Press.
Fan Gang (1996). Inter-enterprise Debt and Macroeconomic Performance in China. *Jingji Yanjiu (Journal of Economic Research)*, March/April. Beijing: National Economic Research Institute of China [in Chinese]. Also available in English as *NERI Working Paper*, No. 96003.
—— and Wing Thye Woo (1993). Decentralized Socialism and Macroeconomic Stability: Lessons from China, *WIDER Working Papers*, No. 112. Helsinki: World Institute for Development Economics Research.
——, Li Yang, and Zhou Zhenhar (1994). *Growing into the Market: China 1978–1992*. Shanghai: Shanghai United Press.
SSRC (State System Restructuring Committee) (1994). *Current Reform Policies*. Beijing: Reform Press.
SSRC (State System Restructuring Committee) (1995). *Current Reform Policies*. Beijing: Reform Press.

Chapter 5

ADB (Asian Development Bank) (1996). *Asian Development Outlook 1996–7*. Oxford: Oxford University Press.
Central Statistical Office (1996). *Impetus and Present Situation of Vietnam Society and Economy After Ten Years of Doi Moi*. Hanoi: Statistical Publishing House.
Dang, Duc Dam (1994). Fighting inflation while sustaining growth and reform momentum in Viet Nam, In *Macroeconomic Management in Southeast Asia's Transitional Economies*, edited by M. F. Montes, R. A. Reyes and S. Tambunlertchai. Kuala Lumpur: Asian and Pacific Development Centre.
Dodsworth, John R., Erich Spitäller, Michael Braulke, Keon Hyok Lee, Kenneth Miranda, Chistian Mulder, Hisanobu Shishido, and Krishna Srinivasan (1996). Viet Nam: Transition

to a Market Economy, *IMF Occasional Paper*, No. 135. Washington, DC: International Monetary Fund.

Dollar, David and Borje Ljunggren (1995). Macroeconomic Adjustment and Structural Reform in an Open Transition Economy: The Case of Viet Nam, Prepared for a Conference on Participation of Reforming Economies in the Global Trading and Financial System, 26–27 May 1995, Helsinki, Finland: UNU/WIDER.

Fforde, Adam and Stefan de Vylder (1996). *From Plan to Market: The Economic Transition in Viet Nam*. Boulder, Colorado: Westview Press.

Jansen, Karel (1997). Economic Reform and Welfare in Viet Nam. Draft paper submitted to the UNU/WIDER project on Welfare in Transitional Asia, January. Helsinki: UNU/WIDER.

Krueger, Anne O., Hal B. Lary, Terry Monson, and Narongchai Akrasanee (eds) (1981). *Trade and Development in Developing Countries: Individual Studies*, Vol. 1. Chicago: University of Chicago Press.

Lee, Keun (1996). An assessment of the state sector reform in China: Viability of legal person socialism. *Journal of the Asia Pacific Economy*, No. 1, pp. 105–21.

Montes, Manuel F. (1995). The private sector as the engine of Philippine growth: Can heaven wait? *Journal of Far Eastern Business*, No. 3, Spring, pp. 132–47.

—— and Keun Lee (1996). Contrasting Northeast and Southeast Asian 'Capitalism': Implications for China, *Asia Journal* 3 (1): 1–35.

Murata, Fuminori (1997). Vietnam turns to private sector to stem rising tide of red ink. *The Nikkei Weekly*, March 10, p. 20.

Naughton, Barry (1995). *Growing Out of the Plan: Chinese Economic Reform, 1978–1993*. New York: Cambridge University Press.

Nguyen, Thi Hien (1994). Savings mobilization in the process of transition in Viet Nam. In *Macroeconomic Management in Southeast Asia's Transitional Economies*, edited by M. F. Montes, R. A. Reyes and S. Tambunlertchai. Kuala Lumpur: Asian and Pacific Development Centre.

Sachs, Jeffrey and Wing Thye Woo (1994). Experiences in the transition to a market economy. *Journal of Comparative Economics* 18 (3): 271–5.

Selden, Mark and William S. Turley (eds) (1993). *Reinventing Vietnamese Socialism: doi moi in Comparative Perspective*. Boulder: Westview Press.

Sun, Laixiang (1996). Emergence of Unorthodox Ownership and Governance Structure in East Asia: An Alternative Transition Path. Paper presented at the UNU/WIDER project meeting on Transition Strategies, Alternatives, and Outcomes, 14–16 November, Helsinki.

Thuyet, Pham van (1995). The Emerging Legal Framework for Private Sector Development in Viet Nam's Transitional Economy, *Policy Research Working Paper* No. 1486. Washington, DC: The World Bank, Transition Economics Division, Policy Research Department.

Van Arkadie, Brian and Manuel F. Montes (1995). Is there an Asian approach to macroeconomic management in the process of transition?, In *Macroeconomic Management in Southeast Asian's Transitional Economies*, edited by M. F. Manuel, R. A. Reyes and S. Tambunlertchai. Kuala Lumpur: Asian and Pacific Development Centre.

World Bank (1993). *Viet Nam: Transition to the Market*. Washington DC: The World Bank, Country Operations Division, East Asia and Pacific Region.

World Bank (1995*a*). Viet Nam: Poverty Assessment and Strategy, *World Bank East Asia and Pacific Region Report*, No. 14645-VN. Washington DC.

World Bank (1995*b*). Viet Nam: Economic Report on Industrialization and Industrial Policy, *World Bank East Asia and Pacific Region Report*, No. 14645-VN. Washington DC.

Chapter 6

Andreff, Vladimir (1989). Economic reforms in North Korea and Viet Nam. *Seoul Journal of Economics* 2 (1) (March): 87–107.

Chun, Hong-Tack (1996). *System Transformation of North Korea and Issues in Economic Integration of the Two Koreas*. Seoul: KDI.

—— and Sang-Ki Kim (1996). Realities and implications of the food crisis in North Korea. *KDI Policy Forum*, No. 101 (29 January) [in Korean].

Chung, Joseph S. (1983). North Korean industrial policy and trade. In *North Korea Today: Strategic and Domestic Issues*, edited by R. Scalapino and J. Kim. Berkeley: Institute of East Asian Studies, University of California.

De Melo, Martha, Cevdet Denizer, and Alan Gelb (1995). Patterns of transition from plan to market. *World Bank Economic Review*, Vol. 10, No. 3.

Eberstadt, Nicholas (1995). *Korea Approaches Reunification*. New York: M. E. Sharpe.

—— (1997). Hastening Korean unification. *Foreign Affairs*, Vol. 76, No. 12.

—— and Judith Banister (1992). *The Population of North Korea*. Berkeley: Institute of East Asian Studies, University of California.

Economic Dictionary (1985). Pyongyang: Social Science Press.

FAO (Food and Agriculture Organization) and WFP (World Food Programme) (1997). Joint Report on the 1996 Harvest and Food Supply Situation in North Korea. *Kukji Sik-lyang-Nong-up*, Vol. 39, No. 1 [in Korean].

Gomulka, Stanislav (1994). Obstacles to recovery in transition economies. In Obstacles to Enterprise Restructuring in Transition, edited by P. Aghion and N. Stern. *EBRD Working Papers*, No. 16, pp. 8–10.

Hyun, Myung-Han (1989). Several problems regarding the uses of circulating capital. *Kulloja*, No. 4, pp. 30–33 [in Korean].

Ickes, Barry, Randi Ryterman and Stoyan Tenev (1995). On Your Marx, Get Set, Go: The Role of Competition in Enterprise Adjustment, *World Bank Working Papers*. Washington, DC: World Bank.

Kang, Myoung-Kyu (1989). Industrial management and reforms in North Korea. In *Economic Reforms in the Socialist World*, edited by S. Gomulka, Y. Ha and C. Kim. London: Macmillan.

—— and Keun Lee (1992). Industrial systems and reforms in North Korea: A comparison with China. *World Development*, No. 7, pp. 947–58.

Kim, Chul-Sik (1986). The associated enterprise in our country is a new form of the socialist enterprise organization, *Kulloja*, No. 2, pp. 70–6 [in Korean].

Kim, Sang-Gyum (1994). *Foreign Trade and External Economic Policy in North Korea*. Seoul: KIEP [in Korean].

Kim, Woon-Keun (1994). The Current Status of North Korean Agriculture and the Prospects of Inter-Korean Agricultural Trade. Paper presented at the seminar organized by the Forum on Agricultural Research, August [in Korean].

Kim, Yon-Chul (1996*a*). Prospects of economic reform in North Korea. *Trends and Prospects*, No. 31 [in Korean].

—— (1996*b*). Food crisis leading to reform in North Korea. *Hangyerye Daily*, 7 October.

KUB (1994). *Assessment of the Third Seven-Year Plan in North Korea*. Seoul: Korean Unification Board, Government of Korea [in Korean].

Kwon, Oh-Yun (1996). A study of change in economic policy in North Korea. In Hyondai Research Institute, *Today and Tomorrow of the North Korean Economy*. Seoul: Hyundai Research Institute [in Korean].

References

Lee, Chan-Woo (1996). Results and prospects of the Rajin-Sunbong investment forum. *Unification Economy*, No. 22 (October) [in Korean].

Lee, Hy-Sang (1990). North Korea's August third programme: The hidden reform. *Proceedings of the Fourth International Conference of Korean Economist*. Seoul: Korean Economic Association.

Lee, Keun (1993a). *New East Asian Economic Development: Interacting Capitalism and Socialism*. New York: M. E. Sharpe.

—— (1993b). Property rights and agency problems in China's enterprise reform. *Cambridge Journal of Economics*, July.

—— (1994). Making another East Asian success in China. In *From Reform to Growth*, edited by C. Lee and H. Reisen. Paris: Organization for Economic Cooperation and Development.

Lee, Pong S. (1987). Interaction of Economic Reform and Political Goal: A Case of North Korea. Paper presented at the Conference, Economic Systems and Reforms in a Changing World, Institute of Social Sciences, Seoul National University, Seoul.

Lee, Sang-Sul (1986). Carrying out the Dae-An model and the associated enterprises. *Kulloja*, No. 7, pp. 46–56 [in Korean].

Lee, Seok-Ki and Sinlim Choi (1996). *Conditions of the North Korean Economy and Prospects of North and South Korean Economic Cooperation*. Seoul: KIET.

Lin, Justin (1996). *The China Miracle: Development Strategy and Economic Reform*. Hong Kong: Chinese University Press.

Merrill, John (1989). North Korea's Economy Today: The Limits of Juche. Paper presented at the Fourth Korea–US Conference on North Korea, August, Seoul.

Murrell, Peter (1996). How far has the transition progressed? *Journal of Economic Perspectives*, No. 2, pp. 25–44.

Than, Mya (1996). Economic Reforms in Transitional Economies of Mainland Southeast Asia. Paper presented at the International Conference, System Transformation of the Transition Economies: Europe, Asia and North Korea, Institute for Korean Unification Studies, 14 September, Seoul.

UNIDO (UN Industrial Development Organization) (1995). *Investigation Report Concerning Selected Projects for the Action Programme for the Development of Light Industry*. Translation in Korean published by KDI in 1996.

Chapter 7

Alesina, A. and A. Drazen (1991). Why are stabilizations delayed? *American Economic Review* 8 (5): 1170–88.

Alvarez, Elena C. (1997). Cuba: Potencialidades de Recuperacion y Desarrolo. Paper presented at XX Congress of the Latin American Studies Association, April 17–19, Guadalajara, Mexico.

Cardoso, Eliana and Ann Helwege (1992). *Cuba After Communism*. Cambridge, Massachusetts: The MIT Press.

Castañeda, Rolando (1993). Cuba: Central elements of a stabilization programme. In *Transition in Cuba: New Challenges for US Policy*, A project by the Cuban Research Institute, Latin American and Caribbean Center: Florida International University: 419–61.

Deere, Carmen Diana (1996). Reforming Cuban Agriculture: Toward the Year 2000. Paper presented to the First Annual Meeting of the Latin American and Caribbean Economic Association, 17–19 October, Mexico City: ITAM.

Deere, Carmen Diana, Niurka Pérez, and Ernel Gonzáles (1994). The view from below: Cuban agriculture in the 'special period in peacetime'. *Journal of Peasant Studies* 21 (2): 194–234.

Dominguez, Jorge (1993). The transition to somewhere: Cuba in the 1990s. In *Transition in Cuba: New Challenges for US Policy*. A project by the Cuban Research Institute, Latin American and Caribbean Center, Florida International University.

Everleny Perez, Omar (1998). Cuba: La Evolucion Economica Reciente: Una Valoracion, mimeo.

Feinsilver, Julie M. (1992). Will Cuba's wonder drugs lead to political and economic wonders? Capitalizing on biotechnology and medical exports. *Cuban Studies*, No. 22, pp. 79–114.

Figueras, Miguel Alejandro (1991). Structural changes in the Cuban economy. *Latin American Perspectives* 18 (2): 69–85.

Fitzgerald, Frank T. (1995). The Cuban revolution in crisis: From managing socialism to managing survival. *New York: Monthly Review Press* 239.

Gonzalez, Edward (1996). *Cuba: Clearing Perilous Waters?* Santa Monica, CA: The Rand Corporation.

Joglekar, Gitanjali and Andrew Zimbalist (1989). Dollar GDP per capita in Cuba: Estimates and observations on the use of the physical indicators method. *Journal of Comparative Economics* 13: 85–114.

Maingot, Anthony (1993). The ideal and the real in Cuban political culture: Identifying preconditions for a democratic consolidation. In *Transition in Cuba: New Challenges for US Policy*. A project by the Cuban Research Institute, Latin American and Caribbean Center, Florida International University.

Mesa-Lago, Carmelo (1993). The social safety net in the two transitions. In *Transition in Cuba: New Challenges for US Policy*. A project by the Cuban Research Institute, Latin American and Caribbean Center, Florida International University.

—— (1995). Cuba's Raft Exodus of 1994: Causes, Settlement, Effects, and Future, *The North-South Agenda Papers*, No. 12. Miami, FL: University of Miami, North-South Center.

—— and Horst Fabian (1993). Analogies between East European socialist regimes and Cuba: Scenarios for the future. In *Cuba After The Cold War*, edited by C. Mesa-Lago. Pittsburgh, PA: University of Pittsburgh Press.

Pastor, Manuel Jr and Andrew Zimbalist (1995a). Waiting for change: adjustment and reform in Cuba. *World Development* 23 (5): 705–20.

—— —— (1995b). Facing the Future: External Shocks, Economic Crisis, and the Dynamics of Transition in Cuba. *NACLA Report on the Americas*, Vol. 29, No. 2.

—— —— (1998). Has Cuba turned the corner—and if so, which one? Macroeconomic stabilization and the implications for reform in contemporary Cuba. *Cuban Studies* 27: 1–20.

Pérez-López, Jorge F. (1991). Bringing the Cuban economy into focus: Conceptual and empirical challenges. *Latin American Research Review* 26 (3): 7–53.

—— (1995). *Cuba's Second Economy: From Behind the Scenes to Center Stage*. New Brunswick, NJ: Transaction Publishers.

—— (1996). Foreign Direct Investment in the Cuban Economy: A Critical Look. A Paper prepared for presentation at the First International Meeting of the Latin American and Caribbean Economic Association, October 17–19, Mexico City.

—— (1998a). The Cuban economic crisis of the 1990s and the external sector. *Cuba in Transition—Volume 8*. Washington, DC: Association for the Study of the Cuban Economy.

—— (1998b). Economic reforms in a comparative perspective. In *Perspectives on Cuban Economic Reforms*, edited by J. F. Pérez-López, and M. F. Travieso-Diaz. Tempe, AZ: Center for Latin American Studies, Arizona State University, Special Studies No. 30.

References

Peters, Philip and Joseph L. Scarpaci (1998). *Cuba's New Entrepreneurs: Five Years of Small-Scale Capitalism*. Arlington, VA: Alexis de Tocqueville Institution.

Ritter, A. R. M. (1990). The Cuban economy in the 1990s: External challenges and policy imperatives. *Journal of InterAmerican Studies and World Affairs* 32: 117–49.

Roca, Sergio (1993). Cuban privatization: Potential path and implementation. In *Transition in Cuba: New Challenges for US Policy*. A project by the Cuban Research Institute, Latin American and Caribbean Center, Florida International University.

Rodrik, Dani (1991). Policy uncertainty and private investment in developing countries. *Journal of Development Economics*, No. 36, pp. 229–42.

—— (1994). The rush to free trade in the developing world: Why so late? Why now? Will it last? In *Voting for Reform: Democracy, Political Liberalization, and Economic Adjustment*, edited by S. Haggard and S. B. Webb. New York: Oxford University Press.

—— (1996). Understanding economic policy reform. *Journal of Economic Literature* XXXIV (1): 9–41.

Rosenberg, Jonathan (1992). Cuba's free market experiment: Los mercados libres campesinos, 1980–1986, *Latin American Research Review* 27 (3): 51–89.

Sanguinetty, Jorge (1993). The transition towards a market economy in Cuba: Its legal and managerial dimensions. In *Transition in Cuba: New Challenges for US Policy*. A project by the Cuban Research Institute, Latin American and Caribbean Center, Florida International University.

Suchlicki, Jaime (1999). Castro's Cuba: More Continuity Than Change. Paper prepared for the Americas Society, April 15.

Turtis, Richard (1987). Trade, debt, and the Cuban economy, In *Cuba's Socialist Economy Toward the 1990s*, edited by A. Zimbalist. Boulder, CO: Lynne Reinner.

Zimbalist, Andrew and C. Brundenius (1989). *The Cuban Economy: Measurement and Analysis of Socialist Performance*. Baltimore: Johns Hopkins Press.

Chapter 8

Aoki, Masahiko and Hyung-Ki Kim (eds) (1995). *Corporate Governance in Transitional Economies*. Washington: The World Bank.

Aghion, Phillipe and Olivier Blanchard (1998). On privatization methods in Eastern Europe and their implications. *Economics of Transition* 6 (1) (May): 87–99.

—— —— and Burgess, S. (1994). The behavior of firms in Eastern Europe, pre privatization. *European Economic Review*, 38: 1327–49.

Aukutsionek, Sergei *et al.* (1998). Dominant shareholders, restructuring and performance of privatized firms. *Communist Economies and Econ. Transformation* 10 (4): 495–518.

Ben-Ner and Derek C. Jones (1995). Employee participation, ownership and productivity: A theoretical framework. *Industrial Relations* 34 (4) (October): 532–54.

Bevan, Alan A., Estrin, Saul and Schaffer, Mark E. (1998). Determinants of Enterprise Performance During Transition, mimeo, Centre for Economic Reform and Transformation, Heriot-Watt University, Edinburgh.

Bim, Alexander S., Jones, Derek C., and Weisskopf, Thomas E. (1993). Hybrid forms of enterprise organization in the former USSR and the Russian federation. *Comparative Economic Studies* 35 (1): 1–37.

References

Blasi, Joseph R. (1994). Russian labor-management relations: Some preliminary lessons from newly privatized enterprises. In *Proceedings of the Forty-Seventh Annual Meeting*, IRRA Series, edited by Paula B. Voos. Madison, Wisconsin.

―― Joseph M. Kroumova, and D. Kruse (1997). *Kremlin Capitalism*. Cornell, Ithaca: ILR Press.

Bolton, Patrick (1995). Privatization and the separation of ownership and control: Lessons from Chinese enterprise reform. *Economics of Transition* 3 (1): 1–13

Bonin, John (1976). On the design of managerial incentive systems in a decentralized planning environment, *American Economic Review* 66 (4): 682–7.

Boycko, M., A. Schaefer, and R. Vishny (1996). A theory of privatization. *Economic Journal* 106 (March): 309–19.

Buck, Trevor, Igor Filatotchev, Mike Wright, and Vladimir Zhukov (1999). Corporate governance and employee ownership in an economic crisis: Enterprise strategies in the former USSR. *Journal of Comparative Economics* 27 (3) (September): 459–74.

Carlin, W. and M. Landesmann (1997). From theory into practice? Restructuring and dynamism in transition economies. *Oxford Review of Economic Policy* 13 (2): 77–105.

Claessens, S. and S. Djankov (1997). Managers, incentives and corporate performance: Evidence from the Czech Republic. Paper prepared for the WDI Conference on Labour Markets in Transition Economies, 17–19 October 1997.

Commander, Simon, Qimiao Fan, and Mark E. Schaffer (1996). *Enterprise Restructuring and Economic Policy in Russia*, EDI Development Study. Washington: World Bank.

Earle, J. and S. Estrin (1998). Privatization, Competition and Budget Constraint: Disciplining Enterprises in Russia. SITE Working Paper No. 128, March 1998. Stockholm School of Economics: Stockholm, Sweden.

―――― Jones, David and J. Svejnar (eds) (1996). Workers self management in transitional economies. In *Advances in the Economic Analysis of Participatory and Labor Managed Firms*, Vol. 6, pp. 3–28. Greenwich, Conn.: JAI Press.

―――― and L. Leshchenko (1996). Ownership structures, patterns of control and enterprise behavior in Russia. In *Enterprise Restructuring and Economic Policy in Russia*, edited by C. Simon, Q. Fan, and M. E. Schaffer, EDI Development Study. Washington: World Bank.

Estrin, Saul (ed.) (1994). *Privatization in Central and Eastern Europe*, London: Longmans.

―― and Adam Rosevear (1999). Enterprise performance and ownership: The case of Ukraine. *European Economic Review* 43: 1123–36.

―― and Mike Wright (1999). Corporate governance in the former Soviet Union: An overview. *Journal of Comparative Economics* 27 (3) (September): 398–421.

Filatotchev, Igor, Irena Grosfeld, Judith Karsai, Mike Wright, and Trevor Buck (1996). Buyouts in Hungary, Poland and Russia: The financial issues. *Economics of Transition* 4 (1) 67–88.

―― Mike Wright, and Mike Bleaney (1999). Privatization and corporate governance in Russia: Analysis and policy implications. *Economics of Transition*, vol. 7.

Fitzroy et al. (1998). *Employee Ownership in Privatization*. Budapest: ILO.

Frydman, R., C. Gray, and A. Rapaczynski (eds) (1996). *Corporate Governance in Central Europe and Russia*. Budapest: CEU Press.

―――――― and M. Hessel (1997). Private ownership and corporate performance: Some lessons from transition economies. *World Bank Policy Research Papers*, No. 1830. Washington D.C.: The World Bank.

Groves, Theodore, Y. Hong, J. Macmillan, and B. Naughton (1994). Autonomy and incentives in Chinese state enterprises. *Quarterly Journal of Economics* 109 (1): 183–209.

────── and B. Naughton (1995). China's evolving managerial labour market. *Journal of Political Economy* 103 (4): 873–92.
Hinds, M. (1990). Issues in the Introduction of Market Forces in Eastern and Central European Socialist Economies. Washington, World Bank, March.
Jefferson, Gary H., and Thomas G. Rawski (1994). Enterprise reform in Chinese industry. *Journal of Economic Perspectives* 8 (2) (Spring): 47–70.
Jones, Derek C. (1998). The economic effects of privatization: Evidence from a Russian panel. *Comparative Economic Studies*, XXX (2) (Summer): 75–102.
────── (1999). Privatization and restructuring in Russia: A review and micro evidence from St Petersburg. In *Reconstituting the Market: The Political Economy of microeconomic transformation*, edited by P. Hare, J. Batt and S. Estrin. Harwood.
────── and K. Ilayperuma, (1998). The determinants of employee participation during fading communism and early transition. *Advances in the Economic Analysis of Participatory and Labor Managed Firms*, Vol. 6.
────── and Takao Kato (1996). The determinants of executive compensation in transitional economies: Evidence from Bulgaria. *Labour Economics* 3: 319–36.
────── and Niels Mygind (1998). Ownership patterns after privatization in transition economies: Evidence from the Baltics. *Baltic Journal of Economics* 2.
────── ────── (1999). The nature and determinants of ownership changes after privatization: Evidence from Estonia. *Journal of Comparative Economics* 27: 422–41.
────── ────── (1999a). The effects of privatization upon productive efficiency: Evidence from the Baltic Republics. *Annals of Public and Cooperative Economy*. CEES Working Paper Series, No. 22 (30 pages).
────── ────── (1999b). Ownership and Productive Efficiency: Evidence from Estonian Panel Data mimeo, Hamilton College.
────── and Jeffrey Pliskin (1997). Determinants of the incidence of group incentives: Evidence from Canada. *Canadian Journal of Economics* 30 (November): 1027–45.
────── and Tom Weisskopf, (1996). Employee ownership and control: Evidence from Russia. *Proceedings of the Forty Eighth Meeting of the Industrial Relations Research Association*, pp. 64–76.
──────, Takao Kato, and Svetlana Avramov (1995). Managerial labor markets in transitional economies. *International Journal of Manpower* 16 (10): 14–24.
──────, M. Klinedinst, and C. Rock (1998). Productive efficiency during transition; evidence from Bulgarian Panel Data. *Journal of Comparative Economics* 26: 446–64.
Kato, Takao and Mark Rockel, (1992). Experiences, credentials and compensation in the Japanese and U.S. managerial labor markets: Evidence from new micro data. *Journal of the Japanese and International Economies* 6: 30–51.
Kornai, Janos (1992). *The Socialist System: The Political Economy of Communism*. Princeton and Oxford University Press.
Li, David D. (1996). A theory of ambiguous property rights in transition economies: The case of the Chinese non-state sector. *Journal of Comparative Economics* 23 (1) (August): 1–19.
Mygind, Niels (ed.) (1995). Privatization and Financial Participation in the Baltic Countries mimeo, Copenhagen Business School.
Nuti, Mario (1995). Employeeism, Corporate Governance and Employee Ownership in Transitional Economies, mimeo, London Business School.
Pinto, Brian, Marek Belka, and Stefan Krajewski (1993). Transforming state enterprises in Poland. *Brookings Papers on Economic Activity* 1: 213–70.

Pohl, Gerhard, Robert E. Anderson, Stijn, Claessens, and Simeon Djankov (1997). Privatization and Restructuring in central and Eastern Europe: Evidence and policy Options, World Bank Technical paper 368, Washington DC.
Smith, Stephen, Beom-Cheol Cin, and Milan Vodipevic (1997). Privatization incidence, ownership forms and firm performance: Evidence from Slovenia. *Journal of Comparative Economics* 25 (2) (October): 158–79.
Standing, Guy (1997). *Russian Unemployment and Enterprise Restructuring: Reviving Dead Souls*. London: Macmillan.
Sun, Laixiang (1996). Emergence of Unorthodox Ownership and Governance Structure in East Asia: An Alternative Transition Path. Paper presented at UNU/WIDER Project Meeting on Transition Strategies, Alternatives and Outcomes, 14–16 November, Helsinki.
Uvalic, Milica and Daniel Vaughan-Whitehead (eds) (1997). *Privatization Surprises in Transition Economies: Employee Ownership in Central and Eastern Europe*. Cheltenham, UK: Elgar.
Vaughan-Whitehead, Daniel (1998). Profit sharing in Albania. In *Advances in the Economic Analysis of Participatory and Labor Managed Firms*, Vol. 6, pp. 91–114.
Weitzman, Martin and C. Xu (1994). Chinese township-village enterprises as vaguely defined cooperatives. *Journal of Comparative Economics* 18 (2): 121–45.
Woodward, Richard (1998). Various Forms of Employee Participation in Polish Employee Owned Companies. In Jones, D. and J. Svejnar (eds.) *Advances in the Economic Analysis of Participatory and Labor Managed Firms*, Vol. 6, pp. 57–90. Greenwich, Conn.: JAI Press.
World Bank (1996). *World Development Report: From Plan to Market*, Washington.

Chapter 9

Bai, Chong-En, David D. Li, and Yijiang Wang (1997). Enterprise productivity and efficiency: When is up really down? *Journal of Comparative Economics* 24 (3): 265–80.
Blair, Margaret (1995). *Ownership and Control: Rethinking Corporate Governance for the 21st Century*. Washington, DC: Brookings Institute.
Borys, Bryan and David B. Jemison (1989). Hybrid arrangements as strategic alliances: Theoretical issues in organizational combinations. *Academy of Management Review*, No. 14, pp. 234–49.
Bourdet, Y. (1995). An economic evaluation of the Lao transition mix. *Economic Policy in Transitional Economies* 5 (1): 29–51.
Brada, Josef C. (1996). Privatization is transition, or is it? *Journal of Economic Perspectives* 10 (2): 67–86.
Buchanan, James M. (1979). *What Should Economists Do?* Indianapolis, IN: Liberty Press.
Campbell, John L. and Leon N. Lindberg (1990). Property rights and the organization of economic activity by the state. *American Sociological Review* 55 (5) (October): 634–47.
Carroll, Glenn R., Jerry Goodstein, and Antal Gyeses (1988). Organizations and the state: Effects of the institutional environment on agricultural cooperatives in Hungary. *Administrative Science Quarterly*, No. 33, pp. 233–56.
CTVEs Net (various). Global Net of Chinese Township-Village Enterprises. (<http://www.ctve.com>: CTVEs Net).
Demsetz, Harold (1967). Towards a theory of property rights. *American Economic Review* 57 (2) (May): 347–59.

Dodsworth, J. R., E. Spitaller, M. Braulke, K. H. Lee, K. Miranda, C. Mulder, H. Shishido, and K. Srinivasan (1996). Vietnam: Transition to a Market Economy, *IMF Occasional Papers*, No. 135. Washington, DC: International Monetary Fund.

Dollar, David (1994). Macroeconomic management and the transition to the market in Vietnam. *Journal of Comparative Economics* 18 (3) (June): 357–75.

Dong, Xiao-Yuan and Louis Putterman (1997). Productivity and organization in China's rural industries: A stochastic frontier analysis. *Journal of Comparative Economics* 24 (2) (June): 357–75.

Dore, Ronald (1983). Goodwill and the spirit of market capitalism. *British Journal of Sociology* 34 (4): 459–82.

Evans, Grant (1988). Agrarian Change in Communist Laos, *Occasional Papers*, No. 85. Singapore: Institute of Southeast Asian Studies.

Fforde, Adam and Stefan de Vylder (1996). *From Plan to Market: The Economic Transition in Vietnam*. Oxford: Westview Press.

Frydman, Roman, Cheryl W. Gray, and Andrzej Rapaczynski (eds) (1996). *Corporate Governance in Central Europe and Russia, Vol. 2: Insiders and the State*. Budapest: Central European University Press.

Funck, Bernard (1993). Laos: Decentralization and economic control. In *The Challenge of Reform in Indochina*, edited by B. Ljunggren. Cambridge, MA: HIID, Harvard University.

General Statistics Office (1996). *Impetus and the Present Situation of the Viet Nam Society and Economy after Ten Years of Doi Moi*. Hanoi: Statistical Publishing House.

Granick, David (1990). *Chinese State Enterprises: A Regional Property Rights Analysis*. Chicago: University of Chicago Press.

Gui, Shiyong (1999). A crucial and urgent task: Remarks on the reform and development of state-owned enterprises. *People's Daily*, 14 October [in Chinese].

Gurkov, Igor (1997). 'Russian enterprises' adaptation to new economic realities. *MOCT-MOST* 7 (2) (June): 57–89.

Hart, Oliver (1995). *Firms, Contracts and Financial Structure*. Oxford: Oxford University Press.

Havrylyshyn, Oleh and Donald McGettigan (1999). Privatization in Transition Countries: A Sampling of the Literature, *IMF Working Papers*, No. WP/99/6. Washington, DC: International Monetary Fund.

IMF (1998). Lao People's Democratic Republic: Recent Economic Development, *IMF Staff Country Reports*, No. 98/77. Washington, DC: International Monetary Fund.

IMF (1999*a*). Vietnam: Selected Issues. *IMF Staff Country Reports*, No. 99/55. Washington, DC: International Monetary Fund.

IMF (1999*b*). Vietnam: Statistical Appendix. *IMF Staff Country Reports*, No. 99/56. Washington, DC: International Monetary Fund.

IMF (1999*c*). Cambodia: Statistical Appendix. *IMF Staff Country Reports*, No. 99/33. Washington, DC: International Monetary Fund.

Irvin, George (1995). Vietnam: Assessing the achievements of Doi Moi. *Journal of Development Studies* 31 (5) (June): 725–50.

Jefferson, Gary H. and Thomas G. Rawski (1994). Enterprise reform in Chinese industry. *Journal of Economic Perspectives* 8 (2) (Spring): 47–70.

———, John Z. Zhao, and Lu Mai (1998). Reforming property rights in Chinese industry. In *Reform, Ownership and Performance in Chinese Industry*, edited by G. H. Jefferson and I. Singh. New York: Oxford University Press.

Jiang, Zemin (1997). Political Report to the Fifteenth National Congress of the Communist Party of China. *People's Daily*, 22 September.
Kornai, János (1980). *The Economics of Shortage*. Amsterdam: North Holland.
Laky, Teréz (1979). Enterprises in bargaining position. *Acta Oeconomica* 22 (3–4): 226–41.
Leff, Nathaniel H. (1964). Economic development through bureaucratic corruption. *American Behavioral Scientist* 8 (3): 8–14.
Li, David D. (1996). A theory of ambiguous property rights in transition economies: The case of the Chinese non-state sector. *Journal of Comparative Economics* 23 (1) (August): 1–19.
Lin, Justin Y., Cai Fang, and Li Zou (1996). *The China Miracle: Development Strategy and Economic Reform*. Hong Kong: Chinese University of Hong Kong Press.
Lin, Nan (1995). Local market socialism: Local corporatism in action in rural China. *Theory and Society* 24 (3): 301–54.
Liu, Yia-Ling (1992). Reform from below: The private economy and local politics in the rural industrialization of Wenzhou. *China Quarterly*, No. 130, pp. 293–316.
Macaulay, Stewart (1963). Non-contractual relations in business: A preliminary study. *American Sociological Review*, No. 28, pp. 55–67.
McCarty, A. (1993). Industrial renovation in Vietnam, 1986–91. In *Vietnam's Dilemmas and Options: The Challenge of Economic Transition in the 1990s*, edited by M. Tan and J. L. H. Tan. Singapore: Institute of Southeast Asian Studies.
Milgrom, Paul and John Robert (1990). Bargaining costs, influence costs and the organization of economic activity. In *Perspectives on Positive Political Economy*, edited by J. Alt and K. Shepsle. Cambridge, UK: Cambridge University Press.
────── (1992). *Economics, Organization and Management*. Englewood Cliffs, NJ: Prentice Hall.
Naughton, Barry (1995). *Growing Out of the Plan: Chinese Economic Reform 1978–1993*. Cambridge, UK: Cambridge University Press.
Nee, Victor (1992). Organizational dynamics of market transition: Hybrid forms, property rights and mixed economy in China. *Administrative Science Quarterly* 37 (1): 1–27.
Nelson, Richard R. and Sidney G. Winter (1982). *An Evolutionary Theory of Economic Change*. Cambridge, UK: Cambridge University Press.
O'Brien, Kevin J. (1994). Implementing political reform in China's villages. *Australian Journal of Chinese Affairs*, No. 32 (July), pp. 33–59.
Oi, Jean C. (1996). Local state corporatism: The organization of rapid economic growth. In *Chinese Rural Industry Takes Off: Incentives for Growth*, edited by J. C. Oi. Berkeley, CA: University of California Press.
Otani, Ichiro and Chi Do Pham (eds) (1996). The Lao People's Democratic Republic: Systemic Transformation and Adjustment. *IMF Occasional Papers*, No. 137. Washington, DC: International Monetary Fund.
Parker, David and Pan Weihwa (1996). Reform of the state-owned enterprises in China. *Communist Economies and Economic Transformation* 8 (1): 109–27.
Parris, Kristen (1993). Local initiative and national reform: The wenzhou model of development. *China Quarterly*, No. 134 (June), pp. 242–63.
Pejovich, Avetozar (1990). *The Economics of Property Rights: Towards a Theory of Comparative Systems*. London: Kluwer Academic Publishers.
Perotti, Enrico, Laixiang Sun, and Liang Zou (1999). State-owned versus township and village enterprises in China. *Comparative Economics Studies* 41 (2–3) (Summer/Fall): 151–79.

Probert, Jocelyn and S. David Young (1995). The Vietnamese road to capitalism: Decentralization, de facto privatization and the limits to piecemeal reform. *Communist Economies and Economic Transformation* 7 (4) (December): 499–525.

Raiser, Martin (1996). How are China's State-owned Enterprises Doing in the 1990s? Evidence from Three Interior Provinces. *Kiel Working Papers* No. 781. Kiel, Germany.

Rana, Pradumna B. (1995). Reform strategies in transitional economies: Lessons from Asia. *World Development* 23 (7): 1157–69.

Sabel, Charles and David Stark (1982). Planning, politics and shop-floor power: Hidden forms of bargaining in Soviet-imposed state-socialist societies. *Politics and Society*, No. 11, pp. 439–75.

Stark, David (1996). Networks of assets, chains of debt: Recombinant property in Hungary. In *Corporate Governance in Central Europe and Russia, Vol. 2: Insiders and the State*, ed. R. Frydman, C. W. Gray and A. Rapaczynski. Budapest: Central European University Press.

State Bureau of Industrial and Commercial Administration and Theoretical Department of Beijing Daily (1984). Notice of the Central Committee of the CCP Concerning Rural Work in 1984. *Geti Laodongzhe Shouce (Individual Labourers' Handbook)*. Beijing: Daily Press and Gongshang Press.

SSB (State Statistical Bureau) (various years). *Statistical Yearbook of China*. Beijing: China Statistics Press.

Sun, Laixiang (1992). A survey on the economic efficiency of state-owned enterprises. In *The Functioning Mechanism of China's Commodity Economy*, ed. Li Yining. Beijing: China Economy Press [in Chinese].

—— (1997). Emergence of Unorthodox Ownership and Governance Structures in East Asia: An Alternative Transition Path, *WIDER Research for Action*, No. 34. Helsinki: UNU/WIDER.

Svejnar, Jan (1990). Productive efficiency and employment. In *China's Rural Industry: Structure, Development and Reform*, ed. W. Byrd and L. Qingsong. New York: Oxford University Press.

Thanh, Ngo Kim (1995). Public enterprise reform in Vietnam's transition: Problems and policy implications. The Hague: Institute of Social Studies. MA thesis.

Walder, Andrew G. (1994). Corporate organization and local government property rights in China. *Changing Political Economies: Privatization in Post-Communist and Reforming Communist States*, ed. V. Milor. Boulder, CO: Lynne Rienner.

—— (1995). Local governments as industrial firms: An organizational analysis of China's transitional economy. *American Journal of Sociology* 101 (2) (September): 263–301.

Wank, David L. (1996). The institutional process of market clientelism: Guanxi and private business in a South China city. *China Quarterly*, No. 147, pp. 820–38.

Weitzman, Martin L. and Chenggang Xu (1994). Chinese township-village enterprises as vaguely defined cooperatives. *Journal of Comparative Economics*, 18 (2): 121–45.

Williamson, Oliver E. (1991). Comparative economic organization: The analysis of discrete structure alternatives. *Administrative Science Quarterly*, No. 36 (June), pp. 269–96.

Wong, Christine (1992). Fiscal reform and local industrialization. *Modern China* 18 (2): 197–227.

—— (1995). *Financing Local Government in the People's Republic of China*. Manila: Asian Development Bank.

Wong, John, Ma Rong, and Yang Mu (1995). *China's Rural Enterprises: Ten Case Studies*. Singapore: Times Academic Press.

Woo, Wing T., Hai Wen, Jin Yibiao, and Fan Gang (1994). How successful has Chinese enterprise reform been?: Pitfalls in opposite biases and focus. *Journal of Comparative Economics* 18 (3) (June): pp. 410–37.

World Bank (1994a). Lao People's Democratic Republic. *Country Economic Memorandums*, No. 12554-LA. Washington, DC: World Bank.

World Bank (1994b). China: Macroeconomic Stability in a Decentralized Economy. *Country Economic Memorandums*. Washington, DC: World Bank.

World Bank (1996). *World Development Report 1996: From Plan to Market*. New York: Oxford University Press.

Yearbook of China's Township and Village Enterprises (various years). Beijing: Agriculture Press [in Chinese].

Young, Susan (1994). Ownership and obligation in China's rural enterprises: Community interests in a non-legalistic environment. In *Chinese Economy in Transition*, edited by Yanrui Wu and Zhang Xiaohe. Canberra: National Centre for Development Studies, Australian National University.

Zhang, Weiying and Yi Gang (1995). China's Gradual Reform: A Historical Perspective, *China Centre for Economic Research Working Papers*, No. E1995001. Beijing: Peking University.

Zou, Liang (1992). Ownership structure and efficiency: An incentive mechanism approach. *Journal of Comparative Economics* 16 (3) (September): 399–431.

Chapter 10

Alesina, Alberto and Roberto Perotti (1996). Income distribution, political instability, and investment. *European Economic Review* 40: 1203–28.

—— and Dani Rodrik (1994). Distributive politics and economic growth. *Quarterly Journal of Economics* 109: 465–90.

Atkinson, Tony and John Micklewright (1992). *Economic Transformation in Eastern Europe and the Distribution of Income*. Cambridge, UK: Cambridge University Press.

——, Lee Rainwater, and Timothy Smeeding (1994). *Income distribution in OECD Countries: The Evidence from the Luxembourg Income Study* (LIS), mimeo, 18 May.

Benabou, Roland (1996). Inequality and growth. In *NBER Macroeconomics Annual 1996*. Massachusetts: The MIT Press.

Boltho, Andrea (1992). Growth, Income Distribution and Household Welfare in the Industrialized Countries since the First Oil Shock. *UNICEF ICDC Innocenti Occasional Papers, Special Subseries—Child Poverty in Industrialized Countries: EPS26*. Florence: UNICEF International Child Development Centre.

Braithwaite, J. D. and T. E. Heleniak (1989). Social Welfare in the USSR: The Income Recipient Distribution. Washington DC: Centre for International Research, US Bureau of the Census.

Cornia, Giovanni Andrea and Sandor Sipos (1991). *Children and the Transition to the Market Economy*. Aldershot: Avebury.

Flemming, J. and J. Micklewright (1999). Income distribution, economic systems and transition. *Innocenti Occasional Papers, Economic and Social Policy Subseries, EPS70*. Florence: UNICEF International Child Development Centre.

Goskomstat (various years). *Narodnoye Khozyaistvo SSSR* (National Economy of the USSR), *Rossiysky Statistichesky Yezhegodnik*. Moscow: Russian Statistical Yearbook.

Harrold, Peter (1992). China's reform Experience to Date, *World Bank Discussion Papers*, No. 180, Washington DC: The World Bank.

Honkkila, Juha (1997). Privatization, Asset Distribution and Equity in Transitional Economies, *UNU/WIDER Working Papers*, No. 125. Helsinki: UNU/WIDER.

Hussain, P., P. Lanjouw, and N. Stern (1991). Income Inequality in China: Evidence from Household Survey Data, China Programme Technical Report, No. 18, STICERD. London, London School of Economics.

Kakwani, Nanak (1980). *Income, Inequality and Poverty*. Oxford: Oxford University Press.

Kolodko, Grzegorz, W. (1986). The Repressed Inflation and Inflationary Overhang under Socialism, *BEBR Working Paper*, No. 1228. Urbana-Champaign: University of Illinois.

Kornai, Janos (1980). *Economics of Shortage*. Amsterdam: North Holland.

Lehmann, Hartmut, Jonathan Wadsworth, and Ruslan Yemtsov (n.d.). The Distribution of Earnings in Transition: Is Russia Really So Different? mimeo. Washington DC: World Bank.

McAuley, Alistair (1994). 'Social Welfare in Transition: What Happened to Russia, *World Bank Research Paper Series*, No. 6. Washington, DC: World Bank.

McKinley, Terry and Mark Brenner (1998). Rising Inequality and Changing Social Structure in China: 1988–95, mimeo. Helsinki: UNU/WIDER.

Milanovic, Branko (1993). Cash Social Transfers, Direct Taxes, and Income Distribution in Late Socialism, *World Bank Policy Research Working Paper*, No. 1176. Washington, DC: World Bank.

—— (1995). Poverty, Inequality and Social Policy in Transition Economies, *World Bank Policy Research Paper Series*, No. 9. Washington, DC: World Bank.

—— (1998). *Income, Inequality, and Poverty during the Transition from Planned to Market Economy*. Washington, DC: World Bank.

Pelphs-Brown, H. (1977). *The Inequality of Pay*. Oxford: Oxford University Press.

Ping, Zhan (1997). Income Distribution during the Transition in China, UNU/WIDER *Working Paper*s, No. 138. Helsinki, Finland: UNU/WIDER.

Pryor, F. L. (1973). *Property and Industrial Organization in Communist and Capitalist Nations*. Bloomington: Indiana University Press.

Roxborough, I. W. and J. C. Shapiro (1994). Employment Incentives of Taxes Based on the Average Wage, mimeo. London: Goldsmith College.

Rutkowski, Jan (1994). Labour Market Transition and Changes in the Wage Structure: The Case of Poland, mimeo. Princetown: Centre for International studies, Princetown University.

—— (1999). Wage Inequality in Transition Economies of Central Europe: Trends and Patterns in the Late 1990s, mimeo. Background document prepared for the World Bank ECA Pov 2000 Project, ECSHD. Washington, DC: World Bank.

Standing, Guy and Daniel Vaughan-Whitehead (1995). *Minimum Wages in Central and Eastern Europe: From Protection to Destitution*. Budapest: Central European University Press.

UNICEF (1994). Crisis in Mortality, Health and Nutrition, *Economies in Transition Studies*, Regional Monitoring Report No. 2. Florence: UNICEF International Child Development Centre.

UNICEF (1995). Poverty, Children and Policy: Responses for a Brighter Future, *Economies in Transition Studies*, Regional Monitoring Report No. 3. Florence: UNICEF International Child Development Centre.

Vecernik, Jiri (1994). Changing Earnings Inequality under the Economic Transformation: The Czech and Slovak Republics in 1984–92, mimeo. Prague: Academy of Sciences.

Venieris, Yannis and Dipak Gupta (1986). Income distribution and socio-political instability as determinants of savings: A cross-sectional model. *Journal of Political Economy* 94 (4): 873–83.

World Bank (1994). Poverty in Poland, *World Bank Report*, No. 13501-PO. Washington DC: World Bank.

Zamfir, Catalin (1995). Social Policy in Romania in Transition, Report prepared for UNICEF-ICDC, mimeo. Florence: UNICEF International Child Development Centre.

Chapter 11

Aghion, Philippe and Peter Howitt (1992). A model of economic growth through creative destruction. *Econometrica* 60 (2): 322–52.
Balcerowicz, L. (1995). *Socialism, Capitalism, Transformation*. Budapest: Central European University Press.
Borner, S., A. Brunetti, and B. Weder (1995). *Political Credibility and Economic Development*. New York: St. Martin's Press.
——, M. Kobler, and C. Winiker (1996). Institutional Uncertainty and Economic Growth in the Baltics, *WWZ Discussion Paper*, No. 9606. Basel: WWZ.
Boswell, Jonathan (1990). Community and the Economy. The Theory of Public Co-operation. London and New York: Routledge.
Byrd, William and Lin Qingsong (eds) (1990). *China's Rural Industry: Structure, Development, and Reform*. Oxford: Oxford University Press.
Campos, J. Edgardo and Hilton Root (1996). *The Key to the Asian Miracle: Making Shared Growth Credible*. Washington, DC: The Brookings Institution.
Coleman, James (1988). Social capital in the creation of human capital. *American Journal of Sociology* 94 (Supplement): S9–S120.
DIW *et al*. (Deutsches Institut für Wirtschaftsforschung Berlin, Institut für Wirtschaftsforschung Halle, Institut für Weltwirtschaft Kiel) (1996). Gesamtwirtschaftliche und unternehmerische Anpassungsfortschritte in Ostdeutschland, *Report No. 14, Kiel Discussion Papers*, No. 227/228. Kiel: Institute of World Economics.
EBRD (European Bank for Reconstruction and Development) (1996). *Transition Report* London: EBRD.
EBRD (European Bank for Reconstruction and Development) (1997). *Transition Report Update*. London: EBRD.
Elster, Jon (1989). Social norms and economic theory. *Journal of Economic Perspectives* 3 (4): 99–117.
Fan, G. (1994). Dual track transition in China. *Economic Policy* 9 (4): 99–102.
Friedman, Eric and S. Johnson (1996). *Complementarities and Optimal Reform*, mimeo. Durham, NC: Duke University.
Frye, Timothy and Andrei Shleifer (1997). The Invisible Hand and the Grabbing Hand, *American Economic Review*, Papers and Proceedings, 87 (2): 354–8.
Grabher, Gernot and David Stark (eds) (1996). *Restructuring Networks in Post-Socialism*. Oxford: Oxford University Press.
Granick, D. (1990). *Chinese State Enterprises. A Regional Property Rights Analysis*. Chicago: University of Chicago Press.
Greenlagh, S. (1990). Land Reform and Family Entrepreneurialism in East Asia. In *Rural Development and Population: Institutions and Policies*, edited by G. McNicoll and M. Cain. New York: Oxford University Press.
Greif, Avner (1994). Cultural beliefs and the organization of society: A historical and theoretical reflection on collectivist and individualist societies. *Journal of Political Economy* 102 (5): 912–50.

Greif, Avner and Eugene Kandel (1995). Contract enforcement institutions: Historical perspective and current status in Russia. In *Economic Transition in Eastern Europe and Russia: Realities of Reform*, edited by E. Lazear. Stanford: Hoover Institution Press.

Habermas, Juergen (1988). *Theorie des Kommunikativen Handelns*, Vol. 1. Frankfurt a. M.: Suhrkamp.

Heinrich, R. (1993). On the merits of spontaneous privatization. *Institute of World Economics Discussion Papers*, No. 201. Kiel: Institute of World Economics.

Johnson, Simon, Daniel Kaufman, and Andrei Shleifer (1997). Politics and Entrepreneurship in Transition Economies. *The William Davidson Institute Working Paper*, No. 57. Ann Arbor: University of Michigan.

Kaufman, Daniel (1997). The Missing Pillar of a Growth Strategy for Ukraine: Institutional and Policy Reform for Private Sector Development, mimeo. Cambridge, MA: Harvard Institute of International Development.

Kolodko, Grzegorz and D. Mario Nuti (1997). *The Macroeconomics of Transition: The Polish Alternative Model*. Paper prepared for WIDER project meeting on Transition Strategies, Alternatives and Outcomes, May 15–17, Helsinki: UNU/WIDER.

Kornai, J. (1980). *The Economics of Shortage*. Amsterdam: North-Holland.

Lipton, David and Jeffrey Sachs (1990). Creating a market economy in Eastern Europe: The case of Poland, *Brookings Papers on Economic Activity*, 0 (1): 75–133.

Marcincin, A. (1996). Slovakia: The family circles privatization, mimeo. Bratislava: Centre for Economic Development.

—— and S. van Wijnbergen (1997). The impact of Czech privatization methods on enterprise performance incorporating initial selection-bias correction. *The Economics of Transition* 5 (2): 289–304.

Mummert, Uwe (1997). German economic, monetary and social union and the theory of institutional change. In *The German Currency Union of 1990: A Critical Assessment*, edited by S. Frowen and J. Hoelscher. Basingstoke and London: MacMillan Press.

Murrell, P. (1992). Evolutionary and radical approaches to economic reform. *Economics of Planning* 25 (1): 79–95.

Naughton, Barry (1996). China's macroeconomy in transition. *China Quarterly* 144 (4): 1083–1104.

Nelson, J., J. Kochanowicz, K. Mizsei, and U. Munoz (1994). *Intricate Links: Democratization and Market Reforms in Latin America and Eastern Europe*. Washington, DC: New Brunswick: Transaction Publishers for the Overseas Development Council.

North, Douglas C. (1981). *Structure and Change in Economic History*. New York and London: W.W. Norton.

North, Douglas C. (1991). Institutions. *Journal of Economic Perspectives* 5 (1): 97–112.

Pinto, B., M. Belka, and S. Krajewski (1993). Transforming State Enterprises in Poland: Microeconomics Evidence on Adjustment. *Transition and Macro-adjustment: Policy Research Working Papers*, No. 110. Washington, DC: World Bank.

Platteau, Jean-Phillipe (1994). Behind the market stage where real societies exist—Part I: The role of public and private order institutions. *Journal of Development Studies* 30 (3): 533–77; Part II: Trust and generalized morality. *Journal of Development Studies* 30 (4): 754–817.

Prior, Richard (1997). Development and Trends of Organised Crime in Business in the Former Soviet Union. Paper presented at the EBRD Seminar on Sound Business Standards and Corporate Practises, 13 April, London: European Bank for Reconstruction and Development.

Putnam, Robert (1993). *Making Democracy Work*. Princeton, NJ: Princeton University Press.

Qian, Y. and G. Roland (1994). Regional Decentralization and the Soft Budget Constraint: The Case of China, *CEPR Discussion Papers*, No. 1013. London: Centre for Economic Policy Research.

Raiser, Martin (1997). Soft Budget Constraints and the Fate of Economic Reforms in Transition Economies and Developing Countries, *Institut für Weltwirtschaft an der Universität Kiel, Kieler Studien* No. 281.

Riskin, C. (1987). *China's Political Economy: The Quest for Development since 1949*. Oxford: Oxford University Press.

Rose-Ackerman, Susan (1996). Why is Corruption Harmful? Background paper for the 1997 World Development Report, *The State in a Changing World*. Washington, DC: The World Bank.

Rose, Richard and Christian Haerpfer (1996). Change and stability in the new democracies barometer, *Studies in Public Policy*, No. 270. Glasgow: Centre for the Study of Public Policy, University of Strathclyde.

——, William Mishler, and Christian Haerpfer (1997). Getting real: Social capital in post-communist societies, *Studies in Public Policy*, No. 278, Glasgow: Centre for the Study of Public Policy, University of Strathclyde.

Sachs, J. D. and W.-T. Woo (1994). Structural factors in the economic reforms of China, Eastern Europe and the former Soviet Union. *Economic Policy* 9 (1): 101–45.

Shleifer, Andrei (1996). Government in Transition, *HIID Discussion Paper*, No. 1783. Cambridge, Massachusetts: Harvard Institute for Economic Research.

Sinn, H. W. and G. Sinn (1993). *Kaltstart: Volkswirtschfltiche Aspekte der deutschen Vereinigung*, 2. Auflage. München: Deutscher Taschenbuch Verlag.

Sudgen, Robert (1989). Spontaneous order. *Journal of Economic Perspectives* 3 (4): 85–97.

Sun, Laixiang (1996). *The Emergence of Unorthodox Ownership and Governance Structure in East Asia: An Alternative Transition Path*. Paper presented at the WIDER workshop on Transition Strategies, Alternatives and Outcomes, 14–16 November, Helsinki.

Wallis, John and North, Douglas C. (1986). Measuring the transaction sector in the American economy. In: *Long-term Factors in American Economic Growth*, edited by S. L. Engerman and R. E. Gallman. Chicago: University of Chicago Press.

Watson, Andrew (1992). The management of the rural economy: The institutional parameters. *Economic Reform and Social Change in China*. London and New York: Routledge.

Whyte, M. K. (1996). The social roots of China's economic development. *China Quarterly* 144: 999–1019.

Index

A-firms 188, 190
accountability 116
accounting wages 201
'advantages of backwardness' 32
aerospace 41, 52
after-tax income 185
aggregate distortions 8
Aghion, P. 154, 221
agrarian reform 65
agriculture 39–40, 60, 67, 85, 97, 117, 127
Agroprombank 54
aid 129, 134
Akmola 62
Albania 8, 160, 164–5
Alesina, A. 17, 216
Alfa Bank 50
alienation right 176
Almaty 62
Alvarez, E. C. 143
Andreff, V. 116
Aoki, Masahiko 154
Aral Sea 55–6
arrears 201, 203, 227
Ashgabat airport 76
'Asian crisis' 97
Asian Development Bank (ADB) 129
'Asian tigers' 21, 129
'Asian-type responsibility' 48
Åslund, A. 7, 33, 35
asset(s) 47
   distribution 48
   inequality 16–17, 36, 216
   leasing 172
   stripping 24, 209
associated enterprise 116
   model 116
Atkinson, T. 193
attenuation 176
auction-privatized firms 16
'auctioning property for money' 46
'auctioning property for vouchers' 46
'August Third Campaign' (1984) 118
Aukutsionek 157
autarchy 52, 76
autarkic trade regimes 21
authoritarian regimes 20, 24, 29, 37, 44–5
autonomy 116, 127, 166, 177, 181–2
Azerbaijan 45

Bach Ho oilfield 104
Bai, Chong-En 172
balance-of-payments crisis 44
Balcerowicz, L. 218
Banister, J. 123
banking and finance 48
bankruptcies 112, 203
banks 62, 64, 156
barriers to entry 195, 197
barter trade 56
'barterization' 33
base wage 156
BAT 60
Belarus 21, 45
Ben-Ner 154
Benabou, R. 17, 216
benefits rights 173
benefits 185, 197
Berezovsky, B. 53
Bevan, A. 160
'big bang' theorists 35
Bim, A. S. 154
birth rates 66
black market exchange rates 33
black market 135–6, 229, 231–2
'black plots' 122
Blair, M. 190
Blanchard, O. 154
Blasi, J. R. 47, 159
Bofinger, P. 19
Boltho, A. 193
bombings 143
Bonin, J. 155
bonuses 110
book-to-market ratio 47
Borner, S. 231
Borys, B. 174
Bosnia-Herzegovina 45
Boswell, J. 223
Bourdet, Y. 178
Boycko, M. 154
Brada, J. C. 172
Braithwaite, J. D. 196
Brenner, M. 206
Breton, P. 33
Brezhnev era 57
bribes 231–2
Bruno, M. 18

264 Index

Buchanan, J. M. 174
Bulgaria 48, 159, 163, 166
bundle of rights 175
business ethics 48
business performance 160
Byrd, W. 226

Cambodia 172
Campbell, J. L. 176
Campos, J. E. 223
Campos, N. F. 11
capital 97
  flows 137
  incomes 207
  inflows 85
  markets 45
  productivity 19, 30, 39
  stock 32
  transfers 100, 183
capital–labour ratio(s) 53, 123, 185
capital/output ratio(s) 8, 32
capitalism 47–52
capitalist economies 194
Cardoso, E. 135
Carlin, W. 160
Carroll, G. R. 175
Castañeda, R. 145
Castro, Fidel 133, 139
Castro, Raúl 139
cement 105
Central Asian Republics (CARs) 55
Central European countries, *see* countries by name
central planning 10, 32, 37, 73, 90, 116, 174, 178
Central Statistical Offices 200
central–local coordination 91
centrally planned economies (CPEs) 13, 25, 30, 115, 154
'champion of isolationism' 52
Chernobyl disaster 56
China
  agriculture 32, 195, 226
  GDP 11, 52
  gradualism in 3, 6, 10, 29, 78, 224
  health care/education in 79
  income inequality in 17, 194, 205–6
  property rights reform in 178
  reforms in 3, 8, 78–92, 142, 149, 198, 225–7
  SOEs 172, 176, 197
  township and village enterprises (TVEs) 23, 26, 32, 85, 166, 173, 183–6, 225
Chinese strategy 45
Chubais 156

Chun, Hong-Tack 123
Chung, J. S. 115
Ciolko, M. 34
CIS 3, 5, 10–11, 41, 235
  see also countries by name
Citrin, D. A. 19, 42
civil institutions 234
civil unrest 135
CMEA 103, 106, 134
cobalt 150
Coleman, J. 220
collapse 115, 122, 131, 150
collective(s) 188
  farms 117, 226
  ownership 183, 195
Comecon 56
Commander, S. 159
commitment 25
commodity-exchange business 48
communist(s) 42
  regime 25, 114, 132
compensation 155–6, 165–7
  packages 23
competition 20, 107, 150, 172, 188, 191, 226
competitive markets 20
concentration coefficient 206
construction 104
consumer goods 118
  sector 128
consumer(s) 44, 195
  subsidies 41
consumption 41, 44, 196
contract responsibility system 175, 179
contracts 186
control 154–5, 158–60, 162
  right(s) 154, 173, 175
  rights in 184
cooperation 25–6, 220
cooperative(s) 60, 65, 102, 110, 136, 144
  equilibrium 220
  shareholding (CSH) 93
  shareholding corporations 88
Cornia, G. A. 66, 95
corporate financing and control 49–50
corporate governance 162
corporatization 87
corruption 48, 57, 229
cotton 56, 58, 70, 74
credibility 36, 229, 233, 235
crime 5, 26, 67
  rate 48
criminals 26, 230–1
Croatia 8
cronyism 5
Cuba 5, 132–47
Cultural Revolution 78
currency collapse 43
current account deficits 99

Czech Republic 25, 164, 236
Czechoslovakia 150, 193

Daewoo 60
Dang, Duc Dam 98
data quality 201
De Melo, M. 7, 33–4, 126
de Vylder, S. 103, 178
de-collectivization 226
death rates 66
debt 142
  financing 44
debt–asset ratio 87
debt–service payments 44
decentralization 81, 86, 91, 101, 115, 130, 225, 229
'Decisions on Economic Reform' 93
defence expenditure 31, 148
'deliberation councils' 223
democratic regimes 20, 24, 44–5
  see also strong and weak democratic regimes
Democratic Republic of Vietnam (1954–75) 177
democratization 12, 35
demonetization 33, 36
Demsetz, H. 175
depoliticization 157
deregulation 33
Desai, P. 42, 44
desert 56
devaluation 98, 196
development 95–7
  level 8, 79
direct foreign investment (DFI) 60, 72
direct subsidies 41
discounted bills of exchange 227
disincentives 16, 183, 215
distortions 32
distribution rights 175
distrust 229
dividends 185, 195
DIW 227
Dmitriyev, M. 49
Dodsworth, John R. 100, 172
Doi Moi reform process 98–103
Dollar, D. 98–9, 182
dollarization 33, 99, 141
dollars 136, 149
domestic 44
  prices 31, 43, 71
'domestic multinationals' 83
dong 98
Dong, Xiao-Yuan 185
Dornbush, R. 43
downsizing 156
dual-track pricing system 179
dual-track transition 78, 82–8, 173

Earle J. S. 45, 154
East Asian (growth) model 114, 128–9
East Asian model 111
East Germany 227
Easterly, W. 18
Eastern European countries, *see* countries by name
Eberstadt, N. 123
EBRD 25, 41, 229
economic and technological development areas (ETDAs) 86
economic development 8, 32, 90, 115, 219–20
economic efficiency 117
economic growth 79, 97
economic liberalization 35
economic performance 6, 10, 13, 65–7, 95, 114, 118–19, 153–69, 233–5
economic sanctions 129
economic structure 83–8
education 60, 62
Edwards, S. 43
efficiency 16, 24, 127, 190
elections 35
electric energy 39
Elster, J. 219
embezzlement 112
emigration 67, 135
employee(s) 154, 158–9
  influence 170
  ownership 153–4, 156, 163
  participation 153, 155–6
employers 36
employment 40, 45, 108, 123, 172
energy 41
engineering 31
'enterprise localism' 116
enterprise(s) 85, 98, 116, 144, 184, 186, 203
  rationalization 142
  sector 45–6, 203
environmental degradation 56, 108
environmental factors 12
equality 141, 146
equipment 39
equitized firms 108
equity 25, 146
Estonia 11, 158, 162, 165
Estrin, S. 154, 158
ethnic composition 35, 77
ethnic groups 67, 77
ethnic tensions 122
European Union (EU) 47, 215
'European-type responsibility' 48
Evans, G. 178
Everleny Perez, O. 149
ex-communist parties 35
excess wage tax 211
exchange controls 69

exchange rate(s) 19, 59
  policy 18
exchange-rate-based stabilization 19, 42, 44
executive compensation 156, 167
exogenous shocks 223, 238
explanatory power 12
export(s) 32, 43, 107, 128, 133–4, 137, 184
  orientation 21
  promotion 21
  quotas 40
  sector(s) 36, 107
  tariffs 40
  taxes 40
export-oriented growth 52
export-oriented manufacturing firms 37
export-oriented oligarchy 37
exporters 44
extended family 226
extent of liberalization 34
external borrowing 44
external finance 3
external shock(s) 133–5, 181
external trade 48

family allowances 45, 195, 212
family businesses 226
'family' restaurants 139, 150
famine 119–22, 180
Fan, G. 223
farmers 37, 60, 82, 85, 136, 226
farmers' markets 148
Feinsilver, J. M. 135
'fence breaking' 180
Fergana Valley 56
fertilizers 106
Fforde, A. 103, 178
Fifteenth Party Congress 180
Filatotchev, I. 157
financial institutions 50
financial sector reform 64
financing 44
firm cannibalism 24
firms 108, 111, 127, 142, 145
fiscal decentralization 17, 197, 206, 225
fiscal deficit(s) 99, 135
Fish, M. S. 35
Fitzgerald, F. T. 149
fixed assets 32
fixed-term leasing 183
Flemming, J. 200
flexibility 57, 81
floods 119
food 106, 119, 135
  crisis 119
foreign debt 120, 125
foreign direct investment (FDI) 24, 83, 128, 197

foreign exchange 59, 132, 134, 142
foreign investment 42, 85, 97, 128, 132, 135 137, 148, 182, 216
foreign investors 24, 60, 72, 81, 127, 142–3, 190
foreign joint venture(s) 85, 104, 127
foreign ownership 163
foreign trade 61, 82, 120, 125
formal institutions 25–6, 219, 221
former Soviet Union (FSU) 29, 202–5
free riding 23, 215
free trade zone (FTZ) 128
Freedom House political freedom index 34
Friedman, E. 223
frontier approach 163
Frydman, R. 161, 172
Frye, T. 49, 232
'FSU effect' 33
fuel 39, 104
Funck, B. 178
Fyodorov, B. 42

Gaidar, Y. 42
game theory 220
Gazprom 40, 52
GDP 30, 65, 135, 137, 140, 172
  per capita 10, 32, 149
German big bang model 131, 138
German invasion (1941) 56
German Monetary Union 227
Germans 77
Gerschenkron 32
Gini coefficients 16–17, 193, 200–1, 206, 214
'giving property to work collectives' 46
global interests 116
GNP 120
  per capita 140
gold 59, 74, 99
Gomulka, S. 127
Gonzalez, E. 149
goods 9, 95, 106, 175
Gorbachev era 57, 157, 193
Gorbachev reforms 30, 36
governance features 188
governance issues 23
governance structures 24, 171, 183–6
government(s) 34, 43, 50, 70, 73, 89, 136, 223
  expenditure 11, 19, 36, 51, 62
  revenues 12–13, 19, 34, 36, 79
  spending 60
  type 35
Grabher, G. 228
gradualism 10, 29–30, 58, 138, 144, 224
grain 58, 71
Granick, D. 176, 226
Greenlagh, S. 226
Greif, A. 231
Griffin, K. 57

gross earnings 208–12
gross national expenditure (GNE) 57
group activities 155
group-based incentive schemes 155
Groves, T. 166
growth 16, 19, 43, 80, 85, 94, 97, 106, 145
  equations 161–2
  rate(s) 30, 144, 185
Gui, S. 180
Gupta, D. 17, 216
Gurkov, I. 172

Haerpfer, C. 233
Hainan 86
hard budget constraint 133, 226
hard currency 126, 134, 142
  shortages 128
'hard landing scenario' 131
Harrold, P. 197
Hart, O. 190
Havrylyshyn, O. 172
health 60, 62
heavy industry 8, 118, 123
Heinrich, R. 236
Heleniak, T. E. 196
Helms–Burton legislation 139, 142
Helwege, A. 135
Hernandez-Cata, E. 35
Heybey, B. 34
high-technology industries 41, 52
'hire-purchased' 183
Holmes, S. 10
home repairs 110, 150
honesty 220
Hong Kong Stock Exchange 184
Honkkila, J. 17, 207
horizontal integration 116
household budget surveys (HBS) 200–1
household enterprises 186
household responsibility system 65, 82, 194, 226
Howitt, P. 221
human capital 108, 132–3, 141
human development (HD) 161
Hungary 8, 25, 34, 45, 49, 150, 164, 193, 195, 201
Hussain, P. 194
hybrid governance structures 174
hyperinflation 65, 69
Hyun, Myung-Han 117

Ickes, B. 34, 114
ideology 89, 221
IED–GDP ratio 87
Illarionov, A. 42
'illiberal democracies' 12

IMF 58, 65, 68, 70, 129, 172
immigration 135
import(s) 107, 134, 137
  capacity 134
  substitution policy 41
import-substituting industrialization 21
'in-household work teams' 118
incentives 146
  microeconomic 13–16, 23
income distribution 48, 65, 149, 193–206
income inequality 16–17, 36, 67, 92, 145, 201–6, 215
  see also income distribution
income redistribution 37, 44
incomes 172, 212
inconsistent gradualism 77
'inconsistent shock therapy' 77
indirect subsidies 41
'individual business family' policy 188
industrial policy 91, 103–8, 206
industrial restructuring 127
industrial strategy 39–41
industrial structure 51, 124
industrialization 79, 91
industry 31, 74, 76, 102, 133, 140
inflation 6–7, 36, 41–4, 197, 201
  control 18
  rates 98
  tax 44
informal economy, see second economy
informal institutions 25–6, 122, 219–37
informalization 141, 207
infrastructure 129, 133, 186
initial conditions 55–7, 78–82, 114
  institutional 5, 9–13, 232
  structural 5, 7–9, 113
input 95, 117
insider ownership 153–5, 157–8
insider privatization 24, 235
insider-privatized firms 16
'insiders' 47, 75, 87, 156, 235–6
institutional capacity 149
  of the state 5, 11–12, 24, 30, 34, 36, 45, 111, 224, 238
  index 10
institutional change 223
institutional collapse 10, 29, 33, 36
institutional continuity 24, 226
institutional decline 36–9
institutional economies 24–6
institutional efficiency 11
institutional factors 24
institutional investors 49
institutional reforms 224–9
institutional transition 90
institutions
  formal rules (legal system) 25, 220–1, 223
  informal rules (social norms) 219–24

inter-enterprise debt (IED) 87
inter-regional inequality 17, 215
inter-republican trade 32
interest rate(s) 59, 98
international specialization 51–2
intra-regional inequality 17, 215
investment(s) 17, 30, 80, 128, 143
  rate 97, 100
Iraq 125
Irvin, G. 182

J-firms 188, 190
Jansen, K. 111
Japan 129
Jefferson, G. H. 166, 178
Jemison, D. B. 174
Jiang, Zemin 180
Johnson, S. 223
joint ownership 183
joint ventures 182–3, 190
Joint-Venture Law (1984) 128
Jorge, D. 147

Kakwani, N. 206
Kandel, E. 231
Kang, Myoung-Kyu 115
Karimov (President) 70
Kato, T. 156, 166
Kaufman, R. R. 36, 44
Kaufmann, D. 230
Kazakhstan 5, 55–77
Kazaks 67, 77
Kim Il-Sung 115, 130
  era 123
Kim Jong Il 118, 122, 130
Kim Chul-Sik 116
Kim Hyung-Ki 154
Kim, S. 128
Kim, W. 117
kiosks 77
'kitchen plot' 117
Klugman, J. 60
Koen, V. 42
kolkhozni 200
Kolodko, G. W. 196, 232
Kombinaten 116
konzertierte Aktion 223
Kornai, J. 156, 174, 196, 218
Krueger, A. O. 111
Kruger, G. 34
KUB 118
Kumtor gold project 72
Kwon, Oh-Yun 118
Kyrgyzstan 3, 55–77

labour 95, 110
  force 78, 82, 91, 127

market 108–11, 215
  mobility 48
  productivity 39, 53, 153, 161
  shedding 142
  shirking 16, 23, 215
Lahiri, A. K. 42
Laky, T. 174
Landesmann, M. 160
Lao People's Democratic Republic 178
Laos 172, 182–3
Latvia 11, 158, 164
law and order 36, 48, 61, 74
layoffs 142–3, 145, 182, 203, 210
leases 82
leasing 183
  contracts 190
Lee, Hy-Sang 115
Lee, Pong S. 115
Leff, N. H. 188
legal norms 219
'legal person socialism' 113
legislation 157, 181
Lehmann, H. 209
Li, D. D. 158, 173
liability 188
liberalization 3, 6, 34–6, 114, 127
  indices 35
  domestic prices 82, 99
  of foreign trade 61
  of labour markets 94, 126, 197, 214
light industry 117, 123, 127
Lin, J. Y. 114, 176
Lin, N. 186
Lindberg, L. N. 176
Lipton, D. 224
liquidation 236
Lithuania 11, 158, 164
Liu, Yia-Ling 188
living standards 65
Ljunggren, B. 98
loan rates 98
loans 129
local government property rights 176
local interests 116
Logovaz 54
losses 112, 181

Macedonia 8
machinery 39
macro-level distortions 32
macroeconomics
  approach 18–20
  conditions 3
  policy 41–4
  populism 43–4
  stability 113
mahalla 61, 69, 74
mainstream approach 18

majority ownership 165
malnutrition 148
management contracts 190
managers 22, 60, 87, 112, 117, 156–7, 166, 179, 235
manat 64
Marcincin, A. 236
market 174
  forces 133
  imperfections 8
  information 186
  liberalization 82
  models 73–6
  reform(s) 6, 20, 144, 194
  transition as 174
market-type reforms 30
marketization 81, 94, 117–18, 127
Marrese, M. 42
mass privatization 236–7
Mayer, G. 21
McAuley, A. 200
McCarty, A. 181
McGettigan, D. 172
McKinley, T. 206
'median voter theory' 216
Menatep 50
Mercedes Benz 60
Merrill, J. 117
Mesa-Lago, Carmelo 135
Miami 143
Micklewright, J. 193, 214
micro-level distortions 32
migration 18, 67, 92, 215
Milanovic, B. 17, 203
Milgrom, P. 175, 190
militarization 30, 32
modernization 81, 127
Moldova 3, 45
monetary overhang 7, 81, 136, 144, 149
money-based stabilization 19
Mongolia 8, 57
Montes, M. 43
moral norms 219, 221–2
morality 220–2, 232
'muddling-through' scenario 143–4
multiple exchange rates 33
multiplier effects 128
Mummert, U. 227
Murrell, P. 34, 114
Mygind, N. 158

nationalism 42, 76, 122
Naufor 49
Naughton, B. 10, 34, 112, 172, 227
Nazarbayev (President) 70–1
Nee, V. 175
Nelson, J. 223
Nesporova, A. 23

New Democracies Barometer 233
New Economic Policy 51
new market institutions 30
new private sector (NPS) 22–3, 127, 145, 198, 236, 239
Nguyen, Thi Hien 98
nominal exchange rate 18
non-ferrous metals 39
non-policy-related factors 30–4
non-priority goods 115
non-resource sector 43
non-state enterprises 62, 112
non-state institutions 10, 33
non-state sectors 80, 83–6, 91, 102
non-tradable sector 133
non-tradables 95, 97
North Korea 5, 114–31, 129
North Vietnam 103
North, Douglass 25, 218
Nuti, D. M. 232

O'Brien, K. J. 185
'objective' factors 35
OECD 49, 201, 235
Oi, J. K. 177
oil 104, 106
oil and gas industry 40, 44
'one factory–two systems' method 127
open-door policy 128–30
optimal policy approach 18
'ordinary government expenditure' 10
organizations 154
Otani, I. 173
output 42, 65, 95, 106, 134, 164, 172
  loss 140
  performance 5, 7–9
  quotas 181
output–labour ratios 185
outsider ownership 154, 157
'outsiders' 47
over-industrialization 30, 32, 140
overvalued exchange rate 43–4
owner(s) 22, 87, 154, 173, 184
ownership 154, 156–8, 162, 171, 175–6, 183–6
  right 175
  structure(s) 83, 87–8, 108, 190

Paniccà, R. 66
Pérez-López, J. F. 148
parallel markets 150
Parris, K. 188
paternal role 74
path dependence 22, 174, 238
patron–client ties 188
Paufor 49
payroll taxes 196
peasant associations 65

peasant markets 117
peasants 110, 117, 226
Pejovich, A. 175
pensions 45, 195, 199
performance 6, 24, 30, 45, 65–7, 108, 155, 161, 170
performance-based pay 156
perks 195
Perotti, E. 184
Perotti, R. 17, 216
peso 141
'petty plots' 117
Pham, Chi do 173
Phelps-Brown, H. 194
Ping, Z. 17
Pinto, B. 166, 236
planners 51
planning 51
Platteau, Jean-Phillipe 220
Pliskin, J. 155
Pohl, G. 160
Poland
  (transition) performance of 3, 25
  income inequality in 193, 201
  private sector 195, 232
  privatization in 45, 164, 236
  stock market in 49
policies 20–6, 57–65, 127
policy choices 18–26
policy options 34–47
policy-related factors 30–4
political credibility index 235
political elites 239
political freedom, see democratization
political institutions 234
political revolution 232
political tensions 81, 122, 139
political uncertainty 129
politico-economic factors 24–6
Polterovich, V. 10
Popov, V. 42, 43, 71
population(s) 66, 108, 123
populist model 76
populist policies 43–4, 216
post-communist economies 47
'post-Washington' consensus 20
poverty 65, 67, 149
power groups 139
Poznanski, K. 25
predatory activities 16
price(s) 59, 61, 97–8
  control(s) 43, 45, 58, 69, 98
  deregulation 40
  liberalization 61
  mechanism 5
  reform(s) 57–8, 63, 75, 113
  subsidies 41
primary industry 123

primary producers 56
Prior, R. 231
private enterprises 108, 173, 186–8
private farms 60
private investors 97
private ownership 24, 133, 144, 153, 165, 183
private plot 117
private sector(s) 91, 111–12, 142, 146
privatization 3, 15, 20, 24, 45, 57, 61, 63, 65, 78, 94, 101, 112, 117–18, 144–6, 154–5, 157, 171, 235–7
privatized SOEs 22–3
Probert, J. 177
producers 44
production 195
  functions 163
  possibilities frontier diagram 95
  possibility frontier curve(s) 95
'production team contract system' 117
productivity 95, 117, 155–6, 160, 170, 185
  gap 31, 39
profit(s) 181, 195
  targets 179
profit-sharing 165
profitability 160, 167
property 145–6
  claims 145
  registers 150
  rights 116, 146, 150, 171, 175, 178–83
  rights reform 174
property rights regimes 24
  orthodox 13–16, 171
  unorthodox (new ownership forms) 171–91
Pryor, F. L. 193
public goods 9, 19, 36, 50
public ownership 89
Putterman, L. 185
pyong 117
Pyongyang 117

Qian, Y. 225
Qingsong, L. 226
'quasi cooperative sector' 15

radical reform(s) 78, 127, 130, 179
radical reform parties 35
Rajin 128
Rana, P. B. 182
raw materials 97
  industries 39
Rawski, T. G. 166, 185
real exchange rate 18, 43–4
recession 29, 203
redistribution 195
redistributive policies 36
redundant employment 186
reform(s) 35–6, 115, 138–40

paths 55–77
  strategies 224
regional differences 92
regression(s) 12–13, 33–4, 160
  equations 8
relative prices 31, 40, 71
religion 35
remittances 132, 137, 141–2, 150
remuneration 110
rent(s) 43, 52, 75, 195, 230
  redistribution 43
  seeking 16
repressed inflation 7
resource(s) 96
  endowment 68
  sector 39–40, 43, 52
resource-based industries 31, 52
restructuring 32, 39, 43, 80, 127, 164
return right(s) 154, 175
reunification 103, 224
revenue/GDP ratio 11, 38
rice 98, 106
rights 154
riots 73, 135
  urban 67
Riskin, C. 226
Robert, J. 175, 190
Roca, S. 149
Rockel, M. 156
Rodriguez, J. L. 139
Rodrik, D. 10, 17, 21, 216
Roland, G. 225
role of the state 94, 111, 145, 224–9
Root, H. 223
Rose, R. 233
Rose-Ackerman, S. 223
Rosevear, A. 158
Rostowski, J. 42
rouble 19, 40, 43, 57
rouble zone membership 7, 58
Roxborough, I. W. 212
'rule of law' 12, 81
rural collectives 82
rural industrialization 186
rural private enterprises 187
rural reform 82
rural–urban balance 133
Russia
  (inconsistent) shock therapy in 5
  economic performance of 10, 30–4
  exchange rate(s) in 19, 21, 42–4
  GDP 8, 11
  income inequality/redistribution in 17, 43–4, 48, 193
  institutional decline in 19, 36–9
  privatization in 45–7, 162, 172
  resource sector 39–40
  shock therapy (inconsistent) 29–53

stock market in 49
wage dispersion in 210
Russian Longitudinal Monitoring
  Study 200, 209
Russians 77
Rutkowski, J. 209
Ryterman, R. 114

Sabel, C. 174
Sachs, J. D. 32, 43, 98, 223
'safety valve' 43
Sanguinetty, J. 150
savings 41, 44
  ratio 17
Schieber, G. 60
'second economy' 174, 193
secondary industry 123
secondary manufacturing 31, 39
  industries 52
security firms 231
Seilschaften 229
Selden, M. 103
self-employment 136, 144–5
separation allowances 109
serfdom 226
service sector 31
severance scheme 109
shadow economy 11, 36, 48, 229
Shandong 88
Shanghai 87, 179
Shapiro, J. C. 212
shareholding corporations 91, 113, 127
'shares for loans' auctions 49
Shenzhen 85, 87, 179
Sherritt 143
Shleifer, A. 232
Shmeler, N. 31
shock therapy 18, 30, 33, 42, 98–9, 224, 227–9
  see also inconsistent shock therapy
'shortageflation' 196
Sinn, G. 225
Sinn, H. W. 225
Sipos, S. 195
Slavs 77
Slovenia 8, 164
slow-reform parties 35
Smith, S. 163
smuggling 107
social burdens 186
social capital 173–4, 220, 223–4, 229–35
social cohesion 19, 25, 215
social mobility 226
social norms 219, 221
social policies 45
social sector reforms 108–11
social security 60, 91
social services 48, 133, 186

social spending 133
social tensions 17, 216
social transfers 9, 50, 195, 197, 215
social trust 187, 233–5
socialism 8, 113, 226
socialist economies 7, 10, 80, 95, 115, 117, 125, 132, 194
socio-political instability 17, 216
SOE reforms 83–8, 116
soft budget constraint 117, 134, 171
'soft landing scenario' 130
solidarity 222
South Korea 114, 129
South Vietnam 103
Soviet-type economies (STEs) 155
special economic zones (SEZs) 86, 128, 197, 206
speed of liberalization 5, 33–4
speed of reform 29
shareholding 87
stabilization 3
　macroeconomic 18, 42, 59, 62–3, 196
stable leadership 24
stagnation 115, 122
Stallings, B. 36, 44
Standing, G. 161, 211
Stark, D. 172, 228
starvation 135
state enterprises 8, 60, 86–7, 91, 98, 100, 108, 110, 112, 116, 127, 142
state farms 60, 63, 65, 136, 146
state firms 108, 143
state institutions 33
state ownership 89, 165
state sector(s) 78–9, 102, 173
State Statistical Bureau (SSB) 172
state-owned enterprises (SOEs) 13, 22–3, 78, 87, 94, 171–2, 176, 226
Stewart, F. 23
Stiglitz, J. 10, 18, 20
stock exchanges 87, 154, 179, 184
Stolychniy Bank 54
'stop and go' approach 42, 132, 178
strong authoritarian regimes 12
strong democratic regimes 12, 30, 46
structural adjustment 133–5
structural change 39
structural distortions 7, 29, 33
structural reforms 196–8
subcontracts 186
subsidiaries 127
subsidies 38, 41, 58, 87, 111, 134, 142, 182, 195
subsidization 38, 41
Suchlicki, J. 140
sugar 133, 143
Sugden, R. 219
Sun, L. 108

Sunbong 128
supervision costs 22
support 173
'surrogate' financing 38
Suutela, P. 15
Svejnar, J. 185

Taiwan 114
Tajikistan 45, 55
'tariff jumping' 83
Tarr, D. 68
Tashkent 56
tax(es) 40, 139, 144–5, 181, 196, 198, 230
　evasion 198
　reform 94
　revenue 112
tax/GDP ratio 11
Tengiz oilfield 68, 71
textiles 97, 106
Thailand 108
Than, Mya 114
Thanh, Ngo Kim 181
'the red directors' 46
three-plan system 181
threshold levels of liberalization 13
Thuyet, Pham van 108
time wages 155
tourism 132, 135, 137, 141–3
town and village enterprises (TVEs) 15, 23, 85, 183–6, 190, 225
tradable sector 133
tradables 95, 134
trade 30, 56, 91, 118, 126, 133
　deficits 32, 137, 140
　dependency ratio 125
　embargo 132, 135, 142
　flows 32
　issues 103–8
　openness 84
　policy 111
　protection 111
　'under-openness' 140
traditional property rights theory 184
transaction costs 25, 219–20, 226–7
transfers 57, 195, 212
transformational recession 6, 30, 103, 140
transition 94–7, 140–7, 150
　strategies 18–26
'transitional democracies' 44
trust 25–6, 34, 155, 220, 222, 233–5
Tumen river 128
Turkic Central Asians 77
Turkmenistan 21, 45, 55
Turley 103
TVE sector 173
two-tier banking system 98

Ukraine 21
underdevelopment 30, 96, 111
undervalued exchange rate 43
UNDP 60, 65, 128
unemployment 67, 110
UNICEF 197
UNIDO 123
unification 33, 131, 227–9
unions 142
urban private enterprises 186
urbanization 79, 91, 186
  ratio 123
use-rights 57
user fees 111
utilization right 175
Uzbekistan 3, 5, 10, 25, 45, 55–77
Uzbeks 67

value-maximization principle 190
Van Arkadie, B. 99
Vaughan-Whitehead, D. 160, 211
'VAZ' autoplant 54
Vecernik, J. 209
Velvet Revolution (1989) 237
Venieris, Y. 17, 216
Vietnam's Company Law (1991) 108
Vietnam
  GDP 11, 99
  health care/education in 111
  property rights reform in 180–2
  reforms in 3, 8, 33, 98–103
  shock therapy in 6, 10, 29, 98–9
  SOEs 172, 177, 197
  trade policy in 21, 107–8
voting shares 157
voucher privatization (scheme) 156, 236
voucher privatization method 237

wage flexibility 96
wages 156, 194, 197
Walder, A. G. 176
Wallis, J. 220
Wank, D. L. 187
war destruction 7, 8, 12
Warner, A. 35, 44

Washington consensus 95
Watson, A. 226
weak democratic regimes 12, 37
weak institutions 47–52
Weisskopf, T. 159
Weitzman, M. L. 158, 184
welfare 196
  state 17, 36
West Germany 227
Whyte, M. K. 226
Wijnbergen, S. van 236
Williamson, O. E. 174
Wong, C. 177
Wong, J. 184
Woo, Wing Thye 32, 86, 98, 185, 223
Woodward 164
work collectives 46–7
work ethics 48
worker cooperatives 146
workers 22, 36, 40, 46, 67, 87, 98, 110, 136, 155, 157, 165, 210, 235
workers' collectives 15
World Bank 10, 16, 46, 64, 68, 70, 98, 109, 129, 173, 209, 235
World Development Report 6, 108
world prices 31, 40, 58, 71
WTO 91

Xiamen 85
Xiaoping, D. 179
Xu, C. 158, 184

Yeltsin, B. 157
Yeltsin reforms 30
Yi, G. 177
Young, S. 177
Young, S. 187

Zakaria, F. 12
Zamfir, C. 210
Zettermeyer, J. 19, 43
Zhang, W. 177
Zimbalist, A. 145
Zou, L. 175